SOCIAL PROBLEMS AND WELFARE

Rajendra Kumar Sharma

ATLANTIC
PUBLISHERS & DISTRIBUTORS (P) LTD

Published by

ATLANTIC

PUBLISHERS & DISTRIBUTORS (P) LTD

7/22, Ansari Road, Darya Ganj,
New Delhi-110002
Phones : +91-11-40775252, 23273880, 23275880, 23280451
Fax : +91-11-23285873
Web : www.atlanticbooks.com
E-mail : orders@atlanticbooks.com

Branch Office
5, Nallathambi Street, Wallajah Road,
Chennai-600002
Phones : +91-44-64611085, 32413319
E-mail : chennai@atlanticbooks.com

Printed in India at Nice Printing Press, A-33/3A, Site-IV, Industrial Area, Sahibabad, Ghaziabad, U.P.

SOCIAL PROBLEMS AND WELFARE

Preface

This book covers university syllabi in Sociology in the papers Social Problems; Social Welfare; Social Security and Welfare etc. Analytic in presentation of matter drawn from authentic sources; holistic in interpretation and conclusions, with examples drawn from Indian situations and narration in simple language with questions for exercise at the end of each chapter, this book has been planned as a textbook for students and reference manual for teachers.

The book has been divided into three parts. Part I entitled *Social Problems* includes chapters : Social Problems; Population Problems; Social Tensions; Casteism; Untouchability and Minorities; Problems of Hindu Marriage; Tribal Problems; Problems of Urbanisation; Rural Disorganisation and Problems; Democracy and Its Problems; Poverty; Beggary; Problems of Industrialisation; Unemployment; Labour Problems; Student Unrest and Youth Tensions.

Part II entitled *Deviance* includes chapters on Crime; Criminal Tribes; White Collar Crime; Juvenile Delinquency; Prostitution; Suicide; Alcoholism and Drug Addiction.

Part III entitled *Reform and Welfare* includes chapters : Social Reform Movements; Labour Welfare; Rural Reconstruction; National Emotional Integration and Welfare of Backward Classes.

Suggestions for improvements are invited from indulgent readers.

RAJENDRA K. SHARMA

Contents

PART III — REFORM AND WELFARE

SOCIAL PROBLEMS

SOCIAL PROBLEMS

1

Social Problems

The term social problem involves two terms 'social' and 'problem.' Therefore, social problem is a problem which is social in nature. Thus it is different from economic, political, metaphysical and other types of problems. The term social means concerning society, social relationships, social structure, social organisation etc. On the other hand, the term problem means undesirable, conflicting, incongruous, improper and difficult situation condition or behaviour. Therefore, social problems are the undesirable situations, conditions or behaviour concerning society, social institutions, social relationships, social structure, social organisation etc. It is always disintegrating and disorganising. It is pathological. It is harmful. It has to be cured.

Definitions of Social Problem

Besides the above literal definitions of social problem, some definitions by eminent sociologists are as follows:

1. *Raab and Selznick.* It is the problem of social relationships which challenges the society itself or creates obstacles in the satisfaction of important ambitions of many people.

2. *Bernard.* Social problems are the conditions which demand solid often reformative activities in society due to humanity, utility or inactivity.

3. *Arnold Rose.* A social problem may be defined as a situation which has influenced a good majority of people, i.e. they believe that this situation itself is responsible for their difficulties or displeasures which may be reformed.

4. *Richard and Richard.* When most of the members of society accept a particular condition and behaviour pattern as undesirable and objectionable, it is called social problem.

5. *Nisbet.* These are called social since these are directly related to human relationships and the accepted system of society. We may call them problems since these create hurdles in expected plans and point out upheavals in the regular life of community.

NATURE OF SOCIAL PROBLEM

From the above definitions it is clear that social problem is a condition creating crisis and upheaval in generally established and current valuers of society. The social problem is connected to majority of the members of society. According to Bernard, the repressive and tense condition consequent of social problem may be involving three types of elements: (i) Tension factors which challenge some value of society, (ii) Social valuers which are being challenged, and (iii) Intense reaction of individuals and groups to challenge. The following characteristics exhibit the nature of social problems.

1. Disintegrative. Social problem, directly or indirectly disintegrates social system. It seriously effects values. Therefore, it may be, more properly, defined in the context of social ideals and values. Due to its relation to values, it is possible that what we call social problem may not be so in a different society since each society has different ideals and values.

2. Multiple causes. Social problem is a term when the humanity in social organisation is jeopardised and social ideals, values and norms are obstructed.

3. Many Remedies. Hence the solution of the complex social problem requires varied and multisided remedies.

4. Dissimilar importance. Different social problems have dissimilar importance. The number of persons affected by a social problem is not a necessary index of its importance. A problem connected with few persons may be more serious than a social problem influencing a good majority of people in a society, thus a social problem is evaluated not by the number of people it impresses but the severity of danger or challenge it poses to the existence of social organisation.

5. Functional Value. Social problem, though disintegrative, has functional value since its cure leads to social problem and social development.

6. Inter-connected. Social problems are inter-connected due to which. these become serious. For example, unemployment, poverty and crime are inter-connected.

7. Two Viewpoints. Social problem may be interpreted from two different viewpoints. From the individual viewpoint it leads to maladjustment of the individual to society. From the community viewpoint it may be harmful or disintegrative of the community. Hence social problem should be takled both on individual and community level.

METHODS OF STUDYING SOCIAL PROBLEM

1. Historical Method. This method is used in studying societies, civilizations, communities and incidents in a time period or in a time sequence. It is used to study the origin, development and transformation of social phenomena. It is very useful in determining the origin and evolution of a social problem. It was used by early sociologists.

2. Individual Life Study Method. In this method a social problem is viewed as a whole from the perspective of individual life. It clarifies different aspects of a social problem. Therefore, it is a useful method of study.

3. Community Study Method. In this method, as is clear from the nomenclature, attempt is made to understand communal and tribal problems, the problems of particular communities, minority problems, labour problems, problems of women, problems of backward classes etc.

4. Ideal Type Analysis Method. Max Weber used this method in studying causal relationships. Ideal type is a concept which helps the investigator to measure similarities and dissimilarities in actual incidents. Problems which involve analysis in study are particularly studied by this method.

5. Quantitative Method:

(i) *Social Survey.* Social problems cover in a large section of people in society are studied by survey method to determine the extent or quantity or number of persons involved. Survey method has been successfully used in studying social problems like crime, beggary, unemployment, poverty, over-crowding etc. This method is particularly utilised to study problems of a particular community such as labour problem, minority problem, problems of women etc.

(ii) *Statistical Method.* This method is a useful instrument for comparing past, present and future state of a social problem. In it statistical techniques are used giving reliable and exact data concerning a social problem.

(iii) *Sociometry.* According to J.L. Moreno and Helen Hall Jennings sociometry is used to determine social distance and mutual relationships among individuals and groups. It finds out harmony and disharmony, attraction and repulsion, friendship and enmity among persons and groups.

APPROACHES TO STUDYING SOCIAL PROBLEM

1. Social Problem Approach. In this social problem is studied through survey method after dividing it in separate classes. J.L. Gillin has used this approach in his study of social problems.

2. Social Disorganisation Approach. Elliott and Merrill have used this approach in which a particular social problem is discussed from the viewpoints of social disorganisation.

3. Cultural Lag Approach. According to. W.F. Ogburn the main cause of social problem is cultural lag in which while a culture evolves in a particular direction it lags behind in a different direction. This is due to the fact that different elements of a culture do not change or evolve in the identical speed or in the same direction and often some element lags behind others.

4. Community Study Approach. In this approach, as is clear by the nomenclature, social problem is studied from the view point of community studies. This approach has been particularly used in anthropological studies of tribes.

5. Value Structure Approach. In this attempt is made to study as to how far conflict of values creates social problems and how far it hampers their remedies.

MAIN CAUSES OF SOCIAL PROBLEMS

Various diagnoses

Different sociologists have presented various diagnoses of social problems. According to Elliott and Merrill the main cause behind the political problems and social problems is the sinfulness of human beings. Ceaser Lombroso has emphasised the biological factors in causing social problems. According to Talcott Parsons the main cause of social problems is the inadequate adjustment between man and his physical resources. Wolf has considered population as the main cause of social problem. According to Ogburn cultural lag is the main cause of social problems. According to Raab and Selznick, when the social organisation fails to systematise social relationships resulting in disintegration and disharmony, social problems arise.

REMEDIES TO SOCIAL PROBLEMS

1. Control of Tension Factors. Social problems may be remedied by control of tension factors so that tension may be eliminated or minimised. This is particularly important in remedying the problem of communalism, casteism, linguism, regionalism etc. in contemporary Indian society.

2. Change in Behaviour. Change in human behaviour through education, propaganda, reform etc. is always a necessary remedy in solving social problems concerning family, marriage, inter-community relationships etc.

3. Legal Control. One of the most effective remedy of social problem is social legislation. The government should not only punish those violating the legal provisions but also try the rehabilitation of those relinquishing crime, delinquency, prostitution, beggary etc.

4. Change in Social Structure. Solution of social problems as that of casteism, untouchability etc., require change in social structure.

5. Establishment of Socialist Society. According to socialist and community thinkers the best remedy to social problem is the establishment of socialist pattern of society since most of the problems are due to inequality.

6. Religious Education. According to so many thinkers irreligion atheism and materialism are the main causes at the root of social problem. These thinkers suggest compulsory religious education as a necessary remedy. According to P.A. Sorokin and Arnold Toynbee social problem may be remedied by the acceptance of religious values.

7. Social Service. An important remedy to social problem is the propagation and advancement of social service through voluntary organisations.

8. Efforts by Elite. The intellectuals, authors, sociologists, educationists, social workers, psychologists and psychiatrists together with government officials and administrators should make effort to remedy social problem.

From the above discussion of etiology and remedy of social problem, it is clear that since social problems have multiple causes these should be attached from different sides and by men and women from different walks of life.

SCOPE OF SOCIAL PROBLEMS

Social relationships might be institutional such as familial, marital etc. They may be communal such as rural, urban etc. They might be structural or concerned with social classes. These classifications of social problems determine the field or sphere of social problems. Marital problems are the problems of tensions between males and females or opposite sexes. These lead to marital disorganization, divorces, prostitution etc. Familial problems are due to familial tensions. These include family disorganisation or broken families resulting into crime, juvenile delinquency, alcoholism and drug addiction etc. The tensions in social stratification, the imbalance among social classes lead to classism, casteism, untouchability etc. Besides, some economic maladies, imbalances, tensions and malpractices disrupt normal and healthy social relationships and create social problems such as beggary, unemployment, poverty, problems of industrialization and urbanization and finally the labour problems. Then, there are problems due to group tensions. These groups may be racial, regional, geographical or national etc. Tensions among them lead to the social problems of regionalism, linguism, communalism, racialism etc.

The above explanation of the nature of social problems shows the need of their remedies. Of course, most of the social problems can be solved by increasing natural understanding among members of society. Increase in integrative processes of social interaction is the most important means of the solution of social problems. Of these the most important are cooperation, accommodation, assimilation and adjustment etc. Negatively, the disintegrative processes of social interaction such as conflict, maladjustment etc., should be removed. All this involves social education.

But the members of society themselves can solve a social problem only by mutual agreement. If this is not forthcoming, the state may help by enacting social legislations. Thus modern welfare states help in solving social problems through enacting social legislations concerning family, marriage, inheritance, divorce, child marriage, widow remarriage, civil marriage etc. Social legislations are enacted to ameliorate the condition of backward classes, untouchables, destitutes, orphans, displaced persons, handicapped persons etc. Besides, legislations are enacted to counter exploitation of some one group by another. These include laws concerning beggary, prostitution, alcoholism, drug addiction, juvenile delinquency, crime, etc.

In the end, social problems can be solved by a cooperation between the people and the welfare state.

QUESTIONS FOR EXERCISE

1. What is social problem? Discuss its nature.
2. Explain the methods of studying social problem.
3. Analyse the main causes and remedial measures of social problems.
4. Write short note on Scope of Social Problems.

2

Population Problems

SOCIAL CHANGE DUE TO DEMOGRAPHIC FACTOR

Population is a significant factor in social change. This fact can be clearly understood and its importance realized if we study the consequences of population growth on society. A steep rise in the population in any country gives rise to various social problems. Many a change in the society is due mainly to population increase. For example, if there is such a rise in the population that male population outnumbers the female population, the value of women will rise. If the female population outnumbers the male, sexual promiscuity is likely. As a result of wars in the past there used to be sharp decline in young and healthy males, and this used to result in widespread prostitution and lesbianism. This was the case in post-war Germany. In social change, the increase in population has the following effects:

1. Increase of Poverty. This point hardly needs labouring. We are witnessing this phenomenon in India these days. As observed by Malthus the population increases in geometric progression while the economic sources increase in arithmetic progression. Thus we find that the pace of growth in the economic resources is very slow and gradual. Accordingly the sharp increase in the population is bound to put extra pressure on the available resources and lead to impoverishment.

2. Famine. As noted above, according to Malthus, the natural resources fall much behind the increase of population. Unless a new technology intervenes to boost the production or war occurs to destroy considerable number of people, the conditions of famine are likely to occur. As we know there were so many famines in India and other parts of the world. In the famine of 1896-97, 75 lakh people died and crores were affected. Three years later another famine occurred in India. The famine of 1899-1900 took the toll of 12 lakh human lives and affected crores of people.

3. Fall in the Living Standards. This fact is a corollary of the above facts. If as a result of population rise there is general impoverishment of people, the cost of living is bound to rise and the capacity for purchase reduced. Thus it is likely that the money now will buy less than it used to be. This means people will be buying less goods now than before and this means fall of living standards.

The population rise means more pressure on space and therefore, housing problem becomes acute. In the past two decades though there has been 2 to 4 times increase in the wages the cost of living has gone up 10 times or more in India. Naturally the living standards have declined by 100% or more.

4. Decline in Health. More population means more pollution and more disease. The slums grow rapidly and morals loosen. Prostitution for livelihood becomes a feature of crowded living conditions. What is more, unhygienic conditions prevail. Health declines and diseases become rampant. It has been calculated that in India the number of people dying of various diseases every year is very large.

5. Distribution of Agricultural Holdings. The increase in population leads to distribution of agricultural holdings and ultimately they become uneconomic. This can be illustrated by a model. Suppose A has 10 acres of land. At his death this is distributed among his five children. Each gets 2 acres. Now, if these persons have their children, 4 each. At the time of their death their children will receive 1/2 acre land each, which is wholly uneconomic.

6. Dissolution of Family. When people suffer from want and disease, they are unhappy, morose and bitter. They are liable to blame others for their ills and this means tension and bitterness in family will grow. This tends to assume proportions where divorces, suicides and other ills abound. All this leads to breakdown of family. As noted above slum conditions breed corruption and prostitution. There are slums in India and abroad in which prostitution is so common that family has become a farce.

7. Personal Disintegration. Poverty is the chief breeder of crimes and when criminal tendencies are fanned in individuals the personality of the concerned individuals is adversely affected. It is a common knowledge that juvenile delinquents come from poor families and crowded slums. In an overcrowded home children have no separate rooms for study and no indoor games to keep them engaged. This sends them to streets where they roam like vagabonds and develop abnormal personalities. Besides early exposure to sex makes them take to homosexuality, prostitution and promiscuous sexuality. These factors naturally distort the personality. Another effect of poverty is that children growing up in rural surroundings when become adults feel compelled to move to cities for employment. The drastic change from rural environs to urban environs makes them prey to multiple vices and diseases. Thus they fail to grow balanced personalities. Even a balanced person subjected to stresses and strains of poverty becomes irritable and querulous. He may take to liquor. This complicates the problem still further. This gives rise to all sorts of mental and physical ills which in turn, leads to disintegration of the personality.

8. Marital Disintegration. Indirectly, the cudgel of poverty, falls rather heavily on the stability of marriage. As population rises the disintegration of marriage sets in. The population rise leads to poverty and poverty gives rise to tensions of all sorts. Due to stress and strain husband may take to liquor and wife to vagrancy. All this leads to marital disintegration.

9. Social Disintegration. The disintegration of family, personal and marital disintegration leads to social disintegration. The traditions and mores loosen their hold fast. People become selfish, tense, anxious and bitter and become misfits. They are unable to carry out their work efficiently, with the rise in urban population the feeling of communal togetherness declines and with the rise in the rural population the exodus to cities begins.

TABLE 2.1

Population in India

Census year	Member	Increase
1981	683,329,097	+24.66
1991	846,302,688	+23.85

TABLE 2.2

Population in India

S.No	State/UT	Population 1991	% of Total Population 1991	% of Total Population 1981
1	2	3	4	5
1.	U.P.	13,91,12,287	16.44	16.22
2.	Bihar	8,63,74,465	10.21	10.23
3.	Maharashtra	7,89,37,187	9.33	9.19
4.	West Bengal	6,80,77,965	8.04	7.99
5.	Andhra Pradesh	6,65,08,008	7.86	7.84
6.	Madhya Pradesh	6,61,81,170	7.82	7.64
7.	Tamil Nadu	5,58,58,946	6.60	7.08
8.	Karnataka	4,49,77,201	5.31	5.43
9.	Rajasthan	4,40,05,990	5.20	5.01
10.	Gujarat	4,13,09,582	4.88	4.99
11.	Orissa	3,16,59,736	3.74	3.86
12.	Kerala	2,90,98,518	3.44	3.72
13.	Assam	2,24,14,322	2.65	2.64
14.	Punjab	2,02,81,969	2.40	2.46
15.	Haryana	1,64,63,648	1.94	1.89
16.	Delhi	94,20,644	1.11	0.91
17.	Jammu and Kashmir	77,18,700	0.91	0.88
18.	Himachal Pradesh	51,70,877	0.61	0.63
19.	Tripura	27,57,205	0.33	0.30
20.	Manipur	18,37,149	0.22	0.21
21.	Meghalaya	17,74,778	0.21	0.19

1	2	3	4	5
22.	Nagaland	12,09,546	0.14	0.11
23.	Goa	11,69,793	0.14	0.15
24.	Arunachal Pradesh	8,64,558	0.10	0.09
25.	Pondicherry	8,07,785	0.09	0.09
26.	Mizoram	6,89,756	0.08	0.07
27.	Chandigarh	6,42,015	0.08	0.07
28.	Sikkim	4,06,457	0.05	0.05
29.	Andman and Nicobar	2,80,661	0.03	0.03
30.	Dadra and Nagar Haveli	1,38,447	0.02	0.01
31.	Daman and Diu	1,01,586	0.01	0.01
32.	Lakshadwip	51,707	0.01	0.01

Source : Census of India, 1991.

All the above mentioned social effects of population rise can be observed in modern India. This is the main reason why government is propagating family-planning so lavishly. According to some scholars the population rise affects even the form of the government.

POPULATION PROBLEM IN INDIA

India was the first country to launch an official programme of family planning as early as 1952. During the period 1951-87, almost Rupees 3500 crores have been spent on the programme. The current pace of annual expenditure is estimated at Rs. 600 crores per year or Rs. 44 per eligible couple per year. In spite of the fact that there has been a substantial increase in the programme expenditure over the years from 1976, the birth rate has been hovering between 30-33 births per 1000 population per year. There appears to be diminishing return to investments in family planning programme mostly because of the emphasis on sterilization which attracts couples with wife of age 30 and above after they have achieved their desired family size. There is a need to revamp the family planning programme to make it acceptable by younger age and lower parity couples by encouraging spacing methods.

The socio-economic picture that emerges for the country as depicted in 1991 census figures, is far from optimistic and definitely frustrating. During the decade 1981-91, India has added a whooping 160.7 millions to its population, which is almost equal to the combined population total of France, United Kingdom and Italy. During the decade, the population has increased by 23.50 per cent or at an annual rate of 2.11 per cent, compared to 24.66 per cent or at an annual rate of 2.22 per cent in the 1971-81 decade. Though the population growth rate shows a small decline during 1981-91 compared to the earlier years when it was steadily rising, the decline has been very slow and even by 1990 the barrier of 2 per cent growth in the population was not breached for the country as a whole, does not seem to have been overcome. However, the picture seems to be different when we consider the figures separately by states. Kerala, Tamil Nadu and Goa have registered a decadal growth rate of 13.98, 14.94 and 15.96 percentages respectively, far lower than the national level of 23.50 and are also the states which have recorded substantial decline in their growth rates compared to the earlier decade. On the other hand, among the large Hindi speaking states of Uttar Pradesh, Bihar, Madhya Pradesh and Rajasthan (which have been euphemistically referred to as "Bhimaru" states), the growth rates continue to remain quite high, with the decadal increases of 25.16, 23.49, 26.75 and 28.07 percentages respectively. These states together constitute almost 40 per cent of India's population and prevalence of high growth in such a wide area largely determines the national scene. The demographic differences between the states are accentuating over time and at present in many demographic parameters the large Hindi states are lagging behind by 15-20 years. Demographic polarisation of states into two groups are likely to have political and other repercussions. Another cause for serious concern is the sex ratio of the population. The result of the 1981 census was welcomed by those who were interested in improving the status of women in this country, since it indicated for the first time the reversal in the trend of declining sex ratio of the population (number of females per 1000 population of males) since the beginning of the century. The sex ratio of the population declined almost steadily from 972 females per 1000 males in 1901 to 930 females per 1000 males in 1971, but in 1981 this declining trend in the sex ratio was arrested and marginally increased to 934 females per 1000 males. Credit was given to the special emphasis given by the Government on provision of mental and child health care services, legal measures to control atrocities on women such as due to dowry deaths, improvements in female literacy and emergence of a strong leadership group from women. However, the 1991 census seems to have, at the first sight, shattered this hope with the sex ratio declining once again to 929 females per 1000 males.

Growth rate of metropolitan cities have revealed some surprising trends in the census. The population of Greater Bombay has increased from 8.24 million in 1981 to 9.91 million in 1991 registering an annual rate of growth of 1.84 per cent, in comparison with 3.25 per cent experienced in the previous decade, 1971-81.

There appears to be a substantial dispersion of Bombay's population into New Bombay and this has been really a laudable achievement by the Maharashtra Government in reducing the rate of growth of population in Greater Bombay. Among the cities, Hyderabad has recorded a maximum rate of growth, with population increasing from 2.50 million in 1981 to 4.27 million in 1991, with an annual rate of growth of 5.35% per year. This is followed by Delhi which has increased its population from 5.70 million in 1981 to 8.38 million in 1991, recording an annual growth rate 3.85 per cent. Similarly, Bangalore city has also substantially grown with an annual growth rate of 3.54 per cent per year during the decade 1981-91. These cities can benefit from the experiences of Bombay which has been successful in developing residential city.

India cannot afford the present rate of growth of 2 per cent per year in its population without inviting the Malthusian checks of famine, epidemics and conflicts to control its population. Not only the economic imbalances within the states are aggravated by the continuing growth of population, but also the imbalances between the states which are polarising demographically as more advanced and less advanced states, lead to increase in political tensions. There is an urgent need to implement innovative and imaginative programmes to reduce fertility levels as quickly as possible; otherwise mortality levels are bound to go up.

FAMILY WELFARE PROGRAMME IN INDIA

Population explosion in developing countries is a matter of international concern. For India with 16% of the world's population and 2.4% of the global land area, it is a problem of serious magnitude. Its current population growth rate of 2.03% (SRS 1981) with an annual addition of 1.6 crores presents a formidable scenario. India's population size has increased from 34.2 crores at the time of Independence to 84.4 crores as per the 1991 Census. Already there is tremendous pressure on our resources for providing even the basic needs, such as food, housing, education, health, to the country's large population. If the present growth of population is unchecked, the demand for even basic facilities and services would far outstrip their supply and there would be a serious impact on our socio-economic development, the quality of the lives of the people and the environment. Indeed, population control has to be the foremost national priority.

Although India was the first country in the world to launch the National Family Planning programme in 1951; over the years many other developing countries like Thailand, Indonesia, China, Sri Lanka etc. have achieved much greater degree of success in controlling population. China has an annual growth rate of 1.44% (1989) and Indonesia 1.5% (1989). The National Health Policy adopted by the Parliament in 1983 envisages that by the year 2000 AD, the Net Reproduction Rate would be Unity, with the population growth rate at 1.2% birth rate of 21 per thousand, death rate of 9 per thousand, infant mortality rate at below 60 per thousand live births and couple protection rate of 60%. The latest figures available indicate that while due to the efforts made in providing better and more extensive health care, the death rate has come down to 10.2 per thousand, the birth rate is still very high at 30.5 per thousand. The population is increasing at an unacceptable rate of 2.03%. The infant mortality rate has come down, but is still high at the rate of 91 per thousand. The couple protection rate at 44.1% is also much below the target. A sustained national effort, therefore, called for to achieve the goal of balanced population profile by the turn of the century.

The family planning programme in India is being promoted on voluntary basis, as a people's movement in keeping with the democratic traditions of the country. The two children norm is being promoted through independent choice of the family planning method best suited to the acceptor. The programme in the field is implemented by the State Governments and Union Territories Administration and there is very wide disparity in the success rate. While it has had considerable success in the southern states, specially Kerala and Goa where the birth rate has come down to about 19 per thousand, its impact in the large northern states like U.P., Bihar, Madhya Pradesh and Rajasthan, has been limited and the birth rates in these States are still in the range of 33 to 37 per thousand.

It is realised that the people respond to the family planning programmes more readily, if they are assured of the survival of their children. Therefore, for many years family planning is being pursued as a part of the integrated Programme of Family Welfare with special attention to the health and well-being of the family, specially mothers and children. A vast rural and urban infrastructure has been established to implement the Family Welfare Programme in the country. Immunisation Programme has been universalised to ensure better prospects of child survival which in turn would create the right psychological ambience for the small family norm. The desire for large families, specially male children in the prevailing socio-cultural and economic milieu, characteristically low status of women, low female literacy, early marriage of girls and high infant mortality rate are stumbling blocks in the progress of the Family Welfare Programme. The lack of popular commitment and will inhibit its faster tempo. The Programme is perceived as a Governmental programme, devoid of popular participation. Quality and out-reach of its service-delivery network are deficient in many parts of the country. Overemphasis on terminal methods lead to inadequate coverage of younger couples with high fertility potential. Communication systems are not effective enough to dispel the prevailing apathy, ignorance and misconceptions about the programme among the masses.

Confronted with the grim prospects of population explosion and the inadequacies of the present strategies, radical and innovative strategies are called for to revamp the programme and bring about a more rapid decline in fertility. Population Control and Family Welfare Programme needs to have a national consensus, cutting across political, religious and cultural differences. It needs to be based on active community participation and has to be transformed from a governmental programme into a people's movement. A differential need based strategy needs to be developed in the 206 low performing districts in the country which are mostly in the four North Indian States, viz. U.P., Bihar, Madhya Pradesh and Rajasthan to create an immediate impact. The status of women and female literacy are key factors for fertility decline, as seen in the State of Kerala and elsewhere. Age of marriage of girls is yet another crucial factor. In the four large North Indian States mentioned above, the average age of marriage for girls is well below the national average of 18.3 (1981) and the statutory minimum age of 18 years. Studies indicate that if the average age of marriage of girls in India is pushed up by two years, it may result in lowering the birth rate by about 25%. Besides, a comparatively higher age of marriage would bring down maternal and infant mortality.

Information, Education and Communication (IEC) effort is vital to the Population Control Programme. Fortunately, there has been a quantum jump in female literacy (24.8% in 1981 to 39.42% in 1991) during the last decade, thanks to specific measures undertaken by the Government. Population education should be a part of school and college education. It should also form an important ingredient of adult education and non-formal education. Communication strategies should be so devised as to be effective enough to bring about attitudinal changes and dispel apathy, ignorance and misgivings about family planning and small family norm. All non-governmental organisations — private sector, voluntary agencies, private medical practitioners and practitioners of Indian Systems of Medicines, Local bodies and Panchayati Raj Institutions should be fully involved in a massive effort of community participation. The service delivery system and its out-reach should be expanded with emphasis on quality of service. A package of effective incentives and disincentives should be formulated specially for younger couples in high reproductive range who require spacing methods of contraception. New generation contraceptives should be introduced in the country to make an impact on younger couples.

Thus, there is an imperative need to develop an integrated multisectoral strategy to handle the population problem in all its dimensions. Given strong political will, commitment of the people and vigorous implementation of revamped strategies, there is no reason why India should not be able to contain its population within manageable limits and open the way for utilisation of its resources for improving the quality of life of its people.

QUESTIONS FOR EXERCISE

1. Discuss the role of demographic factor in social change.
2. Discuss the population problem in India as revealed by census 1991.
3. Discuss critically the Family Welfare Programme in India.

3

Social Tensions : Regionalism, Linguism and Communalism

Group tensions may arise if there is any contradiction between two groups on questions of language, community, residence, culture, social or economic status etc. In this way, one may trace group tensions to a variety of causes such as physical, religious, social, cultural, economic and political, etc. Tensions increase when groups differ from each other in these or in other respects. Gardner Murphy gives it the name of the sin of being different. It must of course be kept in mind that group tensions cannot the attributed to the mere fact of dissimilarity. It is not inevitable that groups that differ from each other must also have tense relations. The fact of difference is further supplemented by some psychological factors, so that it leads to tension. It has been pointed out earlier that many prejudices, beliefs and attitudes are the root cause of tensions. Krech and Crutchfield have recognised physical, psychological and social causes of tensions. On the other hand, Kimball Young has laid greater stress on the cultural causes and factors that lead to tension.

CAUSES OF SOCIAL TENSIONS

Roughly speaking, the following causes may be said to contribute to the growth and development of tensions:

(1) Physical Causes. In this particular case physical is almost synonymous with geographical. People who live in different geographical regions are naturally apt to differ from each other in respect of their habits, diet, mode of life, anatomical features, according to the differing geographical conditions to which they have to adapt themselves. The result is that this difference leads them to look upon all people brought up in different geographical regions as foreigners. It is only natural that one should love a person of one's own nationality and avoid a foreigner whom he does not know and cannot understand so well. If this mutual distrust is further comingled with some other factors and when this distrust becomes more serious it leads to tensions between people of different regions.

(2) Social Causes. In social relationships the factor of social distance is very important. In every society, there is a stratification as a result of which each particular kind of group has a special status and certain roles in society that devolve upon it and its members by virtue of their status. The relationships between two groups are determined by their respective social status. To take an example near at hand, in Indian society the Brahmins occupy the highest position in the social stratification while the untouchables are at the other end of the ladder. Consequently, the social distance between the Brahmin and the Shudra is greater than the social distance that separates the Brahmin and the Kshatriya. The person who occupies a higher status because of social distance regards the group belonging to the lower status as mean and contemptible. The offsprings of people of different status are endowed with certain prejudices at their birth peculiar to the respective statuses. If a Brahmin child even touches the child of a scavenger, he is immediately bathed with the result that the child forms the belief that touching a scavenger results in defilement. It is evident that prejudices of this kind should lead to the development of tensions between the various social groups.

(3) Cultural Causes. Culture is expressed in language, literature, patterns of living and thinking or ideational activity. The differences in respect of any one of these factors will lead to a cultural difference between groups. People tend to recede into themselves and away from people who differ from them culturally since communication of idea and other cultural factors is impeded by lack of conformity. Each individual regards his own culture as the highest while he looks with disdain and contempt at another's culture which he regards very much lower than his own. Thus people who harbour deep love and respect for ancient Indian culture naturally hate and mistrust people who have taken to Western culture. In Bengal it is this very cultural difference that led to tense relations between the Brahmins and other groups. Group tensions can originate on any disputed element in culture. Now in India itself, we find tensions running high between people who speak Hindi and the people who do not, between people who speak the Assamese tongue and those who speak Bengali, and between the Punjabi population and those who would like to foist Hindi on them.

(4) Religious Causes. People who have faith in different religions naturally differ in respect of their ideas about God, the world hereafter, heaven, hell, soul, etc., and other matters of religious interest. They have faith in different saints. Their methods and places of worship differ. This difference often leads to communalism since most of the religious people are convinced that it is only their own religion that preaches that truth while all other religions are no more and no less than a tissue of lies. As a result of this communal feeling the Hindus and Muslims view the actions of each other with distrust, while they are fully convinced of each other's unmitigated folly. This only leads to more staunch communalism, and it sometimes reaches such a stage that actual conflict becomes inevitable.

(5) Economic Causes. Difference in economic status will directly and apparently cause a difference in the dress, standard of living, modes of behaviour, customs and ideational activity of social groups. In the materialistic culture of today, the increased importance of monetary wealth has led to social status being determined by financial success. Hence it is that social distance increases when economic differences become more and more accentuated. This has the result of promoting conflicts and tensions between people belonging to different classes. Tensions of this nature can be witnessed the world over between labourers and industrialists, the rich and the poor, and the exploiters and the exploited.

(6) Political Causes. The Communist party has played the greatest part in encouraging and increasing the tensions that already existed between different economic classes. Similarly, the political organisation known by the name of DMK in the South had done much to promote the regional conflict between the North and South in India; in fact, it is responsible for it in the first place. The communal tensions between the Hindus and Muslims had been much increased by various communal and political parties such as the Muslim League, the Hindu Mahasabha, etc., that have aimed at political objectives. In much the same manner different political groups augment the tensions existing between various lingual groups by constantly harping on this sensitive question. In the present political set up in India the various communal organisations are very important. In the last general election many of the candidates elected claimed communal conformity and collusion of sympathies of the electorate and thereby secured votes that ensured their passage into the parliament where they, in utter faithfulness towards the electors, further encouraged communalism since by only this method could they ensure a return to their present happy position. In this manner, political parties usually have a major hand in promoting and creating caste, political and communal tensions.

(7) Psychological Causes. Finally, the most important and the most prominent causes at the root of social or group tensions are psychological. In fact, they are the direct causes of group tensions. Physical, social, religious, cultural and economic differences cannot inevitably lead to group tensions unless mutual jealousy, hatred, contradictory beliefs, attitudes of conflict and prejudices are not implanted in the minds of members of the various groups. The presence of these psychological elements tends to accelerate the normal rate of growth of group tensions. Injury to one's self-respect normally leads people to harbour feelings of hatred for the group that is responsible for this injury. The tension between various groups is further increased by the sense of self-expression. Groups that fear each others are naturally always on the look out of opportunities in which they may inflict injury upon the hated group. In this way, the psychological causes are the root causes of group tensions.

From the above description of the various causes due to which social or group conflicts and tensions are aroused, it is evident that no one cause is responsible for group tensions. There may be various causes that lead to the development of various tensions between sundry groups under all kinds of differing circumstances. In this connection, it is essential to maintain an open mind and a Catholic attitude. At the same time it must be remembered that usually more than one cause is mixed up with any type of group tensions. Many different causes and all kinds of circumstances co-operate to create an atmosphere that is conducive to the growth and development of group tensions.

Once some definite tensions are created between different groups, it is not easy to rid them of these tensions. Group tensions are the outcome of certain definite circumstances and situations. Group tensions then obviously cannot be eliminated so long as these conditions are allowed to remain. In this way, then the permanence of these group tensions is maintained for a fairly long period of time.

WAYS OF RESOLVING SOCIAL TENSIONS

As a general rule, it can be stated that the method of eliminating group tensions would involve all the causes that cause and inflame group tensions. The causes that are responsible for these group tensions are of the social, economic, political, psychological and a variety of other kinds. Hence, any attempt at eliminating them would involve social, economic, political and psychological means. What appears to be more reasonable and practicable is that efforts should be made to remove the various prejudices harboured by the members of these groups. They should be made to realise that the members of the other groups are just as much human beings as they themselves, that they too have the sense to realise the importance of co-operative effort, that their life is as strewn with difficult boulders as their own and is not the bed of roses and that they must be compassionate and that they too are desirous of extending their circle of acquaintances and friends. The group tensions that exist between various groups can be removed if their members are made to realize and feel the bond of unity that binds one human being to another. Here it is feasible to mention only the major means of putting an end to group tension.

(1) Education. The most important single cause at root of group tensions is ignorance. This ignorance takes two forms, education being one of them. Group tensions grow easily among uneducated people and linger there. The other form of education is ignorance concerning various other social groups. The result of this lack of information is that people from all kinds of misconceptions regarding the members of the other group. The Muslim is inclined to think that the Hindu is interested only in gaining ascendency over them while the latter labours under the misconception that Muslims seem to have nothing more than negative mechinations to occupy their time with. The white-skinned people seem to have decided once for all that the negroes are mean, contemptible, uncultured and unintelligent. There seems to be no reason to suppose that the negroes are any the more charitable or are too reticent to think base thoughts of the white skinned people. The natural ignorance only serves to augment the existing tension. Hence, the most important method of eliminating group tensions is the propagation of common ideals through the medium of education. This education should be of both kinds. On the one hand, it is necessary to develop the personality of every individual in the nation by a comprehensive programme of education, so that it will induce in them a charitable and broad attitude. They will learn benevolence. It should be seen carefully that no discrimination is exercised in educational institutions with regard to admission, scholarships or appointments on the basis of caste, religion, community, region, or any other basis. It is to be regretted that no precautions are taken to prevent this malpractice in India. Throwing light on the problem of casteism in the Mysore state Dr. M.N. Srinivas has written that the principle of casteism is the guiding principle not only in any and every appointment within the state but it also governs the division and distribution of seats in schools and colleges. If casteism is to be routed from the Indian scene, then all terms relating to and smacking of casteism should be removed from the vocabulary of the people. Efforts should be made to develop benevolence and toleration in the people through education. Sports and extra curricular activities should be so devised that the student may be conscious of taking part not only in a competitive sport but also in one in which he learns to co-operate. In addition to this the student should also be acquainted with the moral ideas, customs, etc., of other social groups so that he may literally be immunized against all attacks of prejudicial and misleading propaganda. Indian students should have knowledge of the various people living in different parts of the country.

(2) Creation of healthy literature. Education is not only confined to schools and colleges but rather is the province of literary matter with the result that books and magazines also share the burden of educating the country's youth. One comes across many propaganda machines called by the name of magazines whose only aim is to spread false information adding to the group tensions already existing. Besides these, there is also much in literature and much of the kind of literature that promotes group tensions. There are some social groups who use the medium of cheap literature as an organ whose one and only confessed aim is to deride all other groups and to praise its own proponent. It is of the essence that literature of this nature should be subjected to the strictest control. There should be very strong controls foisted on communal organs. The positive step in this direction would be the practical and continuous encouragement of good and healthy literary activity in the country. Magazines and papers that aim at correct information will always reduce group tensions and increase tolerance, co-operation and friendship in society. It is magazines and papers such as these that should receive the encouragement from the state.

(3) Preparation of healthy public opinion. In fact, the total removal of group tensions calls for the growth of a healthy public opinion. To attain this end, in addition to magazines and newspapers, radio and public platforms should be used for propaganda calculated to lessen group tension. Programmes that help to reduce casteism, regionalism, linguism and communalism and to promote nationalistic feelings should be broadcast over the radio. Propaganda can also be employed to put an end to the misleading ideas imbeded in the minds of the public.

(4) Improving social adjustment. One important cause of group tensions is social maladjustment. People who fail to find proper adjustment with the conditions of their existence harbour, and are prey to feelings such as hatred, fear, obstinacy, opposition, disgust, etc., and they are constantly on the lookout for an opportunity when they may be able to give vent to them against the other groups. Group tension is also a kind of adverse adjustment. Hence, one method of getting rid of it is to encourage and introduce proper social adjustment between various groups.

(5) Reducing social distance. And social adjustment between various groups can be introduced only when the social distance between them is reduced so much that there is possibility of fruitful social intercourse between them. They should be encouraged to improve their mutual contacts. Social or group tensions can be considerably reduced by increasing the mutual contact and intimacy between members of various groups. The best and the most effective method of removing untouchability is to increase the contact between the higher castes and untouchables. This contact will help to remove the feelings of disgust and hatred for the untouchables in minds of members of higher castes while the untouchables will be able to regain some of their dignity and self-respect and along with it their self-confidence. Much good in the direction of removing casteism permanently from the country can be achieved by establishing mutual intimate relationships between the various castes by encouraging inter-caste marriages between them.

(6) Balanced development of personality. Groups are conglomerations of human individuals. At the root of group imbalance there is individual imbalance. Hence, one other method that can reduce group tension is the balanced and proper development of the personality of the members of various groups. This work should start first of all with educational institutions. In educational institutions, the help of a psychologist can be enlisted for progress in this direction. Besides the educational institutions, another social institution that has much importance for the developing personality is the family. The individual's character or personality is also susceptible to influences emanating from the improvement of social associations. In brief, all methods that can help in the development of balanced personalities within society will also help reduce group tension indirectly.

(7) Youth Organization. Youth has much importance both in social conflict as well as in co-operation in society. It is essential to make special efforts in the groups of youths in order to reduce group tensions. For this it is necessary to form youth organisations formed at the national level, and the formation of which does not bow to any considerations of religion, community, language, region, etc. One example of this kind of youth organisation is the annually held Youth Festival in almost all Indian Universities. Youth festivals of this kind can be arranged in every town and every village. It is necessary to organise Indian rural population, particularly the younger generations, so that community life in villages may prosper and progress. If this is not achieved then it will become impossible to establish co-operation after removing group tensions.

(8) Propagation of national objectives. One other important cause at the root of group tensions is the lack of comprehensive aims and objectives. It usually happens that most of the time each group is busily engaged in attaining its own selfish interests. Every religion, community and caste is busy finding and devising ways and means whereby it can benefit its own members. It is only natural that under these circumstances group tensions between various religions, communities and castes should increase. But if all these various individual groups are presented with some national objectives and some programmes of national security and emancipation then these comprehensive programmes will have the desired effect of reducing group tensions.

(9) Removal of economic disparity. Another cause of group tensions is economic disparity or inequality. Economic disparity leads to the formation of economic classes. Of these classes the higher classes exploit the lower. This only leads to an increase in mutual bitterness, and it can even culminate in class struggles. Besides, economic insecurity spreads unhappiness and unrest and dissatisfaction. Hence, economic security is essential to the removal of group tensions. This fact is accepted by communist and non-communist thinkers alike.

(10) Social emancipation. Many group tensions are maintained in status quo by virtue of many social causes that contribute to this end. For example, the idea of untouchability and the restriction on inter-caste marriage have both been instrumental in maintaining casteism at a fairly high level. If casteism is to be removed, it is necessary that both these evils be removed at the root.

(11) Formal or constitutional means. Finally it is justified to resort to all constitutional provisions to get rid of group tensions since it sometimes becomes necessary to enforce any new suggestion by the force of law to get over the natural obstinacy of the people. Constitutional methods can be usefully employed to prevent all communal activity. In India much reform was achieved when untouchability was pronounced a legal offence since it made the people respect this reform measure. In much the same way casteism can also be declared an offence and even if this is not considered a very practical step, good precedents and examples can be created by taking stern action. Wherever there appears to be any corruption this is alleged to be the outcome of casteism. Legal prohibition and restriction can be applied to all magazines and other media of mass communication that serve to increase group tensions.

(12) Specific studies of group tensions. Group tension is a psychological fact. All the methods for its elimination that have been hitherto enumerated can be successful only if particular attention is paid to its psychological aspect. Psychologists can be employed to make some special studies in this connection. For example, Gardner Murphy guided some researches in connection with communal tensions in India. Similarly specific psychological research can be ordered in connection with casteism, linguism, regionalism and other kinds of tensions. These psychological researches can serve the purpose of suggesting practicable methods of removing these tensions. But once these methods have been evolved, what is needed is some strong steps on the part of the government and willing co-operation on the part of the public.

Having made a general study of group tension, it is not proposed to turn to the description of problems at the root of which exist social or group tensions. In India, one can come across this kind of social conflict in regionalism, linguism and communalism. They will now be described individually.

REGIONALISM

Of course, regionalism has always been present in India in one or the other form but never has it attained such magnitude as it possesses today and neither was it ever as detrimental to any national interest as it is in the present context. When there were so many states in the country it was not harmful to have regionalism in them but when the entire country has become one nation, regionalism poses a serious threat to national unity and integration.

What is Regionalism?

Regionalism is the sense of affection and attachment for people belonging to one's own region and hatred for those who belong to some other region. As a result of this, people of one region in India have started looking at people from some other part of the country in the same light in which they are prone to regard foreigners. They want that only people of their own area should run the government in their region while they do not want to make any place for people who have migrated from some other region irrespective of the period for which they may have been living there. In this way, some people have demanded the formation of a separate state of Nagaland in the Naga area. The Akali party of Punjab has demanded the formation of a Punjabi Suba. It was on the basis of region that the state of Bombay was divided into two separate states, those of Gujarat and Maharashtra. In addition to these antics of the politicians some people are demanding that the South should be formed into an entirely separate unit. India is a union of the states. The functions of government have been divided between the central government and the respective state governments. All these states are free to act on all domestic matters. Hence, the unity of the nation can be maintained only so long as the people regard the entire country as one nation and their own country. If all the people are going to lay their faith in their own respective regions and will not accord any consideration to the interests of the nation then it will become difficult for the union government to continue functioning. In this way, regionalism has become a serious problem for the interests of the nation.

Causes of Regionalism

There are many causes at the root of this regionalism in the country, the major ones being the following —

(1) Geographical causes. The main cause of regionalism is geographical. There is some essential difference between the food habits, languages, life, etc., of every region and the people who live there. By virtue of these differences they come to regard each other as foreigners and they acquire an attitude of fear and hatred for each other.

(2) Historical causes. As has been indicated earlier, there are some historical causes also as the root of regionalism. For example, there has been some difference between the people of the North and South ever since the time of the Aryans and it has continued. Many of the kings of the North have won over the South while there have been few kingdoms in the South which have extended to the Northern part of India. Because of this, many South Indians look upon Northern India as separate entity from Southern India.

(3) Political causes. But if the situation is carefully and minutely observed, it will be seen that the main cause at the root of regionalism present in the country is of a political nature. In different regions some people have demanded the formation of regional governments and in this they have been inspired by regional interests and by aims of gaining power. In this direction a major part has been played by the revolutionary Naga party guided by Phizo, the Akali party of Punjab, the D.M.K. party of the South and other political parties. The truth is that the leaders of these political parties are responsible for having propagated regionalism in their respective areas. Not only this, even some representatives of different areas who are members of political parties give prime importance to the interest of their own regions even in the face of national interests which are ignored by them.

(4) Psychological causes. Finally, the psychological causes have contributed no less to the development and stability of regionalism. It is the wish of most of the persons that it be their area that progresses the most. This idea in itself is neither bad nor detestable but when they disregard the national interests and those of other regions for the attainment of this, then this feeling takes on a form of regionalism. Besides this, there are many individuals encouraging regionalism who express the hatred, jealousy, fear, anger and other feelings contained in them in this manner.

(5) Other causes. There are some other causes besides those mentioned above that promote regionalism. For example, it is only rarely that one comes across married couples among whom one belongs to Bengal and the other to Punjab or to Rajasthan or to Chenai, for that matter. As a general rule, people belonging to different regions do not marry and hence the occasion for close contact between the two does not arise. In addition to these there are some economic causes of regional tension. In the country there are some regions that are backward in comparison with some other regions. As a result they are often seen possessed of a sense of inferiority and they become jealous of others. People belonging to some particular sphere are seen to be particularly successful in some vocations. For example, in India, the most successful business men are seen to belong to Marwar, Gujarat and Punjab, and in this sphere they have a practical monopoly. In this too they are hated by some people who try to turn them out from their own regions.

Means for the Abolition of Regionalism

The following means can help to end regionalism or at least to dilute it to some extent:

(1) Encouragement to transport and communication. If regionalism is to be eliminated, the people should be encouraged to indulge in travel and to increase contact with people belonging to different regions of the country. Recently, a train of religious hermits toured the country and similarly many farmers belonging to Rajasthan travelled all over the country. In India, the tradition whereby people are induced to visit places of religious importance is a good one inasmuch that it helps people to travel all over the country and meet different people. In going to different corners of the country the people realise that India is a large country and regional sentiments can be removed or rendered less effectual by encouraging transport and communication in the country.

(2) Propaganda of the national history. The history of the nation should be propagated all over the country so that the people may clearly realise that the history of the individual regions of the country is only a part of the history of the nation to which all the regions have made an important contribution. The propagation of the national history will help to eradicate the sense of regionalism.

(3) Prevention of regional political parties. It is essential for national unity and integration that the political parties propagating regionalism and regional interests should be prevented from doing so. If they indulge in unrestricted campaigns for promoting regional interests they should be declared illegal. Although in a democracy every individual has the right to form a political organisation in order to express his views but if it tends to harm the interests of the nation this right must be curbed.

(4) Propagation of the national sentiment. Finally, in order to remove the psychological causes at the root of regionalism an effort should be made to propagate the sentiment of nationalism in the country. It is necessary to resort to all the various media of propaganda to obtain results in this direction. Efforts should be made to remove the regionalistic tendencies from all spheres such as government service, educational institution, etc., and the sentiment of nationality should be encouraged.

Regionalism is a complex problem. If it is to be solved it must be attacked from all sides and furthermore such a task requires co-operation from the government and the people. Only then can this problem be solved.

LINGUISM

India is a multi-lingual state in which many languages are spoken. Practically every state has its own language and sometimes more than one languages are spoken in the same area. Some of these languages are English, Hindi, Punjabi, Marathi, Tamil, Telugu, Malayalam, Kannada, Urdu, Bengali, and many others besides these. Probably, the greatest number speak Hindi which is also the national language, and their number is on the increase. But the literatures of the various other languages have also been appropriately developed. For example, the literature of Bengali, Punjabi, Tamil, etc., are by no means of a lower intellectual stature than that possessed by Hindi. The presence of many languages in a country is no defect in itself. An increase in the literature of the various languages is an increase in the literary wealth of the nation itself. When the people try to develop the language that they speak and do not attend to other languages it is not a matter that is likely to cause concern to one who has the interests of the nation at heart but when the difference of languages becomes a pretext for tension between people speaking different languages then it does become a grave matter. When one language is considered superior to the other languages which are considered both inferior and detestable, and there is a blind and unconsidering acceptance of such a view, then this tendency is christened linguism. Like all the other isms that one is apt to run across, this linguism is also harmful for the communal interest.

Problems of Linguism

During the past decade or so, linguism has been gathering momentum and force till now it has become a definite threat to the unity and integrity of the nation. In Punjab, the problem of choice between Punjabi and Hindi has created a lot of conflict and tension while in Assam the language question has even resulted in bloodsheds. In Bengal, Bengali has been opposed to Hindi and a serious problem in linguism has thus taken shape. Besides the problems of regional languages, the proponents of Hindi, English and Urdu are creating tension in the entire country. It often happens that the language movement is only a disguised political move and on close observation it will become clear that there are not many literary persons but mostly politicians who cause lingual movements. For example, the movement for the Punjabi language in the Punjab was attached to the demand for a Punjabi Suba.

Causes of Linguism

What are the causes at the root of linguism? As it is, linguism is a complex problem and it is difficult to make a complete analysis of all its various causes. Nevertheless, the following are some of the important causes briefly stated:

(1) Geographical causes. Linguism is like the other tensions mentioned previously inasmuch that it too has a geographical causes. Different languages are spoken in the different parts of India and these individual languages also have a lot of varieties since the dialect differs from one town to another. Language is the medium through which people express their thoughts and feelings and make them know each other. And it is through language that they come to know each other. Hence, it is natural to feel a bond of intimacy with one who speaks some one's own tongue while one feels lost among people who speak some other language than one's own. Every language has its own literature. This literature is everywhere influenced by the local geographical conditions, rivers, plains and mountains, local vegetation, animals and local culture. It reflects the life of the people who speak that language. Hence, literature bears a very definite relation to its geographical demarcation. The familiarity that a person finds in the literature of the language that he speaks is not available to him in any other literature. Hence, it is natural for a person to wish for the development and progress of the language of his own region and he does not appreciate it if the language of another region is forced on him. When this mental tendency grows more vicious and strong, when the individual acquires a sense of hatred for the other languages and people who speaks them then tension is created.

(2) Historical causes. Some of the causes of linguism are also historical. India has been attacked by one foreigner after another. These foreigners came equipped with their own respective languages. The Mughals came and brought Persian which mixed with the local languages and became Urdu. The Britishers put in their appearance with the English language up their sleeves. These languages found the Indian soil suitable and they prospered and grew, and their Indianization also occurred. Many Hindus also wrote in Urdu. If the people had recourse to reason there need have been no occasion for the problem of Urdu or Hindi to have arisen but people who turned to ancient history for their inspiration did not accept the Indianization of Urdu and kept the language as it was, with an abundance of Arabic and Persian words. It was not confined to this because the literature that they created had a foreign soul.

(3) Psychological causes. And yet, the most important and the primary causes at the root of linguism are of a psychological nature. At its root are the hatred for the other languages and those who speak them in addition to the respect and admiration of one's own language. At its root is the narrow-minded self-respect of the individuals. If the prejudice concerning the other languages is removed from the mind and a comprehensive and sympathetic view-point is adopted, it becomes possible for any number of languages to prosper.

(4) Political causes. Linguism is also inspired by the political interests and aspirations of different politicians and political groups. Many communal political parties raise the language issue, instigate their people and want to win their votes during the elections. The problem of linguism has gained in complexity because of its affiliations with politics.

(5) Economic causes. There are some economic causes that also inspire linguism. Some languages are financially assisted by the government which aims at their progress but people seeking other languages object to this and thus linguism increases.

(6) Social causes. Linguism is encouraged by some social factors also. Some myths and legends, customs and traditions prevail in every society. That language is respected in society which provides a place for these. It also is the language that is adopted by the society. On the contrary, the languages that do not respect and accept these or the languages that cater to contrary presumptions are objected to. In this manner linguism spreads.

Suggestions for the Eradication of Linguism

Having studied the causes that cause linguism, it is now possible to turn to the means for its solution and elimination. In this context the following suggestions can be made:

(1) Development of the national language. In the event of their being one national language, and literature, that have been developed people speaking the different languages which have an opportunity to communicate with each other through the medium of this national language and the tension existing between them will be sensibly lessened.

(2) Encouragement to all major languages. In addition to the development of one common national language and literature the main regional languages should also be encouraged. No language can be forced upon any region and neither can a language be developed by putting stress upon it. The language automatically develops through the medium of usage. Once this is clearly understood much of the tension caused by linguism would come to an end. In this way, the government should encourage all the important regional languages. The government should see to it that Punjabi is developed in the Punjab, Bengali in Bengal and Assamese in Assam and so on in addition to which Hindi should be propagated in all parts of the country.

(3) Opposition of communalism. In order to obliviate the political causes of linguism it is necessary to vigorously oppose communalism in the country.

Finally, it should be remembered that in order to solve the problem of linguism it is necessary to adopt a comprehensive viewpoint. Each language should be encouraged by the government and in every region particular attention should be paid to the regional language and its development. The political intrigues that instigate the problem of linguism should be kept in strict check and a national language and national literature should be developed so that contact between groups of people speaking different languages increases and linguism decreases.

COMMUNALISM

India's independence was announced on 15th August 1947 and it was on that day that in every corner of the country Hindus and Muslims shed each other's blood. The inhuman behaviour seen during these communal riotings has probably no equal in the entire history of the world. Entire villages were set on fire and living children were thrown into the conflagration; women were taken in processions beaten with whips while they were naked. At many places entire trainloads of human beings were put to death. Millions were rendered homeless while millions of others lost their property and earnings; but the worst part of the whole deal is that in spite of such a costly and terrible sacrifice communal tensions have not been put to an end. It is only recently that there were communal riotings in Bengal and other Eastern states. This spark is one that is apt to catch fire at any moment. There are some special causes at its root. Knowledge of the ways in which communalism can be removed from the country can be had after these causes are known.

Causes of Communal Tension

The following are the main causes of communal tension:

(1) Geographical causes. One main cause of communalism is a geographical one. There is great communal tension wherever the Hindus, Muslims, Christians and others live in separate sections because in the modes of life and conduct of the different religious groups exist wide differences.

(2) Historical causes. Another important cause of communal tension is of a historical nature. It is an established historical fact that Muslim religionists came to India as foreigners and started converting Hindus to Islam with the force of the sword. Many of the Muslim rulers inflicted much injustice and misery on the Hindus while on the other hand, some Hindu kings retaliated in an equally violent manner to these activities on the part of Muslim kings. It is hundreds of years since these goings on took place and after that period there have been numerous occasions on which the Hindus and the Muslims co-operated with each other. In the war of freedom of 1857, Hindus and Muslims made a combined effort to win the freedom of the country. In the Congress, in the Indian National Army, the Muslims stood by the Hindus in opposing the Britishers but in both the communities many people have been unable to forget the past in which the dictatorship of Aurangzeb posed a threat to the very existence of Hindu religion by his injustice and cruelty. There was a time when the Muslim women of Punjab and Kashmir quietened their children by making them think of Harisingh Nalva. This had the cumulative memory result in maintaining communal tension. And not only this, some people went so far as to form political parties based on communal interest which indulged in all sorts of petty quarrels. They also inflamed the minds of both the communities against each other. The Muslim League demanded the formation of Pakistan. Pakistan was formed and yet communal tensions were not dissipated fully.

(3) Psychological causes. The main cause of communal tension is of a psychological nature. Communal rioting breaks out between the Hindus and the Muslims in the country whenever the hatred and disgust that they have for each other reaches feverish pitch due is nominal misunderstanding. There are some perceptive and misleading dogmatic concepts at the root of this mutual hatred. Hindus are prone to believe that the Muslim is a born traitor while the Muslims feel that they are in constant danger from the Hindus. Tension increases because of such fallacious thought based on ignorance.

(4) Social causes. Some social causes also promote communal tension. Even today there are many restrictions that hinder any profound relationships between Hindus and Muslims. The Muslims slaughter cows and this injures the religious feeling of the Hindus while the Hindus find it objectionable to form too close a relationship with the Muslim because they profess a different religion. Many of the customs respected by the two stand in complete contradiction. Hindus grow their religious tuft of hair which the Muslim do not. Their respective dresses differ widely. In washing hands the Hindus pour the water so that it proceeds from the direction of the elbow to that of the wrist while the Muslim so pour it that it flows from the wrist to elbow. These things are well nigh insignificant but because of them the two are prone to look at each other as slightly mad. At present inter-caste marriages are exceptions in the country and it is unthinkable for the people to think in terms of marriages between different religious groups.

MEASURES TO RELIEVE COMMUNAL TENSIONS

A study of the forementioned causes of communal tensions provides a clue to the means to their solution. The following are the important ways of eliminating communal tensions:

(1) Propagation of the national history. If communal tensions are to be eliminated it is necessary that those aspects and times in history should be emphatically propagated in which the Hindus and Muslims combined to act in the interests of the nation and made sacrifices to this end. The employment of this measure will serve to remove the historical causes of communal tensions while it will simultaneously encourage nationalist emotions.

(2) Mutual contact. In order to remove the psychological causes at the root of communal tensions it is necessary to improve the mutual contacts between the two communities. Youth organisations should be formed in every village and every town in which the youths of every community should participate and actively take part in different programmes. In addition to this other associations of this kind can also be formed in which members of the different communities get the opportunity to meet and know each other.

(3) Discouraging communal parties. The government should keep a vigilant and stern eye on the activities of the communal parties while it should be progressively tried to put an end to these parties. In India many communal parties promote communalism while acting in the guise of cultural and religious associations. The government should attend to them, and if found, they should immediately be stopped.

(4) Formation of healthy public opinion. Newspapers, lectures, radio programmes and the cinema should be utilised in forming a healthy national public opinion and the use of these for communal propaganda should be declared illegal.

(5) Encouragement to national festivals. In the country the national festivals and occasions should be encouraged in such a manner as to enable people of all communities to participate to the fullest extent. What can be done in this direction is to declare the important festivals of both communities such as Holi, Diwali, Id, etc., to be national festivals so that Hindus and Muslims should both take part. This mutual contact will help to reduce communal tensions.

From the foregoing treatment of the various methods of eradicating or at least lessening communal tensions it is evident that in this direction it is necessary to resort to all social, scientific and psychological methods. It is necessary to make a concerted effort. Both the government as well as the people will have to co-operate if any success is to be achieved in this direction. The element of communalism has been in the country for such a long time that great effort will have to be made if this poisonous weed is to be removed.

QUESTIONS FOR EXERCISE

1. What do you understand by social tensions? Analyse the causes of their growth in India and suggest suitable remedies.
2. Write short note on Regionalism.
3. Write short note on Linguism.
4. Point out the causes of Communalism in India and suggest remedies.

4

Casteism

Casteism is partial or onesided loyalty in favour of a particular caste. When any mode of thinking assumes the form of an ism, it becomes rigid and partial. The sense of caste when it implies a specific status in society does not pertain to casteism. The sense of caste is converted to casteism only when consideration of superiority between castes and the tendency to consider the interest of one's own caste as opposed to the other castes are attached to it. In this manner the members of one caste do not hesitate in dealing fatal blows to the interests of the other castes, if the interests of their own caste are furthered in so doing.

DEFINITION OF CASTEISM

It is necessary to define casteism if its form and nature are to be clearly and precisely understood. Some main definitions are the following:

(1) Loyalty to the sub-caste. In the words of K.M. Panikkar, "In this way it is only because of casteism that the Smiths want to benefit only the Smiths while the Joneses want to come to the aid of the other Joneses. It matters little if the members of the other castes are irreparably harmed, if it does not cause any concern to the Smiths and Joneses."

(2) Loyalty to the caste. But casteism is apparent also in the form of loyalty to the caste. In the words of D.N. Prasad, "In this way, caste has been dragged into the political arena in the form of casteism such as 'brahmanvada' and 'kayasthavada'.

(3) Blind group loyalty. In this opinion casteism is the blind and irrational loyalty to the community. In this all considerations of proper or improper, justice or injustice, etc., are thrown to winds in the face of the interest of one's own caste, and these must be achieved. In the words of Kaka Kalelkar "Casteism, therefore, is an overriding, blind and supreme group loyalty and ignores the healthy social standards of justice, fair play, equity and universal brotherhood."

In this way, then putting it briefly, casteism is a blind group loyalty towards one's own caste or sub-caste which does not care for the interests of other castes and seeks to realise the social, economic, political and other interests of its own group. This definition of casteism includes all the preceding definitions of the concept and tends to classify further the political aspect of casteism.

CAUSES OF CASTEISM

Now-a-days, casteism is at its height in India, the culmination of many causes. Some of the many causes are as follows:

(1) Sense of caste prestige. The most important cause of casteism is the desire of people belonging to a particular caste to enhance the prestige of their caste and in so doing see no wrong in adopting even the most downgraded and deleterious methods. But prestige of the caste can be maintained only on the ground that every opportunity be availed of and utilised in order to improve the social status of members. In order to achieve this objective every caste provides its members with all possible privileges in order to raise their social status. This tends to increase casteism.

(2) Marriage restrictions. The second cause that encouraged the development of casteism in the restriction on marriage that prevails in Hindu society. Under the caste system the restrictions that apply to marriage turn every caste into a monogamous group in which each individual looks upon himself as related in some way to all the others and for this reason everyone pays proper attention to the interests of others. Such action encourages casteism.

(3) Urbanization. With the advent of the tendency to urbanization it becomes possible for all castes to collect in large numbers in towns. At the same time the lives of members of various castes became beset with problems as a result of which it became necessary to provide security for them on a communal basis. Casteism is spreading because of the necessity to fulfil this need of security.

(4) Increase in the means of transport and propaganda. One factor that has assisted the development of casteism is the increase in the means of both transport and propaganda because this improvement has led to the establishment of relation between members of a caste who were previously separated because of geographical distances. And the feeling of casteism is being rapidly propagated through the medium of newspapers and communal magazines.

CONSEQUENCES OF CASTEISM

On the one hand, casteism serves to further the interests of a small number of individuals but, on the other hand, it is proving harmful to the nation as a whole. Some of the major consequences of casteism are following:

(1) Hindrance in the development of nationalism. Casteism hinders the growth and development of nationalism. On the one hand, casteism has divided Indian society into many parts while, on the other hand, many tensions and conflicts between these various parts have been created on the basis of casteism.

(2) Hindrance to democracy. Many of the professional leaders in the political field exploit casteism and at election time ask the people to vote for them on communal considerations and they also succeed in their evil designs. This sometimes results in the election of unscrupulous individuals who do not hesitate in crushing common interests in the consideration and promotion of caste interests. In practice, the glories of casteism are sung even behind the scenes where there is professedly inequality. In this way, casteism is fatal to democracy. According to K.M. Pannikar, "In fact no organisation of society on the basis of equality is possible so long as the sub-caste and the joint family exist."

(3) Corruption. People inspired by the sense of casteism try to provide all kinds of facilities to people who belong to their own castes and in doing so they resort to all kinds of immortal and improper activities. In this way extreme corruption in the society is increasing.

(4) Hindrance in technological efficiency. Because the appointment to government and private services is done on the basis of caste, there seems to be continuing increase in the number of inefficient and worthless people. On the other hand, the efficient and able individuals do not get the opportunity to find employment. Thus a great obstacle is placed in the path of the nation's industrial and technological advance.

REMEDIES TO CASTEISM

The following are some suggestions concerning the solutions of the problems arising out of casteism:

(1) Proper Education. The greatest need for a solution of the problem of casteism is proper education. The educational institutions should be able to provide an atmosphere in which caste distinctions are not encouraged while at the same time children are allowed to develop a distaste for this kind of discrimination. A healthy point of view in the public against casteism can thus be generated. Casteism can be destroyed only by the development of new psychological tendencies and behavioural patterns.

(2) Inter-caste Marriage. Another way of combating the continuing increase in casteism is the encouragement of inter-caste marriage. Inter-caste marriage provides an opportunity for two families belonging to different castes to come together not only for two individuals, one male and the other female, to do so. In this way, the seed of casteism shall be unable to strike root and even if it does the resulting sapling will be so weak that it will subsequently be wiped out.

(3) Lesser use of the word 'caste'. One way of solving the problem of casteism is to make less frequent use of the word 'caste' so that there may be no traces of it left in the minds of the impressionable children and they should not be imbued with the idea of caste distinction. In this way, at least it will become possible to destroy the notion of casteism in the coming generations.

(4) Cultural and economic equality. Another way of facing problem of casteism is to introduce cultural and economic equality in the minds of the members of the various castes. Inequality in the sphere of cultural and economic welfare between the races promotes jealousy and competition among them which later assumes the form of casteism. Hence, the restoration of cultural and economic equality of various castes is an important step towards the abolition of casteism from the society.

SUGGESTIONS FOR THE ABOLITION OF CASTEISM

Mahatma Gandhi has compared casteism to the appendix in the human body. As long as it continues to enjoy health it serves its purpose but when it becomes diseased the only course is to eliminate it because if it is not removed it poses a threat to the existence of the entire organism. In this way, it is opined by some people that this conflict can be eliminated from democracy only when the caste system is completely removed from it. But in the present context, in which the castes have taken on the form of classes and casteism is on increase, it seems impractical to harbour any hope for the complete removal of casteism from society. Casteism cannot be legalised and then infringed. It is the foundation of Hindu Society. A strong and tremendous revolution is needed to get rid of it. But the artificial stimulation of a revolution proves harmful in the long run of time. Hence, as long as the society is not prepared to change the system and adopt some other social order in its place, it is best to confine oneself to corrections and improvements. In this connection different scholars have expressed different views and have made various suggestions. Some of the important suggestions are the following :

(1) Dr. Srinivas' view. In Dr. M.N. Srinivas' opinion most of the shortcomings of the caste systems can be removed and the door opened to democratic equality through adult franchise, five year plans, the provision of education, constant progress of the backward classes and the influence of the culture of higher castes on the living standards of the backward and lower castes.

(2) Dr. Ghurye's suggestion. According to Dr. Ghurye, the conflicts originating in casteism can be removed by encouraging inter-caste marriages. Co-education should be introduced at the primary level and boys and girls should be given the opportunity to come together. This will lead to improvement of the behaviour between different sexes simultaneously with which casteism will be actively refuted. Inter-caste marriage will be encouraged and the individuals marrying out of their own castes will be instrumental in creating an atmosphere that will be fundamentally opposed to casteism.

(3) Dr. Rao's opinion. According to the suggestion put forward by Dr. V.K.R.V. Rao, in order to put an end to casteism and to deprive it of its very basis, the creation of some optional groups should be encouraged in which the communal tendencies of the individual can be manifested and organised. Casteism will decrease as the number of these groups increases because the individuals will have the opportunity to express their instincts and motives outside the caste.

(4) Suggestion by Mrs. Karve. It is suggested by Mrs. Iravati Karve that in order to put an end to the conflict arising out of casteism it is necessary to create economic and cultural equality between the castes.

(5) Prabhu's view. According to P.N. Prabhu, the conflicts created by casteism can be ended only when the internal aspects of conduct are influenced. For this it is necessary to try and develop new attitudes in the people. The cinema can do much towards the creation of these attitudes.

The notion of caste has been existent in Indian society for almost thousands of years. Today it has become an impediment in the progress of the country. It is necessary to change its form in order to ensure the development of national sentiment and the progress and success of democracy in the country. But this cannot determine the extent to which caste system should be developed and then all governmental and non-governmental sources in the country should be employed for the achievement of that level of development. The first step would be to remove the idea of caste discrimination from the minds of the future generation. Co-education will encourage inter-caste marriages. Further, the idea of eliminating words that indicate caste from names should also be propagated and made popular. Caste committees and associations should be prevented legally and the Government should prevent appointments being made to posts on the basis of caste, whether in government or non-government organisation. In this way, it is necessary to make efforts in every direction for improvement of this horizon.

QUESTIONS FOR EXERCISE

1. Analyse tho evils of casteism.
2. Discuss the various ways in which caste sentiments get strengthened in modern India.
3. Examine the causes of caste conflicts in Rural India.

5
Untouchability and Problems of Minorities

In 1935 the Government of India prepared a list of castes. This list included 429 castes whose total population numbered 5.35 crore people. According to the 1981 census the population of scheduled castes in India was 10,47,54,623. These castes were called scheduled castes by virtue of their inclusion in the list. These are called untouchables. The problem of untouchability is a serious social problem in the Indian society.

Definition of Untouchability

It is extremely difficult to define untouchability. Actually, untouchability implies those disabilities which were imposed upon the Harijan castes by the superior castes. In Untouchability Offences Act, 1955, the word 'untouchability' was given this connotation. In this way according to the above law "It is an offence to prevent any person on the ground of untouchability: (a) from entering any place of public worship which is open to other persons, professing the same religion, (b) from worshipping or offering prayers or performing any religious service in any place of public worship or bathing in or using the water of any sacred tank, well, spring or water-course in the same manner as is permissible to other persons professing the same religion, and (c) from access to or use of a shop, hotel, public restaurant or place of public entertainment or public conveyance or hospital, dispensary or educational institution or charitable trust." Dr. Bhim Rao Ambedkar and Mahatma Gandhi have also defined untouchability on the basis of some disabilities. In this way disabilities are a sign of untouchability. Dr. D.N. Majumdar has written, "The untouchable castes are those who suffer from various social and political disabilities many of which are traditionally prescribed and socially enforced by higher castes." In brief, untouchables are those castes which are subject to some disabilities in every walk of life social, religious, economic and political. This definition will be further classified by a detailed description of the disabilities.

Disabilities of Harijans

Untouchables suffer from the following disabilities:

(A) *Religious disabilities.* In India the Harijans were subjected to various religious disabilities in the society. They were prevented from entering temples, monasteries and cremation grounds, and were not permitted to make use of them because it was believed that these places would become impure by their touch. In this way the Harijans could not worship in the temple. Their presence was considered sufficient to defile gods, let alone their worshippers.

But the disabilities imposed upon the Harijans in India are pre-eminently social and economic, the removal of which will, in itself, eliminate their backward condition in respect of political status. Actually, the religious disabilities of the Harijans are also their social disabilities.

B. *Social disabilities.* In the social sphere the disabilities of the Harijans are the following:

1. Prevention from the use of public roads. Hudson has written that the presence of a particular untouchable caste in Tamil Nadu was considered so derogatory that their members were prevented from using the public roads in the daytime and consequently they were obliged to do their work at night. Their shadow was enough to defile the members of the higher castes. Thus, upon seeing the members of the higher castes the Harijans would adopt a prostrate posture upon the ground so that their shadow may not fall on the members of the higher castes.

2. Prevention from the use of public wells. In almost all Indian villages the Harijans were forbidden the use of the well for drawing water, and this convention was enforced with a greater or lesser degree of strictness. In Bengal they were permitted to come near the well but not allowed to draw water from it. Only a higher caste Hindu could draw water from them. In some other states the untouchables were not permitted even to approach the well.

3. Prevention from entering schools. The Harijan children did not have the right to enter the schools because if they sit down to study beside other children it would have defiled the children of the higher castes. On the other hand there were no separate schools for the Harijans. Actually, education was not even considered necessary for them. If they insisted upon being taught then they had to sit out in the open sun in order to study. In many religious texts education has been forbidden for the shudras.

4. Other social restrictions. The disabilities of the Harijans were not restricted only to the social sphere but these extended into the economic sphere too. Due to their social disabilities they could not retain any interest and enthusiasm for their occupation. They did not have the permission to engage in the professions of the higher castes. And even as it is their conventional occupations were dirty and soiled and their means for earning their bread and butter were limited. Even now there is next to no education among the Harijans. They are burdened with debt while poverty and famine conditions prevail among them. They live in dirty slums in which new diseases are always making their life miserable. There is no medical provisions for them, since the high caste doctor becomes defiled merely by touching them.

Caste and Untouchability

There are many racial, religious and social causes of untouchability in

India. The major cause is the caste system. The untouchable castes are the most inferior among the numerous castes in Hindu community. To the caste system is attached the sense of high and low, which is the fundamental cause of untouchability. Another cause of untouchability is the prevalence of many taboos in the caste system. Just as there are taboos for the higher castes intermarrying, eating and mixing with the lower castes, in the same way taboos were created for preventing, touching and even seeing of the lower castes which did the dirty work, as a consequence of the feeling of superiority and inferiority. These castes came to be called the untouchables. In this way untouchability in India is based upon the caste system. Untouchability is the result of the sense of superiority and inferiority and social taboos. In *Caste and Class in India*, Ghurye has written that in Poona, during the reign of the Marathas the untouchable caste Mahar and Mang were not allowed to enter the gates of towns between three O'clock in the afternoon and nine in the morning because the shadows are at their longest at this time and there is the fear of the higher Brahmins being defiled. In Maharashtra the Mahar caste could spit only in small containers tied around their neck because where they spit upon the road it might defile some superior Hindu by touching his foot. Often if some Brahmin passed their way the Mahars had to destroy the imprints of their feet with brambles and lie down at a distance in order to protect the Brahmin from their shadow. In Malabar the Shanar had to keep a distance of twenty-four feet from the Brahmin, the Tiya a distance of thirty-six feet and Pulayan a distance of more than ninety-six feet. It is obvious that the biggest cause of untouchability is the segregation of relations within the castes.

Causes of Untouchability

But all this does not mean that untouchability is caused solely by the caste system and the elimination of the later would mean the automatic eradication of the former. Actually there are other causes of untouchability beside the caste system. In '*Caste in India*' J.H. Hutton writes, "The origin of the position of exterior caste is partly racial, partly religious and partly a matter of social custom."

In this way, the three fundamental causes of untouchability are 1. Racial, 2. Religious, and 3. Social custom.

1. Racial Factors. The fundamental causes of untouchability are racial factors. The victor always considers himself superior to the vanquished and wants to be spared the latter's influence. This is no less true in the case of races. In the opinion of some scholars the Aryans designated to some derogatory names the non-Aryan races settled in India and considered them untouchable. In Assam the Ao branch of the Naga tribes is not allowed to wear ivory ornaments on both arms. According to Hutton this restriction has been imposed upon the Ao people because they are different from the other Naga tribes from the racial viewpoint. In Garhwal the bride and bridegroom belonging to the artisan and Harijan castes, which had low social status were not allowed the use of the palanquin or the horse. The cause of this has been explained by some sociologists to be the advent of the higher castes from the plains into the native homeland of the artisans and Harijans. These examples prove that racial distinctions have some hand in the origin of the custom of untouchability. Dr. D.N. Majumdar has written correctly, "The disabilities of the so-called 'depressed' castes are not ceremonial but probably founded on racial and cultural differences."

2. Religious Factors. Religious beliefs and conventions are also causes of untouchability. In religion much importance is attributed to purity and divinity. As a result of the religious importance of purity it was considered essential to remain aloof from the people who engage in impure occupation. In this way untouchability originated in the religious factor. In the words of Dr. Ghurye "Idea of purity, whether occupational or ceremonial, is found to have been a factor of the genesis of caste or the very soul of the idea and practice of untouchability." It was the sense of purity which led the sweepers and cobblers being designated as untouchables in Hindu society. Besides purity another cause of the origin of untouchability are the social taboos. Intermarriage among castes, consumption of the object of totem, or its disrespect in any way are forbidden. Besides these there are a number of other taboos prevalent in the castes like avoiding washerman because he washes clothes seeped in secretion of the women's menstrual cycle. Thus in the Vol. 1 of *Census of India,* Hutton has written, "There can be little doubt that the idea of untouchability originates in taboos."

3. Social Factors. The custom of untouchability has its origin in some social factors as well. Social customs and conventions share the burden of maintaining the untouchability of the untouchables recognised by the religious and racial causes. Social conventions are so influential that even the members of the untouchable castes dare not violate the customs of untouchability. In *The Hindu* of 24th December in 1932, it was written about the Puraadavanan castes established in the Tinneveli district of Tamil Nadu that they are not only considered untouchable but even unpresentable and, they cannot leave their dwelling in the day time because there is a fear of their defiling the other castes. They washed their clothes at night. When Thakkar Bapa went to meet them they came out upon extreme entreaty and when they came their entire body was trembling because they were burdened by the social stigma of untouchability.

In this way the racial, religious and social factors are the major ones among many causes of the origin of untouchability and it would be difficult to remove untouchability as long as ignorance in these spheres continues to exist.

EFFORTS TO ERADICATE UNTOUCHABILITY

There have been numerous governmental and non-governmental efforts towards the eradication of untouchability in India and the improvement in the condition of the untouchables. The governmental effort is directed towards the. prevention of untouchability on the one hand and improvement in the condition of the untouchables on the other. In the paragraph 46 of the Indian Constitution much emphasis has been laid upon the spread of education among the backward castes and the protection of their economic interests.

In the Indian Constitution the equality of citizens of India was announced. The following paragraphs in the Constitution provide for the eradication of untouchability.

Paragraph 15. 1. The state will not discriminate against any citizen on grounds only of religion, race, caste, sex, place of birth, or any of them.

2. No citizen shall, on grounds only of religion, race, caste, sex, place of birth or any of them, be subject to any disability, restriction or condition with regard to:

(a) Access to shops, public restaurants, hotels and places of public entertainment, or (b) The use of wells, tanks, bathing ghats, roads, and places of public resort maintained wholly or partly out of state funds or dedicated to the use of the general public.

Para 16. 1. There shall be equality of religion, race, caste, sex, descent, place of birth, residence or any of them, be ineligible for or discriminated against in respect of any employment of office under the state.

2. No citizen shall, on grounds only of religion, race, caste, sex, descent, place of birth, residence of any of them, be ineligible for or discriminated against in respect of any employment of office under the state.

3. Nothing in this article shall prevent Parliament from making any law prescribing, in regard to a class or classes of employment or appointment to any office under any state specified in the First Schedule or any local or other authority within its territory, any requirement as the residence within that state prior to such employment or appointment.

Para 17. 'Untouchability' is abolished and its practice in any form forbidden. The enforcement of any disability arising out of 'Untouchability' shall be an offence punishable in accordance with law.

2. Arrangement under the Directives of Government Policy. The following arrangement has been made for the eradication of untouchability in the Directive Principles of State Policy in the Indian Constitution:

Chapter 6. The government will develop the economic and educational interests of the weakest classes, especially scheduled castes and scheduled backward castes, with special precautions and will protect them from social injustice and all kinds or exploitation.

Article 46. The state shall promote with special care the educational and economic interests of the weaker sections of the people and in particular, of the scheduled castes and the scheduled tribes and shall protect them from social injustice and all forms of exploitation.

Article 164. Provided that in the State of Bihar, Madhya Pradesh and Orissa, there shall be a Minister in charge of tribal welfare who may in addition be incharge of welfare of the scheduled castes and backward classes or any other work.

Article 330. 1. Seats shall be reserved in the house of people for:

(a) The Scheduled Castes;

(b) The Scheduled Tribes except the Scheduled Tribes in the tribal areas of Assam; and

(c) The Scheduled Tribes in the autonomous districts of Assam.

2. The number of seats reserved in any state for the scheduled castes or the scheduled tribes under clause (1) shall bear, of as nearly as may be the same proportion to the total number of seats allotted to that state in the house of the people as the population of the scheduled castes in the state or the scheduled tribes in the state or part of the state as the case may be in the respect of which seats are so reserved, bears to the total population of the state.

Article 332. 1. Seats shall be reserved for these scheduled castes and the scheduled tribes, expect the scheduled tribes in the tribal areas of Assam the Legislative Assembly of every state specified in the Part A or Part B of the First Schedule.

2. Seats shall be reserved also for the autonomous districts in the Legislative Assembly of Assam.

Article 335. The claims of the members of scheduled castes and the scheduled tribes shall be taken into consideration, consistently with the maintenance of efficiency of administration, in the making of appointments to services and posts in connection with the affairs of the union or of a state.

Article 338. 1. There shall be a special officer for the scheduled castes and scheduled tribes to be appointed by the President.

2. It shall be duty of the special officer to investigate all matters relating to the safeguards provided for the scheduled castes and scheduled tribes under this classification and report to the President upon the working of those safeguards at such intervals as the President may direct and the President shall cause all such reports to be laid before each House of Parliament.

Article 340. 1. The President may by order appoint a Commission consisting of such persons as he thinks fit to investigate the conditions of socially and educationally backward classes within the territory of India and the difficulties under which they labour and to make recommendations as to the step that should be taken by the Union or any State to remove such difficulties and to improve their condition and as to the grants that should be made for the purpose by the Union or any State and the conditions subject to which such grants should be made, and the order appointing such commission shall define the procedure to be followed by the Commission.

According to the 17th paragraph of the Indian Constitution untouchability is a punishable crime. In 1955 the Indian Government passed the Untouchability Offences Act in which any person forcing the disability of untouchability can be sentenced to six months imprisonment or a fine of Rs. 500 or both for his first crime. For every subsequent crime the sentence will include both a term in jail as well as a fine. If considered necessary the punishment may also be increased. According to this Act the following activities were declared criminal — preventing entrance into public temples or places of worship, preventing the drawing of water from sacred lakes, wells, falls, or springs, preventing people from the use of dharamshala, inn, hotel, river bank, cremation ground, water tank, water tap, educational institution, public hospital, public restaurant, preventing the Harijans from pursuing any general occupation, doing a barber's job or any general activities and harassing them or discriminating them on the basis of untouchability at such times as religious festivals, residential houses, business or profession.

Besides enacting laws against untouchability the government of India also instigated propaganda against untouchability throughout the country. All the states observe 'Harijan Weeks' and 'Harijan Days'. In states and districts, advisory committees have been made which increase contact between untouchables and superior Hindus. Books, handbills, posters and pamphlets are printed in Hindi, English and regional languages and distributed among the public in large number. Films and radios are also used as means of propaganda against untouchability.

ERADICATION OF UNTOUCHABILITY

1. Tribal Advisory Council in States. The Fifth Schedule to the Constitution provides for the setting up of Tribal Advisory Council in each State having Scheduled Areas and if the President so directs, for constituting such Council in States which have Scheduled Tribes, but no Scheduled Areas.

2. Welfare and Advisory Agencies. A *Commissioner for the Scheduled Castes and Scheduled Tribes* under Art. 338 of the Constitution has been appointed to investigate all matters relating to the safeguards for the Scheduled Castes and Scheduled Tribes and report to the President on the working of these safeguards.

3. Two Central Advisory Boards. One for Tribal Welfare and another for Harijan Welfare, have been constituted to associate members of Parliament and Public workers with matters relating to the welfare of these classes.

4. Welfare Departments in the States. Art. 164(1) of the Constitution requires that in the States of Bihar, Madhya Pradesh and Orissa, Welfare Departments in charge of a Minister should be set up. Welfare Departments have been set up in these States as well as in A.P., Assam, Gujarat, Rajasthan, U.P., West Bengal, Himachal Pradesh, Manipur and Tripura.

5. Representation in Legislatures. Under Articles 330, 332, and 334 of the Constitution, seats proportionate as far as possible to their population in the States have been reserved for the Scheduled Castes and Tribes in the Lok Sabha and the State Assemblies for a period of 20 years from the passing of the Constitution. The Parliament extended by another 10 years reservations in the Lok Sabha and the State Legislatures for Scheduled Castes, Scheduled Tribes and the Anglo-Indians.

6. Representation in Services. 15 per cent of the total vacancies for which recruitment is made by open competition on all-India basis and 16.75 per cent of the vacancies for which recruitment is made otherwise, are reserved for the Scheduled Castes. For the Scheduled Tribes, the reservation is 7.5 per cent in both cases. There are also other concessions as regards age, qualifications, etc.

7. Scholarships and Grants. 10.5 per cent of the merit scholarships granted by the centre for deserving students of the lower income groups and for students in the institutions which are members of the Indian Public Schools Conference, are reserved for backward communities. Some of the State Governments offer similar scholarships.

8. Research. *Tribal Research Institutes* have been set up in Andhra Pradesh, Bihar, Gujarat, M.P., Orissa, Rajasthan and West Bengal.

9. Economic Improvement. Realising the financial problems of the Harijans the Government have taken the following steps in the direction of their financial improvement:

(i) *Laws for escaping debt.* In nearly all the States of India laws have been enacted for defending the untouchables from the creditors. Small debts have been entirely condoned.

(ii) *Laws for defence against the tradition of slavery.* In Bihar and Orissa the Harijans had to become slaves of the creditors in the event of their inability to repay debt. Now this tradition has come to an end due to laws.

(iii) *Distribution of land to Harijans.* In Andhra, Bihar, Orissa, Maharashtra, Tamil Nadu, Uttar Pradesh and Gujarat the Government have turned useless and unoccupied land into cultivable land and have distributed it among the Harijans.

(iv) *Laws making the farmer the owner of the land.* The governments of Andhra, Bihar, Orissa, Assam, Madhya Pradesh and West Bengal have enacted laws by virtue of which the Harijan cultivating the land is to be considered the landowner and cannot be deprived of it.

(v) *Financial assistance to agriculture.* The Government is rendering financial assistance to the Harijans in order that they may be able to buy agricultural implements, animals, manure, superior seeds, modern tools of agriculture etc.

(vi) *Assistance in Agriculture, Cottage Industries and Animal Husbandry.* In Assam, Bihar, Maharashtra, Uttar Pradesh, Andhra and West Bengal the Harijans are being assisted financially as well as otherwise for the development of their cottage industries. Training centres are also being opened for teaching people and making them skilled in cottage industries. Animal husbandry and poultry farming are also being encouraged among the Harijans.

10. Financial Assistance to Non-Governmental Efforts. The Government of India are also providing aid to non-governmental institutions which are exerting efforts for the eradication of untouchability.

11. Educational Facilities. The educational facilities provided by the government to the Harijans take the form of free educational scholarships, books, stationery and other educational needs.

12. Other Government Facilities. According to the Indian Constitution posts has been reserved in government services for untouchables. Not only in central government services but also in state government services these seats were reserved. The condition of the untouchables improved due to the 'Admission to Malabar Mandir Act' and 'Prohibition of Public Disability Act' of the Madras Government. In order to arrange for the progress of the Harijans the Madras government appointed a Labour Commissioner and enacted many laws for defending the Harijans from the landlords and also in order to provide them with land. The governments of other states also followed the lead of Madras government. In Uttar Pradesh two parliamentary secretaries were appointed for improving the condition of the Harijans. Many co-operative societies were also opened for the Harijans. Many Harijan students were given scholarships.

Non-Governmental Efforts

Besides the programme for political awakening, the Indian National Congress made efforts for the eradication of untouchability. The attempts made by Gandhiji in this direction are well known. As a result of his efforts the untouchables slowly got rid of their social disabilities. The doors of the universities, temples, public places etc., were opened to them. In the beginning the superior Hindus opposed these improvements but they later agreed to them. Besides the Congress many other political parties took part in the emancipation of the Harijans. Among them the work done by the Depressed Class Union, The Social Service League, Depressed Classes League, Andhra Deen Seva Sangh, Depressed Classes Conference and Scheduled Castes Federation deserves mention. But the Harijan Sevak Sangh has made the maximum efforts in this direction. In 1932 this Sangh was started under the leadership of Thakkar Bapa. There are many branches of this Sangh in Andhra, Tamil Nadu, Mysore, Gujarat, Maharashtra, Karnatak, Uttar Pradesh, Bihar and Delhi. 120 Boarding Houses are being managed by the Harijan Sewak Sangh. As a result of the efforts made by the Tamil Nadu Sangh 100 big temples were opened for the Harijans. The Sangh achieved much success in opening the public places to the Harijans. Many Harijan students should be thankful to the Sangh for their scholarships which they got mainly due to the efforts of the Sangh. Technological schools have also been opened for imparting training on cottage industries and this too has come about mainly through the efforts of the Sangh. Among these institutions the Harijan Audyogik Grah Delhi, Harijan Audyogik School and Hostel Kadambokam, Harijan Ashram Prayag, Harijan Audyogik School Kanjivaram deserve to be mentioned. Institutions for women include Harijan Balika Vidyalaya Sabarmati, Harijan Balika Sadan Hugli, Anjani Harijan Girls Hostel Bezwada, Kastoorba Balika Ashram Okhla etc.

Suggestions for the Eradication of Untouchability

The methods of eradication of untouchability are now known to all educated people. The following suggestions can be made in this direction:

1. Increasing education among the Harijans. Education should be spread among the Harijans and this should include both general education as well as technical education. Education should be free, coupled with facilities of scholarships, books, stationery, hostels etc.

2. Laws for economic improvement. Laws should be formulated for legal protection from interest upon loans and deprivation of land in order to improve the financial condition of the Harijans.

3. Removal of economic disabilities. The Harijans should be helped in every conceivable way so as to end their economic disabilities.

4. Assistance in agriculture and cottage industries. The Harijans should be provided with land, animals, ploughs, seeds, manure and agricultural tools for agriculture. Financial assistance for cottage industries should he supplemented by technical training.

5. Laws against social disabilities. Laws should be formulated for preventing the Harijans from being subjected to social disabilities.

6. Laws against religious disabilities. Laws removing the religious disabilities which burden the Harijans should also be enforced.

7. Propaganda against untouchability. Platform speeches, radios, newspaper, the press and other means of communication should assist in the propaganda against untouchability.

8. Reserved seats in services. In spite of the enforcement of all the above mentioned measures, it will take the Harijans a long time to achieve equality with the superior castes. Thus, until they do so, same seats should be reserved for them in the government services.

9. Reserved seats in the legislatures. It is necessary that seats should be reserved for the harijans in the legislatures for some time to come. Some people contend that this violates the democratic principle of equality, but the people who have been deprived of equality for hundreds of years need some privileges in order to restore them to the general level. Once they have become equal to the superior castes, the privileges will no longer be necessary.

10. Eradication of the caste system. The eradication of the caste system is very essential for the removal of untouchability. Actually, the caste system is the biggest single cause of untouchability even though it is not the sole cause. Thus the eradication of the caste system will also remove the tradition of untouchability.

11. Contact between caste Hindus and untouchables. It is necessary that there should be an ever increasing contact between the Harijans and the caste Hindus at the same time that all the above measures are being put into practice, so that the tradition of untouchability should he destroyed and the feeling of sheer disgust which the superior Hindus harbour for the untouchables as well as the sense of inferiority of the Harijans should be eliminated. This contact will reduce mutual discrimination and culminate in the untouchables becoming like the other Hindus.

It is a matter of no small pleasure that the central and state governments along with many other political and religious institutions of the country are making tremendous efforts in achieving these improvements. Awakening is also spreading among the Harijans. It is hoped that, with the efforts of the Harijans themselves, governmental and other social institutions, Harijans will become equal to higher castes, and this problem will be wiped off from Indian society.

PROBLEMS OF MINORITIES

Who are Minorities?

We may define a minority as a group of people, who, because of their physical or cultural characteristics, are singled out from the others in the society in which they live for differential and unequal treatment; and who therefore regard themselves as objects of collective discrimination. "Differential and unequal treatment" does not necessarily mean that one is at the bottom. If two well-trained and competent persons compete for a job of high prestige and income and one loses out on the grounds of his group membership alone, this does not indicate a low-class status, but rather a minority group-status. A minority group is a group which, regardless of whether it is on the class ladder, faces barriers to the pursuit of life's values that are larger or greater than the barriers faced by persons otherwise equally qualified. This is a distinction superimposed on the class system. A member of a minority group, then, is not necessarily a member of lower class, but he is lower on the stratification ladder than he would be were it not for his group membership. Wherever there are minority groups there is, by definition, discrimination. It implies the application of standards which are arbitrary and unfair by dominant standards. The central meaning of "minority group" of those who are thus identified is precisely that they are judged by standards which are in violation of major social values.

Distinctive marks of Minorities

The symbols by which minorities are distinguished may be religion, language, national origin, race or some combination of these and other characteristics. All over world the minority-majority scale is prevalent in different degrees of discrimination. The Negros are the popular minorities in U.S.A. even today. In India the term minorities is often applied to Muslims, Harijans and backward classes on account of their general disabilities is accorded by the dominant groups. In India the caste system with the ritual sanction is responsible for the creation of a minority of people who are accorded discriminatory treatment by the bulk of the society. The untouchables and other depressed castes, the scheduled tribes etc. have been the oppressed classes in our society through the ages. The Brahmins who were the dominant castes not only enjoyed a privileged status in society but aimed at an occupational superiority and its retainment as a vested interest so that the untouchable never had sufficient opportunities to rise up the social ladder.

Types of Minorities

Though social scientists contend that minorities do not imply low-classes, in India, the untouchables are an illustration of that group of people who were the ritual minority to begin with in terms of their racial inferiority in comparison to the Aryan race but who subsequently remained the lowest class also on account of their inability to rise up the socio-economic ladder. The scheduled tribes who form a bulk of our population have also been grouped as a minority because of the lack of opportunities to rise up.

Women down the ages have also been considered a minority in India. Inequality of treatment and lack of adequate opportunities for development suppressed the initiatives of this sex. But the status of women has changed significantly in modern times due to the impact of Western culture on Indian thought. The legal sanctions afforded to this erstwhile minority by way of the Widow Remarriage Act, the Sharda Act, and other legal bills prohibiting female infanticide and raising the age of consent for marriage have improved the lot of women in our country. Voluntary organisations and social reform movements have brought about a change in the status of women in our country and even today the interest of this minority group is of main concern to the Constitutionalist.

The Muslim Minority

Muslims are another minority element in our country. To begin with the history of the Muslims dates back to the period of conquests which the Khilji dynasty had inflicted on our population. The relation between the Hindus and Muslims was on a conqueror-conquered scale and the Britishers played their part in their unification or otherwise. In comparison to the Muslim-majority countries like Arabia, Africa, Pakistan etc. in India they are a minority. In *The Muslim Dilemma in India* by M.R.A. Baig, he gives an exemplary exposition of the fix this minority group is in. Is it better for Muslim Indians to assimilate and thereby lose their identity? Or are they bound by Islam to preserve their identity and thereby suffer the mental, physical, social and economic consequences of non-assimilation with the Hindu culture? This, according to the author is the Muslim dilemma. His thesis is that Islam as practised in the Muslim majority countries has to be adopted to conditions in which Muslims are a minority. Theological, historical, sociological, psychological, political reasons have resulted in division of India which culminated in the creation of Pakistan. The dilemma of the Muslim Indians is indeed great since the ability with which one can fit into an entirely opposing social set up of the Hindus in India is not easy. To the Muslims practice of polygamy for example, is repugnant to Hindus. The Indian Constitution though purporting secularism has been accused of framing laws which are Hindu oriented. Polygamy is condemned. Nevertheless this minority group has not been completely rejected through total abolition of the one man-many-women ethic. The Muslim Marriage Act pays special regard to the private and personal sanctions of the community and allows polygamy under varying conditions. So is the case with other features of their social life which is ill fitting in a Hindu society.

Status of Minorities in India

India being a secular nation, the minority groups whether based on religion like the Muslims race and ethnic origins like the untouchables have to be supported. The political recognition of the uniqueness and value of every simple individual in terms of civil liberties has gone a long way in improving the lot of the minorities. The caste drags of the untouchables and other depressed classes have been elevated on the social scale by the passing of the *Caste Disabilities Removal Act*. The Harijans today are the privileged sections of the society. Special privileges are offered to them and reservation of seats in both educational and employment avenues has indeed heralded the growth of this section of the community. Likewise political representation to the minority group in every state on a proportionate basis enables their advancement in political sphere too.

Social progress in general is aimed at through the uplift of the minorities as well as equal opportunities to them for advancement. No discriminatory treatment or segregation is possible under the legal order. Discrimination is indeed punishable. But one has to remark in this context laxity of legality alone on a social set-up.

What India needs today is not laws alone. Social thinking and education should be directed towards a free social intercourse of the majority-minority population without any traditional inhibitions. Safeguards should be taken against any breach of the legal code and a smooth interflow of interaction should be made a national phenomenon rather than a legal force. For, social scientists contend that there is no power less powerful than cohesion and no strength stronger than nationality.

QUESTIONS FOR EXERCISE

1. What are the disabilities of untouchables?
2. Review briefly the anti-untouchability movement in post-independent India estimating its success and failure.
3. Who are the minorities in India? Analyse their problems and suggest remedies.

6

Problems of Hindu Marriage

Due to the influence of Western culture and English education the Hindu marriages system has undergone considerable changes, the important among them being the following:

1. Marriage is not held as compulsory. In Hindu society formerly marriage was considered to be absolutely compulsory for both male and female. According to Hindu scriptures, a person who does not beget a son through marriage cannot attain heaven. The birth of a son was considered to be necessary for the well-being of the ancestors. No man could perform yajna without a wife. Marriage, therefore, was necessary even for religious purposes. But due to the influence of Western culture many males and females do not consider marriage to be necessary these days. Due to economic difficulties also some persons do not enter into matrimony. The modern educated Hindu girl is not prepared to accept slavery of male. She marries for love and if it is not forthcoming she refuses to marry. Many girls, specially those who are in a job, do not marry unless they get a suitable match and if such a match is not available they do not marry at all. The educated men and women do not believe in the ancient religious values and therefore do not consider marriage to be necessary.

2. Breaking of the Taboos of Sagotra and Sapravar marriage. Ancient Hindu tradition forbids the marriage of persons belonging to the same Gotra and Pravar. This very much restricts the field of choice of mate. Therefore, at present the educated persons are gradually violating the restriction. It has been rejected by law.

3. Opposition of child marriages. In medieval India the custom of child marriage was very much in vogue. After the passing of Sarada Act child marriages have become illegal. Another factor leading to the restriction of child marriage in Hindu society is the tremendous increase of women education. Due to the custom of dowry also poor parents fail to arrange for a bridegroom at an early age. The boys also do not marry early because of late settlement in career.

4. Permission of Inter-caste marriage. Formerly, inter-caste marriage was considered to be wrong in Hindu society. It has now been legally permitted. With the increase of co-education, women education and the democratic ideal of equality and liberty inter-caste marriages are now considered to be signs of forwardness. The bonds of endogamy are, therefore, gradually breaking and the number of inter-caste marriages increasing.

5. Prohibition of polygamy. Formerly a man was allowed to marry several women in order to get a son. With the increase of women education the ladies are demanding equal rights in marriage. The Hindu Marriage Act of 1955 has declared polygamy to be illegal. No one can marry a second time while the former spouse is alive.

6. Permission of Widow Remarriage. Due to the untiring efforts of social reformers and educated persons for widow remarriage it is no more considered to be wrong in Hindu society. Consequently its incidence is now on the increase.

7. Provision for Divorce. The Hindu Marriage Act of 1955 introduced a significant change in the institution of Hindu marriage by permitting divorce under certain specific circumstances.

DISORGANISATION OF HINDU MARRIAGE

The above mentioned changes in Hindu marriage are indicative of progress on the one hand and disorganization on the other. The increase in the incidence of divorce, the increase in the age of marriage and rise in the incidence of extra-marital sex relationship are indicative of disorganisation in Hindu marriage. Changes such as the prohibition of polygamy, the restriction of child marriages, the permission of widow remarriage and freedom in the choice of mate are healthy signs of progress. Thus, on the whole, it cannot be said that the changes in Hindu marriage in recent times have led to its degeneration. The sanctity of marital bond has, however, diminished. It is no more unbreakable. It can be broken if there is no love and harmony between wife and husband. In fact the Hindu marriage system is passing through a transitional stage. English education, women education, influence of Western culture, urbanization and industrialization have changed social values of the Hindu male and female. The institution of family is changing fast. The disorganization of Hindu family has created circumstances leading to disorganization of Hindu marriage. Romantic marriages are increasing. This has led to an increase in the number of divorces. In spite of these fast changes it can be safely predicted that there is no immediate danger to the institution of Hindu marriage because of the psychological security which it provides.

PROBLEMS OF HINDU MARRIAGE

The following are the chief problems faced by the institution of Hindu marriage recently.

1. Child marriage. The problem of child marriage was very serious in Hindu society till the passing of Sarada Act. Since then age of the marriage of boys and girls has been gradually increasing so much so that in some cases it is thirty for the boy and more than twenty-five for the girl. In fact the reasonable age for marriage is eighteen to twenty-two in the case of girl and twenty to twenty-five in case of boys. The reasons behind child marriages in Hindu society were religious conservatism, endogamy, Sati custom, the custom of dowry and the joint family. The Hindu Marriage Act of 1955 has fixed the valid age for marriage of the boys and girls at 21 and 18 respectively. These legal steps could not work immediately because of the widespread conservatism among Hindus, incompleteness of prohibitive Act and the absence of female education. With the removal of these difficulties in the way of restraint of child marriages, this problem has appreciably diminished in Hindu society.

2. Widow remarriage. About the condition of widow remarriage in ancient India, A.S. Alteker has written, "Side by side with niyoga, the widow remarriage also prevailed in Vedic society." The custom of widow remarriage, however, disappeared gradually and it was considered to be wrong as early as 200 A.D. The restriction on widows, sexual exploitation of child widows, increase of immorality among widows, increase of prostitutes and the lowering of the general status of women in Hindu society has led to large scale conversion of Hindu widows to Islam and Christianity. Much can be said about the ethical justification of widow remarriage. It gives the fundamental human rights of marriage to the young woman who has untimely lost her husband. It eliminates the possibilities of the increase of immorality and the increase of prostitution. From the social view-point it results in the increase of the number of Hindus, saves the society from evils of religious conversion, immorality and prostitution. From legal view-point it ends the share of the widow in the property of her late husband, while, on the other hand, it gives her all legal rights of inheritance, adoption of child etc., in the house of her new husband.

Due to the untiring efforts of Ishwar Chandra Vidyasagar the Hindu Widows Remarriage Act was passed in 1856. This Act declared its legal validity. At present, though widow remarriage is not very much admired it is not opposed in Hindu society. In the lower castes it was never seriously opposed. In the higher castes it is now gradually being accepted.

3. Dowry. According to Max Radin, "Ordinarily dowry is the property which a man receives when he marries, either from his wife or her family." the Websters new international dictionary has defined dowry as, "the money, goods or estate, which a woman brings to her husband in marriage." In brief dowry is that money, property or valuables which the bride party has to give to the bridegroom party in exchange of marriage. Thus the chief evil of dowry system is that the bride party is compelled to give it in exchange of marriage, otherwise the bride has to suffer the consequences at the hand of her in-laws. It is hence that Alteker has rightly said, "It is now high time for Hindu society to put an end to this evii custom, which has driven many an innocent maiden to commit suicide." Some persons have pointed out to some so called advantages of dowry system. They have maintained that it helps in the establishment of the new household of the newly married couple. It has been pointed out that the lure of dowry helps in the marriage of ugly and uneducated girls. These so-called advantages do not count even for a moment before the glaring evils of dowry system. Some of the gross evils of this system can be seen in the murder of female children, the suicides of young maidens, the late marriages of girls, unmatched marriages, breaking of the settlement of marriage on the question of dowry, the child marriages to avoid dowry, the criminal activities of the fathers of girls and the lowering of the standard of living, increasing family disharmony, immorality, mental diseases and finally in the hindrance to women education. The evil of dowry is persisting because of increase of the value of money, general poverty, unemployment, delimitation of the field of choice of mate, the competition to get the bridegroom from rich family etc. The evil can be restricted only by strict legal measures against it. Recently some sort of legal restriction on dowry was made by an Act passed by the Government. This, however, has not been sufficiently effective. With the increase of women education, the incidence of inter-caste marriages and anti-dowry propaganda, this can be appreciably uprooted from Hindu society.

DIVORCE

Before the passing of Hindu Marriage Act of 1955 the Hindu woman could not divorce her husband even though he made hell of her life. The Hindu Marriage Act has divided Hindu marriages into valid, void and voidable. The age limit in case of boys and girls has been fixed at 21 and 18 respectively. The Act has prescribed monogamy and declared polygamy to be illegal. It has accepted the mother as the guardian of the children along with the father but its more important prescription is with regard to divorce. It permits divorce in the case of adultery, change of religion, suffering from some incurable diseases not contracted from the other spouse, renunciation of the world, not traceable for more than seven years, absence of cohabitation for two years after the decree of judicial separation and not following the decree for the restitution of conjugal rights. The wife can divorce the husband if her another wife is alive or if he has been found guilty of rape, sodomy or bestiality. The application for divorce can be filled after three years of marriage. In the meanwhile judicial separation is allowed on the following conditions:

1. Desertion of the Applicant by another party two years before the date of application.
2. Cruel behaviour.
3. Suffering of another party from leprosy or any other infectious disease, for one year before the date of application but the disease should not have been contracted from the applicant.
4. Madness of the party for two years before the date of application.
5. Co-habitation of either person with some man and woman other than the husband and the wife.

After the court gives permission to divorce the man and woman cannot marry for one year.

The following are the important social legislations passed in India since 1843.

No.	Period	Act
1.	1856	Hindu Widow Remarriage Act.
2.	1870	Female Infanticide Prevention Act.
3.	1866	The Converts Marriage Dissolution Act.
4.	1872	Special Marriage Act.
5.	1928	The Hindu Inheritance Act.
6.	1939	Child Marriage Restraint Act.
7.	1930	The Hindu Gains of Learning Act.
8.	1937	The Hindu Women's Right to Property Act.
9.	1946	The Hindu Married Women's Separate Maintenance Act.
10.	1946	The Hindu Marriage Disabilities Removal Act.

The following are the important social legislations passed in India after Independence:

1. The Hindu Marriage Act, 1955.
2. The Hindu Succession Act, 1956.
3. The Hindu Minority and Guardianship Act, 1956.
4. The Hindu Adoption and Maintenance Act, 1956.

HINDU CODE

The Indian Parliament have passed the following Acts for reform of Hindu marriage family and the status of women in Hindu society: Hindu Married Women's Rights to Separate Residence and Maintenance Act, Hindu Marriage Act, Hindu Succession Act, Hindu Adaptation and Maintenance Act, and Hindu Minority and Guardianship Act. These Acts are collectively known as Hindu Code.

1. Hindu Married Women's Rights to Separate Residence and Maintenance Act, 1946. By this Act the Hindu married women can claim maintenance while residing separate from the husband on the following conditions: 1. If the husband is suffering from some loathsome disease which has not been contracted from the wife. 2. If the husband behaves so cruelly towards the wife that her residing with the husband is undesirable or dangerous, 3. If the husband deserts her without her wish. 4. If the husband marries again. 5. If the husband adopts another religion. 6. If the husband keeps some concubine. 7. Other justifiable causes. But the wife cannot demand maintenance from the husband if she is guilty of adultery or conversion to another religion.

2. Hindu Marriage Act, 1955. This Act applies to all the members of Hindu society. It has made the following important changes in the institution of Hindu marriage:

(a) *Classification of Hindu marriage.* According to this Act Hindu marriages can be divided into three classes — void, voidable and valid.

(b) *Determination of the age for marriages.* By the provisions of this Act the minimum age limit for the boys and girls has been fixed at 21 and 18 years respectively.

(c) *Provision for monogamy.* According to this Act a Hindu male or female can enter into matrimony only if no spouse of either is alive at the time of marriage. Thus the section 5 and clause 1 of the Act provides for monogamy in Hindu society.

(d) *Provision for the guardianship of the mother.* According to this Act the mother will be considered the legal guardian of the minor son or daughter after the father.

(e) *Provision for divorce.* As has been already pointed out in the discussion of the problem of divorce in Hindu society, the Hindu Marriage Act provides for divorce by wife or husband under certain specific circumstances.

3. Hindu Succession Act, 1956. According to this Act the daughter is also given equal right of inheritance in the property of the father, along with the son. The women got right to the use, sale, and mortgage of the property received through inheritance.

4. Hindu Adoption and Maintenance Act, 1956. According to this Act the husband has to take the consent of the wife while adopting a son or daughter. The issueless window also got rights of adoption. The following conditions should be satisfied to make adoption legal: 1. After the death of husband every sound minded adult widow has a right to adopt a son or give her son to another for adoption. 2. Every healthy minded male will have right to adopt a son but this will require the consent of his wife. 3. The unmarried adult woman will also have the right of adoption. 4. The adopted person will be less than 15 years in age and normally unmarried unless there is a custom of child marriage in his or her caste. 5. The daughter can also be adopted and given for adoption. There may be certain undesirable consequences of the adoption of a girl by widower and boy by a widow. Therefore, it has been specified that the widower or bachelor should be at least 21 years old than the girl. Similarly, the widow or the unmarried woman should be at least 21 years older than the son. Again, the age of the boy or girl at the time of his or her adoption should be less than 15 years.

The Hindu Adoption and Maintenance Act provides for the maintenance of the adopted son or daughter, the deserted wife and widow, the disabled old man or woman and the helpless persons. In this connection the following important provisions has been made: 1. The Hindu wife will have the right of maintenance during the lifetime of her husband. The wife deserted by the husband or living separate from him by her own wish will have the right of maintenance under certain specific circumstances. If the husband keeps a concubine, changes his religion, behaves cruelly, suffers from loathsome disease, the wife will have a right of maintenance though living separate from the husband. 2. The widowed daughter-in-law and the granddaughter-in-law will also have right of maintenance. 3. The widow or unmarried daughter will also have right to maintenance by the father. 4. The minor children, even if they may be illegitimate will have a right to claim maintenance from the parents during the term of their minority.

5. Hindu Minority and Guardianship Act, 1956. This Act prescribes for the following provisions in connection with guardianship: 1. The child will remain under the guardianship of his mother upto the age of five years. It is only after it that the father will be considered the legal guardian. After the death of the father the mother will again have the right of guardianship. 2. In the case of unmarried daughter and the illegitimate son the mother will have the right of guardianship and it is only after her death that the father will get this right. The right of the guardianship of the married daughter will vest with her husband. 3. The legal guardian will have right to do all such things which he considered to be necessary for the good of the minor child. But he cannot do anything contrary to his other interests. He will not have any right to spend, sell, mortgage or gift any portion of the property of the minor person under his guardianship. For the purposes of this Act the child below the age of 18 will be considered a minor and under the guardian.

Effects of Hindu Code on the status of Hindu women

The above mentioned Acts under Hindu code have widely influenced the status of women in Hindu society. The following are important points in this connection:

1. Equal right to male and female. The Hindu code provides for equal rights to the Hindu male and female in almost every field of life. With it the females have secured equal rights with the males concerning inheritance of property, adoption of son and daughter, remarrying after the death of husband, divorcing the husband in certain circumstances and marrying again. Thus the code has finished the exploitation of women in Hindu society. They have been given all human rights and thus do not depend on males' mercy.

2. End of male's domination in family. The Hindu code have ended the male's domination in Hindu family. Now, the husband cannot adopt a son or daughter without the consent of the wife. In the case of the daughter the mother is the life long guardian. The husband cannot misbehave with the wife because if he does so she cannot only get divorce from him but also claim for maintenance unless she remarries. The daughter and the widow have right of inheritance of property. The father and mother have equal rights of guardianship of the children.

3. Abolition of polygamy. Before the passing of Hindu Marriage Act the evil of polygamy was widely prevalent in Hindu society. The Hindu Marriage Act has put an end to it. Now the husband cannot keep a concubine or marry another woman in the lifetime of his wife. Thus the Hindu Marriage Act has established monogamy in Hindu society.

4. Restriction of child marriages. The new social legislations have eliminated the evil of the child marriage from Hindu society. The age of legal marriage has been fixed at 21 and 18 for the boys and girls respectively.

5. Increase in the instability of family. With the provision for judicial separation and divorce the Hindu code has made Hindu family unstable. It has given a blow to the joint family. The number of divorces has increased. The marital relations have, however, improved because the wife and husband both take care to behave properly so that a condition of judicial separation may not arise. This has led to progress in the status of Hindu women.

6. Women's rights of inheritance. The Hindu code has given economic equality to Hindu women by providing for their right of inheritance in the property of husband and father.

7. Equal rights of guardianship. The Hindu code has provided for equal rights of guardianship of children to both wife and husband. It has thus established equality in this connection.

8. Life insurance of the old and disabled. By providing for the maintenance of the old, disabled, widows and orphans the Hindu code has established social security in this respect. It is like a life insurance of these persons.

The above discussion of the influences of Hindu code makes it quite clear that it has improved the status of women in Hindu society. It has met their age old demands of inheritance, adoption, maintenance, guardianship, separate residence and divorce. It has placed them on equal footing with the males. Though here and there it may cause the breaking of a family but indirectly it has made marriage and family stronger by placing them on a sound footing.

QUESTIONS FOR EXERCISE

1. Explain the changing pattern of Hindu marriages in India.
2. What are the problems of Hindu marriage? What social legislations have been passed to remedy them?
3. Review briefly the legislative measures that have changed the status of Hindu Woman.

7
Tribal Problems

TRIBAL PROBLEMS

The Indian tribes at present suffer from mainly two types of problems. Firstly, those which are also found in other people of the country and secondly, those which are peculiar to tribal people. In this latter type of tribal problems the following are the most important:

1. Cultural Problems. Due to contact with other cultures, the tribal culture is undergoing a revolutionary change. Due to the influence of Christian missionaries, the problem of bilingualism has developed which has led to indifference towards tribal language. The tribal people are imitating Western culture in different aspects of their social life and leaving their own culture. An important influence of cultural contact is seen in the form of disappearance of youth dormitories, imitation of the western dress and modes of living has led to the degeneration of tribal life and tribal arts, such as dance, music and different types of crafts.

2. Religious Problems. Due to the conversion of many tribal people to Hindu and Christian religion, the tribal groups have been divided into several sects on the basis of religion. This has shattered their collective life and conflicts and dissensions are increasing. The tribal people are gradually forgetting their tribal religion. This has led to social disorganisation.

3. Social Problems. Due to the influence of Hindu community the tribals are facing the problem of increasing bride price. This has encouraged elopement of girls and their forcible lifting by males. Another social problem created by the tribal contact with Hindus is the evil custom of child marriage. The contact with the civilized society has increased the number of premarital and extramarital sexual relationships in tribal society and the number of dissolution of marriages. This has also increased the incidence of prostitution and venereal diseases.

4. Economic Problems. The contact with the civilized world has disintegrated the entire economic system of the tribal people. They have forgotten their ancient crafts. Most of them are working as labourers in plantations, agriculture farms, factories and other jobs. The employers every where misuse the ignorance of the tribal people, take maximum work from them and give them minimum money in return.

TRIBAL WELFARE

The Indian Constitution has made important provisions for the welfare of tribal people. Posts have been reserved for them in public services, in States and Centre. Seats have been reserved for their representatives in the Legislatures of different States and in the Indian Parliament. Special provisions have been made regarding their administration. District and regional councils have been established to carry out their welfare. The government have given special attention to their educational and economic development. This has not appreciably improved the condition of tribal people. The following suggestions can be made in commotion with tribal welfare:

1. Economic reforms. Efforts should be made to encourage tribal people to permanently establish for cultivation, because the shifting cultivation practised by them results in much wastage. The co-operative forests utilization societies can help the tribal people in utilizing the forests in which they live. The Government should arrange for technical help and education to improve the condition of tribal crafts and provision should be made for the marketing of the goods produced by them. Laws should be strictly enforced in tribal areas.

2. Educational reforms. At the base of the fallen state of tribal society is their widespread illiteracy. Educational expansion, therefore, should be given primary consideration. The tribal education should be given through their own language and in their own cultural background. Colleges should be established to safeguard the tribal fine arts. Provisions should be made for technical and commercial education in the tribes. Along with education the tribal music, dance, plays and recreation should be encouraged. Religious dogmatism and superstitions should be removed through scientific education.

3. Reform in the level of health. Efforts should be made to improve the level of health of tribal people. This will require provision of medicines, pure water, nutritive food, clean and properly ventilated houses and generally healthy atmosphere.

4. Social reforms. Whatever may be the opposition from certain vested interests, efforts to carry out social reforms in tribals must be realized. The evil customs of bride price, magic and ritualism, child marriage, prostitution etc., should be removed. These social reforms can be carried out only after economic reforms.

5. Political reforms. It is a pity that the government officials posted in tribal areas misuse the ignorance of tribal people and exploit them for different purposes. They ignore the tribal culture and are completely indifferent to their welfare. The government should appoint such officials as are conversant with the tribal culture and intend to improve the condition of tribal people.

In free India the State and Central Governments have made incessant efforts in the direction of tribal welfare. At the central level a commissioner attached with Home Ministry takes care of tribal welfare. Under him there are several Regional Assistant Commissioners whose number has now increased to 16. In the States, there are special Directorates of tribal welfare. In Assam five

District and Regional Councils have been established for tribal welfare. Tribal Research Institutes for the study of tribal culture and language are working in Bihar, Madhya Pradesh, Orissa and other states. Efforts are being made to expand educational facilities in tribal areas. Thousands of scholarships have been granted by Central and State Governments. Provisions have been made for special seats for tribal people in medical, engineering and technical colleges. Posts have been reserved for them in public services. Primary and Secondary Schools have been established in tribal areas where there is provision for free education.

In the political field the tribes send their representatives to State and Central Legislatures, some of whom have risen to the rank of Deputy Ministers and Ministers. Some tribal youths qualify in All India Services and their number is gradually increasing.

For the economic regeneration of the tribes, the Government has enforced rules regarding land ownership and utilization of land. Crores of rupees have been spent for the development of cottage industries. The Community Projects have been established everywhere. Grain shops have been opened which provide for improved type of seeds. Laws in connection with debt have been enforced. Special multi-purpose tribal blocks have been created. Shifting cultivation is restricted and tribal families have been permanently established on suitable land. Efforts have been made to provide housing facilities in some tribal areas. Hospitals have been opened which provide free medicines, check epidemics and cure all types of diseases. Research institutes have been opened for the study of tribal culture and language. New roads have been made and old roads improved in the tribal areas. Personnel working for tribal welfare are given special training for this purpose. Institutes for their training have been established in Madhya Pradesh, West Bengal, Assam, Rajasthan, Maharashtra and other States.

The above brief outline of the State and Central Governments' efforts in the direction of tribal welfare shows the extent of work that has been done in different Five Year Plans. This has definitely led to some improvement in some directions. The solution of tribal problems, however, requires a multi-sided planning. To quote D.N. Majumdar, an authority on Indian tribal problems, "There is no one solution to tribal problems, there is no common platform to demand it. There are levels of cultural development and there are different patterns of life that the tribes own. In any scheme of rehabilitation of tribal life, the attitudes and configurations of culture must be known to work out plans, and what is true of one culture area may not be so for a second."

QUESTIONS FOR EXERCISE

1. Outline the chief problems of tribal people in India.
2. Contact with civilisation is responsible for tribal discomfort everywhere. Briefly examine the important effect of such contact with reference to Indian tribal life.
3. Write note on Tribal Welfare.

8
Problems of Urbanization

In almost all cities of the world there is progressive increase in the population consequent upon industrialization. This is a simple and quite easily understandable phenomenon. Whenever some new industry is put up a large labour force and a sizeable managerial cadre are required. In order to meet this demand there is influx of population to the city where an industry is being set up. In flourishing cities of the world, every day some or the other new industrial unit is coming up. Therefore there is continuous influx of population to cities. This progress in the population has resulted in the problems of overcrowding. The industrialization and mechanization have given rise to a host of social problems.

PROBLEMS OF URBANIZATION

(1) Decline in Social Sympathy. The first consequence of overcrowding and increasing population is the decline in fellow-feeling and sympathy. In villages we find a lot of sympathy and communal feeling. A villager knows almost every other man in his village; knows about his problems, joys and sorrows. He feels for them. On the other hand, the question of knowing others does not arise in cities. And obviously we can have little sympathy for those who are unknown to us. In cities everyone is concerned about himself or his friends and lacks sympathy for others.

(2) Lack of Social Control. With the decline in fellow-feeling, sympathy and concern for others, there is also decline in the social control in cities. As the population increases in cities there is decline in control of family and caste on the behaviour of an individual. The infection of no control and arbitrary behaviour in cities is catching even rural population. Now-a-days the control of caste and panchayat has declined considerably in villages.

(3) Decline in Family Control. The rise in the urban population has led to decline in family control. The family ties have lost their orthodox value and have become rather lax. In cities there are a number of families where both husband and wife go to work. In such families in the nature of things, control over children. Lakhs of labourers live in cities without their families. Obviously, there is no question of family control over their behaviour. After coming to cities they start indulging in licentious behaviour because there is no one there to check them. They start going to cinemas and also visit houses of ill repute.

(4) Decline in the influence of Religion. In cities the philosophy of materialism is ascendant. Everybody has become self-centred and is madly pursuing his self-interest without any consideration for others. All this is a direct result of the decline in the influence of religion in the urban life.

(5) Change in the Status of Women. There has been considerable change in the status of women in cities. There is great awakening among women. They are on the way to achieving economic independence. They are no longer slaves to their husbands. Commenting on this great change in the status of women in cities, Earnest R. Mowrer writes, "The husband is no longer the head of the household in many families, in spite of the fact that he still provides the family name. The wife, on the other hand, finds herself quite equal of her husband in the family circle, if not superior." However there is an evil side of this awakening among women. There is rise in the incidence of illicit sex-contacts, divorce, and pre- and extra-marital sex.

(6) Changes in the institution of marriage. In India marriages used to be contracted by the parents of bride and bridegroom. But now-a-days there is an increasing tendency to choose one's life partner freely and of one's own accord.

(7) Changes in Family Structure. In cities the institution of joint family is disappearing. Everywhere there is an increasing tendency to have limited families confined to husband, wife and their offspring.

(8) Superiority of Male ratio in Population. The reasons for the greater number of males in the urban population are quite clear. In cities lakhs of labourers live single, their families live in their villages. Hence in cities males out-number females.

(9) Professionalization of Entertainment. In cities relaxation and entertainment are not natural. One does not participate in it but merely enjoys it passively. Of course, one has to pay through his nose for this entertainment. One can go to a cinema, to a hotel to see a cabaret or even to a brothel to see dance or buy sexual pleasure. In short, entertainment in cities is commercial and one has to pay for the entertainment.

(10) Scarcity of Living Accommodation. In cities there is acute shortage of accommodation. More industrialized a city is less is the living accommodation in it. In cities like Mumbai, Calcutta and Delhi people are compelled to sleep on footpath. Even those who find a roof overhead live like cattles. Ten to twenty persons may be staying in a single room. Naturally this gives rise to all sorts of evils.

(11) Slums. This really follows what has been said above. As a consequence of shortage of living space, there are sprawling slums in big Indian towns. In Kanpur these slums are called *Ahatas*; in Delhi *Basti;* in Bombay *Chawl* and in Madras *Cheri.* These slums are a blot on the fair name of India. What is rather distressing is that along with slums we find grand mansions of mill owners.

(12) Changes in Moral Values. There is change in the moral attitudes of city dwellers. The industrialization leads to mechanization and as a consequence of mechanization man becomes an automation and loses his independence and moral autonomy. The industrialization has produced a man who functions in the manner of a component of a machine. He feels himself a victim of circumstances and is unwilling to assert his will. The attitude of working girls towards sexual relations has changed considerably. As industrialization has created great demand for working hands, women get work along with men. Due to this they have achieved economic independence and are no longer prepared to play a second fiddle to their husbands. The old moral values have crashed. New gadgets have given household women great deal of time to pursue their interests. All this has brought about great change in moral thinking and moral values.

(13) Breakdown of Joint Family. In cities the joint family system has broken down. In cities most families consist of husband, wife and their offsprings.

(14) Increase in Evil Profession. In cities many an evil professions flourish. Due to frustrating working conditions in the factory workers drink, gamble and go to prostitutes.

(15) Increase in the incidence of crime. As R.K. Mookerjee has very aptly observed, in industrial centres manhood is unquestionably brutalized, women dishonoured and childhood poisoned at the very source.

(16) Increase in Juvenile Delinquency. In cities there is a sharp increase in juvenile delinquency due to industrialization, unscrupulous employers engage child labour. This is an important factor in producing juvenile delinquency. Besides, the children of those parents who go to work are not properly attended to by their parents. They are left to their own design and tend to become juvenile delinquents.

(17) Corruption, Conflict and Competition. In cities we find cut-throat competition in economic field. Not only among businessmen but among mill-owners there is furious competition. When this competition becomes fierce, evil practices are resorted to. Blackmarket is a direct consequence of this fierce competition.

The above mentioned social impact of industrialization is to be found in all countries. Some effects are desirable, while others are undesirable. To control the undesirable effects there is town planning in advanced countries.

QUESTION FOR EXERCISE

1. Write note on Problems of Urbanization.

9

Rural Disorganisation and Problems

Rural Disorganisation is the disorganisation in rural social structure, rural family, rural marriage, rural social conventions etc. Such a state can be seen in Indian villages near big cities. Here the community consciousness in village life is steadily decreasing. The control of the caste panchayats is almost non-existent. The villagers who work in the towns as labourers acquire such habits as drinking, prostitution, telling lies, unnecessary show and needless boasting etc., and when these villagers return to their native village they spread extreme immorality. The village youths studying in the towns also become addicted to irresponsibility and sedantry habits and when they exhibit the same habits in their villages the other simple-minded adolescents are also corrupted. The village belle living in the town is even more adept at the use of cheap cosmetics and on her return to the village she spreads this habit among her sisters in the village. Now-a-days, the villagers are using cosmetics and other means in a larger measure than before and the level of health in the villages is fast deteriorating because milk and its bye-products from the villages are sold in the towns, and, secondly, the money thus earned is being wasted on useless things. Though education is spreading in the villages, educated have turned their back to the old ideal of simple living and high thinking. Even though they may appear plain in their dress and way of living due to poverty and simple due to insensitivity, they are not the least scrupulous in adulterating commodities which they sell.

The convention of hospitality is no longer observed. Sex relations are marked by a lack of responsibility. The joint family is fast disintegrating. The number of thefts, abortions, murders, assaults, litigations etc., is steadily increasing. The old customs are being violated. The bonds of caste and society are disregarded. Similarly, family ties are also being discarded. Individualism, materialism and rationalism are increasing. Hence the only elements which now characterize village life are agriculture which is the major occupation of villagers, small population, lack of transport facilities, lack of scientific comforts, mud houses, unmetalled roads and natural environment etc.

AREAS OF RURAL DISORGANISATION

During the British rule the caste system suffered a severe shock in the village. Due to the British economic policy and new laws different castes abandoned their traditional occupations and adopted other professions. Many Brahmins and Kshatriyas started farming. The members of the untouchable castes became agricultural labourers. The control of caste panchayat weakened. It is seen in the villages, now-a-days that the status of an individual in the villages is determined not only by his caste but also by his personality, financial condition and activities as well. Although the Brahmin is addressed respectfully, the wealthy untouchable is not the recipient of any the less respect even though he belongs to a lower caste. And at some places it may even be that he may be respected even more than the poor Brahmin. Being assisted by government laws the lower castes no longer look upon themselves as inferior and in south India at some places the untouchables consider themselves defiled if they touch a Brahmin. If any Brahmin happens to come into their sector he is assaulted with brooms and in extreme cases strict measures are taken to purify the place which he has defiled by his touch.

In this way in the present age the members of each caste are engaged in strengthening their own organisations. Some castes have formed their own welfare organisation, by holding meetings they mobilize their brethren for the protection of their interest. But even then the power of the caste panchayat; exercised in the form of control over the individual's behaviour, food habits, ways of living etc. has gradually disappeared. Even in such villages where the laws regarding touchability in the caste are necessarily observed, freedom is given towards violating them in the towns. Although marriages are still contracted within the same caste even then there is no obstacle to behaviour, eating, conversing etc. between different castes. But although in this way the caste system appears to be growing weak on the one hand it seems to be gaining in strength upon the other. Casteism is increasing due to vested interests. In recent times it is seen that most of the people vote for the member of their own caste. Even political parties issue tickets only to those members whose caste was in majority in that electorate. The same had been the case in the previous election and some elected persons had even tried to gain advantage for their own caste. In this way due to political and other interests casteism is increasing. Most administrative authorities in government and non-government factories, offices, colleges and other works think it very necessary to employ only the members of their own caste.

1. Jajmani Disorganization. In this way, in regard to the caste system both weakening and strengthening tendencies are in evidence but the jajmani system is undoubtedly crumbling. Jajmani system was based on the exploitation of the Kameen by the Jajman. As a result of the declaration equating all the citizens of free India and the efforts of the government to improve the backward classes, the backward classes have now gained a certain degree of self-respect and their Jajmani relations with other castes are in the process of being broken off. Secondly, the circulation of many in place of services in the villages has also had a degenerating effect upon the jajmani system. Thirdly, the jajmani relations are also dying out because the caste panchayats have lost their power and the occupations are no longer based on caste. Mobility is also increasing in the rural areas due to an increase in the facilities of transport. All these causes have together worked towards the detriment of the jajmani system; but, this does not mean that the jajmani system has been completely eliminated from the villages. Remnants of the jajmani system have been found in all the recent studies of the rural communities although signs of their growing disability are also evident in most studies.

2. Family Disorganisation. Although the joint families are still viewed with respect they are no longer the unit of rural community, having been replaced by single families. Groups based upon similar interests are becoming stronger in place of the group constituted from kinship. With the increase of individualism the families are becoming smaller and smaller and the control exercised by the family over the individual member is also decreasing. But the kinship group has not yet lost its power over the family completely. In the villages, as is wont to be in the towns, many of the activities of the family are being taken over by other agencies. For example, in the villages where a grinding machine has been installed, the wheat is ground in the mill instead of at home. The women are progressively being more educated and being given many social, economic and political rights with the result that they are conscious of their position in the family which is continuously improving.

3. Marital Disorganisation. The institution of marriage, much the same as the family, is changing. The scope of marriage possibilities is increasing. Although there are not many examples of intercaste marriage, even then marriages are contracted within the same village and between members of neighbouring villages. Although the marriages are decided upon by the parents it is considered quite proper to take the assent of the boy and girl, in particular the boy. The number of love marriages and divorces is negligible in most villages in India. The basis of the selection of the other party is also changing. Although the ancestry is still an important factor in marriage, more importance is now attached to the personal financial condition and education of the boy and the qualities of the girl. In the Hindus the demand for dowry is increasing and so is that of Mehar among Muslims. At the same time much wasteful expenditure in marriage ceremonies is now being avoided and the party accompanying the bridegroom is smaller. The customs of marriage are also undergoing change. Although it is difficult to present any universal pattern in this respect, marriages now take place between parties reveal improved awareness of marital obligations. The system of child marriage is in its last throes and widow remarriage is accepted.

FACTORS OF CHANGE

Even though it is very difficult to analyse the direct and indirect causes of change in a community, rural or otherwise, it nevertheless is possible to recognise the major factors in change in the rural sphere which may be placed in the following classes:

1. Natural factors
2. Technological factors

3. Social factors
4. Economic factors
5. Cultural factors
6. Political factors.

It would be advantageous to make a brief study of factors which cause change in rural life:

1. Natural factors. The natural factors of change in the rural community include all those natural elements which are found in the region in which that specific rural community exists. For example, the villages which have sprung up close to the rivers and the villages prospering in the mountains show apparently the effects, respectively, of the rivers and the mountains. The social, economic, cultural and political life of the rural community settled in the bamboo forest exhibits the effects of the bamboos. In places frequented by seismographic disturbances the houses are constructed of wood. The vegetation and the animals peculiar to any place are most frequently consumed and employed in their native land. In the same way, the cottage industries which develop in any place bear a direct co-relation to the minerals found in that area. In this way rivers, seas, floods, storms, rain, hailstorm, earthquakes, mountains, vegetation and animals etc. are the natural factors which influence the rural community. Whenever anyone of them changes, the life of the rural community also changes. The geographists have written numerous books on the subject of the impact of geographic environment upon human life. The natural factors shape the geographic environment. Their effects are universally known. If the Ganges river alters its course miles away from the one which it was previously pursuing then not only the economic life but also the other aspects of the rural community stranded upon the old banks of the river will be changed.

2. Technological factors. The natural environment alone does not transform human communities, because man constructs a fair portion of his environment for himself, and these also have widespread effects upon his life. Man creates a novel environment with the assistance of the technical factors and adapts natural environment to himself. These technological factors include all the inventions. Wherever electrical power has been made available to the villages, it has completely transformed thc rural community. According to Prof. Ogburn the invention of the radio alone has resulted in nearly 150 major changes in rural social life. Machines have not been used as much in the Indian villages as they are in the villages of the West. But even then the work of grinding wheat and ginning cotton has lost its flavour for the rural families since the machines for such purposes were intalled in their villages. This has influenced the life and condition of the women. With the invention of steam and electrical power all the aspects of human life have undergone some change or the other.

3. Social factors. The social factors have comprehensive effect upon the social life of the rural community. For example, the existence or the inexistence of Sati custom, child marriage, negation of widow remarriage have some effect upon the life of the rural community, its effect being particularly evident in the condition of the female population. The major social factors which influence the life of the Indian rural community are caste system, joint family, Jajmani custom, various laws of marriage as well as social and religious customs and traditions etc. Any change in any one of these factors results in a change in the rural community. For example, when the caste panchayats grow weak or lose power completely the intercaste relations in the villages undergo continuous change. In the same way changes can also be seen in the mutual relations between different castes due to the Jajmani relation having been broken off.

4. Economic factors. The economic factors include those which are related to agriculture, business and industries. As a result of the pressure upon land having increased in the villages, many people have migrated to the towns in search of employment. Living in the towns the moral life and values of a rural youth undergo changes which have their influence upon the moral life and values of the other people in the village when he returns to the village. Wherever factories or mines have been established in the villages the relations between men and women have been influenced by their working together. Poverty is an economic factor and its widespread effects upon the life of the community are only too well known.

5. Cultural factors. Cultural factors include beliefs, assumptions, values etc. Changes in them have repercussions in the entire social life. In India wherever the Hindu, Muslim and Christian culture have had an opportunity to meet, the cultural life of the influence of Western culture, the institution of youth dormitory is vanishing from many tribal villages. In rural girls and boys who are influenced by Western culture the tendencies of individualism, materialism and irresponsibility intrude and these exert important influence upon rural institutions like family, marriage, caste system etc.

RURAL PROBLEMS

Now-a-days the condition of the villagers in India is very much unsatisfactory. The villages which were once like heaven on earth are today the very incarnations of poverty, hunger, disease, disunity and disorganization. Not only assault but even incidents of armed robbery and murder are commonplace in the villages. Litigation is resorted to even over the merest trifles and this creates persistent mutual enmity. The dry and gloomy faces of the villagers advertise their low state of health. The villages which were once famed for honesty today give shelter to people who surpass their urban brothers in deceit. In the villages where at one time the ideal of morality was very high today, corruption, moral degeneration and social deviance pass all limits. Superstition, ignorance, lack of education, poverty, unemployment etc., have turned the village into detestable places to live in. The problems of agriculture and economic problems of the Indian villages are grave, the social problems are no less serious. Of these the chief ones are the following:

1. Agricultural Problems

In India the condition of agriculture is very bad. The major problems in this respect are:

(i) *Old and unskilled methods.* In India the progressive methods of farming have not yet been popularized so that the farmers persist with the old methods. Ploughing, sowing, harvesting other allied activities still follow the old pattern. As a result greater labour yields less.

(ii) *Old kinds of tools.* Besides the methods of farming, Indian agriculture is further handicapped by the use of old and out-moded tools. Modern implements like tractors, sowers, mowers and harrow have not been introduced on the scene for the respective agricultural activities. The reason for this backwardness is that the farms are sub-divided into small pieces and the farmers have no adequate knowledge of the tools nor the resources to purchase them.

(iii) *Undeveloped varieties of seeds.* Not much has been achieved in India towards the improvement of the varieties of seeds and whatever little has been done does not spread over any considerable area. Most of the villagers use undeveloped and degenerate seeds on their farms. As a result the yield per acre is extremely low.

(iv) *Small and Scattered Farms.* Most of the farms in India are small and scattered. Due to the fact that the succeeding sons have equal right to their deceased father's property, the land is divided among the heirs. In this way as the land is further subdivided in each succeeding generation the resulting pieces of land become uneconomic holding, which means that they do not yield food crops in proportion to the efforts expended upon them.

(v) *Shortage in the means of Irrigation.* There is a serious shortage of the means of irrigation in India. The crop is not good because the plants do not get water at the proper time. Mostly agriculture depends upon the rains for water, which makes it a gamble based upon the monsoon. If the rains come at the proper time and in proper quantity the crop is good, otherwise it is a failure.

(vi) *Shortage of Manure.* There is a considerable shortage in the supply of good manure in adequate quantities to the villages of India. Consequently, India cannot have the same number of crops every year as those which are possible in some other countries. Most of the farmers are ignorant of even the ways of manufacturing manures. Knowledge of chemical manures is almost negligible and even where the chemical manures are available, the quantity is insufficient to meet the needs of the farmers.

(vii) *Destruction of Crops by Insect.* In India the villagers are not acquainted with the modern methods of preventing and curing diseases to which the plants are susceptible. Thus small insects do heavy damage to the crops. Besides insects, animals like rats, monkey and foxes and even some birds help themselves to a good part of the crops.

Besides the above mentioned special problems the villages of India are faced with such other agricultural problems like the complete ignorance of the farmer regarding the new scientific research upon agriculture, etc.

2. Economic Problems

The economic problems are also very serious in the Indian villages. The major problems are the following:

(1) Lack of proper sale Organisation. There is no proper organisation for the sale of the produce of agriculture and cottage industries in the villages of India with the result that the producers do not get proper remuneration for their labour and their enthusiasm does not get any incentive. In the villages of U.P. 65% produce is sold in the villages.

(2) Indebtedness and high rates of Interest. Indebtedness has reached a very high level in the Indian villages and the villagers do not get any relief from it because the rate of interest is extremely high. Sometimes the money-lender goes to the extent of taking possession of the animals of debtor and legally dispossessing him of his land as well. As a result of the extremely high rate of interest the progress of agriculture is not possible and at the same, neither is possible any increase in the small scale industries. According to the 1951-52 All India Rural Credit Survey, the rate of interest in villages is between 20 and 40%. The burden of debt upon the villagers would be approximately Rs. 100 crores.

(3) Lack of Facility in the means of Transport and Communication. In the villages of India the road surfaces are not at all pleasing and neither is there any proper facility of motor vehicles for the transportation of goods. And in some places even the letters in the post offices are distributed only once a week. The trade activity moves at a snail's pace because there is no facility in the means of transport and communication.

(4) Assistance to Small Scale and Cottage Industries. The cottage and rural industries of India are in a hopeless condition. They neither have adequate knowledge of the scientific instruments of production, and nor have these instruments easily available, and even if they are available there is not enough money with the producer to enable him to purchase them. The produced goods cannot compete with the goods produced in the factory, thus the rural industries are continually degenerating. The economic condition of the villages cannot be improved without solving the problems of the rural industries.

(5) Problems of landless Agricultural Labourers. The condition of the landless labourers in the agricultural sphere is very deplorable. Their annual income is less than rupees one thousand per family and they are occupied only for 218 days in the year. Among them 61% labourers are employed for almost the entire year. The number of agricultural labourers in India is 490 lakh and this number is continuously increasing. The Planning Commission had admitted that the problem of these labourers is undoubtedly big and complex which has not only an important relation with the village economy but which, in the next 15 to 20 years, will have a serious influence upon the entire economic and social development.

(6) Problem of Cattle. The problem of the cattle in the villages of India is also serious because they neither get sufficient fodder nor are they protected from diseases. There is a great shortage of cattle of a good breed and no adequate measures are being implemented to improve it. Many of the animals consume fodder even though they are completely useless because killing them is forbidden by religious dogmas.

(7) Undeveloped Vegetation. Another problem of the rural economy is the lack of an adequate use of the forest wealth. The forests are neither properly protected nor properly developed and proper use is also not made of them.

Besides the above mentioned problems of thé villages some other problems also assume serious proportions for example, the problems of famine, floods, monsoon failure etc.

3. Social Problems

There are many serious problems in the social sphere of the villages as well. The most important among them are:

(1) Illiteracy. In the Indian villages the problem of illiteracy is very serious. Even today the large number in the rural population is uneducated and illiterate. In respect of the technical and agricultural training, the picture is even more gloomy because there is extreme shortage of it. This not only breeds superstition and dogmatism, it also hinders economic progress.

(2) Poverty and Unemployment. The problem of poverty and unemployment in the villages is no less serious. All the people in the villages do not get even two square meals a day. In some extreme cases many people do not have even adequate cotton clothing let alone the luxury of woollens. The houses are small, inadequate and uncemented. The number of people in the villages who are employed throughout the year is extremely small. Even the farmers do not work all the time in many months of the year while at certain periods they are completely unoccupied. Poverty and unemployment have together spread corruption, filth and moral degeneration in the villages.

(3) Bad Condition of Health. A very serious problem in the villages is the extremely bad condition of health. In India the birth rate as well as the death rate are the highest as compared to the other countries and the span of life is the shortest. The rates of child birth and infanticide are also the highest in the world. Due to inadequate and malnutrition there is hardly any resistance to epidemics which are very common and there is no proper system or arrangement for eradicating them. The houses are very much insanitary while the use of intoxicating drugs makes the state of health even worse.

Besides the above problems other defects like superstition, religious dogmatism, casteism, untouchability, factionalism, disunity and litigation etc. are to be seen in the villages. There is a lack of political awakening. The means of communication not being available, the villagers are ignorant of the national and international problems which arise from time to time. Due to the forementioned defects, the condition of village panchayats is not satisfactory.

MEASURES TO SOLVE RURAL PROBLEMS

Effort is needed to supplement the inadequate planning for eradicating these defects from the Indian villages. In this respect certain positive measures may be suggested, of which the major ones are:

(1) Improvement in Agriculture. The first step towards the reconstruction of the Indian villages should be an improvement in the state of agriculture. The following suggestions can be made:

(i) The new methods of agriculture and farming should be exhibited and made popular.

(ii) Pointing out the shortcomings of the old implements the use of the new kinds of tools should be disseminated, and these tools should be made available in the villages at reasonable prices.

(iii) Improved seeds should be cultivated on government farm and be made available to the farmers at reasonable prices.

(iv) The scattered farms should be unified and the fragmentation of farms beyond a certain limit should be prevented by enacting laws to this effect.

(v) There should be proper provision of tubewells, wells, canals etc.

(vi) The advantages of chemical manure should be propagated and broadcasted, besides making them available in the villages at reasonable prices. The process of making compost manure from cowdung should be popularised. In this respect the panchayats should be assisted by the Government.

(vii) Measures for protecting crops from harmful insects should be exhibited on Government farms and broadcast in the villages. Insecticides and pesticides should be made available in the villages at reasonable prices.

(viii) The Government should distribute medicines for curing the plants of the diseases which they may have contracted.

(2) Economic Reconstruction. The second important step in the direction of solution of problems is economic reconstruction. The following suggestions on the subject can be put forward:

(i) There should be arrangement for the sale of the village produce through cooperative societies.

(ii) The farmers, business men and other people engaged in small industries should be able to get the necessary capital at a low rate of interest from the co-operative bank.

(iii) Insurance schemes and other schemes for saving should be circulated among the villages.

(iv) The roads in the villages should be reconstructed and heavy vehicular traffic should be used for transporting the goods. As far as practicable, the railways should be placed near the villages.

(v) The Government should extend special encouragement and assistance to cottage and small industries. New tools and capital at a low rate of interest should be made available to them, proper assistance being given to facilitate the sale of goods which they produce.

(vi) It is necessary to organise business fairs and exhibitions in the villages at regular intervals so that business may be encouraged and industrial knowledge increased.

(vii) Maximum efforts should be diverted towards the reduction of middle men like landlords and moneylenders from between farmer and labour, on the one hand and the producer and consumer on the other.

(viii) The Government should provide improved strains of cattle for improving the breed of cattle in the villages. Necessary training for poultry farming and fish farming should be imparted. The improved cattle should be exhibited along with the methods of improving the strains of cattle.

(ix) Efforts should be made to provide the landless labourers with the maximum of land by encouraging the Bhoodan Movement. Laws should also be passed in respect of the wages of agricultural labourers.

(x) The Government should construct dams at strategic points in order to prevent floods and also construct canals to reduce the probability of floods. During times of floods and similar natural catastrophic happenings Takavi should be distributed and the farmer exempted from the revenue.

(xi) The village panchayats should develop the pastures and forests contiguous to the village and they should also enact laws for their protection,

(3) Social reconstruction. The problems of village cannot be solved without resorting to social reconstruction. The major suggestions in this respect are the following:

(i) Social education centres and adult education centres should be opened in the villages for the dissemination of literacy. Basic primary education should be made free and compulsory.

(ii) Efforts should be made to provide employment for the unemployed while efforts are being made for removing poverty. Some control over the rate of interest should be exercised and wasteful expenditure curbed.

(iii) The basic laws of health should also be made known to the villagers and contamination of foodgrains prevented.

(iv) Adequate provisions of hospitals and maternity homes should be made in the villages where the poor should be treated free of charge. Measures for the prevention of infectious diseases should be implemented.

(v) It is necessary to remove insanitary condition from the villages if disease is to be prevented. The drain should be widened and cleanliness should be propagated among the villages. This can also be done by donated or contributed labour.

(vi) There is need for social propaganda for the eradication of untouchability, factionalism and superstitions etc.

(vii) In order to reduce the extent of litigation the panchayat should be given the right of considering matters of minor importance.

(4) Political awakening. The problem of rural improvement is not so simple as to be successfully solved by the government alone and unaided, thus there is a great need for political awakening.

INDEBTEDNESS

The money-lenders hold an important place in the rural economic system. In most areas the term 'sahukar' is used for a person who loans money although other words, peculiar to their place of origin, are also used to designate the same person. In ancient India the system of lending money and taking loans was not based on laws. It was based on the individual and conventional relationships between the two parties. Thus both the debtor and creditor had good mutual relations. With the advent of English people when new laws were made for arrangements, the creditors got the opportunity of getting rich quickly. Now the relations between the debtor and the creditor were no longer individual. Their basis now became law and money.

Although the condition of the cultivators in ancient India was quite good, their financial situation became deplorable in the English period and has continued to be such to the present day. The cultivator in India is generally poor. But, at the same time he wants to maintain his dignity in the social and community circles, for which purposes he often does not hesitate in spending far beyond his means on such occasions like marriage. Thus indebtedness is omnipresent in India. In all the states of the country there are large numbers of people who have been under the burden of debt for many generations. Further, the modes of expenditure are also increasing. With every increase in the population the pressure on the land is proportionately increasing. Usually the village people take loans when they marry off their daughters, and not many of them are able to repay this loan. The condition of the cultivator of India has further deteriorated under the impact of some very serious famines in the country not so very long ago. The famines had the effect of placing the unfortunate agriculturist in an even more unfortunate plight as far as his indebtedness was concerned.

Problem of Indebtedness

Loans used to be forwarded on the basis of individual relationships. Now the loans have come to be given or taken against secured land. Both the Indian Agreement Act as well as the Civil Procedure Code worked towards the detriment of the debtor and the betterment of the creditor. These gave the creditor not only of right of taking possession of the mortgaged land in the event of the debtor's failing to repay the loan but also the authority to take possession of the domestic articles and animals of the debtor. He could prosecute them and get them imprisoned. The Registration of Documents Act of 1864 and the Transfer of Property Act of 1882 both helped to increase the number of mortgaged immovable properties in the form of land. The creditors grew continuously richer while the lands of the debtors passed into their hands. The number of creditors grew and so did the quantity of loan. According to Sir Edward

Maclagan, the total rural debt in British India in 1911 was of the order of rupees 300 crores. In 1920 Sir M.L. Derling estimated it at rupees 600 crores. In 1930 this debt was of the order of rupees 900 crores according to the estimates of the I.C.B.I. Committee. In 1955 according to the Dr. Radhakamal Mukerji the debt amounted to rupees 1200 crores. In 1938 total debt in British India was rupees 1800 crore according to S.E.V.S. Manium. It is evident from these statistics that the extent of loan increased sixfold between 1911 and 1938 in British India. Since the latter date this indebtedness continued to increase.

Causes of Indebtedness

This increase in the indebtedness has been attributed to a multitude of causes, the major of which are the following:

(1) Absence of necessary laws. The greatest cause of indebtedness was the absence of laws for protecting the debtor. Due to his special superior status the moneylender would not let the poor man go out of his clutches once he had got hold of him. The cultivator in the village became so involved in it that once he had taken a loan, the burden to debt increased continuously.

(2) Neglect by the government. The English government did not make much efforts to protect the ingenious farmer from the evil design of the moneylender, although many people directed the attention of the government towards the problem.

(3) Economic Upheaval. As a result of the economic disturbance of 1929 the condition of the farmers deteriorated further and they could not prevent themselves from sinking further into debt.

(4) Extravagance. Although most of the people are poor in the rural sphere they do not hesitate in availing themselves of the facilities and taking loans to spend upon such occasions like marriage or the observance of the rituals and anniversaries. This obviously tends to increase the burden of loan.

(5) Facility in taking loan. The facility with which loans could be taken also helped to increase the tendency of taking a loan. Often the moneylender of the village would encourage the villager to take loans by taking ingratiatingly.

(6) Tricks of the moneylender. The tricks of the moneylender had also much to do with the indebtedness in India. Often the moneylender would maintain such a high rate of interest that the debtor could not easily pay it. While providing the loaned money the moneylender would take away the amount of interest at the start. Consequently, the farmer receives a very small amount of money. In a few years the loan would be doubled and trebled with the result that, principal aside, it became difficult to pay even the interest. As a result of the religious tendency most of the rural people feel it necessary to repay even the loan incurred by their predecessors. Consequently, the loan continued through generations. The illiteracy of the village farmer is also a major cause of his indebtedness. Taking unfair advantages of his ignorance the unscrupulous moneylender would give an amount to the farmer while he wrote a different one upon the paper. This malpractice has been known to go to the extent of the farmer being compelled to put his thumb impression upon a blank paper which would otherwise be used for divesting the poor creature of his entire stock of belongings. In the Indian village the moneylender usually belonged to the higher caste. Thus the creditors did not have the strength to oppose them due to his high social status, which was used to keep the poor in their places.

Result of Indebtedness

Many results of this increasing indebtedness are manifest in the villages of India. Some of the major consequences are the following:

(1) Slavery. The worst result of indebtedness was seen in an increase in the number of landless labourers. As has been mentioned earlier, the moneylenders took advantages of the ignorance and helplessness of the farmers to dispossess them of their land. Consequently, the farmer became a labourer and started ploughing his own land for the moneylender. Sometimes the debtor had to serve the moneylender in return for his loan, in which situation his condition was no better than that of a servant. In some villages it has been a custom that the parents take a loan from the moneylender and send their children to work for the moneylender as unpaid employees. The condition of these children is worse even than slaves. In this way the system of debt has indirectly compelled thousands of people in the villages to spend a life of slaves.

(2) Increase of Poverty. The most explicit result of indebtedness is the increase in the poverty of the farmer because once he became entangled in debt he remains poor no matter how much he may exert himself. It was no easy matter for them to repay their loans so that, in some families, the lives of generations was spoiled in repaying the debts incurred by their grandparents.

(3) Deterioration of Agriculture. As a result of indebtedness the condition of agriculture also deteriorated because most of the farmers had to work on their moneylender's land as servants. Obviously, they could not take that interest in their work which they would have taken had they owned the land.

(4) Low Standard of Health. The farmer, burdened with a heavy debt was continuously growing weaker because he was beset with the problem of repaying it. Many people tried to repay the loan by working extremely hard but when they failed to do so even after the maximum of efforts they sank into a premature decrepitude. In this way indebtedness is one cause of the fall in the level of health in the Indian villages.

Suggestions for Removing Indebtedness

Many suggestions have been put forward for eradicating indebtedness from the village. Of them the major ones are the following :

(1) Government Loan at Low Interest. The government should make arrangements for giving loans to the farmers at low rate of interest.

(2) Communal Societies and Banks. In order to arrange for loans in the villages, communal societies and banks should be created.

(3) Arrangement for declaration of Bankruptcy. There should be some arrangement by which the farmer can be declared bankrupt when the loan increases beyond his capacity to repay it.

(4) Laws for preventing dispossession of land. Laws should be enacted which may prevent the moneylender from taking possession of farmer's land.

(5) Control over the rate of interest. The maximum rate of interest in the village should be determined and punishment should be met out to any one charging a higher rate of interest.

(6) Checking the accounts of the moneylenders. The government should carry out a check of the registers and accounts of the moneylenders from time to time and punish the moneylenders if any discrepancy is found.

(7) Registration and licensing of moneylenders. Only the registered and licensed moneylenders should have the right to provide loans.

Efforts for the Prevention of Indebtedness

In 1815 a very large number of people forced individuals of the moneylenders class in 45 villages of Poona district and 22 villages of Ahmed Nagar district to handover the papers of the cultivators which were than publicly put to fire by the villagers. The Commission which was appointed to look into these disturbances recommended, that laws should be made to prevent the farmers from being dispossessed of their land. On the basis of the recommendation of this Commission the Deccan Agriculturists Act was passed in 1880, which was the first government step towards improving the condition of the debtors. Following this, Acts were then passed at intervals for improvement in this direction besides a number of commissions which were appointed. As we have had the occasion to mention earlier, both the Registration of Documents Act, 1854 and the Transfer of Property Act, 1882 worked in favour of the moneylender who embarked on large scale exploitation of the poor debtors. In 1874 in Punjab alone ten lakh acres of land were secured and by 1891 this had risen to forty lakh acres. Between 1875 and 1893 moneylenders in the different parts of Punjab Province took possession of 11 lakhs 89 thousand acres of land. In order to put a stop to this exploitation, the Punjab Land Alienation Act was passed in 1900. Similar steps were taken in 1902 in U.P., in 1904 in the North West Frontier Provinces and in 1916 in the Central Provinces. According to these Acts the mortgaged land could remain with the moneylender only for a short period after which it was to be necessarily returned to the farmer. These Acts gave the Collector and the Deputy Commissioner the right to negotiate a settlement between the moneylender and the debtor. But the provisions did not go a long way in achieving any material success because the moneylender had the right to dispossess the cultivator of his land. Thus these laws did not solve the problem of indebtedness in any of the provinces.

Besides these Acts the Government also made certain laws for checking the business of the moneylenders. The Accounts Regulation Act was passed in 1930 in Punjab. Following this, rules were made in every province by which the moneylender was obliged to keep an account of his business. It was provided that these accounts could be checked at any time and the moneylender was to be held responsible if no such accounts were kept and any unwritten business was not be considered official and was to be discounted. According to these Acts the moneylender had to keep the debtor informed about the state of his debt and also to issue receipt for every amount received. But even these Acts did not prove particularly beneficial since the illiterate farmer could not make use of them and the moneylender was apt to solve his problems without having recourse to judicial procedure.

Many laws were also enacted for the purpose of limiting the rate of interest. But the moneylender used to uncover some loopholes in these laws to crawl through in order to continue their nefarious activities. The notable feature of efforts in this direction is the Agriculturist Relief Act of 1934. In many provinces the respective governments tried to finalize the rate of interest but it did not bring any positive result.

The government also took steps to have the moneylenders registered and licensed but not many moneylenders complied with the move. In 1939 only one thousand of the five thousand moneylenders in Punjab were registered. In the laws which provided for this registration the term moneylender was not clearly defined. This too served to obstruct the improvement in the existing situation. Debt Conciliation Act were passed in many provinces for the mutual resolution of loans. Such Acts were passed in 1933 in the Central Province, in 1934 in Punjab and 1936 in Assam, Bengal and Madras as well as in some other Indian States. These Acts provided for the appointment of Conciliation Boards for achieving settlements between the moneylenders and the debtors. Upon disregarding the decisions of the said boards the moneylenders had to suffer numerous disabilities. This system proved beneficial to the Farmers. In 1940, in Punjab alone 26 thousand applications concerning rupees 2,46,000.00 for the settlement of loans were disposed of. Of the amount rupees 91.45 lakh represented the actual debt, of which the debtors were prepared to pay rupees 35.35 lakhs. In the same way these Acts also had good results in other provinces as well. But this system of settlement did not include all kinds of loans so that in many cases advantage could not be derived from it. Besides, some cases of corruption in the Boards also came to light. In some Boards completely unlettered people had been included, who were totally incapable of discharging their duties.

Defects in the Preventive Measure

Besides the above Acts the provincial government passed many laws for the essential reduction in the debt as well as for a moratorium. These Acts were called the Debt Relief Acts. By means of these statutory measures the government sought to control the rate of interest and improve the conditions of the debtors in a number of ways. There is no need for a detailed description of all these Acts. It can briefly be said that due to a number of causes these Acts did not prove as beneficial as they should have been. The major causes among them are poverty, ignorance and illiteracy of the farmer which prevent him from taking full advantage of these Acts. Secondly, even the government did not help and protect the debtor adequately enough. Thirdly, these Acts contained such defects that the moneylenders managed to carry on their activities without being endangered. Finally, it may be said that the laws made for solving the problem of indebtedness have proved completely inadequate. They undoubtedly did achieve a certain degree of improvement but they could not put an end to the immoral and corrupt practices of the moneylenders. Even though they have helped the cultivator to some extent in some places, the moneylender has again managed to get into control of the situation because the cultivator is compelled to come back to the moneylender because the government has not provided proper arrangements by which the farmer can avail himself of loan.

Since the country attained independence the solution of the problem of indebtedness has been receiving special attention of the Indian government. For this the Co-operative Credit Societies Act has been passed. According to this Act co-operative credit societies, State and Central Co-operative Banks have been established. In order to supply grains to the cultivator grainbanks have been established. Land mortgage banks have been established in order to provide the farmer with long-term loans. The present situation and progress of all these co-operative societies and banks will be described in detail in the study of co-operative societies in the context of rural reconstruction.

QUESTIONS FOR EXERCISE

1. Point out the areas of change in present rural India. What are the factors leading to rural disorganisation?
2. Discuss the problems of Indian rural life.
3. Suggest measures to improve the condition of rural life in India.
4. Briefly discuss the problem of indebtedness in rural India.

10

Democracy and its Problems

Democracy was defined by Abraham Lincoln as the government of the people, by the people, for the people. In democracy it is the public that rules. Generally, the representatives of the public are chosen by adult franchise and the governmental functions are performed by these representatives. The ideals of democracy are liberty, equality and fraternity. Democracy establishes political, economic and social equality. In it, every individual has the right to express his thoughts, make associations and indulge in all constitutionally permissible activities. The ultimate objective of democracy is not only a successful government but the establishment of an ideal state in which there is the maximum scope for the development of fraternity. Democracy aims at the evolution of conditions which allow for the maximum possible and the best development of the human personality.

PROBLEMS OF DEMOCRACY

But while on the one hand, democracy has been praised it also on the other hand has been ridiculed and criticised. Oscar Wilde has gone so far as to say that democracy means no more than the beating with sticks of the people, by the people, for the people. This criticism of democracy, however, is not logical nor supported by facts. And yet there can be no denying the fact that the institution of democracy is beset with some fundamental difficulties. Roughly speaking, these difficulties may be put into the following classes :

(i) Difficulties concerning elections,

(ii) Difficulties concerning representation,

(iii) Psychological difficulties.

(i) *Difficulties concerning elections.* The following are the difficulties concerning elections that face a democratic institution or government :

(1) Political groupism. In a country governed on the democratic pattern there are more than one political parties all of which constantly indulge in propaganda to further their respective political interests and sometime do not care even if the public stands to lose by their actions. And sometimes political groupism can even result in storms of violence and bloodshed. In the face of political gain no consideration of the propriety of the means employed worries the parties and recourse is had to the worst means if they further the interests of the party.

(2) Forgetfulness of the objectives of election. In fact, in democratic countries the various contestants fight for election only in order to gain power and are the blissfully unaware of the actual objectives of election. Neither the contestants nor the electing public pay any heed to the aims and objectives that are at the root of the election. On the one hand, the aim of democracy is the establishment of equality and fraternity. But on the other hand, in the days of elections one sees a preponderance of mutual hatred, competition and jealousy. Votes are solicited in the name of caste and group relationships, and are also cast on these bases by the public. And sometimes votes are even bought by the force of money. Sometimes people are bribed out of their political convictions by offers of subsequent facilities in return for the votes. In this way, the interests of the nation are thrown to the winds while limited and narrow interests of political power and economic liberty rule the roast. Communal tensions are aroused and class struggles are made even more bitter.

(3) Evil effects of propaganda. In the democratic pattern propaganda is indulged in to give currency to opinions. And propaganda is the best means of educating the public but when at the time of elections the very objectives of the elections are forgotten then the propaganda at that time is hardly calculated to educate the people and is more likely to deceive and mislead them. In these campaigns of propaganda all kinds of falsehood are circulated in order to turn the public opinion into their own favour. This has the cumulative effect of electing those people who are completely inefficient and corrupt while it also deprives the deserving and efficient person of success. At the time of election the propaganda is calculated to rouse the passions and prejudices of the people rather than to educate the people.

(4) Misuse of money power. As has been pointed out earlier, often votes are bought and the democracy is reduced to being a puppet in the hands of the capitalists who exploit the public in order to gain their own interests.

(5) More rejection than election. In fact just as H.G. Wells has pointed out one finds more rejection than election in democracy. What happens is that the voter instead of selecting turns more to the rejection of candidates. He does not turn to the consideration of the efficient and able candidates but think in terms of bad qualities, hatred and possibilities of loss because of the election of a particular candidate. In this way, he proceeds from one to the other rejecting each one in turn and ultimately selects the one against whom he can find nothing or from whom he can hope to benefit in some way or the other. In this manner, then, there is more rejection than election in an electoral campaign in a democracy.

(ii) *Difficulties concerning representation.* In addition to the above mentioned difficulties of election there are some difficulties of representation that characterise a democracy. In fact the main difficulty among them is the absence of good and proper representation. Now-a-days the states are quite big entities and in a people running into a few millions it is not possible to have direct election. It is for this reason that indirect election is resorted to. And even in this there is the difficulty of it being doubtful as to the extent to which a particular individual may represent the public that has elected him for this very purpose. Evidently, in a society some people become the rulers while the rest are only the ruled. Then how can it be called the government of people ? Sometimes it also happens that the leader of the powerful group takes over the administration. In this way, in its practical form democracy does not appear to be very different from aristocracy. It is a matter that needs thought. After all how can the people be represented at all adequately by an individual who is a leader coming from a higher social strata and who only rarely comes into direct contact with the public except for a short time during the days of elections. And even if they do attend to the problems of their electors it is only to provide security for opinions and the vested interests.

SOLUTION OF THE PROBLEMS OF DEMOCRACY

To some extent, the problems of democracy can be solved. The difficulties of efficient representation can be removed by dividing the areas of election on the basis of efficiency. The difficulties of election can be eliminated by political education. The time taken in the discussion of problems by the parliament can be materially reduced if committees constituted of expert persons are formed for the solution of various problems. The public itself can prevent undesirable changes in the established leadership. Many of the psychological defects can be removed by developing the national character and the sense of co-operation. Roughly speaking, the following conditions are essential for a successful democracy.

(1) High level of general election. If a democracy is to be a success, a high level of general election is very essential. The cities cannot make a success of democracy as long as they do not introduce a high conception of public life. This education can be imparted in two ways, mass education and political education. In mass education what is of particular importance is the newspaper in addition to speeches and the freedom of forming associations. The leaders of mass education are independent, knowledgeable and impartial newspapers. It is necessary to educate the citizens in connection with the elements of communal life at an early age. The practical education concerning democracy is imparted to the citizen when he takes part in democratic institutions, panchayats, municipalities, and the elections of the union and state legislatures.

(2) Equality. Social, political and economic equality is absolutely necessary if democracy is to be a success. As a general rule, no individual or class of individuals should be possessed of special privileges over and above those available to the people in general. But equality does not imply that there should be no distinction on the basis of skill and qualities or on any other basis. Actually, the real implication of equality is the equality of opportunity. The differences between the individuals cannot be eradicated in the name of equality. Haldane is only too correct in his statement that you cannot make men equal because Nature is too powerful. One woman is born beautiful while another is born ugly and this creates a major difference. One man comes into this world possessed with large resources of grey matter while another is completely devoid of them. One individual enjoys good health while another suffers from poor health. In a democracy some particular classes can be endowed with special prerogatives and privileges in order to rid them of their backwardness and bring them upon the mark of the rest of the population. But these measures should continue to be exceptions and should not be permitted to become the rule. In this way, then, all the posts in the government should be open to all who have the appropriate ability and skill. All adults should have the right to vote in a democracy in order that adult franchise should be established. In the economic sphere each individual should be employed and the employment should bestow on the individual a sufficient income by virtue of which he may spend a superior and comfortable life. Conditions of unemployment, poverty, famine and unhealthy conditions of life are not in any way conducive to democracy. On the contrary, they are destructive of democracy.

(3) Liberty. Liberty is a fundamental condition of democracy. J.S. Mill considers the liberty of the individual to be the most important. But liberty does not imply the right of the individual to behave in any manner that he pleases. Liberty implies self-control and not irresponsibility. Mill who lays so much emphasis upon the individual's liberty, advises the control of the individual in all cases where effect is to have repercussions in society and influence other individuals. Liberty means that the individual has the opportunity to develop himself to the fullest extent and he is not obstructed in any way from realizing his self. What is necessary for the liberty of all is that no individual should have unlimited power in his hand, no individual should indulge in the misuse of the power and authority allotted to him.

(4) Fraternity. In order that the democracy may be a success and should also be rid for its psychological difficulties it is necessary that the ideal of democracy and fraternity, should be achieved. The real problem is the establishment of a democratic society ,and not a democratic government, the latter being only a means to the establishment or achievement of the former. The main characteristic of a democratic society is fraternity and co-operation is the main basis of the activity of individuals belonging to a democratic society. Fraternity should be encouraged in all spheres in order to hasten the establishment of a democratic society.

From the foregoing description of the nature, difficulties and the means to the achievement of democracy it is evident that in it progress is comparatively slow but ultimately the most beneficial.

NEED FOR EDUCATION IN DEMOCRACY

Aldous Huxley has remarked, "If your aim is liberty and democracy, then you must teach people the arts of being free and of governing themselves". Democracy can never be successful without education. Wherever democracy has been unsuccessful, it has been so because of the lack of education. In a democracy the government is composed of the elected representatives of the people and if the people are uneducated they can never elect the right leaders and consequently can never create the right kind of government. In fact, it is impossible even to hope for democracy in the absence of education. It is difficult to expect a citizen to behave responsibly if he is not even aware of his rights and duties. Bertrand Russell has commented, "Democracy in its modern form would be quite impossible in a nation where many men cannot read." The truth of the matter is that education is a prerequisite of democracy. Only after proper education should the citizen be invested with his democratic rights. As Fichte, the German philosopher has commented, "Only the nation which has first solved in actual practice the problem of educating perfect men will then solve the problem of the perfect state." Although Fichte made this comment in the context of autocratic states, it cannot be doubted that the perfection of even a democratic state can be judged only by the extent to which it contains educated people. As Hetherington puts it, "Democratic government, at least, demands an educated people." Throwing light on the objectives of education in the 1949 meeting of the Universities Commission, Dr. Radhakrishnan stressed the fact that the democratic state recognises the importance of this individual, and it is the process of development of this individual which is called education. Hence, education is absolutely necessary for establishing a democratic society. Dewey has pointed out that democracy is inconceivable without education, because education alone can generate and instill the qualities which democracy demands as a prerequisite. Philosophers of the ancient Greek city state were aware of the significance of education. Both Plato and Aristotle laid stress on the importance of education for the success of democracy. Ernest Barker comments, "To Plato education was the most important function of the state and the department of education is the most important state department which was particularly advocated for producing the philosopher kings to improve the men's minds for becoming virtuous beings". Plato, in his famous text, *Republic*, stressed not only the importance of education for democracy but even formulated a plan for the education of men and women which made all kind of development — physical, mental, moral and aesthetic — possible. Aristotle was of the opinion that the aim of the state is to make possible the achievement of the highest moral level and this can be reached through education alone. Thus, education is the most important function of the state. From one point of view, the state itself is a school in which the individual learns citizenship, for Aristotle suggested that the aim of education was to produce good citizens. These truths were known not only to the Ancient Greeks but also to Indian thinkers of ancient times. India has been the home of democratic ideals and principles from ancient times. Hermitages, and places of worship, were used as schools in which the sages tried to produce ideal citizens who could become useful members of society. But the modern age needs democratic education far more than was given in ancient Greece or ancient India because modern democracies are so vast and their problems so complex that the education of citizens is even more imperative today.

IMPORTANCE OF EDUCATION IN DEMOCRACY

The importance of education for a democratic state is fairly evident from the foregoing account. The following things can be stressed in this connection:

(1) Knowledge of rights and duties. If democracy is to be a success, it is essential that every citizen should be aware of his rights and duties because only then can he take active and productive part in the affairs of the state. The knowledge of rights and duties can be obtained only through education. Education socializes the individual so that he develops consciousness of duty.

(2) Development of humane qualities. If the ideal of brotherhood is to be achieved by a democratic state, it is necessary for it to develop humane qualities in its members. Kant's moral concepts, quoted earlier, throw important light on this. Only through education can such qualities as a high moral character, sociability, benevolence, patience, pity, sympathy and brotherhood, etc. be developed in the individual.

(3) Faith in democratic ideals. In order to make democracy a success, it is essential that its citizens must have faith in the democratic ideals. And this can be brought about only when they are adequately educated because it is only the educated person who realizes that the sole purpose of life is not the satisfaction of gross physical desires. The ideals of freedom, liberty, brotherhood, are more valuable and necessary. No one but the educated individual can understand the circumstances and needs of another person before passing judgement on him. Only such a person can accept the ideal of equality after recognizing human values as being the end to be achieved.

(4) Fulfilment of political duties. In a democracy the government is elected by the people, and hence the responsibility for electing a good government devolves upon them. And, if the people are unable to understand their political rights or to fulfil their political responsibilities, it is foolish to hope for a democratic government. This ability to recognise where one's duty lies can come only through education. Educated people can properly assess the qualities and shortcomings of the various individuals who are fighting the elections, and of the various political parties and their plans and policies which they profess. In India, the absence of education is a big handicap in creating a truly democratic state because during elections the ignorant people are persuaded to vote for the wrong person, with the result that the governance of the country has failed time and again. Corruption is rampant. The Mudaliar Report points out that if democracy is anything more than voting blindly, then every individual must accept the task of independently thinking about all social, political and economic problems before deciding upon the party he wishes to support. But this is possible only when the entire electorate is educated to think independently.

(5) Protection and transmission of culture. In any state, ideals can be achieved only when change is accompanied by a parallel continuity, and this continuity with the past is maintained only through culture, the social heritage, which is passed on to the new generation through the medium of education.

Hence, education is also required for transmitting culture to future generations and for protecting it.

(6) Preventing exploitation. The ideals of democracy are opposed to exploitation of every kind, but if political, social and economic exploitation is to be eliminated from society, it is essential to have universal and compulsory education. In its absence, the rich and powerful people will never give up their advantage and habit, while the poor will never become sufficiently conscious of their rights or their ability to organise together and counter this exploitation. Educated people in a country are aware of their rights and they have the intelligence and training to fight exploitation or violation of their rights. Hence, education is the only real foundation on which democracy can be based.

EDUCATION FOR DEMOCRACY IN INDIA

All these important aspects of democratic education hold true in India also. India is not merely a modern democratic state but a country which is traditionally inclined towards democracy. A democratic constitution was adopted after independence. In 1938 Jawaharlal Nehru had said, "The Indian National Congress stands for independence and a democratic state." This objective was achieved after independence with the establishment of a democratic society. The Indian Constitution seeks to establish a popular government in the country on the basis of democratic principle outlined earlier. For this every citizen must participate in the administration, through his right to vote and to be elected. Every individual is guaranteed and given equal status and opportunity, because no one is discriminated against on the basis of religion, race, caste, community, sex, or on any other grounds. The government is responsible to the people and its elected representatives.

In order to achieve this objective of democracy, education is as necessary in India as anywhere else, a truth which the Indian people have been quick to realise. In the words of Dr. F.W. Thames, "Education is no exotic in India. There has been no country where the love of learning had so early an origin or has exercised so lasting and powerful an influence. From the simple poet of the Vedic age to the Bengali philosopher of the present day there has been an uninterrupted succession of teachers and scholars." Not only did the Indian Constitution accept the ideals of democracy, it considered education the prime responsibility of the state. In Article 45 of the Constitution it has been stated that every state must arrange for the provision of free and compulsory education to all children upto the age of 14, within ten years of the date of inception of the Constitution. After the achievement of independence, a new phase began in the history of education. Articles 29 and 30 of the Constitution give fundamental rights to every individual in connection with education and cultural development. According to Article 29, every Indian national living in any part of India will have the right to maintain his own specific language, script and his culture. No person can be refused right of admission to any educational institution, established by the state, by reason of religion, race, caste, language or any other similar consideration. According to Article 30, every minority community will have the right to establish and maintain educational institutions of its own choice, irrespective of whether the minority is a linguistic or religious one. The state will also not refuse aid to any such institution created by a religious or linguistic minority. Articles 45 and 46 determine the policy for education as part and parcel of the directive principles. According to Article 45, the state will make every effort to provide free and compulsory education, within ten years, to every child below the age of 14. According to Article 46, the state will pay special attention to the educational and economic interests of all backward classes, especially the scheduled castes and scheduled tribes. It also entrusts the state with the duty of protecting such tribes from social injustice and exploitation of every kind. The Indian Constitution laid the foundation for a *federal government* in which the functions of the state and central governments are distinctly defined. Both the central and state governments have some duties with respect to education.

QUESTIONS FOR EXERCISE

1. Explain the problem of democracy in India, suggest remedies.
2. Discuss the objectives of education in a democratic society.

11
Poverty

According to Gillin and Gillin, "Poverty is that condition in which a person either because of inadequate income or unwise expenditures, does not maintain a scale of living high enough to provide for his physical and mental efficiency and to enable him and his natural dependents to function usually according to the standards of society of which he is a member."[1] Thus, poverty is a condition of extremely lower standard of living. In it even the necessary wants are not fulfilled. As Goddard puts it, "Poverty is insufficient supply of those things which are requisite for an individual to maintain himself and those dependent upon him in health and vigour."[2] Therefore, a man is called poor when he is unable to gather the means to keep himself and his family in health. But poverty is a relative concept. It can be more or less. Its increase or decrease can be ascertained by the more or less proportion of the necessary things of life for the individual and his family. In the words of Adam Smith, "Man is rich or poor according to the degree in which he can afford to enjoy the necessaries, the conveniences and the amusements of life."[3] Hence in different countries the criterion of poverty also differs. In U.S.A. a person earning Rs. 400 a month will be called poor, while in India a person earning Rs. 50 a month will be called poor. But in fact a condition of the absence of the fulfilment of the minimum necessities of life should be called poverty everywhere. The form of these minimum necessities, however, changes according to place and time.

CAUSES OF POVERTY

Different thinkers have pointed out to different causes of poverty. According to Henery George, the main causes of poverty are the personal ownership and monopoly of the individual on the land. He writes, "In the great cities, where land is so valuable that it is measured by the foot, you will find the extremes of poverty and of luxury. And this disparity in condition between the two extremes of the social scale may always be measured by the price of the land."[4]

1. Gillin and Gillin, *Cultural Sociology,* The Macmillan Co., New York, (1950), p. 785.
2. Goddard, J.G., *Poverty Its Genesis and Exodus,* p. 5.
3. Adam Smith, *Wealth of Nations,* Book I.
4. Henry George, *Progress and Poverty,* Condensed edition, (1939), The Hogarh Press Ltd., London, p. 5.

According to Marx the main cause of poverty is the exploitation of the labourers by the capitalist. To quote him, "He creates surplus value which for the capitalist has all the charms of a creation out of nothing."[5] According to Malthus, poverty increases because while the food production increases in arithmetical progression, population increases in geometrical progression.

All the above mentioned views lay emphasis on certain one particular cause of poverty. But modern thinkers consider poverty the result of multiple causes. In the present complex economic organisation fate or the efforts of an individual are not the sole causes of poverty. As Landis and Landis have correctly said, "In a world where economic hazards are so numerous, the individual cannot always be blamed for poverty." Hence, besides the personal causes there are geographical, economic and social causes of poverty.

Personal Causes

Though one may not believe in fate in the modern time but no one can deny the importance of personal capacity, efforts and characteristics, in the economic status of the person. The important personal causes of poverty are as follow:

(i) *Sickness.* Hunter has written, "Poverty and sickness form a vicious partnership each helping the other to add to the miseries of the most unfortunate of mankind."[6] Due to sickness while a man is unable to work and his income decreases, a major portion of his income is also spent on the cure of the disease. Thus sickness increases poverty and poverty also increases sickness since hard labour in the absence of sufficient nutrition increases many diseases among the labourers.

(ii) *Mental Diseases.* Due to mental diseases also a person becomes incapable of doing anything. This decreases his income and increases poverty. On the other hand, poverty also increases mental disease since it is difficult to maintain the balance of the mind in a state of utter poverty. As Pashley rightly points out, "Poverty alone directly produces a very large proportion of the whole number of cases of insanity among the indigent poor."[7]

(iii) *Accidents.* Accidents either make a person entirely incapable of work or considerably reduce his capacity for it. If the earning member of a family is involved in some serious accident the whole family becomes poor.

(iv) *Illiteracy.* Poverty and illiteracy are mutually related. Illiteracy increases poverty since the capacity to earn of an illiterate person is very low. On the other hand, many persons are compelled to remain illiterate because of poverty. Thus poverty and illiteracy together form a vicious circle to increase the troubles of the poor people.

(v) *Idleness.* Idleness is also a cause of poverty. Many persons, in spite of

5. Karl Marx, *Capital,* Vol. I, Foreign Languages Publishing House, Moscow (1854), p. 217.
6. Hunter, R., *Poverty*, p. 144.
7. Pashley, R., *Pauperism and Poor Laws,* p. 124.

sufficient opportunity to work, do not work because of idleness and hence remain poor. In hot countries idleness is an important cause of poverty and backwardness.

(vi) *Extravagance.* It is well known that an extravagant person can waste any amount of money in no time. In fact the cause of poverty is not a lower income but excess of expenditure over income. Some persons are so much extravagant that they always remain poor in spite of whatever they earn. In India extravagance on the festivals and marriages can be easily observed everywhere, with the result that sufficient money is not available for education, sanitation, light, medicine and other necessities of life.

(vii) *Demoralisation.* Demoralisation or the lowering of character and morale leads to personal disorganisation and finally to poverty. Drinking, prostitution, gambling and other evil habits reduce to poverty even the persons of sufficiently high economic status. They reduce the capacity and cause escapism thus leading to poverty.

(viii) *Other personal causes.* Besides the above mentioned personal causes of poverty there are some other important personal causes. If a man has too many children to bring up, his standard of living is definitely lowered, and he becomes relatively poor. This is the main cause of poverty in India. Old age, death of the earning member, natural calamities, also lead to poverty. In rural India constant fragmentation of land leading to uneconomic holding is a serious cause of poverty among the agricultural class. Abnormalities of personality also cause poverty by creating maladjustment. Such a person cannot stay in one job at a particular place. In fact, every defect of personality reduces man's capacity to work and thus leads to poverty.

Geographical Causes

Besides the above-mentioned personal causes, the following geographical factors are also responsible for increasing poverty:

(i) *Unfavourable climate and weather.* Favourable climate and weather is very much necessary for work as well as for production both agricultural and industrial. Hence in the extremely cold climates and weathers the amount of work and production is considerably lowered. This increases poverty.

(ii) *Absence of natural resources.* No country can become rich in the absence of sufficient natural resources, e.g. fertile land, sufficient water, minerals and other natural products. In the absence of natural resources the inhabitants of the deserts, high mountains and extremely hot and extremely cold countries generally remain poor.

(iii) *Natural calamities.* Besides unfavourable climate and weather, natural calamities such as the eruptions of volcanoes, typhoons, floods, earthquakes and lightning cause serious damage to property and agriculture. In Japan earthquakes cause serious damage to property. In China floods are a major cause of damage to agriculture. In India the, absence of timely rains, excessive or deficient rains cause serious damage to agriculture. This increases poverty everywhere.

(iv) *Pests.* Pests are a major cause of damage to agriculture and movable property such as books, furniture, etc.

Economic Causes

Besides the geographical causes the main causes of poverty are economic. Of these the important one are as follows:

(i) *Agricultural causes.* Absence of sufficient manure, improved tools, implements and machines, means of irrigation and cattle of high breed; diseases, absence of sufficient means to protect the fields from pests and animals; superstitions; exploitation of farmers by the landlords and constant fragmentation of land are some important agricultural causes, which increase the poverty among people of the agricultural class.

(ii) *Unequal distribution.* Even if production is sufficient, millions of farmers and labourers remain poor in the country where distribution of wealth is unequal. In the capitalist system, the rich go on becoming richer and the poor poorer.

(iii) *Economic depression.* Economic depression causes decrease in trade and commerce, lockouts of mills and factories and unemployment of millions of labourers and small traders. Thus it is a serious cause of poverty.

(iv) *Unemployment.* Unemployment is the most serious economic cause of poverty. In India it is a major cause of the lower standard of living of the people both in urban and rural areas.

(v) *Unproductive hoardings.* If a major portion of the wealth of the country is hoarded in unproductive forms such as jewellery, etc., the economic development of the country is seriously handicapped. This is a serious cause of poverty in India.

(vi) *Unwise economic policy.* Sometimes in spite of the presence of sufficient resources and manpower in a country, the people remain poor because of the unwise economic policy of the government. This was an important cause of economic backwardness of India under British rule.

Social Causes

Besides the above mentioned economic causes the following social causes also increase poverty:

(i) *Faulty educational system.* An important social cause of poverty is faulty educational system. It is because of this that in India thousands of educated persons are unemployed and leading a life of poverty. A grave defect in Indian system of education is lack of sufficient opportunities for technical education. Another defect is the high cost of education and absence of sufficient scholarships.

(ii) *Faulty and insufficient housing.* In India due to faulty and insufficient housing, millions of people are forced to live in dirty and unhealthy slums. This reduces their capacity to work by increasing diseases and frustrations. Hence it leads to poverty.

(iii) *Absence of training in home science.* Mismanagement of household is a serious cause of poverty everywhere. This is because of lack of sufficient training to women in home science. Without such a training many middle class families remain poor.

(iv) *Evil customs and traditions.* Evil customs and traditions in society are an important social cause of poverty. In India, for example, the system of dowry compels many families to remain poor in spite of all the efforts of their menfolk to earn.

(v) *Insufficient provision of medical aid.* Insufficient provision of medical aid causes delayed cures, prolonged diseases, permanent displacements and untimely deaths. All these increase poverty.

(vi) *War.* War devastates prospering lands and rich countries. It leads to heavy loss of property and manpower. It upsets the balance of society by disrupting the moral standard and socio-economic system. It gives a serious blow to trade and commerce both national and international. Epidemics spread after war thus adding to the misery of the people. All these lead to poverty.

The above mentioned personal, geographical, economic and social causes do not exhaust all the causes of poverty. In fact they differ from man to man and society to society. But the above mentioned are the important causes of poverty everywhere. Eradication of poverty requires removal of all these causes. This requires efforts from the government as well as from the people.

QUESTIONS FOR EXERCISE

1. Define poverty. Mention steps to eradicate it.
2. Describe the main causes of poverty with special reference to Indian condition.

12
Beggary

The beggary is a curse for any society under any conditions and circumstances; but in a poor country like India it is not only a curse but a great financial burden, too. At present there are more than one and a half million beggars in India and if we include among these those persons who occasionally beg the number will swell into few millions. The beggars perform no useful social function; their existence is parasitical. They contribute to the impoverishment of the country. But the problem of beggary is not economic only it has social and moral aspects also. As a rule the beggars are chronically diseased physically and they are morally corrupt. It is a very common sight to see swarms of ill-clad but apparently healthy young women carrying young babies in their arms and continuously nursing them. The beggars are a fruitful source of disease spreading and also spread reprehensible moral ills. The beggars represent a section of society which has rotted and is petrifying. This requires drastic and immediate tackling; otherwise the beggars would contaminate the whole of society. The foreign press and television have put India to shame by graphically showing pictures of beggars fighting like dogs for few coins, swarming like bees for food left overs of hotels and restaurants, naked women sleeping on floor and children suckling. Such scenes show India in very nauseating colours. When in past India was a land of plenty and economic prosperity existed, there were no doubt beggars in India. But there is a difference between contemporary beggars and the beggars of past days. The beggars of today are either too ill to do any useful work or too idle for that; they, therefore, prefer to beg to fill their bellies to doing work. But the mendicants of ancient times were dedicated souls who had renounced all material goods and performed the vital function of maintaining and sustaining the moral standards of the society. They were spiritual seekers who were supposed not to earn livelihood and were permitted to beg for day-to-day needs of food. The Hindu scriptures and moral codes provided for living by alms for celibates and those who had renounced the world. But the beggars of today have adopted beggary as a profession. They do nothing except begging and leading a life of horrible moral corruption. Moreover, due to less productivity and all round backwardness, even a labourer in India is unable to earn enough to have two square meals a day in spite of day long toil and moil. It is a fact which cannot be over-emphasized that our society cannot afford to have social parasites. Only those who do some productive labour should be fed; none has a right to food without putting in adequate work. Though many superstitious and orthodox Indians consider it a moral duty to give charity; but any intelligent man can easily appreciate the fact that giving of charity amounts to perpetuation of social and moral cancer in the body of society. If we seriously consider the social and moral aspect of beggary, we cannot help concluding that beggary must be uprooted from a society that wants to progress.

DEFINITION OF BEGGARY

Before attempting a detailed study of the problem of beggary in India, it is necessary to define the terms Beggar and Beggary. Two important and illuminating definitions of these problems are given hereunder:

(1) The Bombay Beggary Act, XXXIII of 1945. "A person without means of subsistence and wandering about or found in public places or allowing himself to be used as exhibit for the purpose of begging is covered by the definition". According to this definition three features are to be observed in a beggar: (1) No apparent means of livelihood; (2) to beg at public places; and (3) exhibition of one's suffering, bodily defects etc. in order to elicit public sympathy.

(2) The Mysore Prohibition of Beggary Act, XXXIII of 1944. "Begging includes wandering from door to door, soliciting alms, exhibiting or exposing sores, wounds, bodily ailments or deformities, or making false pretence of them for exciting pity for securing alms." This definition has the same elements as the earlier one though it lays special emphasis that beggars exploit their physical miseries and gross and repelling bodily defects for the purpose of eliciting pity in others and that such exhibitions may not be genuine. Usually elaborate make up and artificial devices are employed to put on an appearance of blindness, mutilated limbs, bleeding open sores and such other bodily afflictions.

BEGGARY IN INDIA

There are about one million beggars and loafers in India. In thickly populated areas the number of beggars is much more than in sparsely populated areas. Usually, temples, mosques, railway roads and bus stations, fairs, shrines, bathing ghats are the popular haunts of beggars. There are of course many roving beggars who move from door to door. Many beggars beg collectively and in an organized manner. They come in large numbers and by sheer shouting and aggressive postures compel people to give them some coins. The places where many people come and go daily are the favourite haunts and like specially located shops carry pugree or overhead price. The beggars also distribute between them mohallas or localities. They live on pavements or in the open under improvised hutments. The beggars are found both in villages and towns. In India the places of pilgrimage are the most prized haunts of beggars.

SURVEY OF BEGGARS

Now-a-days many non-governmental social research institutions have carried out survey of beggars in order to assess the real dimensions of this problem. In this connection a reference has already been made to Madras School of Social Work. The J.K. Institute of Social Work, Lucknow made a survey of 300 beggars. The following facts were revealed by this survey:

(1) Age. The sample had beggars between ages of 5 and 73. The maximum portion was of beggars in 35-43 age group.

(2) Sex. The male-female ratio was 6 to 1, that is, there was one female to every six males. Among children males outnumbered the females. Most children were in 10-15 years age group. The majority of women beggars were in 30-40 age group.

(3) Religion and Caste. Little over 66% of beggars were Hindu and little over 30% were Muslims. Among Hindu, only 1/10 belonged to higher castes; rest were low-caste.

(4) Education. 6% beggars were literate.

(5) Family Status. The 60% of beggars had anomalous family status. The unmarried, widower, widow, married, separated, that is the beggars belonged to all categories.

(6) Earning. 59% beggars earned one Rupee per day, 30% earned Two Rupees per day and the rest between 3 to 5 Rupees per day.

MODE OF BEGGARY

There are many ways to beg. All beggars try to arouse pity in others so that they may be moved to relieve the miseries of beggars or try to make an appeal to the religious sentiment of the people. Giving of alms is considered a laudable act by the religious traditions and it is claimed that by giving alms one earns merit and secures a place for himself in the heaven. The beggars learn to exploit all these techniques. Some women beggars manage to get fake bogus certificate in which the mention is made of the tragedies that have befallen the holder of the certificate and a fervent appeal for all out help is made. There are of course many blind and deaf among beggars. There are lepers who extract money by the chorus of their pitiful and heart rending cries. Some beggars kidnap children and mutilate their limbs in order to use them for beggary. A survey conducted by Chenai School of Social Work revealed that out of 5,000 beggars in Chenai city, as many as 3,500 were able-bodied. Some beggars are in league with thiefs and dacoits and provide them useful clues to enable them to rob and burgle successfully. Some beggars beg by claiming that they have been ruined by drought, flood or earthquake. Some beggars beg by singing songs and claiming payment for their services.

CLASSIFICATION OF BEGGARS

As referred to earlier, a number of surveys have been conducted into the problem of beggary. These surveys have revealed the variety of beggars. Broadly, the beggars may be divided into following categories:

(1) Religious Beggars. In this category are included those who have renounced the world and are carrying on the orthodox tradition of spiritual seeking and enlightenment of the householders. They are Yogis, Sanyasis, Sadhus, Dervish, Fakir, Vairagi, Udasi etc.

(2) Pseudo-Religious Beggars. The pseudo religious beggars are those who have no spiritual quest and belong to no order of sadhus. They merely put on the saffron garb as a convenient way of receiving alms.

(3) Tribal Beggars. These are professional beggars who beg by singing folk songs and giving dance performance on the road side.

(4) Able-bodied Beggars. They are healthy persons who prefer beggary to work as it suits their queer temperament. They are usually in league with bad characters and act as agents of thiefs and dacoits.

(5) Invalid Beggars. These are the persons who cannot earn their livelihood because they are too ill to work. They include lepers, old-aged and chronically ill.

(6) Physically-Handicapped Beggars. These are the beggars who are blind, deaf or dumb or one-legged or legless. They easily are able to arouse public sympathy and pity and are considered deserving of public help. However, in this category are also beggars who have been subject to most inhuman and cruel treatment by other beggars. As mentioned before, many beggars kidnap children and mutilate them in order to use them as their pawns in beggary.

(7) Mentally Unsound Beggars. These include psychotics, schizophrenics, idiots, morons etc.

(8) Child Beggars. The children in misery arouse great pity. They cry, whine and wail so pathetically that they are given alms simply in order to be free from their painful presence. Many clever beggars pretend blindness, hunch-backness or old-age and use children for beggary.

(9) Professional Beggars. Those who are either physically unable or mentally disinclined to do any work and will only beg are called professional beggars.

(10) Part-time Beggars. These beggars are those who are engaged in some petty works and beg in spare time.

THE CAUSES OF BEGGARY IN INDIA

(1) The Economic Factor. Poverty and unemployment are the most crucial causes of beggary. The persons who cannot get any job of any kind are left with little option but to beg, borrow or steal. The latter two are rather difficult. Borrowing requires credit which is unthinkable in the case of indigent person and stealing is unlawful and risky; it needs a mental attitude which is not easy or common. Accordingly begging appears to be the safest course left for indigent and impecunious.

(2) Religious Factors. The widespread and ever growing incidence of beggary in India is very largely due to the religious superstition of the common masses that by giving alms one earns special merit and attains righteousness. This attitude of people renders the task of beggars not only easy but least painful. Thus many persons who have to toil and moil hard and sweat or are forced to earn livelihood feel tempted to join the ranks of beggars. In particular, at the places of pilgrimages huge army of beggars bee line the routes and people going there consider it a sacred duty to offer them alms.

(3) Physical Causes. In India there is no adequate provision for the treatment and social rehabilitation of blind, deaf, dumb or handicapped. In the absence of any reasonable alternative such persons feel compelled to beg.

(4) Social Causes. There are a number of social factors responsible for generating begotry. As a common knowledge, Indian society is highly orthodox and traditionalist. The widows are not allowed to remarry and are often maltreated by their in-laws, hence in order to escape mental torture they move out of family. If, unluckily, they possess no skill or education they are left with little else except prostitution or beggary. The old have not even the first option. The women who get raped or themselves commit some offence are unacceptable to both parents and husbands.

(5) Mental Causes. The idiots, morons and psychotics, unless cared for by society or relatives, have no option but to beg.

(6) Natural Calamities. The earthquake, flood and drought compel people to leave their homes. Many such persons fail to find any work and feel compelled to beg to control the hunger pangs.

Following suggestions can be made for the prevention and eradication of beggary:

(1) Eradication of Unemployment and Poverty. In order to eradicate beggary its root cause must be removed, that is, we must provide everyone a right to work and also raise the minimum wages. In the absence of these essential steps, no other measure can be effective. You cannot ask a person to die of starvation but not to beg. You can ask him not to beg provided you can arrange for his food and shelter.

(2) Legal Sanctions. Every state must pass the law to declare beggary a legal offence.

(3) Centres for Cure of Chronic Diseases. There should be special hospitals to take care of those who are unable to pay their own expenses.

(4) Care of Orphans and Handicapped. The orphans and handicapped should all be taken care of by opening rehabilitation centres.

(5) Treatment of Mentally Ill. The poor persons suffering from mental ailments should be given free treatment in psychiatric centres.

(6) Rehabilitation Home for Fallen Women. The women who become unacceptable to their relatives should not be left to the mercy of rogues and scoundrels; but should be given shelter in rehabilitation centres.

(7) Public Opinion Against Beggary. Inasmuch as Indian people suffer from the religious superstitions that by feeding poor one can buy ticket to heaven, the people should be educated about the causes of beggary and harmful effect of their current practices.

It is a great pleasure to find that the Indian government is alive to this problem and taking every possible steps to eradicate beggary.

GOVERNMENTAL MEASURES TO ERADICATE BEGGARY

The Criminal Procedure Code applies to vagrants and vagabonds alike and provides penalties under Sections 65(i)(b) and 109(b). Beggars may be proceeded against under Section 133 as those committing public nuisance. Beggary within railway premises was prohibited by law on February 15, 1951. Special Acts have been passed by most of the States to prohibit begging in public places. In others, municipal and police acts provide measures against begging. To deal effectively with persons who kidnap children for the purpose of exploiting them for begging, the Indian Penal Code (Amendment) Act, 1959, was enacted.

At present most of the states in India have passed laws declaring Beggary a legal offence. In the year 1959, the Government of India amended the Indian Penal Code so as to make beggary and abuse of children culpable crimes. Prior to this amendment in the Indian Penal Code by the Government of India, various states had passed laws making beggary a legal offence. Some of the important Acts are quoted below:

(1) The Hyderabad Prevention of Beggary Act, 1941.

(2) The Bengal Vagrancy Act, 1945.

(3) The Mysore Prevention of Beggary Act, 1945.

(4) The Bombay Prevention of Beggary Act, 1945.

(5) The Madras Prevention of Beggary Act, 1945.

(6) The Cochin Vagrancy Act, 1945.

(7) The Travancore Prohibition of Begging Act, 1945.

(8) The Bhopal Prevention of Beggary Act, 1947.

(9) The Bihar Prevention of Beggary Act, 1952.

All the above mentioned Acts declare beggary an offence and provide for punishment of going to jail or payment of fine. They have also classified the beggars into various categories. The provision of punishment, its nature and severity is made in accordance with the categories of beggars. Besides the above Acts, the municipal acts of Punjab, Madhya Pradesh, Uttar Pradesh also prohibit beggary and declare it a legal offence. In the big Indian towns like Calcutta, Mumbai, Chenai, Delhi and Bangalore where foreigners come in large numbers there are strict laws against begging and begging at these places is not tolerated. In order to check the problem there are poor homes in these towns where beggars are kept. They are given food and shelter and encouraged to do some useful work or learn some skill. Several states are now seriously thinking to completely ban beggary and provide some sort of alternative employment to beggars.

QUESTIONS FOR EXERCISE

1. Define Beggary. Suggest remedies for its eradication.
2. Write a short essay on Beggary in India.
3. Beggary is inextricably related to social forces impinging upon the individual. Examine the statement critically.

13
Problems of Industrialization

Though industrialization in India is making rapid strides, it is still far behind the industrial growth in Western Countries. After India became independent in 1947, the government of India paid particular attention to industrial growth. It helped the local industry to grow rapidly. In order to put India on industrial map fast, the government decided to enter the field of heavy industry which demanded huge investments. The government set up many heavy industrial complexes all over India in order to promote a balanced growth and also to help the ancillary industry to expand fast.

As a result of fast industrialization, the process of urbanization too, is growing fast and this is having deep impact upon society. The industrialization is not only pushing up the urban population but is also affecting the social conditions in nearby villages.

THE SOCIAL IMPACT OF INDUSTRIALIZATION

The important consequences of industrialization in India are as follows:

(1) Urbanization. As a consequence of industrialization the population in the cities has gone up. This will be clearly seen in the following table:—

TABLE 13.1

Year	Urban Population (% of Total)	Increase
1872	8.8	—
1881	9.3	+0.5
1891	9.4	+0.1
1901	10.0	0.6
1911	9.4	–0.6
1921	11.3	+1.9
1931	12.1	+0.8
1941	13.9	+1.8
1951	17.3	+3.4
1961	18.0	+0.7
1971	19.0	+1
1981	23.0	+4
1991	26.0	+3

(2) Impact of Urbanization. The process of industrialization increases the urban population. It is on account of industrialization that there is progressive rise in the population of cities in India. Whatever social impact is due to the urbanization is indirectly due to industrialization. Therefore, the impact of industrialization and the impact of urbanization are in fact two facets of the same underlying process, namely, industrialization. The following are some of the important social influences of urbanization:

(i) *Decline in the sense of Sociability.* The first and foremost impact of urbanization in India is the increase in the population of the cities, and this, in turn, has resulted in the progressive decline in the sense of sociability. In villages the sense of sociability is stronger than in the cities. Therefore, the loss of village population and increase of city population results in the decline of sense of sociability.

In cities the activities of almost everyone are self-centred and governed by the calculus of self-interest and personal gain. Therefore, no one really bothers about other people except insofar as their association is helpful in promoting self-interest. Thus people in cities prove to be calculating and display little altruism.

(ii) *Decline in Social Control.* With the decline in the sense of sociability there is consequent decline in Social control. Due to lack of community feeling and the fear of social disapproval people are bound to become increasingly individualistic and even arbitrary in their conduct. Thus we find in towns today a glaring neglect of tradition and contempt for social approval. Everybody wants to do whatever pleases him.

(iii) *Decline in Family Control.* As the population of cities has grown the cities have expanded. This has resulted in there being great distances between the places of work and places of residence; between educational institutions and homes. This has meant that people stay away from home environments for the best part of the day. Small wonder, then, that under these circumstances there is progressive decline in the control of family over its members. The modern education, the excitement of cinema, fashion, clubs and societies have contributed greatly to this trend.

(iv) *Decline in the Influence of Religion.* The increase in the population of the cities leads not only to the decline of social and family control but also leads to decline in the influence of religion. In metropolitan towns the life is highly materialistic and individualistic. This in turn promotes atheism. This means that people in cities are not guided by tradition and are indifferent to religious belief. Their conduct is governed by rational or personal considerations. Thus the life in cities is relatively devoid of the influence of religion.

(v) *Change in the Institution of Marriage.* The increase in urban population has resulted in certain changes in the institution of marriage. Generally, care is taken to take into confidence the spouses before marriage. Whereas, in village, marriage is an affair between families rather than individuals; in cities today no marriage can be solemnized if any of the spouse is opposed to it. The incidence of love marriages is growing.

(vi) *Change in the Institution of Family.* Another impact of urbanization is the gradual extinction of the joint family system and its replacement by nuclear family. Now-a-days, most families consist of husband, wife and their progeny.

(vii) *Change in the Condition of Women.* With the changes in the institution of family, there is also change in the pattern of family. Women are becoming increasingly independent and the education among them is also spreading. They are becoming increasingly conscious of their rights and privileges but along with it there is also a tendency to arbitrary and wilful conduct. The incidence of illicit sexual relations, divorce etc. are also on increase. The ostentation and intense fashion have also become the order of the day.

(viii) *Increase of Male-ratio.* A significant impact of urbanization of the population is that the ratio of male population is increasing. The main reason for this phenomenon is that due to shortage of housing millions of people are forced to live single in cities. The evil of this phenomenon is that this gives rise to sexual corruption.

(ix) *Commercialized Entertainment.* On account of industrialization there has been widespread growth of commercialized entertainment. The cinemas are tremendously popular, prostitutes do roaring business. Indeed, there is a charge on every kind of entertainment in the cities.

(x) *Housing Shortage.* The growth in population in cities is so fast that it is not possible to provide people with adequate residential accommodation. Indeed pressure on space in cities is so tremendous that most people are forced to live on roads or in shabby accommodation in cities like Bombay. The shortage of residential accommodation compels people to stay without families. The persons coming from villages are unable to bring their families with them. This phenomenon, as observed earlier, leads to inevitable sexual corruption.

(xi) *Growth of Slums.* Industrialization has resulted in shortage of accommodation and this, in turn, has given rise to slums, overcrowded shabby living quarters. These slums are populated by workers and other indigent people. The persons living in these slums are constantly exposed to all kinds of diseases, are liable to become social deviates and criminals the loss of morals is an inevitable consequence of living in slums. The *Ahatas* of Kanpur, *Bastis* of Delhi, *Chawls* of Bombay and *Cheris* of Madras are stigmas on the face of India. Their shabby quarters are worse than stables of horses and pens of cattles. There is no ventilation, no drainage, no drinking water. A besmirched raggled piece of jute hanging in front of homes is an eloquent testimony of their pitiable condition. The glaring contrasts in the palatial lives of industrialists and the dirt laden existence of workers testify to the hollowness of our socialism and democratic life. Pandit Nehru was so moved emotionally on seeing slums that he wanted them to be burnt down and the persons responsible for them to be hanged. They symbolize extreme moral and physical decline — the nadir of all that is bad in life. According to Dr. Radhakamal Mukherjee, "In the thousand slums of India's industrial centres manhood is, unquestionably brutalized, women dishonoured and childhood is poisoned at its very source".

THE ECONOMIC CONSEQUENCES OF INDUSTRIALIZATION

The following are the important consequences in the economic field of industrialization in India:

(1) Growth of Capitalism. As a result of industrialization there is tremendous concentration of wealth in few hands. Due to industrialization one man can control a business of crores of rupees and go on amassing wealth unabated. Thus like other countries industrialization in India has also given tremendous fillip to the growth of capitalism.

(2) Mass Production. As a result of industrialization there is production on large scale. In India steel, cement, sugar, jute, fertilizers, electrical equipment, rail roads are being produced on mass scale. India, with its vast population, is now self-sufficient in these commodities, nay, it exports many of these.

(3) Growth of Trade. On account of vast production there is unparallel growth in trade and commerce. The development of fast means of communication has contributed a lot towards this end. The foreign trade has also shown tremendous rise.

(4) Division of Labour and Specialization. An economic impact of industrialization is the division of labour and specialization. Gradually, the number of technocrats and highly skilled personnel is growing.

(5) Rise in the Standard of Living. As a result of industrialization there is a certain rise in the living standard. Today, electric fans, gas, radio and television are common household goods.

(6) Economic Crisis and Unemployment. But whereas means of comfort and luxury are now easily available there is, on the other hand, grave economic crisis. The mechanization of all production has thrown millions of people out of work. Due to industrialization, there is glut of many commodities. This leads to grave economic crisis.

(7) Industrial Disputes and Accidents. The industrial disputes and accidents arc incvitable accompaniments of industrialization. Wherever there is industry, there are thousands of workers. It is a natural tendency of workers to expect more and more for their work; on the other hand, the industrialists want more production for less wages. Under these circumstances there are bound to be clashes of interest resulting in industrial disputes. The working conditions in Indian industry are not of high standard and accidents are very common.

(8) Problems of Workers. Besides strikes and lockouts, workers have some other problems. An important problem in this connection is that of rest and relaxation. Firstly, they have to work for long hours so that they get little rest. Secondly, whatever rest they get there are no adequate sources of healthy entertainment available.

(9) Spread of Socialism and Individualism. The industrialization has promoted both socialism and individualism. As a result of it capitalism grew and with it spread the ideas of individualism and *laissez faire*. On the other hand, the ideology of socialism also spread as a result of industrialization. The industrial workers organized themselves into trade unions and political parties in order to gain their support to profess socialism.

(10) Class Conflict. Like other countries industrialization in India has given rise to class conflicts and class war. There is continuous tension among the poor and rich. However, the class-war in India is as yet not very intense.

(11) Decline of Rural Industry. As a result of industrialization the goods of daily use were produced on mass scale. The quality of machine-made goods is of good standard and they are cheap. This resulted in large inflow of goods into villages and this ruined the cottage industry of the villages.

INDUSTRIALIZATION AND SOCIAL DISORGANIZATION

Industrialization gives rise to many such processes which lead to social disorganization. The industrialization produces many problems at family, individual and community level. Industrialization induces individual and family disorganization. Industrialization gives rise to such causes as are responsible for social disorganization. Following are such causes:

(1) Causes of Individual Disorganization. The industrialization gives rise to facts which cause disorganization in the individual. Millions of workers migrate from villages to towns for jobs. As there is acute shortage of accommodation in towns and the life is otherwise costly also, they are unable to bring their families to cities. Therefore after a day's hard work they can get neither any healthy entertainment nor the peace of home. Lacking all suitable alternatives they take to drinking, prostitution etc. This leads to their moral degeneration. The gaudy and exciting urban environment and materialistic outlook of life also contribute to moral degeneration. This produces disorganization not only among workers but in other persons, too.

(2) Unemployment. While industrialization has created employment opportunity for millions, it has also lead to unemployment. The mechanization of production greatly reduces the need for workers. Whenever a new sophisticated machine is installed in any factory hundreds of workers are thrown out of job. Many rural women come to cities in search for job but unable to find one are forced into prostitution. The unemployment in turn leads to social disorganisation.

(3) Crime and Immorality. The process of industrialization has also led to rise in the incidence of crime and immorality. As referred to earlier, thousands of workers in the town are unable to find suitable accommodation or are unable to cope with high expenses of urban life. They are forced to lead secluded existence. Being not highly morally trained they succumb to the twin lure of wine and woman; they drink country liquor and visit lowly prostitutes. The industrialization has also given rise to factionalism, materialism and mechanical character of life. All these things have encouraged crime. As a result of industrialization small boys and girls take to work and they are easily spoiled.

(4) Factionalism and Heterogeneity. The industrialization has contributed to factionalism and given rise to economic disparities. This is proving highly subversive of social cohesion and unity. The difference between rich and poor keeps growing and both classes tend to develop anti-social tendencies. Whereas industrialists live in fully air-conditioned palatial mansions, the poor are constrained to sleep on footpath and whereas the former live a luxurious life the latter are unable to make their both ends meet. The economic disparity is productive of social disorganization.

(5) Cultural Lag. The process of industrialization results in cultural lag. This is due to the fact that industrialization leads to fast progress in materialistic things. The manner and modes of life outwardly changes very rapidly but there is no progress of inward culture. Thus inward change does not keep pace with outward changes and this contradiction results in cultural lag.

(6) Changes in Values. Industrialization has resulted in change in values. On account of industrialization jobs are now available to women and children. This has resulted in changes in relations of husband and wife and children. Women are no longer chattle pieces of men. They enjoy now relative economic independence and their outlook on life has changed. The relations between various people are no longer based on tradition but are guided by the calculus of self-interest.

(7) Family Disorganisation. Industrialization has resulted in disorganisation of family life also. The husband and wife go their respective places of work and there is no one back home to care and look after children. Where children also do jobs there can be no proper provision of education. Due to changes in values and consequent change in the attitudes the cohesion of family life is severely distributed. If husband and wife both stay out of home chances of disharmony among them increase. If women and girls go out of home for job the chances of illicit sexual relations increase. On account of all these factors family disorganization results.

(8) Urbanization. An inevitable consequence of industrialization is the increase in urbanization. Due to urbanization big cities spring up with populations far in excess of their capacity. As a result a large number of persons have to live in one or two room quarters. In this situation there is disaffection among married couples and unmarried persons get frequent opportunities to peep upon sexual activities of married persons. This has evil effect on impressionable young persons and they indulge in premature sex. Many a time queer sexual intimacy among family members is the outcome of this hopeless and helpless situation. The relations among individuals in cities are of impersonal character. The urbanization results in loosening of social control. The community life is disrupted. The gaudy and exciting life of cities produces imbalance in social and personal relations. The freedom of contact between sexes also disturbs family life. The life in clubs and society is a life of rebellion against social traditions and restrictions. The slums, the epidemics, immoral and amoral outlook have all combined to knock the bottom out of harmonious and peaceful life in cities.

STEPS TO CHECK ILL EFFECTS OF INDUSTRIALIZATION

From the above discussion of social and economic effects of industrialization, it is quite clear that industrialization has given rise to a number of evil effects. These include housing shortage, labour problems, unnatural life, increase in crime and exploitation, ruin of rural industry etc.

Following measures should be taken to counteract the evil influences of industrialization:

(1) Town Planning. The industries should be at a reasonable distance from the residential colonies and the main centres of the city. The slums should be cleared and replaced by good hygienic houses.

(2) Planning of Factories. The factories should be well-planned. They must be well-ventilated and have all amenities. They should be so structured and equipped that the chances of accidents are minimal.

(3) Enactment of Labour laws. There must be well laid down rules for the workers. Their wages, bonus, working hours, gratuity, pension, leaves etc. should be governed by laws enacted by the government and these should be strictly enforced.

(4) Promotion of Rural Industries. The government should encourage rural industries. It must give liberal loans for their development.

(5) Decentralization. Many an evil effect of industrialization is due to the fact that there is usually concentration of industry at one place. This should be avoided and there should be diversification of industries.

(6) Development of Cottage Industry. A number of evil effects of industrialization are due to mechanization and specialization. This lopsided development can be greatly averted by promotion and encouragement of cottage industries.

(7) Housing. As a result of industrialization there is acute housing shortage in industrial towns. Numerous evil effects flow from the shortage of housing. These can be avoided by giving building of houses top priority.

(8) Healthy Entertainment. The increase in the incidence of crime, juvenile delinquency and prostitution in industrial towns is due to lack of healthy entertainment. If we know the cause of a phenomenon it is easy to control it. Thus by providing healthy entertainment we can counteract the above-mentioned evils.

All the above-mentioned suggestions for the improvement of urban areas and for counteracting the ills of industrialization have been in one form or the other accepted, at least in principle, by Government of India. Fortunately, industrialization in India is still not so intense and concentrated as to produce alarming problems. If some advance steps can be taken at this stage it is possible to mitigate the most severe types of ills consequent upon industrialization. The acute problems of industrialization are in India confined to few metropolises like Calcutta, Mumbai, Kanpur etc. Of course the efforts being made at these centres to mitigate the evil effects of industrialization leave much to be desired. The existence of slums is a glaring fact of all industrial centres. It is an indelible blot on our society. The working conditions of labour are neither healthy nor hygienic. There is no provision of wholesome entertainment. The government needs pay special attention to this aspect. The closing down of red-light areas is no solution of the problem. The government alone does not have resources to solve the monumental problems posed by industrialization. It needs the co-operation of local-self-government and also the efforts of the industrialists.

QUESTION FOR EXERCISE

1. Discuss critically the social consequences of industrialization in India.

14

Unemployment

Defining unemployment, Karl Pribram has written that "Unemployment is a condition of the labour market in which the supply of labour is greater than the number of available openings."[1] According to Fairchild, "Unemployment is forced and involuntary separation from remunerative work on the part of the normal working force during normal working time, normal wages and under normal conditions." Generally speaking, unemployment means the non-availability of work even though there is a desire to do it.

FORMS OF UNEMPLOYMENT

The forms of unemployment have been given different names by different scholars. Some main forms in this connection are the following:

1. Cyclical unemployment. It is that unemployment which results from trade cycles, profit and loss and fluctuations in the price level. For example, when there is a depression in trade, thousands of people are thrown out of work.

2. Sudden unemployment. That form of unemployment which is in evidence in those businesses which engage workers periodically for example, workers are turned out from time to time when the work in the factories decreases.

3. Unemployment arising from failure in industry or business. Many factories close down after a short period of existence and their workers are left without work.

4. Unemployment resulting from deterioration in industries. When industries deteriorate due to lack of success in competition or one of the variety of causes, many people become unemployed.

5. Unemployment arising from seasonal business. Seasonal business stops when season comes to an end. As a result, the people engaged in it are thrown out of work.

From the standpoint of factors affecting unemployment, it may be divided into the following two types:

(i) *Subjective unemployment.* This is caused by physical or mental shortcomings of the individual.

1. Pribram, K., *Encyclopaedia of Social Sciences*, Vol. XV, p. 147.

(ii) *Objective unemployment.* This is caused by factors beyond the control of the individual and is related to objective circumstances.

Distinctions of Objective Unemployment

Objective unemployment may be divided into the following four forms:

1. Seasonal unemployment. This is the unemployment caused by the shutting down of seasonal industries.

2. Cyclical unemployment. This is due to the cyclical economic inflation and depression.

3. Structural unemployment. This is due to the defects in the economic structure, for example, while thousands of people are unemployed in Kanpur there may be a heavy demand for labour in Delhi. In this situation the unemployment is not due to the excess of supply over demand but rather due to the defeat of the economic structure.

4. Normal unemployment. This form of unemployment prevails in almost all countries. In a complex economic organisation it is difficult to provide full time employment for everybody.

UNEMPLOYMENT IN DIFFERENT FIELDS

Besides the above mentioned types the following three forms are accepted according to the fields of unemployment:

1. Agricultural unemployment. This form includes the unemployment of the people engaged in the agricultural sphere.

2. Technological unemployment. This includes the unemployment resulting from advances in technological techniques. For example, as the machines in any industry or factory increase they continually displace human beings.

3. Educational unemployment. It includes the unemployment of all those people who are educated in some respect or other.

Of the above mentioned types of unemployment the first is the most important in India. This will be now discussed in sequence.

Agricultural Unemployment

According to the Royal Agricultural Commission the farmers in the villages of India remain unemployed for three to six months. According to the report of the National Income Committee published in 1951 the per capita income of people engaged in agriculture was estimated at rupees 180 while the income of people engaged in other professions was estimated at two and a half times this figure, i.e., rupees 450. The cause of this difference in income is agricultural unemployment. During the decade between 1941 and 1951 many people left the villages and came to the towns in search of employment. These people either had no land or, if they had, it was insufficient, and even if it was adequate it was not fertile. Dr. Radhakamal Mukerji has estimated that the number of landless labourers among the people dependent upon agriculture in India is between six and seven crores. According to a survey conducted by the Uttar

Pradesh Government the farmer in the Eastern areas works no more than three or four months in the year while the farmers in the Western area, which has canals, works for 258 to 280 days.

Causes of Agricultural Unemployment

It is obvious from the foregoing statistics that there is a lot of unemployment in the agricultural sphere in the villages of India. Of the many causes of this state of affairs the major ones are the following:

1. Excessive increase in the population. Nearly 50 lakh people are added every year to the already large population of India. According to Mr. Gopalaswami, this increase will be of the order of 80 lakhs annually. The agricultural production in the country is not keeping pace with this stupendous increase in population and the result is that even now about 69 per cent of the population is dependent upon agriculture. This leads to increased pressure upon the land and an increase in the number of the unemployed.

2. Limited Land. On the one hand the population is increasing while, on the other, the land is limited. Even to begin with there was great pressure upon the land. Now the further increase in the population is leading to increased unemployment.

3. Seasonal nature of agriculture. In India seasonal unemployment is extremely widespread because agriculture here depends to a very large extent upon the weather. According to Dr. Salter, the agriculturist in South India engaged in agriculture for only five months in the year and as for the other seven, he simply whiles away his time. In the same way, the same conditions prevail all over the country and the farmers are unemployed for long periods as agriculture is not carried on throughout the year.

4. Lack of subsidiary industries. If the farmer would employ this time in some other occupation, there would be no unemployment; but this cannot be done in the absence of subsidiary industry. The result is that the landless farmer, or one who has less or unfertile land, remains unemployed.

5. Agriculture depends upon rain. In India agriculture is a gamble with the rains. If the rains arrive at the right time and are neither excessive nor scarce, the harvest is good. But if the rains fall at the wrong time or in insufficient quantity they spell disaster for agriculture. The farmer is disabled due to a lack of adequate means of irrigation. In the absence of rains, famines occur and thousands of people become unemployed.

6. Unscientific and obsolete methods of cultivation. In India the old unscientific method of farming is still being preserved. Consequently, the farmer cannot feed properly many people by the produce of his farm and he is unable to provide his children with proper education or to engage them in any profession.

7. Subdivision of land. In India the land is already divided into small parts and is in the process of being further subdivided. Sometimes these small portions are scattered far and wide. As a result of this sub-division and fragmentation of land the produce falls very low and sometimes the land becomes an uneconomic holding.

8. Disorganisation of agriculture. Actually the biggest cause of agricultural unemployment is that, in India, agriculture is extremely unorganised and diversified.

Major Remedies for Agricultural Unemployment

The major remedies for removing agricultural unemployment in the villages are the following:

1. Improvement in the agricultural system. In order to eliminate agricultural unemployment it is necessary to improve agriculture in the country. The important steps suggested in this context are the following:

(a) In order to improve the system of agriculture the first thing which must be done is to end the uneconomic holdings and to prevent the further subdivision of land into even smaller pieces. The scattered portions of land should be consolidated. This will result in the creation of economic holdings as well as a welcome increase in the output.

(b) The prevailing methods of agriculture do not exploit the natural resources to the fullest extent of their potentiality. Thus the method of intensive cultivation will have to be adopted.

(c) The produce will increase when proper rotation of crops is followed and will also provide employment for a longer period.

(d) Good seeds, good tools, good manure and good animals must be arranged for if the production is to be increased.

2. Proper arrangement of irrigation. A major cause of Agricultural unemployment in India is the dependence of civilization upon the rains. Thus there should be a proper and good arrangement of irrigation through minor and major projects.

3. Increasing the cultivable land. It is also necessary to increase cultivable land in the country, for which it will be necessary to make barren land fertile by scientific methods. Much sandy and rocky land and even marshes and grass lands can be converted into cultivable farm lands by using scientific methods and labour.

4. Development of subsidiary industries. But an improvement in agriculture, not supplemented by any other corrective measure, cannot provide employment to the increasing population. Besides the agriculturist should also get some work during that period of the year when he is not engaged in cultivation. In the village the other men and women are generally idle. In order that all these people should be provided with jobs it is essential that some subsidiary industries should also develop. In this kind of subsidiary industry, such cottage industries like dairy farming, bee-keeping, poultry farming, furniture making, weaving, spinning, match stick making, weaving baskets and ropes, etc., can help to a considerable extent in removing unemployment.

5. Public construction. Besides developing the cottage industries the unemployed people of the villages can be provided with work by engaging in public construction like road building, drain digging, etc.

6. Arrangement for transport of labour. It sometimes happens that at a particular place there is a great demand for labour while in another place, at the same time, there is a great abundance of labour. When such conditions exist the government should make arrangement for transport of labour to provide employment. In the same way arrangements should be made for transporting people from the areas of thick population to the areas where the density is comparatively less.

7. Organisation of agricultural market. If conditions for marketing agricultural produce do not favour the cultivator, the increase in production will not alleviate the problem of agricultural unemployment. The organisation of the agricultural market will increase the income of the cultivator as well as improve the situation with regard to unemployment.

In brief, no one remedy will be adequate to remove the agricultural unemployment. Remedies for all the causes of agricultural unemployment will have to be found. It is a matter of delight that the Indian government is making efforts in this direction. The problem of agricultural unemployment can be solved only through the pooling of governmental and non-governmental efforts.

NEHRU ROZGAR YOJANA

The Nehru Rozgar Yojana has been designed to provide employment to the urban unemployed and under-employed poor. The employment contemplated is of two types: one relates to the setting up of self-employment ventures and the other type relates to provision of wage employment through the creation of socially and economically useful assets and shelter upgradation programmes in urban areas.

The programme has three schemes: (i) scheme for setting up micro enterprises and providing training and infrastructure support for urban poor beneficiaries. This scheme is operative in all urban settlements; (ii) scheme of wage employment for creation of socially and economically useful public assets in the jurisdiction of urban local bodies. This scheme is applicable in (a) towns with less than 20,000 population and (b) towns with population from 20,000 to one lakh, (iii) scheme of employment through housing and shelter upgradation in low income neighbourhoods mainly for the urban poor and economically weaker sections and training and infrastructure support for promotion of construction skills among beneficiaries. This scheme is applicable in settlements with population between one lakh and twenty lakh.

While the target group of the Yojana is urban poor, women beneficiaries and beneficiaries belonging to scheduled castes and scheduled tribes will constitute special target groups. The main achievements of the scheme for the period ending December 1992 are as such (I) Scheme of Urban Micro Enterprises (SUME): Subsidy to the tune of Rs. 63.97 crore and institutional finance (in the form of bank loans) to the tune of Rs. 190 crore (approximately) i.e., three times of the subsidy have been sanctioned to the beneficiaries since the inception of the Yojana in 1989. Under the Training and Infrastructure Support component, 76,960 beneficiaries have been trained/are undergoing training for skill upgradation; (II) Scheme of Urban Wage Employment (SUWE): Under this scheme, the states/UTs have reported expenditure of Rs. 139.85 crore till 31 January 1993 on creation of public assets in low income neighbourhoods and 238 lakh mandays of wage employment has been generated for the urban poor; (III) Scheme of Housing and Shelter Upgradation (SHASU): HUDCO has sanctioned schemes from various states/union territories worth Rs. 275.89 crore (subsidy of Rs. 56.52 crore and loans upto Rs. 219.37 crore) involving upgradation of more than seven lakh dwelling units till 31 January 1993.

Central Public Works Department

The Central Public Works Department (CPWD) is the official agency of the Government of India for construction and maintenance of all Central government buildings except those of the railways, communication, atomic energy, defence services and All India Radio. The spectrum of the activities of the CPWD is very wide, ranging from the selection of site, architectural, structural and landscape planning, design, execution, including budgeting, monitoring and quality control to completion and post-completion maintenance. Contract management and defending arbitration cases are also done by the CPWD. The CPWD handles a wide-range of projects like housing and commercial complexes, educational institutions, hospitals, workshops, factories, foodgrain storage structures, airports, roads, bridges, sports complexes, mints, electronic complexes, National Library and Parliament Library etc.

In recent times, the CPWD has been engaged in providing border fencing, flood lighting and roads along the sensitive Indo-Pak and Indo-Bangladesh borders. The work is being enacted under very severe and hostile conditions and yet keeping up to the tight time schedules laid down by the Ministry of Home Affairs. The CPWD has gained considerable expertise in the study of restoration and rehabilitation of structures damaged by natural disasters. A study on the nature of the Uttarkashi (UP) earthquake and its effect on structures in the area has been conducted by better employment. Number of job-seekers on the live registers of employment exchanges increased from 178.38 lakh as on 31 December 1981 to 363 lakh on 31 December 1991. Table 14.2 gives registrations, vacancies, placements and job-seekers on the 'live register' for the period 1981-90.

QUESTIONS FOR EXERCISE

1. Analyse the causes of unemployment in Indian Agriculture. Suggest major remedies.
2. What special steps should the government adopt for ending the problem of unemployment in India.

TABLE 14.1

Population by Category of Workers

(In crore)

	Rural	Urban	Total
1991 Census			
Total Population	63.13	21.53	83.66
Total workers[1]	24.93	6.56	31.49
Marginal workers[2]	2.77	0.17	2.95
Main workers	22.16	6.38	28.54
(i) Cultivators	10.74	0.32	11.06
(ii) Agricultural labourers	7.04	0.42	7.46
(iii) Household industry workers	0.68	0.36	1.04
(iv) Other workers	3.70	5.28	8.28

Notes: 1. The figures exclude Jammu and Kashmir where the 1991 census has not been held.

2. Figures may not tally due to rounding off.

TABLE 14.2

Registrations Vacancies, Placements and Job-Seekers on the Live Register

Year	(lakh)					
	Number of Employment exchanges[1]	Registrations	Vacancies notified	Placements	Live Register	Percentage increase in Live Register over previous year
1981	663	62.77	8.97	5.04	178.38	10.1
1982	692	58.63	8.20	4.73	197.53	10.7
1983	726	67.56	8.26	4.86	219.53	11.1
1984	745	62.20	7.08	4.07	235.47	7.3
1985	800	58.21	6.75	3.88	262.70	11.6
1986	821	55.35	6.23	3.51	301.31	14.7
1987	835	60.12	6.01	3.34	302.47	0.4
1988	840	59.63	5.43	3.28	300.50	– 0.7
1989	849	65.76	6.00	2.89	327.76	9.1
1990	851	65.41	4.91	2.64	346.32	5.7
1991	854	62.36	4.59	2.53	363.00	4.8

Note : Total may not tally due to rounding off.

1. Including University Employment Information and Guidance Bureaux.

15
Labour Problems

It is a regrettable fact that there have not been sufficient reform and improvement in the conditions of Indian labour. The Indian labour is not properly organized and does not have its own leadership but depends upon outside guidance. The non-labour leaders are politically motivated and are not really interested in the labour welfare. As a matter of fact they more often than not they use the labour unrest as a means to grind their own axes instead of helping the labour genuinely. The government has not paid enough attention to the real problems and needs of labour and though there is much labour legislation intended to help the labour but in actual practice there is little improvement in the condition of labour.

LABOUR PROBLEMS

1. Problem of Migration. One of the main problems of Indian labour is the problem of migration. The increasing pressure on land due to population explosion, the evergrowing army of landless tillers, the social stigma on Harijans, increase in indebtedness, breakdown of joint families, fast means of communication, ravaging of cottage industries and city-oriented education are some of the causes responsible for the exodus of villagers and their influx into industrial town. While by joining the army of industrial labour, there is some improvement in the economic conditions and relenting of pressure on land, the family and social life of these new recruits gets upset. This creates problems of social adjustment, decreases efficiency and comes in the way of the development of healthy employer-employee relationship.

2. Problem of Recruitment. The second main problem of the Indian labour is that of recruitment. As yet there is little direct recruitment. Most of it is done through intermediaries. The services of Employment Exchanges are available to very few. As most of the workers are dependent upon intermediaries and as intermediaries have special type of relationship with the Employers they can afford to behave arbitrarily with the workers. They receive cut-back and have also to be propitiated by other gifts.

3. Problem of Absenteeism. The labour force hailing from villages is usually unable to cope with the alien environment of the city. The fresh food, air and light is not available in cities. Besides slums in which the workers live are extremely unhygienic and great breeders of disease. Accordingly the workers are usually unwell. They consume liquor and visit prostitutes. All these factors combined result in large absenteeism from factories.

The chief causes of absenteeism in India are illness, nightshifts; alcoholism; migrating instinct; industrial accidents; prostitution; laziness; frequency of festivals and litigation. The absenteeism produces adverse economic effects on industrial production and the earnings of labour. Besides it causes rift and tension between employer and employee. The various measures presently taken to meet this problem are grossly inadequate. A Committee set up by the Bombay Textile Mills to investigate the causes of absenteeism and make suitable recommendations for remedying the problem came to the following conclusion: "Proper condition for work in the factory, adequate wage protection from accidents and sickness and facilities for obtaining leave, rest and recreation constitute the most effective means of reducing absenteeism."

4. Problem of Trade Unions. In India the trade union movement is not as yet well organized and developed. The lack of education, susceptibility to religious influence, generally fatalistic outlook, deep indebtedness and opposition by employers and intermediaries are some of the factors responsible for slow and uneven growth of trade union movement. The labour does not have its own leadership and has to depend upon politicians who have furtherance of their own interests rather than labour welfare at heart.

5. Problem of Industrial Disputes. The capitalist economic and social structure, the policy of creating dissension among workers by intermediaries, retrenchment of workers to circumvent labour legislation and paying of compensation are the problems which lead to frequent strikes, lock-outs, gheraoes and sit-in by workers. At times these disputes turn violent and labourers suffer heavily.

6. Problem of Wages. The chief problem of workers is that they are poorly paid. In some cases these are below subsistence level. Due to lack of adequate wages, the labour is unable to give proper education to his children. He cannot maintain his health. This leads to decline in his efficiency and in the ultimate analysis the productivity falls.

7. Problem of Indebtedness. On account of low wages, bribes to intermediaries, drinking and prostitution, most of the workers are permanently and deeply under debt. lt has been estimated that more than 2/3 workers of big industrial towns are under debt and the average amount of debt exceeds their 3 months' salary. Due to heavy indebtedness the worker cannot think progressively and considers whole of his life unrelieved drudgery. The causes of indebtedness are many. Usually the worker is born in debt and due to drudgery becomes desensitized, therefore he takes to drastic and powerful excesses like liquor and woman. This further complicates his problem and desires him to die a pauper in debt.

8. Problem of Low Living Standard. Due to low wages and rising spiral of prices, the living standard of Indian workers has been dropping constantly.

A comparison of wages in India with other countries will bring into relief the pathetic plight of the Indian labourer. The workers in India are underfed and more than 39% suffer from serious malnutrition. In U.S.A. 75 yards cloth is used per head whereas in India it is only 16 yards. There are many causes of low living standard. The main among them are : 1. Low wages; 2. Illiteracy; 3. Population explosion; 4. Intoxication; 5. Lack of skill and 6. Fatalism.

9. Problem of Health. Due to low wages and low standards the workers are unable to eat wholesome balanced diet. What is worse, most of them are addicted to smoking, tobacco chewing, drinking and visiting cinemas and bawdy houses. All these reasons coupled with unhygienic living conditions, inadequate clothing, inclement weather, heavily dispose workers to disease and infection. According to Professor B.P. Adarkar a worker loses 14.6 days a year due to ill health.

10. Problem of Efficiency. According to the report of Tarrif Board a worker in India can handle 180 spindles whereas his counterparts in Japan, England and America can handle 240, 450 to 600, 1220 spindles respectively. As a rule the efficiency of Indian workers is 1/2 or even 1/3 of the worker in progressive countries. Ill-health, lack of education, lack of will to learn and progress, addiction to bad habits are some of the factors responsible for the low efficiency of the Indian workers.

11. Problem of working conditions. The conditions of work of the majority of labour are extremely bad and deplorable and leave much to be desired. Most of the factories are ill-ventilated and the illumination is improper. The living and working conditions are making workers prone to accident. At many places even facilities for drinking water, toilet etc. do not exist. In extreme weather there is no provision to minimize its effects. Due to lack of amenities and hazardous working conditions the efficiency of workers drops and they are exposed to accidents and infections.

12. Problem of child labour. Though it is illegal to employ workers under certain age, these provisions are frequently flouted and circumvented. The problems of child labour in India are the following:

(i) More work and less wages.

(ii) Loss of education of children.

(iii) Lack of proper rest and play essential for proper growth.

(iv) The unhygienic and rigorous working conditions.

(v) Low and below-standard productivity.

13. Problems of women worker. Following are the main problems faced by women workers:

(i) Unsatisfactory conditions.

(ii) Lack of amenities and facilities for maternity leave, child welfare etc.

(iii) Rigorous labour unsuited to delicate constitution of women.

(iv) Mal-treatment and enforced immoral life.

It is a matter of gratification that the Government of India, Trade Unions, progressive and enlightened capitalists and industrialists, state governments and many non-governmental organisations are alive to the above-mentioned problems and are doing everything under their power to remedy them and relieve the conditions of workers.

QUESTION FOR EXERCISE

1. Discuss briefly the chief problems of India Labour.

TABLE 15.1

Consumer Price Index Number for Industrial Workers

Year	Bombay	Ahmedabad	Calcutta	Madras	Kanpur	Delhi	All India	
							All Items	Food
Linking Factor	5.12	4.78	4.74	5.05	4.69	4.97	4.93	4.98
1970-71	182	176	182	170	190	199	186	201
1971-72	190	181	187	182	196	211	192	295
1972-73	203	198	197	203	212	222	207	223
1973-74	233	245	228	229	251	265	250	279
1974-75	289	305	288	301	323	337	317	358
1975-76	300	293	287	314	299	333	313	342
1976-77	298	281	297	288	294	332	301	317
1977-78	318	310	320	311	330	358	324	345
1978-79	325	323	331	318	337	368	331	347
1979-80	359	348	351	350	357	389	360	373
1980-81	400	376	382	388	396	426	401	419
1981-82	460	441	414	446	439	472	451	476
1982-83	502	487	447	475	473	508	486	508
1983-84	564	544	511	550	528	551	547	581
1984-85	609	570	576	576	554	597	582	607
1985-86	654	599	610	630	614	648	620	630
1986-87	717	657	671	681	672	707	674	700
1987-88	791	724	714	756	725	788	736	767
1988-89	856[1]	763[1]	783[1]	802[1]	763[1]	852[1]	786[1]	820[1]
	171[2]	163[2]	172[2]	167[2]	172[2]	177[2]	166[2]	172[2]
1989-90	179	171	178	172	178	182	173	177
1990-91	201	196	203	189	202	201	193	199
1991-92	234	225	223	216	228	225	219	230

1. Average based on six months indices only — April to September 1988 on 1960 base.
2. Average based on six months indices only — October 1988 to March 1989 on 1982 base.

Note: Old Series (1960=100) has been replaced by the New Series (1982=100) from October 1988. Linking factors between 1960 series and 1982 series are operative from October 1988.

Source: Labour Bureau, Shimla.

All-India index is compiled as weighted arithmetic average of centre indices with weights proportionate to aggregate estimate expenditure of each centre.

TABLE 15.2

Consumer Price Index Number for Urban Non-Manual Exployees (Base 1960=100)

Year	Bombay	Calcutta	Madras	Delhi/ New Delhi	All-India
1970-71	168	170	175	174	174
1971-72	172	174	188	180	180
1972-73	183	180	203	190	192
1973-74	204	204	231	217	221
1974-75	241	238	291	262	270
1975-76	246	243	306	273	277
1976-77	255	251	294	274	277
1977-78	269	265	311	288	296
1978-79	285	279	321	303	306
1979-80	315	297	350	321	330
1980-81	347	331	390	352	369
1981-82	393	367	439	395	413
1982-83	440	384	470	428	446
1983-84	493	418	531	468	492
1984-85	538	451	577	508	532
1985-86	568	481	611	551	568
1986-87	612	530	671	597	613
1987-88[1]	666	562	736	645	656
1988-89[2]	130	135	141	135	136
1989-90[2]	139	146	152	143	145
1990-91[2]	154	164	168	156	161
1991-92[2]	180	181	189	177	183
1992-93	204	198	212	196	202

1. Average is based on seven indices (April 1987 to October 1987).
2. A new series of Index Numbers on Base 1984-85=100 has been introduced from November 1987. All-India Index on New Base may be converted to Old Base by multiplying the conversion factor 5.32. Conversion factors in respect of Bombay, Calcutta, Madras, Delhi/New Delhi are 5.38, 4.51, 5.77 and 5.08 respectively.

16

Student Unrest and Youth Tensions

The phenomenon of student unrest started in India with the agitation of 1905 led by Calcutta and Dacca student to oppose the partition of Bengal. This marks student involvement in agitations. As a part of National struggle it was encouraged by all political parties and welcomed by the public. Therefore since then the student's participation in national political movement in India increased at every stage particularly in Quit India Movement in 1942. Most of the national leaders were students during the period of national struggle. They left the colleges and the universities to participate in National Movement at the call of their beloved leaders M.K. Gandhi, J.L. Nehru and B.G. Tilak etc.

Student Unrest in the World

Students' involvement in politics is nothing new. In Germany, Russia and France a large number of students participated in political activities in the 19th century. In 20th century the students' activities in South Korea were effective in changing the Iron regime of Syghman Rhee. In Japan the students demonstrated against Prime Minister Kishi. In Indonesia and Vietnam the students protested against U.S. interference. In England and America one occasionally witnessed student demonstration against expansion of nuclear weapons. Peace marches are a usually scene. A large number of students in Afghanistan are fighting as guerilla against Russians. In Dacca students have several times strongly demonstrated on national issues. In communist countries, however, the phenomenon of disturbed campus is not traceable. On the other hand, in almost all the other countries of the world one finds students' participation in demonstrations, strikes, processions and mass meetings.

Role of Political Parties in India

In India by the participation in national struggle the students learned agitational methods of protest and realised the power of student unity. After the country achieved independence this experience was utilised to highlight student's sentiments on local, regional, national and even international issues. Since the political parties were in the habit of using students as the youth power in political agitations, most of the political parties encouraged students' organisations on political basis. Thus while B.H.U. was dominated by rightist students, J.N.U. was the centre of leftist activities. Congress (I), B.J.P., Janata

Dal and D.M.K. have been maintaining their student wings since independence in India. Therefore, it is quite understandable that the disturbed campus is not a temporary phenomenon. Disturbance is only a symptom, a fruit whose roots are being nourished by all the political parties.

Growth of Youth Power

This, however, does not mean that the students have themselves no political consciousness and that whatever they do is at the instigation of the political parties. Leadership is a phenomenon which is nourished and grown in institutions of higher learning everywhere. This is necessary for the growth of youth leadership in the country. This is most welcome though when it takes wrong turns it becomes a headache to the government and the people alike. In recent years several universities have witnessed growth of student power. In most of the universities the student unions have their own buildings, budget extending to thousands of rupees and all the paraphernalia of a political party. During the period of elections the whole campus and even the city is on siege. All types of methods of propaganda are utilised. Vote catching devises are practised even more shrewdly as compared to the techniques of general elections. Propaganda material worth lakhs of rupees is utilised. Posters come up on all the walls of the city. Hundreds of vehicles of all types are utilised. Money flows from the capitalists and the political parties. And when the winners celebrate they are blessed by the benign presence of the national leaders belonging to the political parties to which they owe allegiance.

The *Modus Operandi*

After the leaders are elected, they take stock of the situation — local, regional and national. If the issues are not pointed enough, even the flimsiest issue is taken up for starting agitation. It is not because there is something to do that the political activities go on but because the leaders have to justify their election and to show their presence that issues are created. This, however, does not mean that all the activities are baseless. Some student activities have undoubtedly cleaned the campus, made the teachers more responsible and kept the administration awake. From time to time the student leaders do the cathartic function of unveiling the mask from the face of the administrators and powerful teacher politicians to show them in their true colours. This service is of single importance.

INDISCIPLINE

Indiscipline is the initial symptom as well as the result of a disturbed campus. While discipline is the adherence to rules and regulations, indiscipline is their contravention. According to the report on the problem of student indiscipline in India in 1960 presented by the committee appointed by the U.G.C. to investigate Student Indiscipline, "Indiscipline is mass moral turpitude and collective defiance of authority and the use of techniques in seeking redress of real or imagined grievances which are not appropriate for students to use." This definition was formulated after a close study of the disturbed campus. The acts of indiscipline noted by the committee involved discourtesy to teachers, misbehaviour towards women students, student riots, damaging the college building, disruption of the normal life of society, squating on tram lines and rail tracks, stopping and burning the buses, physical violence against this or that individual and group and a host of other activities resulting into disruption of the educational process growth of violence and general elimination of peace and order. These acts of indiscipline start on any issue and led by the student leaders followed by thousands of enthusiastic students. The committee called these techniques inappropriate. This is far from convincing since it suffers from the dual standard, allowing the use of these techniques to political leaders and disallowing them to students. This double standard is far from convincing the student leaders.

Multisided Phenomenon

Thus the phenomenon of the disturbed campus is multisided. Physically, it may be seen in acts of violence, damages to property, impediments in the normal working of the educational institutions, mass meetings, hunger strikes, agitations, processions etc. The psychological aspect, however, is more important. This is made of power mongering on the part of the leaders and frustration among the students. So many lapses on the part of the government administrators result in a sense of frustration on the part of the students. One of the most glaring factor creating frustration is the phenomenon of educated unemployment. The student leaders on the other hand are constantly on the look out to rake up an issue to show their power to the student community on the one hand and to the administrators, the government and the public on the other. It is notable that it is from the ranks of these student leaders that some of the most famous national leaders in India have grown. Their example serves to encourage the ambitions of every student leader. By raking up an issue he makes promises to the student community and exercises pressure by threats and coercion upon the administrative authorities.

Psychological Factors

In brief the following psychological factors work at the root of the phenomenon of disturbed campus:

1. Loss of faith in aim of education. As more and more students become disillusioned about the goals of education in the colleges and universities, they withdraw from studies and involve themselves in union activities.

2. Loss of faith in the means. Even if the goals sought by educational institutions may be sound, loss of faith in the means of education may result into frustration. This may be concerning any part of the educational machinery such as admissions, appointment of teachers, discipline among teachers, time table, curriculum, methods of teaching, rules of discipline, rules concerning hostels, efficiency of the general administration and finally the mode and validity of examination and evaluation methods. It is a truism that in India at present all these aspects of education are full of problems which do not appear to be capable of solution in near future.

3. Lack of internalisation of values and attitudes. It is well known that without teachers' involvement in the process of education, no betterment in educational institutions is possible. This involvement, however, requires several conditions. If so many teachers are known to be having side jobs, running tuition shops, doing insurance business or things like that, they can hardly have any involvement with teaching in the educational institutions. This involvement requires more conscientiousness among teachers. The teachers themselves should be free from politics before asking the students to do so. If the teacher unions are functioning like labour unions how can they suggest any thing different to the student unions. The repressive techniques of the research guides can only help to increase frustration rather than any real creative work among the research students. But while the teachers know that there is no necessary correlation between teaching methods and evaluation techniques their enthusiasm in teaching cannot be maintained, unless the teacher-management relationship, the teacher-principal and the teacher-student relationship is improved. The involvement of the teachers is not possible if the teacher taught ratio is beyond a certain proportion. No educational institutions can remain undisturbed without solving this problem. Therefore the values and attitudes demanded from the students should be first created among the teachers. And before asking for involvement on the part of teachers, suitable conditions for its natural growth must of created.

Analysis of the Phenomenon

In *The Sociology of Education in India*, NCERT (1967) Mr. S.H. Asthana and Suma Chitnis have analysed the phenomenon of the Disturbed Campus under two heads as follows:

(A) The Educational System, its Goals, Failure and Indiscipline

1. Goals of education. The minimum goal of education is training for earning a livelihood. The maximum goal of education is socialisation, diffusion of knowledge, values, attitudes and norms of relationships, required for playing adult roles in society. In a healthy system of education both these goals must be realised.

2. Failures of educational system. The above mentioned goals have not been realised. The growing number of educated unemployment clearly shows failure of our educational system to provide livelihood. During British regime even a matric fail could find a job. Now persons with postgraduate degrees are unemployed in a great number. And this number is constantly growing. This failure may be attributed to the following causes:

(i) *No accurate assessment of manpower needs.* As there is no accurate assessment of manpower needs there is no correlation between the number of educated persons growing every year and the number of employment opportunities. Expansion in education has been more rapid than generation of job opportunities.

(ii) *Prejudices.* Caste, region, language, religion and nationality have been the basis of appointment in non-government and even government agencies. Therefore, the organisation has failed to provide livelihood on the basis of merit.

(iii) *Irrelevance of Education to Occupation.* A general criticism of the present educational system is about its irrelevance to occupations other than white-collar jobs. The values created by academic education do not create initiative and necessary qualities of character such as national integration, equality, patriotism, democratic attitude to life, etc.

(iv) *Lack of national integration.* Casteism, communalism, linguism, and parochial tendencies are fast disintegrating Indian society. Far from eliminating these tendencies, the education sometimes encourages them. For example, in most of the colleges and universities linguism, regionalism and casteism are rather the rule than exception. Communalism, though not so much rampant, may also be seen particularly in the educational institutions organised and run by a particular community. Unless national integration is maintained the conflict among various groups of students and teachers is inevitable.

(v) *Absence of democratic values.* It is an irony that the student unions which were primarily established to fulfil the demands of democratization of education have themselves become source of the disturbed campus. Equality may be declared in policy but it is not properly practiced. Liberty takes the form of indiscipline and rowdy behaviour. Fraternity is conspicuous by its absence. In the words of H.S. Asthana and Suma Chitnis, "Democracy, too many, is voicing an opinion. Insisting on one's rights, student unions give an excellent exercise in these qualities. But the more important concept of democracy as a partnership of free men, united in the common purpose of national development, does not emerge."[1]

Unfortunately the example of academic fraternity set by the teaching community is far from encouraging this value among the students. Most of the university departments in every residential university exhibit cut throat factionism among teachers. This factionism sometimes goes to the extent of teacher's activities against the research students and disciples of rival colleagues. Every university department has become a den of favouritism, infighting, casteism, communalism, regionalism, hatred and jealousies. In this atmosphere no youth can learn democratic values. Team work is a phenomena unknown to Indian scholars. While in the West most of the valuable academic advancement has been achieved through team work, in India hardly a group of scholars can see eye to eye on any problem. Seminars exhibit leg pulling and personal aggrandisement, vain show and mannerism rather than any solid contribution to knowledge. Lectures are organised to oblige friends. Examinerships are exchanged. Ph.Ds are distributed on clique basis. Appointments are made on the basis of personal favour. In the face of such a low level of character and behaviour among *gurus*, it is small wonder that the new generation learns that

1. Asthana, H.S. and Suma Chitnis, *The Sociology of Education in India*, NCERT, 1967, p. 323.

opportunism, nepotism, politiking, wire pulling, back biting, cut throat competitions and ruthlessness are the values and traits required for progress in life. It has been rightly lamented by Asthana and Chitnis, "The academic community in India is not a partnership in quest of knowledge. Mutual response between teachers and administrators swings between the two extremes of a callous flouting of authority and a subservience that smothers self-respect. A mood of lethargy and pessimism prevails."[2]

(B) Norms, Sanctions, Values and Attitudes

Change in Norms

Formerly, it was the norm in education that the teachers were respected. According to Indian philosophy of education academic achievements are correlative to respect toward teachers. This norm has been now reversed since education is linked with payment of fees. The modern students have hardly any respect towards their teachers, the idea of serving the teacher is beyond their comprehension. This discourages the teachers to give their best to the student. The modern teacher is stimulated by the challenge he faces in the class. The old teacher was encouraged to give his best because of his love and sentiment of service, dedication and sacrifice for the academic cause. Thus the norms both on the part of teacher and the taught have been reversed.

Change in Sanctions

Formerly, the teacher's attempt to maintain discipline was sanctioned by the administration, the community and even by the students themselves. Even corporal punishment was appreciated. Today attempts to discipline the students do not receive sanction from the community and the students. The administration is helpless against the strength of the student unions. It is a common feature in the universities that rustication of rowdy student leaders is opposed by student unions tooth and nail. It sparks off protests strikes and even violence. The students turn a deaf ear to the teachers, the principal and the vice-chancellor. The parents do not approve punishment any more. Corporal punishment is opposed by the parents.

The most important sanction to discipline in education comes from social ethos. Formerly, the social ethos emphasised reverence for elders. The children were asked to obey their parents and teachers. Today the emphasis is on freedom, freedom to think, freedom to act, freedom to react and even freedom to all kinds of indiscipline. In almost every sphere of life today the only value is self-regard or selfishness. In the absence of the sanction of the social ethos discipline cannot be created in educational institutions.

Change in Values and Attitudes

Indian society was formerly authoritarian. In the wake of democratic values authoritarianism has been substituted by liberty. Not only in the field of education

---

2. *Ibid.*

but in marriage and family modern boys and girls do as they like. The age of marriage is growing, making norm for twenty to twenty-five for girls and 25-30 for boys. Till then boys and girls stay in universities and colleges. Therefore, they learn all types of individual ways of behaviour and conduct. They are not governed either by parents or by teachers. The media, the film, literature, radio, television and everything else are laying emphasis upon personal choice irrespective of what it means to others. Therefore, the values of equality and fraternity have been often set back by liberty. In fact, of the three democratic values, fraternity is the proper basis for equality and liberty. Liberty, on the other hand, cannot be the basis of equality and fraternity. Unfortunately, the modern youth lays emphasis upon liberty as the highest value. Therefore, there is no wonder that he is only concerned with himself.

In Indian axiology *Dharma* was the highest value while *Artha* and *Kama* were subordinate to it. *Moksha* was the ideal of life. This was an integral value system. It has now been substituted by a one-sided value system of *Artha* or *Kama* as the only values to be cherished. According to Indian wisdom while *Artha* and *Kama* are provided by destiny, *Dharma* and *Moksha* are the values to be pursued. In the present world everywhere *Dharma* and *Moksha* are left to destiny and *Artha* and *Kama* are actively pursued. The history of culture in different human societies has shown that mammon worship leads to cultural degeneration and final decay. This is the inevitable result of the present day culture. In such circumstances the youths learn to fulfil their aim by hook or crook. The emphasis is rather on smartness than culture, mannerism than character, general knowledge than scholarship. Therefore, mediocrity is the rule and excellence is exception. Scholarship, simplicity and hardwork are no more necessary values. Not excellence but success is the goal. Not *Dharma* but *Artha* and *Kama* are the aims to be achieved. The modern student aims at enjoyment. The emphasis is on fashion, excitement, novelty, speed and enjoyment. Hetrosexual relationships are gradually breaking all norms of decency and restraint. Student politics knows no level. All means are adopted for self-aggrandisement. The techniques taught by M.K. Gandhi are being used in educational campus all over India for achievement of goals which are directly opposite of decency, discipline and even student welfare.

CONCLUSIONS

The analysis of disturbed campus in India shows several features. While some of it is revolt against oppression most of it may be termed indiscipline. While some of it may be attributed to exuberance of youth, most of it is delinquency, vandalism and even crime. While some of it aims at general welfare of student community, most of it is for the calculated benefit of a clique of student leaders. While some of it may genuinely represent uprising of Indian youth, most of it is due to the inroad of political parties into campus. Most of the union activities are guided not even by the union leaders but by their political mentors outside the campus. While some of the budget of the student unions is covered by contributions from the students, most of it is met by secret donations from political parties and vested interests. Therefore, it goes without saying that the disturbed campus requires corrective measures.

Basically the disturbed campus in India is the result of youth unrest. Youth unrest in India is a phenomenon exhibiting moral perplexity, lack of ideal educators, defective system of education, political gangsterism, groupism among educators, repressive policies of the state, social disorganisation, absence of teacher-parent relationships and finally the psychological defects of character. An analysis of these causes of youth unrest in India will pave the path to the means of curing them.

CAUSES OF YOUTH TENSION IN INDIA

The following are the causes of widespread indiscipline among the youth in the country:

1. Moral perplexity. The youth of today is in a dilemma because he does not know what is right and what is wrong. Most of the teachers express such completely contradictory opinions on moral problems that the educand is confused. On the one hand, he finds very strong arguments being advanced for a materialistic philosophy by some teachers, while other educators are found supporting the cause of idealism with equally valid arguments. The confusion is made worse by the differing opinions on the subject of religion also. Some educators are devout religionists while others are complete atheists. On the one side are the educators who believe in the ancient ideal of abstinence as the sole means of developing character. On the other, one finds more liberal educators who believe that the casual mixing of sexes and social intercourse, etc., are the most important formative influences in character development. They argue that sex is natural and there is no need for any restraint. It is only natural that the educand feels stupefied and is left completely adrift when he is faced with such contradictory alternatives. Consequently, he finds it difficult, if not impossible, to act according to any rational principle. He has no choice but to do as he likes, and one finds that his brutish animal tendencies are being manifested in the form of indiscipline.

2. Lack of ideal educators. Most of the youth forming part of the existing educational structure are completely lacking in ideals. Some of the causes of this materialism are the bad economic conditions of the educators, uneven and often insufferable working conditions, nepotism and favouritism in appointments, absence of any social prestige, etc. But whatever the causes, it cannot be doubted that the majority of teachers at the primary and secondary levels of education are individuals without ideals and principles. In fact, many of them are morally degenerate and there is little cause for surprise if indiscipline among educands increases when they are guided by such individuals. But, it must also be remembered that the government is also very much to be blamed for this situation. Fairly recently, the staff at the primary level went on strike to support its demands for increase in pay. It was argued by the educators that the government could not expect good teaching at the salary it offered to the educator. The government countered this with the suggestion that it wanted the educands taught mathematics and sciences, not ideals. If the government itself exhibits such lack of concern towards the fundamental principles which guide civilized life, it can blame only itself for the difficult situation created in the country by increasing indiscipline.

3. Defective system of education. After India had won her independence, a series of committees and commissions have criticised the existing system of education and pointed out its defects. In spite of this the system continues till today. It was introduced by the East India Company with a view to producing qualified clerical staff. There has been no change for the better, in fact, there has only been a steady erosion of standards. Corruption at all levels is not only rampant but accepted as another fact of life. Accepting bribes to give better marks, cooperating with another educator to give better marks to his candidate, favouritism in the evaluation of doctoral research theses, are some of the common practices. In fact, one can sum up the entire situation by saying that now, there appears to be no correlation between hard work and study, writing the correct answers in the examination answer books and getting good marks. There is, therefore, no occasion for surprise if one finds that the educand's only aim is to secure degree by fair means or foul. Apart from the system of examination, the educational system is further eroded by such defects as an impractical teacher-taught ratio in the class-room, absence of extra-curricular programmes, the prescription of sub-standard text-books, etc. It is only manifesting one's ignorance if one imagines that indiscipline can be removed when the educational system is so beset with defects.

4. Political gangsterism. Most of the colleges and universities in the country have become nothing more than hotbeds of political gangsterism and polemic. Most of the student unions are dominated by stooges of some political parties, and they are concerned only with achieving their own ends by using the student unions. Such influences not only lead to gangsterism in the institution, they also create the possibility of misusing the students for political ends. One finds that during elections, political parties become even more active in their efforts to woo the educands to their side. There is no denying that political parties have played a sufficiently destructive role in bringing about indiscipline and the consequent problems, although it would be unfair to imply that political interference is the sole cause.

5. Groupism among educators. If an individual takes it upon himself to attend the functions and gatherings of teachers' unions of some institution on three or four occasions, he will soon arrive at the conclusion that the groupism found among teachers perhaps exceeds that which is found among the members of any other professional group. Students are not only aware of this groupism, but they are deliberately made aware of this, because in many cases they are directed by one group to observe the activities of the other group of educators and to report it to the first. Thus the educand becomes conscious of existing rivalry between the various groups among his educators. All this has a very detrimental effect on the educand's mind, because he feels that such activity must be justified.

6. Repressive policies at the states. Clashes between the students and police have become a regular feature in almost every state. One hears of many incidents in which the police thrashed the students, carried out a baton charge, entered the college campuses, destroyed property, attacked students inside the colleges, even resorted to firing and killing students. Lack of discipline among the students cannot be compared to revolution and rioting, and it should not be treated as such. At the root of it there are some causes which have to be understood and then eradicated. Adoption of a repressive policy only adds fuel to the fire, and ultimately this fire spreads from one part of the country to another, until it engulfs most of the country.

7. Social disorganisation. Social disorganisation is a condition in which the organisation, control and mutual cooperation that normally exists between various social institutions and committees deteriorates and practically ceases to exist. This kind of disorganisation leads to the disorganisation of such fundamental institutions as marriage and finally, ultimately leading to personal disorganisation. Indiscipline is just one instance of this kind of disorganisation. Hence, one cause of the indiscipline found among students today is the general disorganisation of society.

8. Absence of teacher parent relationship. In a more normal situation, the absence of relationship and contact between teachers and parents is another cause of indiscipline. Both the teacher and the parent are unaware of the difficulties of each other, and thus they blame each other for the defects of the student, without making any effort to improve the student. In fact, the responsibility for the student's indiscipline must be equally divided between the student, the parent and the teacher, but mutual cooperation and contact between the latter two can solve this problem to a great extent.

9. Psychological causes. At its root, indiscipline is a psychological defect of character. Among its more prominent causes are abnormalities concerning sex, inferiority and superiority complexes, feelings of insecurity, absence of any aim, etc. All these factors contribute to the frustration of the educand, which is converted into violence. This violence is manifested in the facts of indiscipline which are universally condemned. The responsibility for giving rise to such psychological symptoms rests upon bad and morally degenerate films and literature, lack of character among the educators, social class distinctions, absence of any normal relations between girls and boys in the college, neglect of moral education, etc.

The most important factor among those outlined above is the defective nature of the system of education, because all other causes have their origin in the basic shortcoming. The existing system of education cannot do with some small changes. It needs to be completely overhauled, in fact, scrapped and replaced by a different system altogether. It should be made to conform to the cultural characteristics of the nation, education should be imparted through the medium of the national language, and it must incorporate better working conditions for the educator, and a more efficacious and reliable system of examination.

MEANS OF CURING YOUTH TENSION

The means of curing youth tension can be gauged from the foregoing account of its causes. The following suggestions have been made in this regard:

1. Improvement in the teacher's condition. This comprehends increase in salary, better conditions of work, more just and impartial selections and appointments, reasonable prospects of advancement, etc. If these conditions are met, the educators will be able to live satisfactory lives, and thus they will be encouraged to impart some idealism to their educands.

2. Presentation of right ideals by the educator. Since almost all educands imitate their educator both consciously and unconsciously, it is necessary that the educator must present the correct ideal in every sphere of conduct. He must in this way lead the educand.

3. Improvements in the system of education. As far as possible, the defects in the system of education pointed out by various committees and commissions should be removed immediately.

4. Improvements in the examination system. Education achieves development of the total personality. The examination, therefore, must test this development, not merely the memory, as it does at present.

5. Preventing political influence in schools. No political party should be given the chance to penetrate school and college life.

6. Control of unwarranted state interference. More often, than not, the vice-chancellors appointed to the universities are appointed on any consideration except that of merit. These appointments are made by the government, and hence are illustrations of undue state interference in education. It is undesirable for the state to interfere in the working of education in this manner.

7. Protection of the independence of educational institutions. Of the many incidents of violence and destruction by the students in the recent past, many were inspired by the entry of the police into college compounds, either without the permission or in violation of the express command of the college authorities. All educationists agree that no government employee has the right to enter the premises of the educational institution with the permission of the principal. If this rule is not violated it would be easier to prevent manifestations of youth unrest from becoming violent and destructive.

8. Contact between educators and parents. Another method of curbing student youth unrest is to encourage contact between educators and parents so that they can meet and discuss the problems of educands and thus remove the causes leading to indiscipline.

9. Moral education. Most thinkers agree that absence of moral education is responsible for youth unrest and character defects of the educands. In any case moral education will definitely curb indiscipline.

10. Creation of proper atmosphere in colleges. The psychological factors at the root of youth unrest can be eliminated by creating the proper atmosphere in schools. As far as possible, the atmosphere should resemble that of a large family in which the relations between boys, girls, educators, students, etc. should be morally psychologically healthy.

Youth unrest is a complex problem having its social, political and psychological aspects. In order to remove it these aspects must be understood and the cooperation of educators, parents and state must be used to solve this problem.

IMPROVEMENT OF STUDENT UNIONS

The role of student leaders in campus is not negative. Student unions cannot run on the pattern of labour unions. Instead of aiming at student's unity and demand of students rights, they should rather aim at furthering the cause of education and strengthening teacher-taught relationship. This, however, requires a periodical survey of the needs and demands of the students by the government and the administration and prompt remedy to them. Restriction on admission of black listed students is a necessary condition for checking indiscipline on the campus. The following suggestions may be advanced for the better organisation of student unions.

1. Student's participation in management. In the colleges governed by managing committees the student leaders may be given representation in the managing committee so that they may get their demands directly fulfilled without any confrontation with the principal.

2. Limitation on expenses. There should be restriction and proper auditing of budget of student unions. If evidence for spending much beyond income is clear, enquiry should be made into the extra source of income.

3. Restriction on activities in public. The activities of student unions should be confined within the campus. They should be restrained to do anything in the city.

4. No permission for litigation. All the controversies concerning students should be decided by the principal, the vice-chancellor or the district administration. At no time the student union may be permitted to go to court for pressing its demand.

5. Proper permission for activities. The student union is governed by campus rules. They should give prior information and seek sanction for every activity from the principal in the college and the vice chancellor in the university. Activities should be organised not only by prior information but prior sanction.

6. Correlation of manpower needs and educational planning. This point has been repeatedly emphasised by every education commission. Educational planning includes educational guidance. Manpower planning depends on vocational guidance. Vocationalisation of higher education is necessary for practical use of educational facilities. Job efficiency should be the criteria for organisation of courses, method of evaluation and modes of instruction.

7. Better teacher-taught relationships. Peace on the campus depends on proper teacher-taught relationships. This requires satisfaction and involvement of the teachers as well as the taught. This depends upon proper policies concerning admission, curriculum, methods of teaching, administration, evaluation, appointments and general facilities.

8. Better socialisation. This requires elimination of parochialism, casteism, communalism, linguism, regionalism and factionalism from the campus. On the other hand, national integration should be propagated by all means.

In the end it should be remembered that a small portion of disturbance is a part of the normal life in the campus. It is only when indiscipline crosses limits then action should be taken. Prevention is always better than cure. This is particularly true in the case of educational campus.

QUESTIONS FOR EXERCISE

1. Write short note on Student Unrest.
2. Discuss the causes of indiscipline in Indian Universities. Suggest remedies.
3. What are the causes of Youth Tensions in India? Suggest curative measures.
4. Write short note on Improvement of Student Unions.

DEVIANCE

DEVIANCE

1

Crime : Definition and Causes

Crime is anti-social behaviour which a group rejects and to which it attaches penalties. In this way all those activities for which the state lays down punishments are crimes. Those activities to which no punishments are attached may be sinful but they would not be criminal. But some thinkers have deemed it comprehensively. In the words of C. Darrow, "Crime is an act forbidden by the law of the land and for which penalty is prescribed."[1] This constitutes a definition of crime from the social viewpoint. From the legal viewpoint, violation of law constitutes crime. In the words of Barnes and Teeters, "The term 'Crime' technically means a form of anti-social behaviour that has violated public sentiment to such an extent as to be forbidden by statute."[2] This definition does not include those anti-social activities which are not prohibited by law. Actually, criminality should attach both to anti-social activities and to activities forbidden by law. Though no punishment is prescribed for anti-social activities, the public opinion always condemns them.[3] According to Garofalo even the actions contradictory of the prevalent conceptions of pity and truth should be considered criminal.[4] To quote Elliott and Merrill, "A crime *ispo facto* implies a disturbance in a social relationship and a social definition as to what such a disturbance is."[5]

CHARACTERISTICS OF CRIME

One extensive analysis has resulted in a description of seven interrelated but overlapping differentials of crime. Ideally behaviour would not be crime unless all the seven differentials are present.

(1) Harm. Before a behaviour can be called crime there must be certain external consequences or 'harm'. A crime has a harmful impact on social interests.

---

1. Darrow, C., *Crime — its Causes and Punishment,* (1934), p. 1.
2. Barnes and Teeters, *New Horizons in Criminology*, Prentice Hall (1959), p. 70.
3. Sutherland, E.H., *Principles of Criminology*, J.B. Lippincott Co., New York (1955), p. 14.
4. Garofalo, R., *Criminology,* Little Brown (Boston), p. 59.
5. Elliott and Merrill, *Social Disorganisation,* Harper & Bros., New York (1950), p. 91.

(2) Illegal. The harm must be legally forbidden, must have been prescribed in penal law. Anti-social behaviour is not crime unless it is prohibited by law.

(3) Malafide Intention. There must be the criminal conduct, i.e., there must be an intentional or reckless action or inaction which brings about the harmful consequences.

(4) Criminal Intention. Criminal intent must be present. Hall suggests that legal scholars have confused between intention and motive. The motives for a crime may be good but the intention is criminal. Thus if a man kills his starving children his motive is good but killing is legally forbidden and so his intention is criminal.

(5) Concurrence of intention and conduct. There must be a concurrence of criminal intention and conduct. For example if a policeman, who goes into a house to make an arrest is not a trespasser from the beginning.

(6) Causal Relationship. There must be a causal relation between the legally forbidden harm and the voluntary misconduct. For example if a man dies of suffocation after being shot at, the relationship between conduct and the harm is not clear cut.

(7) Prescription of Punishment. There must be legally prescribed punishment. The voluntary misconduct must be punishable by law.

Garofalo developed a concept of the "natural crime" and defined it as a violation of the prevailing sentiments of pity and probity. Radcliff Brown defined crime as the violation of usage which gives rise to the exercise of a sanction. The crime is any act which causes harm to man's social interests. The criminal is a person who commits a crime. According to law a criminal is one who has intentionally violated a criminal law. Sometimes a criminal is not treated as such until his criminal acts are proved in court.

The main causes of crime are — (1) Social, (2) Economic, (3) Physical and Developmental, (4) Geographical and (5) Political.

SOCIAL CAUSES OF CRIME

The main social causes of crime are as follows:

1. Family and Crime. The family is the most dominant factor in the social causes of crime in India. Now-a-days family disorganisation is to be seen in India. The control previously exercised by the family over the individual is now lacking. In urban areas, all the members of a family are to be seen pursuing their individual paths. With the lifting of family control there are no restrictions to the criminal tendencies of children. Now that the natural relations between parents and children are devoid of love both young boys and girls are prone to criminal activity. Even in the villages the adolescents and youngmen and women do not respect their elders, and they want to lead a carefree, unrestricted, individual life. Due to all these causes, sex crimes are increasing. One main cause of adultery, abortion, miscarriage, prostitution and juvenile delinquency is the undesirable domestic conditions.

2. Absence of Social Control. A second social cause of crime in India is absence of social control. Previously the caste panchayats in the village kept control over the behaviour and conduct of the members of the caste. It was extremely difficult to conceal crime in the village and when any crime was revealed the caste panchayats meted out very stern punishments, going to the limit of exterminating the guilty persons from the caste. This tended to control and check crime effectively. Today, these social organisations no longer exist. They have been deprived of all their authority. Secondly, with better facilities of transport being available the criminal can commit the crime and abscond from the village to the town or to the village from the town. In urban areas no one is troubled about caste organisations. Now-a-days in big cities, even doing favour to neighbourers is a defunct practice because few have intimacy with their neighbours and social relationships have become impersonal. Any individual can commit a crime and conceal his identity in the city mob. In this way, the disappearance of the control of caste organisations is another cause of crime in India.

3. Defective Education. Modern education in India is very defective. It does not develop the character of students in right direction. Instead it has led to an increase in selfishness, disorderliness and impertinence. Ethical and religious education have no place in the modern education system. Besides this, even after completing his education an individual does not become capable of earning his livelihood and many well educated people remain unemployed for many years. Late employment leads to late marriage. All these causes tend to aggravate criminal activity.

4. Cinema. Cinema has helped in the increase of crime in India. According to Blumen and Hansen, cinemas indirectly influence the male criminals. The cinema arouses criminal tendencies in men by teaching crime techniques, by exhibiting many kinds of crimes, by stimulating the desire for wealth and comforts, by showing ways and means of appropriating them illegally, by arousing the feelings of bravado, toughness and adventure, by arousing profound sexual urges, by stimulating day dreams of criminal jobs. In much the same way it directs or urges many young and inexperienced women to illegitimate relations and crimes by stimulating the sexual desire, the desire for exhibition, love making, independence and variety.

5. Newspapers. Besides cinemas, newspapers also have a hand in increasing criminal activity. Newspapers increase criminal activity by publishing methods of crime through news items, by printing many news items relating to crime, by making crime a general subject, by printing news of major crimes and showing their advantages, circulating the names of criminals, by highlighting causes which tend to increase crime in the name of studies of crimes and by warning and alerting criminals by publishing police methods. The recent wave of dacoits in India was to some extent indirectly assisted by newspapers.

6. Use of Alcohol. The consumption of alcohol also is one of the major causes of crime in India. Drinking is more prevalent among those who have a low standard of life and it is also from among them that the greatest number of criminals are coming. There are large numbers of crimes committed under the influence of alcoholic stimulants. Drinking affects not only the drinker and makes him a criminal but it also has a deleterious influence on his entire family and inclines men, women and children towards crime. In this way drinking increases crime both apparently as well as indirectly.

7. Prohibition of Widow Remarriage. In India widow remarriage is now legally accepted as valid but it is still looked down upon in society. Consequently, many young widows do not remarry for the rest of their lives but such a decision does not annihilate their sexual passion and these rather lie dormant in a corner of the mind and wait for a suitable opportunity. Even if the widow is religious and saintly she is pursued by men and is lured to the path of evil and sin by many threats and cajoling. In this way, there is an increase in adultery, miscarriage, abortion, infanticide, etc. When their sinful deeds public become many commit suicide.

8. Defects of the marriage and dowry system. In India the dowry system also is among the social causes of crime. On the one hand the dowry system urges the fathers of girls to earn money through illegitimate means for their daughter's marriage, it on the other hand, leads to suicide by many young girls who cannot bear to see the degraded condition of their parents, the dowry system has further encouraged late marriages, both in girls and in boys. In extreme cases, the lack of wealth compels a girl to remain unmarried throughout her life or at the most she is married to an old man or to an unsuitable partner. All these also tend to increase sex crimes in society. Very often the parents do not care to ask the girl or boy for opinion and sometimes even proceed against it. This also results in suicide and other crimes.

9. Religion. Religion has also been one of the causes of crime in India. This does not mean that religion itself encouraged crimes but the encouragement has come from the different sects which originated in the differences of opinion between people on matters of religion and in the hatred for other religions. In a general way, of course, communal riots and crimes such as looting, murder and so on, perpetrated in order to increase the number of one's own religion and to injure another religion have always been happening in India. But the crimes committed during communal riots in the name of religion, when the country was partitioned in 1947, are unequalled in the history of the world. Helpless women were denuded and taken in procession through the main roads all the time being whipped. Their breasts were cut off, they were violated and mutilated, their children's hearts were cut out infront of their eyes. The most heinous crimes that can be discovered in the history of criminal activity have been perpetrated in 1947 riots.

10. Changes in Social values. There has been a tremendous change in social values in recent times in India. Now-a-days, new nations such as materialism, individualism, rationalism, the respect for wealth, absence of sex restrictions etc., are becoming very popular in the country. This has led to a disregard of ancient social values and new values have been reinstated in their stead. There is no one common opinion of any kind in them. This disordered state of values also inspires crime because any individual can manage to produce an argument to justify even that which is improper.

Social Disorganization. In preliterate and peasant societies the environmental influences surrounding a person were relatively steady, uniform, harmonious and consistent. But in a contemporary urban society a child is confronted with varying patterns of behaviour even within his own home for not even one's own can act consistently in modern life; the parent himself is the recipient of many alternative roles and behaviour patterns. Similarly groups outside the home have standards of conduct which are often extremely different from those within the home. A great deal of behaviour is in the nature of role playing and when roles are conflicting or ambiguous the behaviour is inconsistent.

Sellin has described the conflicts within contemporary communities. Every person is identified with a number of social groups each meeting some biologically conditioned or socially created need. Each of these groups is "normative" in the sense that within it there grow up norms of conduct applicable to situations created by that group in specific activities. As a member of a given reference group a person is not only supposed to conform to the rules which it shares with other groups, but also to those which are peculiarly its own. A person who as a member of a family group in routine life situations may also as a member of a play group or a work group, political group, a religious group etc. acquire norms which regulate specialized life situations and which sustain, weaken or even contradict the norms earlier incorporated in his personality. The more complex a culture becomes, the more likely it is that the number of normative groups which affect a person will be large and the greater is the chance that the norms of these groups will fail to agree. A conflict of norms is said to exist when more or less divergent rules of conduct govern the specific life situation in which a person may find himself. The conduct norm of one group of which he is a part may permit one response to this situation, the norm of another group may permit perhaps the opposite response.

This condition is considered as social disorganization because the social pressures for conformity on the individual are not uniform and harmonious. In this condition the society does not possess consensus with respect to societal goals or else does not possess consensus regarding means of achieving accepted societal goals. Consequently the individual is confronted with alternative goals or means or one exists under conditions in which the norms of many members of the society are unknown to other members. One finds that behaviour which is correct or proper in one group is wrong or improper from the point of view of other groups in which one has membership.

The processes which result in social disorganization are competition, mobility, conflict and an individualistic ideology which has been logically and intellectually harmonious with a criminalistic ideology.

The preceding exposition on the social causes of crime in India will have brought to light the extent to which the defects of such social organisations as family, caste, religion, marriage etc., have no geographical, economic, political and other causes, but it is intended merely to show the important part played by social organisation in crime.

ECONOMIC CAUSES

The main economic causes of crimes are the following —

1. Poverty. In India one sees extreme poverty. Poverty is a major cause of crime, since a hungry man can do literally anything in order to appease his hunger. One comes across instances where a criminal commits a crime immediately on his release from prison in order that he may be imprisoned again where he is assured of a square meal. Outside the prison he has no such assurance. Dr. Haikerwal has investigated that in the period 1917—1927 thefts increased in number when the prices of wheat went up, and decreased when wheat prices fell. In this way, a close relation is found to exist between the number of crimes and the prices of foodgrains in India. It was found in the course of a study conducted upon the prostitutes of Kanpur that one major cause of prostitution is poverty. Poor girls are easily enticed by men who violate them, take away their virginity and put them on the market. One even comes across news of suicides and murders of families due to poverty.

2. Unemployment. Unemployment, much like property, is a major cause of crime in India. Many young men commit suicides when they are frustrated by extreme poverty and continued unemployment. Among the people who are seen creating disturbances, causing violence, etc., the majority are the unemployed. Most gangsters do not work. Gangsterism is their only occupation.

3. Industrialisation. Industrialisation is also an important cause of crime in India. It has destroyed the family life of millions of labourers. They work very hard for eight to ten hours in the day during which they have to suffer many indecencies and for this they have to live in towns far away from their families. Continued existence of this type leads them to indulge in drinking alcohol and in prostitution and this encourages other crimes. In India, the most prospering centres of prostitution are important industrial towns which, at the same time, foster crimes such as murder, assault, disturbance, robbery, etc. Industrialisation has encouraged crime also due to another reason. Housing becomes a problem in an industrial town when the population increases beyond limits. In some town thousands of families live in houses having no more than one room each. In such conditions the married women have no privacy and children and unmarried members witness happenings which they should not see. This has a bad influence upon them and sex crimes increase among them. Sex crimes increase tendencies to other crimes which then take place. In industrial towns many thousands of labourers and men otherwise are compelled to live alone and this tends to split the ratio of men to women, which consequently encourages sex crimes. Many girls from rural areas are deceived with promises of employment and brought to towns where they are forced to adopt prostitution.

4. Urbanization. Urbanization is the result of industrialization and other causes. Hence all those crimes caused by industrialization are also caused by urbanization. In cities the society fails to exercise control over the individual who looses his identity in the mob after having committed a crime. There is no such facility, however redoubtable in the village. In towns there are better opportunities for picking pockets and practising deception in a crowd. There is absence of healthy recreation in the town and hence the crimes are crowded. Gambling dens, indecent theatres and wine shops provide means of spurious recreation. This encourages crime.

It is evident from the foregoing account of the socio-economic causes of crime in India that here the main causes of crime are social and economic. Absence of reliable statistics makes it difficult to say definitely that the causes of crime here are hardly psychological. But what can be said is that since life in India still lacks some of the velocity and crowdedness of Western life, the psychological causes of crime in India do not compare favourably with their counterparts in America and other Western countries.

PHYSICAL AND DEVELOPMENTAL CAUSES

Physical defects also make a man a criminal because due to deformities he lags behind his fellow beings in many activities and it is in order to remove this difference that he turns to crime. Criminals have usually been found to be extremely ugly. On examining prisoners in the Parkhurst prison, Charles Goring found most of them to be inferior, from the physical viewpoint, to the common individual. Mental defects are just as much causative of crime as are physical defects. Among them feeble-mindedness has particularly been found to be a cause of crime. The percentage of feeble-minded criminals among 948 criminals who had committed crimes of various sorts and were studied by Goring was as follows —

Those who set fire to a heap of wheat	52.9 per cent
Those who set fire to other forms of property	16.7 per cent
Those who robbed and murdered	15.6 per cent
Those who committed unnatural sex crimes	14.3 per cent
Those who were dacoits	10.0 per cent

Gillin calculated that 12 per cent of all prisoners are affected with mental diseases. Besides feeble-mindedness, individuals are also led to crime by epilepsy and emotional disturbances. Of the 1000 young men of Chicago who had repeated their crimes, seven per cent were afflicted with epilepsy. The reason why crimes originate in physical and mental afflictions is that such people are the objects of social derison and mockery because of their impeded and disease-hampered progress, and this social degradation spurs them to engage in anti-social activities. A person who, being very ugly, fails to win a woman's love, tries to gain ascendency over her by the power of money, which he amasses by illegitimate means or by sheer dint of physical power and rapacious activity.

Heredity

Heredity, according to some criminologists, is one main cause of crime. This view is no longer regarded as scientific but there can be no doubt that lineage and descent have some influence upon crime. Early sexual maturity, mental defects and nervous instability etc., are abnormalities an individual inherits, which help in making him a criminal. In a study in Chicago, Healy went into the family history of 668 out of 1000 juvenile delinquents and found that in all 245 of the families were afflicted by one or another mental defects. In 125 cases their ancestors were also found to be criminals. 61 per cent of 823 families which were sampled were found to be suffering from some affliction. But these statistics show the influence of environment at the same time as they indicate the effect of heredity. Some people become criminals due to psychoses. In this way people indulge in criminal activity in order to make up for mental and physical shortcomings. Elliott and Merrill express this by saying that his criminal tendency may be the reaction aiming at remedying shortcomings.

Besides physical defects, factors concerning physical development may also sometimes be causes of crime. As a general rule it can be said that it is between the ages of 17 to 24 that the greatest number of crimes are committed. In old age rape and other sexual crimes increase in number. Murderous crimes are usually committed by young men. Embezzlement, fraud, vagrancy, alcoholic excesses and murder, etc. are peculiar to middle age. Girls who mature early are more prone to become involved in clandestine affairs. In adolescence the aggressive tendency grows.

GEOGRAPHICAL CAUSES

Many geographical causes also stimulate crime. According to criminologists the geographical factors influence crime indirectly. Lombroso has collected evidence and shown that crimes of rape are more common in plains than in the mountains or plateaus. In Italy where malaria is to be found in excess of every other disease the crimes most common are those that are against the individual. According to some criminologists, in hot countries there are more crimes against the person while in cold countries more crimes are committed against property. Lacassagne had formulated a calendar on the basis of seasonal fluctuations in crime. According to this the greatest numbers of cases of infanticide take place in January, February, March and April, of homicide and fatal assaults in July, of patricide in January and October, of rape upon minors in May, July, August, and most of all December, of rape upon young women in June and January. All criminologists do not agree to such a view of the influences of seasons and climates upon criminal activity but the least that can be said is that crimes are susceptible to climatic and seasonal variations in the same degree in which human relationships and tendencies are influenced by them.

POLITICAL CAUSES

Many political causes also encourage crime. Now-a-days many criminals go scot free with prepared legal advice because there is opportunity to prove truth false and falsehood true. This encourages them to engage in further criminal activity. On the other hand, the innocents, who are prosecuted and convicted in their place also become criminals as a reaction. The ill treatment to which the prison inmates are subjected also hardens the softest of criminal. Crimes are further encouraged by the inefficiency, immorality and corruption of the police department. People connected with political groups also unobtrusively assist criminals and make use of them to inflict injury upon and to defame members of opposing groups.

Little research has been done on the relation of political processes to criminal behaviour. Crime statistics present an inadequate picture of the crime situation because politicians juggle the figures so as to 'prove' that their policies have reduced crime. A prominent theory about the influence of politics on crime is that crime is due to the lack of enforcement of laws. There is an anomaly in a great amount of legislation and one finds scant respect for its observance. Clinard has indicated that in America, the general public attitude towards obedience of law is that all laws except those dealing with very serious offences should be violated if one can escape them and laws should be selectively obeyed according to one's interests. Legislative bodies are considered with suspicion and distrust.

Police are regarded as brutal, corrupt and inefficient. Officials charged with law enforcement avoid their responsibility or enforce the laws only sporadically. Moreover, the political machinery supports criminal groups by modifying laws. It supports and promotes large scale white-collar crime to protect its own interest. It also protects groups against injurious legislation. A third form of political corruption is through corruption in governmental contracts. Another form is the operation of patronage system to fill up political offices and also parties practicing fraud in voting. Thus the practice of corruption and crime by the political machinery itself restricts the effectiveness of law enforcement agencies in crime prevention. This is equally true of India as of other countries.

QUESTIONS FOR EXERCISE

1. Do geographical factors influence crime? Critically examine some of the contributions.
2. To what extent political social factors influence crime rate? Discuss.
3. Explain the causes and consequences of crimes.
4. The family is the first great training school in either behaviour or misbehaviour. Discuss the role of family in crime causation.
5. Analyse the role of social disorganization in the incidence of crime.
6. Explain the role of economic and environmental factors in crime causation.

2

Criminal Tribes

A person who violates law for some personal end is called a criminal. And a person who habitually offends and defies the law and has made law-breaking the source of his livelihood and who feels little or no remorse for his misdeeds, in fact, ceases to regard them misdeeds, is a professional criminal. There are certain tribes in India which had been considered habitual offenders or professional criminals for a pretty long time. A criminal tribe is one, the majority of whose members, earn their livelihood by practising crime. The members of these tribes do not look down upon or condemn crime but accept it as a part and parcel of their lives. As a matter of fact, right from the cradle they start teaching their children the tricks of trade and by the time they grow up they become expert criminals and who, therefore, feel nothing to be easier than law breaking for personal profit. Some criminologists believe that crime has become the hereditary property of these tribes and that whosoever is born in such a tribe automatically inherits the predisposition to crime. But there are many scholars of eminence who reject the hereditary theory to account for widespread tendency to crime among the members of criminal tribes. As a matter of fact, it is not so much of a genetic heredity but is certainly a case of social heredity. As the parents of these children are practising crime and, since they feel no shame about what they do, their children are exposed at very impressionable age to crime and pick it up by imitation and learn through experience and trial and error the tricks of the trade. As it is common knowledge that children generally adopt the professions of their parents, it is small wonder that children of the parents who are professionally criminal take to crime.

ORIGIN AND DEVELOPMENT OF CRIMINAL TRIBES

There are a number of criminal tribes in India. The majority of these tribes are nomads and keep moving from place to place. Like gypsies of Europe they have no fixed abode. It is due to this nomadism of these tribes that it is difficult to collect authentic information about the origin and development of these tribes. Therefore there are variety of views among scholars about their origins. According to one view, the Indian tribes also belong to original gypsies of Europe; the criminal Indian tribes also belong to gypsies. According to these scholars the gypsies of Europe spread all over the world and the Indian tribes are therefore European gypsies who migrated to India. There are quite a few scholars who support this view; but there is little scientific evidence in its favour. This view is at best a conjecture.

The second view about the origin of these tribes is that they are actually offshoots of the primitive Indian races. Those members who found a fixed abode and kept pace with the development of civilization and successfully adjusted themselves to changes got amalgamated with the main current of national life. But those individuals, who, for some reasons, could not make adjustments and kept moving from place to place and failed to find a permanent home became nomads and that these nomads are the real ancestors of modern tribes. On account of economic hardships and social ostracisation these people gradually took to crime to keep themselves going and now this has become their habit.

The third view is quite different from the other two views. According to some scholars, these tribals are neither migrants from foreign lands nor have they sprang from primitive races of ancient. But, as a matter of fact, the ancestors of these people belonged to royal household but were forced into exile for some serious crime. In order to escape persecution they kept moving from place to place. It is also claimed that they took to crime as a revenge against their persecutors. In this connection there are many legends and romantic tales about tribals of Rajasthan. It is said that when Maharana Pratap was vanquished, he decided not to settle down anywhere permanently till the defeat was avenged and that his followers kept this vow till recently.

The history of criminal tribes is very old; but the name and classification of these tribes is due to British Imperialist government in India. The British Government passed an Act in 1871, known as Criminal Tribes Act. Between the years 1897 and 1911 the Act was amended twice. According to this Act all the criminal tribes are born criminal and therefore anyone born in this tribe is bound to take to crime. Accordingly all children born in these tribes were enlisted criminal in police records so that a strict surveillance and supervision may be kept over their activities. With the dawn of independence there was great hue and cry against this Act and, as a result, this Act was modified and finally repealed in 1952. However, the long record of criminal activity and propensity could not be abolished by the repeal of Act. Therefore to fill the vacuum created by the repeal of the Act it was filled by passing another Act, known as Habitual Offender's Act. About these tribes T.V. Stephens has written: "The special feature in India is caste system: a family of carpenters will be carpenters, a century or five century hence, if they last so long keeping this in mind the meaning of professional criminal is clear, it means a tribe whose ancestors were criminal from time immemorial, where descendants will be offenders against law until the whole tribe is exterminated."

In modern India, the population of so-called criminal tribes or habitual offenders is about 40 lakhs. According to a recent survey, the break-up for various states is as follows:

S. No.	Name of State	Population
1.	Uttar Pradesh	16,68,845
2.	Maharashtra	6,23,809
3.	Karnataka	2,10,321
4.	Tamilnadu	5,94,440
5.	Madhya Pradesh	76,721
6.	Orissa	74,762
7.	Hyderabad	69,602
8.	Bihar	13,311
9.	West Bengal	2,598
10.	Punjab	76,564
11.	Rajasthan	65,440

CHIEF CRIMINAL TRIBES

In India, there are a number of criminal tribes. The same tribe is known by different names in different parts of the country. In Northern India, the chief among criminal tribes are Sansi, Meena, Kanjar, Bavaria, Boria, Bhedkoot, Bhatoo, Dom, Haboora, Biloch, Karwal, Mahatam, Pakhiwara, Tagco, Harni, Badhak, Bhagaria, Bhil, Baelia, Aheria, Tootia, Bakhar and Nath etc. The chief tribes of Western and Southern India are Bavaria, Chohara, Pardhi and Kanjar. Now we discuss in detail the more important of these tribes.

(A) *Sansi or Sansia.* Sansi is an extremely well-known criminal tribe. Their areas of origin are believed to be Ajmer and Mewat in Rajasthan. The Sansis are broadly divided into two groups, Kalka and Mali. Further these have many sub-classes amongst them. There is another basis for the division of Sansis. Those who are settled in some place permanently and the others who are nomadic and move bag and baggage from one place to another, taking no fixed residence anywhere. In the nomadic Sansis, one group is known as Birthwan and the other group is known as Rheluwala. An interesting feature about these groups is that though they are generally indifferent to moral values, they strictly observe the prohibition against intercaste or intergroup marriage. Some Sansis are settled in Rajasthan. It is believed that they are descendants of notorious dacoit and robber Sahasmal. Some Sansis have settled down in Bengal, too. However the most famous of all Sansis are the Sansis of Punjab. There is a romantic tale about their origin. It is said that a daughter of a certain King was extremely beautiful and passionate. Her sexual adventures lead her to commit a sexual offence — coitus with an outsider, not belonging to royal household. As a result of this she was exiled from the kingdom. In jungle she gave birth to a child who was named Sansi. This bastard is supposed to be the ancestor of Punjab Sansis. As a matter of fact Sansis include persons from all tribes. Some Sansis observe the rites of Moslem religion, while others are Hindus. However they are considered outcastes by Hindus.

(B) *Haboora*. According to some scholars, Habooras are only a branch of Sansis. The word Haboora is connected with Sanskrit word 'hori' which means a dishonest person. Some Habooras trace their origin to Rana Pratap who had taken the vow not to settle down permanently till his defeat of Haldighati was avenged. His followers kept roaming from jungle to jungle and on account of economic pressure felt compelled to take to crime. According to some scholars there are twenty sub-castes among Habooras.

(C) *Dom*. Dom is also a criminal tribe. Their origin is traced to a low Dravidian tribe. Doms are extremely insolvent and slatternly. They are so filthy that no one wants them to come near. Mostly they live outside the cities. It is said about Doms that they are in fact an amalgam of individuals excommunicated by other tribes. The Doms of U.P. try to trace their origin to King Wen; and it is said of Punjab Doms that they belong to a Brahmin tribe which had corrupted itself. It is said that Raja Harishchandra had to do the task of Dom once.

Broadly, there are three categories of Doms. The first type of Doms are nomads; they roam about the jungles of Bihar and Bengal. The second type of Doms are those who live in hills. The third Doms are those who are fond of music and entertain by song and witty talks. They sell small toy musical instruments. They are also known as Dom-Mirasi whose main function was to serve and entertain royal families. According to some schools Dom-Mirasi and Criminal Doms are different peoples.

(D) *Kanjar*. Kanjar is also one of the most notable criminal tribe. Kanjar are further subdivided into, in some areas, in twelve and, in other areas, 23 sub-castes. In earlier days Kanjars used to perform the task of folk entertainers. They were adept in dance and music, and used to entertain feudal lords and royal families by their skills in music and dancing. Later on they were replaced by more skilful entertainers and Kanjars were forced to seek other avenues of earning livelihood. Some Kanjars believe that their ancestors are a sylvan couple residing in woods. This couple was their guru Man and Kanjarani Nathia. They were hunters and dancers and also outlaws. There are many folktales about the ancestors of Kanjars and all of them emphasize their dancing skill. In Punjab a nautch girl is called Kanjari. A Kanjari entertains and a Kanjar acts as an escort. Regarding the origin of Kanjar there is a legend that there was an excellent dancer named Majori. She was the very perfection of dancing skill and was so agile and nimble-footed that she could dance expertly on a tight rope. Her fame was such that many a King were enamoured of her. A certain King offered her the status of Queen and half the Kingdom if she could dance blind-folded on the rope and catch the bangles thrown by him. The performance was arranged and as Majori was about to hold the bangles, another nautch girl, green with jealousy, severed the cord and Majori came tumbling down; was badly hurt and sustained injury and died. But before dying she cursed her rivals that their progeny may be corrupt and being unable to make a living off dancing be condemned to practise prostitution.

FACTORS OF CRIME IN TRIBES

Many a tribe in India is generally regarded to be criminal. From legal point of view these are the ex-criminal tribes. There is not enough evidence, scientifically established or ascertainable, about the origin and development of these tribes. Their origin is shrouded in mythology and folk lore. As regards the question as to why a group as a whole takes to crime as a profession, divergent views have been expressed by scholars. According to one point of view the tendency to do crimes is hereditary and by virtue of being criminal the parents pass on this tendency to their offsprings. However this possibility of genetic heredity of crime is contested by other scholars. The truth of the matter appears to be this; the children who are born in an atmosphere replete and suffused with criminality are bound to be affected. At very impressionable age they learn the various criminal operations and by the time they mature they are expert in criminal techniques. Now nothing appears to them easier than the profession of crime. Being usually illiterate and uncultured they are not suited to any good profession. Little wonder, then, that they are so heavily drawn to crime. Dr. Haikerwal has aptly observed, "The day a baby is born, its parents and others begin to teach it the tricks of trade." How immoral and bad parents spoil their children is illustrated by the story of an American nurse whose sexual habits were perverted. When 13 or 14 she had to be a witness to sexual abuse of her mother by her father who came home drunk. He insulted and abused his wife and forced her to accept penetration per annum. Later he made her and daughter both fellate him and he also mouthed her daughter. This had such traumatic effect on the daughter that normal sex became reprehensible and on account of her perversion she had to suffer sadism of her friends.

On account of their promiscuous sex life the criminal tribes are of highly mixed character and if the genetic theory of crime were true these people should not be criminal,/because children born of these people are usually a cross because women of these tribes are inveterate prostitutes. Below we discuss some of the factors usually considered important for production of criminality in Criminal tribes.

(1) Social and Economic Causes. The social and economic causes play chief role in the production of criminality in the criminal tribes. The individuals or groups which are neglected by the society and are not given their due share in its achievement or accomplishments move away from society and become apathetic to it. If this apathy is not countered by positive social response, it turns into hostility towards society in general and those groups or persons in particular who are directly responsible for the neglect. In order to settle their scores with society such groups operate like undergrounds and keep moving. Besides social factors, economic factors, too, play an important part in helping tribes toward criminality. With the advance of civilization a number of economic problems also crop up. It is well known that with the advancement of civilization, social organizations also become more intricate and complex. In the result, only intellectually and technically resourceful people can find important gainful roles in society. The social changes moreover render many hitherto important and useful persons superfluous. Their skills are no longer worthwhile. Due to these social upheavals many persons and groups become economically sterile. They may go to jungles to lead the life of primitive man — hunting and eating jungle fruits. They may take to begging or singing and entertaining in bazars. In extreme situations they may live off the income from the sale of the bodies of their womenfolk and lastly they may become out and out criminals. Thus we see that economically sterile groups are driven by the society in a phased manner, from vegetation in jungle to prostitution and crime. What is more, well-to-do groups find in them an easy prey to appease their lust.

(2) Extinction of Traditional Professions. The social change has the effect of rendering many a type of services, worthless. The persons so dislocated from their trade find it extremely difficult to adopt alternative trades, particularly if they are past middle-age. For example with the construction of bridges, the jobs of boatmen have become superfluous; with the advent of radio, the street singers are no longer in demand; with the downfall of feudalism and popularity of cinema, the nautch girls are no longer in great demand. Some such tragedy must have overtaken the criminal tribes. The eunuches provide a good illustration. The eunuches at one time enjoyed a place of pride; they were guardians of Zenana or women of royal families or aristocrats. They were privy to many secrets and wielded unusual power. But now they are reduced to the task of putting up grotesque and obscene performances at marriages or births; their status is no more than that of a high class beggar. What is worse, unable to make both ends meet, they act as sodomists, fellators. As a matter of fact they are source of perverse sex. Being sharp witted, they enjoy patronage of both men and women in matters of sex. It will not be surprising if they become one day only purveyors of perverse sex.

(3) Family Disorganization and Degeneration. There are in every society many degenerate families which are morally and culturally so lost that what are considered disvalues by normal persons are regarded values by them. For example they like to have sons who can dishonour women and disrob them. They encourage pick-pocketting and minor thefts. They are proud if their daughters manage to live off a number of men simultaneously even if it leads to mutual destruction among suitors. Such families are breeding grounds for criminality.

(4) Caste System. Each criminal tribe is a specialized organization. This organization is like a Panchayat and this body is usually performing the function and role of a crime polytechnic, that is, it trains its members in the advanced operations of crime. They are imparted expertise in successful cheating. If any of its members is trapped by police and either imprisoned or killed, the members of his family are properly looked after by the Panchayat during the absence of the member.

(5) Corruption among officials. The government normally appoint a high official with numerous subordinates to supervise the activities of criminal tribes.

In each sector there are departments which are supposed to maintain a detailed record of each criminal and the nature of his activity. But there are a number of government servants who are corrupt and become accomplices of these criminals and share the booty of crime. The register of crime record is left unfulfilled and the criminals activity is not reported. Some government servants are successfully trapped by women of these tribes and the lure of free sex deflects many of them from carrying out their duties properly.

From the above discussion it is clear that there are many factors responsible for the inherent criminality of the criminal tribes. Many social and economic factors induce criminality among them; and since they carry the stigma of criminality society is initially prejudiced against them and consider them beyond help and redemption. Accordingly, neither government nor any other public agency thinks about them in constructive terms and draw up some elaborate plan of their rehabilitation. They are at best given lip service by the influential members of government and public. As a matter of fact, certain political and social groups have developed vested interests in their continuance and perpetuation. They furnish them a section of well-trained criminals who can be hired to advance personal motives of the hiring agencies. They also function as receptacle of the overfill or spillover of sex needs of many persons. Their lack of the sense of shame provides opportunity to some enterprising film-maker to produce blue movies. But, above all they are utterly deficient in a desire to reform or improve themselves.

(6) Social Life. Almost all criminal tribes lead an abnormal social life: there are no sets of social and moral values governing their life. Being mostly nomadic there is little fixed social structure and no set of social customs or traditions. As a rule they abide by no fixed laws and perform no definite rites and ceremonies with regard to marriage, birth etc. Their food habits are not also fixed; they have no taboos regarding food and sex. In food, the animal food and liquor are important items. However, they can eat intestines and other parts of animals which are normally eaten by dogs. They usually eat every variety of meat and drink hard liquor. Their sex life is promiscuous. Young boys and girls freely indulge in sex play under the very nose of elders. Most women function as veritable prostitutes. Their economic life is fluid and uncertain; only one thing is certain, they steal whenever possible. Their children are born in open and the function of mid-wife is performed by neighbourhood women. They suckle their young till another is born and are unmindful of suckling two children at the same time. A notable feature of these women is that they are constantly suckling young ones.

(7) Economic Life. The economic life of these tribes is both irregular and uncertain. The members of criminal tribes have no definite means of livelihood and therefore their spending is also erratic. If they somehow are able to lay hand on handsome amount of money, they usually gamble, drink and prostitute. They are found of spending extra money in feasting on meats and hard liquor. There are many small occupations carried on by these people. They collect various materials available in jungle and sell them in towns. These include honey, wax, gum, resin, animal skins and various herbals and animals which are supposedly aphrodisiac and also possess some other medicinal values. There are some criminal tribes which earn their livelihood by putting up public display of monkey-tricks, bear show or performances by snakes and cobras. These people of course make their living by honourable means and should not therefore be referred to as criminal. But, as a matter of fact, all tribals do something or the other. Quite a few of them make sufficient money by their small avocations and are satisfied. They refrain from stealing or other criminal acts. However, there are many who not content with meagre earning are lured into crime to earn easy money. As their moral fabric and sense of social values is weak, being illiterate and exposed from early life to criminality, they are unable to resist the lure of easy money which can be made by theft. Whenever they visit homes of townsmen to sell some articles or repair some ironwares, they would not lose the opportunity of making off with some utensil or other article which they sell for small price. Some of them are really vicious and indulge in child lifting and extorting regular payments from villagers and petty shopkeepers. Some of them run brothels in their huts and offer their females for gratification against money. In short, they can do any fair or foul thing to make money.

COLLECTIVE SOCIAL LIFE

The tribals operate as a well-knit unit. This is an imperative for the success of their criminal operations. They have a central organization called Panchayat where all powers are vested in the headman or tribal chief. The Panchayat organises training in crime expertise of its members. It also provides them with legal and professional aid in the event of abortive criminal attempt. In the event of the death of a member his family is economically provided for and protected by the Panchayat. The headman is empowered to punish any member if he violates the code of Panchayat. There can be excommunication and even extermination if the headman is satisfied that the presence of a particular member is threat to the whole tribe. The headman also enjoys special privileges. He must get whole of the booty of the crime and also has access to every woman.

FAMILY AND PROFESSIONAL LIFE

The homes of criminal tribes are the training centres and prepare the children for their future life of criminality. From early childhood the children are broken into crime and their ears are filled with heroic criminal exploits of their elders and their hearts stuffed and suffused with hatred of other people. They are asked to be brave and courageous and trained to kill animals and birds mercilessly and without compunction. They are told that they belong to a grandfather who had a lifelong record of murder, dacoity and kidnapping but could ever throw dust into the eyes of policemen; the police even was terrorized and badly afraid of him.

From early youth they start a course of practical training and undergo various tests of steeling their nerves. They are trained how to disguise and how to cheat; how to role; how to throw acid; how to escape detection; how to wield knife and firearms. They are also trained to be masculine and remove necklaces and ornaments off women. Another important feature of their training is to operate secretly, be loyal and faithful to the superior and cooperate among themselves. The girls are trained how to use their charms for the criminal purposes. Wrestling, mock-fight, knife throwing are their popular sports. Their first training ground in practical crime is fairs, festivals, crowded railway platforms etc. Thus by phases the child becomes a full-fledged, well-trained criminal.

There is also training in strict discipline in these tribes, though intra-tribal quarrels are not infrequent and they are settled by the headman. But if outsider clashes with any members of the tribe, the whole tribe fights against him as a man, sinking their mutual differences.

MARRIAGE AND MORALS

On account of their nomadic existence and criminal life, the institution of marriage is rather weak and the stable marital arrangements are few; and the divorce is fairly common place. There is no fixed age for marriage; but child marriages are not uncommon. The marriages are usually ceremonized without the assistance of priest. This primarily is due to the fact that Hindus regard these tribes as untouchable and the presence of a priest in the marriages of untouchables constitutes a sacrilege. However tribals celebrate their marriages with great pomp and show; and though, in different tribes different customs are observed, one thing common to all tribal marriages is feasting of meats and hard alcohol. In some gypsies of middle-east marriage is an occasion of great merry-making; and in Turkey all guests have sexual intercourse with the bride. However such licentiousness is not to be found among Indian tribals, though dancing is quite common.

In majority of tribal societies, marriage is by purchase, that is, the bridegroom is required to give bride-money to his father-in-law. There is usually hard bargaining for the price of bride between the bridegroom and the parents of the bride. The bridemoney, as it is called, varies in quantum from one society to the other. As may be expected, a pretty young girl fetches higher price than a fat unseemly. In order to exercise a restraint on the tendency to charge exorbitant prices for brides various societies have fixed such an amount. Bhantu Panchayat fixed the price of Rs. 600 maximum for girls of Dholi, Gaddi, Marwari subcastes and Rs. 500 maximum for girls of Dhapo, Kodan and Charralia subcastes. Among Sansis there is flat rate of Rs. 78 and in Doms it is paltry Rs. 15. In spite of Panchayat there is bargaining particularly if the bride is passionately attractive and adept in sex techniques.

Besides abnormal marriage practices, the moral laws followed by criminal tribes are cock-eyed; these are in fact topsy turvy. What is moral or valuable in normal society is considered to be of no consequence by tribals, they are completely indifferent, even contemptuous, of morals. Thieving, dacoity and killing, are perfectly normal for them. Their sexual morals are equally perverse according to conventional morality. Generally most females of criminal tribes are extremely passionate and fond of sexual intercourse. They not only meet their husbands but freely offer their bodies to others for money or pleasure. They are usually scantily dressed and particularly while suckling, they are completely topless. Usually they are unmindful of covering while bathing etc. They are so unashamed of their bodies that they may be called children of nature or born exhibitionists. Besides normal sex many of them are fond of sodomy. They use their skill at body display and entertainment for espionage for their tribes and thus help in theft and dacoity. Thus we may conclude that morals of tribals are at a low level.

RELIGIOUS BELIEFS AND SUPERSTITIONS

Some tribals subscribe to Moslem faith and others to Hinduism. Those subscribing to Hindu faith are, however, considered to be untouchables by the caste Hindus and not allowed entry into Hindu temples. But Hindu tribals have fashioned out or developed in course of time many deities which are to be placated and whose grace is sought through adulation etc. For example, Bavarian tribals believe in transmigration of souls and they dutifully set apart a certain portion of the booty or looted wealth for the deity. Some tribals are known to worship a deity known by the name of Goodar Por. The water of river Ganga is regarded holy and sacred and plays important part in the lives of the tribals. The swearing by Gangajal is regarded to be final and unalterable commitment. Whenever any ceremony or worship is to be performed, a bottle of Gangajal is kept as a divine witness. At the time of epidemics a ceremonial worship of Kali Devi with elaborate paraphernalia is duly performed. The Bavarians also worship a deity known as Dat. Bhantus also attach great importance to the worship of Kali Devi, they are also sun-worshippers.

The tribals entertain plenty of superstitions some ludicrous and some strange and interesting. Like all primitive races, the Indian tribals attach great importance to the dream phenomenon. Whatever they happen to see in dreams is loaded with meaning for their day-to-day life. They regard the intimation of dream as realities bound to happen and therefore their dreams determine their attitude and responses of life. The dreams may be auspicious or inauspicious depending upon the object seen in the dream. Thus, for example, the sight of a beautiful woman in dream is taken to be extremely auspicious and this may indicate good luck and bring money for feasting and merry-making or may indicate that man will marry a damsel soon; but if a fall of tooth is seen in dream this is most inauspicious as it foretells certain death of a youth of the tribe. As they launch upon criminal operations the Bavarians carefully watch the initial symptoms. The sight of the bird 'Neelkanth' indicates sure success of the operation and is very auspicious. Again a suckling calf or baby is an auspicious sign; but the howl of jackals and sight of menstruating woman is very inauspicious, and the plan is abandoned. Bhantus regard the braying of lamb an auspicious sign; but they regard the sight of a urinating woman a bad omen. The sight of backside is less ominous than the sight of front portion. The sight of pregnant woman may indicate big success or total failure. The sight of the barber, oilvendor, one-eyed person or a policeman in the early morning is regarded very inauspicious. Thus it is clear that tribals entertain plenty of superstitions and are guided in their behaviour by these.

ACTS CONCERNING CRIMINAL TRIBALS

There are a number of criminal tribes in India. Some of them are exclusively engaged in criminal activity, while others are doing some odd jobs but also miss no opportunity to steal and cheat. The latter may be called *Partially Criminal* and the first *Wholly Criminal.* The wholly criminal tribes do no honourable job for making a living. They are most of the time committing crimes or else planning for future crimes. They are always on a lookout for potential centres of crime and are mostly found on crowded railway platforms, fairs and other crowded places to pursue their ends. But partially criminal tribes are either engaged in entertaining by song or dance and animal circus. They also make musical drums, bamboo baskets or small iron wares. There is a legislation regarding all these people, known as *The Criminal Tribes Act.* In India an ordinance known as Indian Penal Code was first promulgated in the year 1760, in which crimes and respective punishment was given in detail. Shortly afterwards Regulation 27 was passed by the East India Company which pertained to criminal tribes. By virtue of this regulation the so-called criminal tribals could be engaged against payment in the construction of roads; and in case any of them deserted duty, he could be sentenced to imprisonment for 6 months. During these days Pindari Thugs were very active and posed serious menace to travellers. In 1839, Government of India established a department known as *Thugee and Dacoity* department. At the same time the activities of criminal tribes came to official notice and various laws regarding them were passed from time to time. The important Acts are listed below :

(a) Criminal Tribes Act, 1871,

(b) Criminal Tribes Act, 1911,

(c) Criminal Tribes Act, 1924,

(d) Habitual Offenders Act, 1958.

Criminal Tribes Act, 1871. The main aim of the 1871 Act was to keep an eye on the activities of the criminal tribes. A constant surveillance over and vigilance about their activity was planned; but it was not the intention or object of this Act to check the nomadism of these people, at that nomadism or moving from one place to another was not regarded in any way objectionable and harmful to the society. It was considered as normal way of life as is the settlement at same fixed abode. The aim of the act was to control the crime and help the members of criminal tribes to reform and rehabilitate themselves. This Act gave wide-ranging powers to the provincial governments. The provincial governments were authorized to declare any group of people who were incorrigible criminals a Criminal Tribe. This Act provided for maintenance of register in which the names and other particulars of all the adult members of a tribe were written. Further they were required to register the information about births and deaths. Some of them were required to report at regular intervals to the police station. From time to time a policeman used to take a round of their colonies and take roll-call of all the members. The 1871 Act had no specific plans for the reform of these people.

In 1879 this Act was amended and it was provided for that government could take the custody of all children of the age 4 and keep them in government schools, away from the pollutant atmosphere of the tribe, upto the age of 18. There, however, were many flaws and loopholes in the Act. Therefore, in the year 1911, it was replaced by a new Act, known as Criminal Tribes Act, 1911.

Criminal Tribes Act, 1911. On account of the lack of success in the control of crime by the criminal tribes and the lack of any improvement in the state of affairs in spite of the 1879 amendment in the Act, the government set up a committee to go into the matters afresh and review the whole thing from all possible aspects. In 1902-3 a high powered Police Commission went into the matters in minute details. On the basis of the report submitted by the Commission, the Government of India passed a new Act regarding Criminal Tribes in the year 1911. In accordance with this Act schedules were prepared for various criminal tribes and these schedules were complete in each respect. In these, there were personal identification marks and the thumb impressions of each of the members of the Tribe. This was done with a view to track down the criminals with ease. Besides the more notorious members of the tribe were put under very strict observation; their activities were minutely watched. Besides, government could remove any child of the age 6 or above from the criminal parents and give them education and training in governmental institutions. Under this act provincial governments were given special instructions for the control of these tribes. The provincial governments were given powers to make suitable amendments in the Act in the light of their experiences.

Criminal Tribes Act, 1924. From many aspects the 1911 Act was defective and contained many loop-holes. Basically in aim and intent it was preventive and not corrective. There were virtually no attempts in it to reform and rehabilitate the present criminals. Of course, there was provision for taking away children and giving them proper education. But there were practical difficulties here, too. Therefore the 1911 Act was replaced by a new Act in 1924. The 1924 Act empowered the provincial governments to declare criminal tribes and prepare a list of their members, having identification mark and thumb impression of each member. Besides, a check was put on the migratory instinct of the tribals. They were not to leave their place without prior permission of the police.

However, the most significant part of the 1924 Act was the provision of the reform and rehabilitation of the criminals. The provincial governments were issued express instruction to draw up elaborate plans to provide relief and rehabilitation to the tribals. They were to be attracted to useful profession and attempts were made to preserve the integrity of their traditional profession and skills.

Habitual Offenders Restriction Act, 1952. Beginning from the year 1871 to the dawn of independence, a number of Acts regarding Criminal Tribes were passed and many amendments thereto made to make them effective and help in checking the crime and control of the activities of the tribals. However, they met with little success and criminality of the tribes instead of being controlled or eliminated, was being perpetuated and the number of crime and criminals went up with population growth of tribals. The idea of checking birth rate among them was alien at that time. After 1947, the national government paid serious attention to the problem and a number of committees were set up to go into the matter. The basic theoretical and practical drawback in all previous thinking on the matter was the fact that these persons were deemed criminal by birth and it was believed that no matter what their opportunities or facilities they could not help being criminal. Therefore nothing could be done to bring them back to normal life and wean them away from criminality. In this connection U.P. Government set up a high power Committee under the Chairmanship of Shri V. N. Tewari to go into the various aspects of the life of criminal tribes. After discussing the pros and cons of various proposals it came to the conclusion that the first and foremost imperative for any possible improvement in the condition of tribals is that the appellation 'criminal' should be dropped. This unnecessarily stigmatized these people and prejudiced others to them. In the words of the Committee: "The removal of the appellation criminal will have salubrious psycho-social impact upon the children of these tribes. This will help to eliminate from the minds of these people anti-social feelings and sentiments, because they will be relieved of the stigma and evil of considering themselves criminals and also relieved of the painful obligation of registering themselves with the police as soon as they attained the age of 15." On the basis of this and many other reports of the committee and recommendations of social scientists and criminologists, the Bombay Criminal Tribes Act was repealed in 1949. This proved a pace-setter and soon all states repealed Criminal Tribes Acts from the respective jurisdictions.

Consequent upon the repeal of the Criminal Tribes Act, a lacuna rather vacuum was felt. It was found that the police were unable to track the criminals on the basis of their records, because these were outdated and the sources of fresh information had dried up. Therefore the Criminal Tribes Act was replaced by Habitual Offenders Restrictions Act, 1952. This filled the gap left by the Repeal of Criminal Tribes Act. But this also removed the most glaring deficiency of the previous Act in so far as the term "criminal" which was a source of stigma against many people and tended to unfairly prejudge them was removed; and yet a mechanism was evolved to maintain strict supervision over the activities of those who, for historical and psycho-socio-economic reasons were predisposed to criminality.

QUESTIONS FOR EXERCISE

1. Write short note on Criminal Tribe.
2. Write short note on Criminal Tribe Act.

3

White Collar Crime

The eminent criminologist E.H. Sutherland has thus defined white collar crime : "White collar crime is committed by a person of respectability and high social status in the course of occupation." Further expatiating the same point Sutherland writes, "The white collar crime is committed in the course of ones economic and fiscal activities." It is evident that in the gamut of white collar crime are included only those crimes which are connected with and are committed in the course of professional and business activity. Normally in the capitalist societies the white collar criminal is not punished. Therefore, the modern criminologists have emphasized this point. In this respect the contribution of Sutherland is significant.

CHARACTERISTICS OF WHITE COLLAR CRIMES

From the foregoing discussion of the white collar crime the following points emerge :

(1) The general traits of white collar crime are similar to those of other crimes. A crime is an act or a complex of activities which are against society and which violate the provisions of law. Similarly, the white collar crime is against society and law. It is obvious that like all crimes the white collar crime is punishable.

(2) The white collar crime is punishable. E.H. Sutherland has written this about the concept of white collar crime: "It does not only emphasize punishment but includes punishability." Thus it is plain that from the view point of penology the white collar crime has the same place and status as any other crime. Mr. Sutherland is very critical of the fact that the law enforcing authorities in capitalist societies tend to ignore or minimize the evil of white collar crime.

(3) The white collar crime is based on violation of trust. According to Sutherland, "White collar crime is based on violation of trust". For example, many a management of educational and other institutions pay much less salary than stipulated by law but compel their employees to put their signatures on false documents; and thus, draw more money from government than actually disbursed. Many financial institutions cheat their subscribers. The Chit Fund and like schemes are instances of such bungling. Many manufacturers boost their sales by offering cheap gifts at nominal cost or free but more than make good their investment by quality deterioration or by reduction of quality. The government is daily cheated of huge sums of money by unscrupulous contractors who grease the palms of concerned officials. Even smuggling is masterminded by highly placed persons who escape detection due to huge pay offs to police. There is slave trade in women controlled and managed by some highly respectable people.

(4) White collar crime is related with differential implementation of law. This is the observation of eminent criminologist Sutherland that white collar crime flourishes and is rarely punished whereas the other criminals are shown no such mercy. This preferential treatment to white collar criminal is due to two facts: (1) White collar crime apparently relates to abuse of money and does not pose threat to life, that is, it is an offence against property and not a physical violation of any one. (2) Since the government and police themselves are susceptible to corruption, they are reluctant to move against persons well-placed and politically and economically powerful. The white collar criminal usually makes it a point to involve governmental agencies in his nefarious activities and, therefore, is protected even upon detection lest government people themselves be exposed.

CONCLUSIONS AND SUGGESTIONS

The above discussion brings into light the fact that white collar crime has assumed serious dimensions in the capitalists societies and is undermining the social and economic health of the society. In order to combat these tendencies it is essential that political corruption be firstly eradicated and that government should refuse to yield to political and economic vested interests. In democracy every government wants to retain power and for this it is very necessary that it may not alienate any powerful political lobby. But if the problem is to be tackled the government should be prepared to take risks. The judiciary should be very well paid and selection should be strictly on merit. The judges must be persons of high intellectual and moral calibre. They should be persons of proven integrity and must be incorruptible. Only by these bold steps can the white collar crime be combated and contained. But it seems that in a capitalist society where golden key opens all locks the eradication of such crimes seems virtually impossible. For effective control and eradication of white collar crime it is very essential that there should be some curb on vast accumulation of money in the hands of individuals, and also monopolization of any trade by private person is not permitted; otherwise the abuse and corruption of money cannot be contained. In socialist countries the white collar crime is not of serious nature and proportion because no men have so much money as to be able to influence or buy the governmental machinery. As a matter of fact the basic cause of these crimes is vast accumulation of wealth in few hands so that even government has to depend upon them for survival. As long as this state of affairs persists there is no hope of any reduction in white collar crime. It is possible to control or at least contain such crimes if liberal labour laws are enforced very strictly and if the government servants are so well paid that they have little temptation to accept bribes.

OCCUPATIONAL CRIMES

The concept of "white collar crime" was introduced in 1939 by Edwin H. Sutherland who used the term to refer to violation of legal codes in the course of occupational activity by persons who are 'respectable' and of high social status. White collar crimes include offences committed by businessmen, politicians, government employees, labour union officials, doctors, lawyers etc. The violations of law include restraint of trade through monopoly, misrepresentation advertising, unfair labour practices, financial manipulations, black-marketing, embezzlement, misappropriation of public funds, illegal prescription of narcotics etc.

A major characteristic of occupational crime is the way in which the offender conceives of himself. Since the offences take place in connection with a legitimate occupation and the offender generally regards himself as a respectable citizen, he does not regard himself as a criminal. At most he regards himself as a "law breaker". The general public are also guided by the same notion. The maintenance of a "non criminal self" concept by the offender is one of the essential elements in occupational crime. The life organization of the occupational offender is not built around a criminal role. He plays a variety of roles particularly that of a respected citizen.

The principle of differential association explains the group attachments of the white collar criminal whereby criminal behaviour "is learned" from others who define the behaviour favourably and isolation from those who do not. Law breaking can be normative in certain business concerns. In some occupations a man may learn the techniques by which law can be violated by building up such rationalization as "business is business". This diffusion of illegal practices is spread from a person already in the occupation. Persons appear to accept or reject opportunities for occupational crime according to their orientations towards their roles and their attitudes toward general social values. Some of these factors are negative attitudes toward other persons in general. The relative importance attached to a status symbol of money as compared with law obedience and the relative importance attached to personal family or business reputations. Some forms of occupational crime are related to the structure of the occupation itself. Occupational crime usually involves some form of organization among the participants. The degree of organization may range from the comparatively simple reciprocal relationships involved in fee splitting among doctors to the more complex procedures involved in the illegal activities of large scale corporations.

Occupational crimes cannot be fully understood without reference to the structure and values of society. The values involved in the regulation of commercial transactions may conflict with those of free enterprise, individualism, or supply demand. Attitude toward selective obedience of law becomes the key to compliance. One of the most important reasons for the high degree of correspondence between some forms of occupational crime and patterns of legitimate behaviour is that many of the activities were not defined as criminal until recent years. Occupational crimes may be viewed as violations of laws which are not part of the values of society or of some groups in society.

QUESTIONS FOR EXERCISE

1. What is white collar crime? Analyse its effects on society.
2. Explain the main characteristics of white collar crimes.
3. Discuss the concept of white collar crime.

4
Juvenile Delinquency

In modern civilized countries a criminal is not looked upon as a sinner or a bad person, but rather as a mentally diseased individual or one who has been victimised by circumstances. There was a time when even small children were severely punished if they committed some crime. But as psychologists proceeded to draw the attention of the civilised world the causes of juvenile delinquency, the tradition of punishing children lost favour, to be replaced by efforts at improving and rehabilitating them. Now-a-days, in every nation efforts are made to correct the juvenile delinquent rather than to punish him. To make the deviant once again a healthy and responsible citizen of society, efforts are made through reformatory schools, probation and other measures.

Legal definition of juvenile delinquency

Legal definition of juvenile delinquency does not conform to its psychological definition, as, from the legal viewpoint, a juvenile delinquent is a person between the ages of 15 and 17 who indulges in anti-social activity. In the U.S.A., the Ohio Code defines juvenile delinquency in some such manner as this: a juvenile delinquent is one who breaks the law, is a vagrant, persists in disobeying orders, whose behaviour endangers his own moral life as well as the moral life of others or one who tries to marry without the consent of his parents. It may as well be pointed out that the age of the so-called juvenile delinquents has not been similarly determined in all countries. It varies from country to country but is within the usual limits of 16 and 20. Normally, it is the 17-year old adolescent who qualifies for this term, but in India according to the prevalent laws, the maximum age of a juvenilc delinquent is fixed at 16. Laws pertaining to this subject have been passed in U.P., M.P., Maharashtra, Tamilnadu, Karnataka, Delhi, West Bengal, Orissa, and East Punjab. In these states in which the juvenile Acts have not been passed, the Reformatory Act of 1897 prevails. In these the maximum age of a juvenile delinquent has been determined at 15. In Maharashtra and Madhya Pradesh it is 17. According to the Reformatory Act, the term Youthful Offender will be appended to any individual below 15 who has been sentenced to life imprisonment or has been convicted of some crime.

Psychological definition of juvenile delinquency

Differing from the legal definition of the controversial term, psychologists lay much emphasis upon the causes of juvenile delinquency in defining it. From the legal viewpoint all those who are not apprehended are not criminals but from the psychological viewpoint all such offenders also are criminals. Consequently, the psychological definition of juvenile delinquency is more comprehensive than its legal definition. According to the psychologists, any and every child, of either sex, between the ages of 15 and 18, who commits a crime, irrespective of the fact that he is apprehended or not, is a juvenile delinquent. In this manner, juvenile delinquent is one who forcibly possesses the property of another or causes it damage, indulges in anti-social activity, creates danger to another's life or hinders the activities of others. Hence a child who throws stones at a car and runs away, one who sets fire without cause, creates dangers for the life of another just for the fun of it, are all juvenile delinquents, from the psychological view point.

Defining juvenile delinquency, Dr. Sethna has written: "Juvenile delinquency involves wrong doing by a child or a young person who is under an age specified by the law (for the time being in force) of the place concerned." Newmeyer puts the same idea in these words, "A delinquent is a person under age who is guilty of anti-social act and whose misconduct is an infraction of law."

Difference between crime and juvenile delinquency

1. Difference of age. The above description of juvenile delinquency makes it apparent that the main difference between a juvenile delinquent and a criminal is one of age but both indulge in anti-social activities. Working of both are subversive and hindering of social relationships. According to Dr. Haikerwal, from the social view point, crime or juvenile delinquency is a form of conduct that acts as an obstacle in the system of human relationships which are believed by society to be its fundamental condition. In this way, if a criminal is below a certain specified age, he will be designated a juvenile delinquent.

2. Difference of actions. But sometimes criminals and juvenile delinquents differ not only in respect of their age but also in respect of the crimes they commit. And in this connection, some actions that young men and children do lead them to be regarded as juvenile delinquents even though their activities are not actually crimes. A classification as wide as juvenile delinquent can include the vagrant, cruel, obstinate or young boys who keep the company of thieves, dacoits, other vagrants and prostitutes, those who keep away from the house for long periods of time without the permission of their parents and those who roam in the lonely streets late at night. It should be remembered here that such activities are, strictly speaking, not illegal or infringing any legal statute. Hence, the juvenile delinquent who chooses to act in these ways cannot be included in the same class as ordinary criminals. Another thing that sometimes happens is that the unemployed, un-housed and wandering child may be included in the category of juvenile delinquents along with the beggar, the farce being carried so far as to present the young person before a court and to try to mend his way.

5. Difference of characteristics. Kohen has distinguished criminal from juvenile delinquents on the basis of the following distinguishing characteristics—

(a) A juvenile's mischief is lacking in utility as he does things that do not benefit him in the least, such as roaming about in the streets without cause. On the other hand, the criminal acts with intent to gain something. A juvenile is sometimes even unaware of the objective of his own actions.

(b) Sometimes a juvenile commits a crime with only an intention to enjoy himself and indulge his sense of humour. It finds expression in practical joking like breaking car glasses, putting boulders on railway tracks or pushing people into a pond of water just for the fun of it. A criminal does not find this a suitable mode of manifesting his sense of humour.

(c) The juvenile delinquent does not commit a crime on a preplanned and well organised basis, being more apt to things on the spur of the moment. A hardened criminal is more inclined to plan his moves and organises crime with a certain show of skill.

Briefly, criminals and juvenile delinquents are to be distinguished by their difference of age, kinds of work, objective of activities, mode of working. Yet normally it is the difference in age alone that is considered the sole basis of marking distinction between the two classes.

METHOD OF DISCOVERING JUVENILE DELINQUENCY

Three kinds of methods have usually been employed to delve into the causes of juvenile delinquency — (1) Statistical, (2) Case history method, and (3) Psychoanalytic method. They have also been used to discover crimes. Now these methods will be described in some detail.

1. Statistical method. The statistical method finds its best exposition in the words of Cyril Burt.[1] He compiled a list of some specific situations or circumstances. And with the help of this inventory he attempted the discovery of circumstances that are peculiar to the healthy ones. Some of these situations are described as follows —

(1) Circumstances of heredity — (a) physical, (b) mental, (c) temperament (also signs of mental diseases).

(2) Circumstances of environment:

(a) Situations in the home — (i) poverty, (ii) defective family relations, (iii) defective discipline, (iv) bad characters in family.

(b) Situations outside the home — (i) neighbours, (ii) conditions outside the home, (iii) friend's circle.

(3) Physical condition.

(4) Mental conditions — (a) intellectual, (b) emotional, (c) interest, (d) emotional aberrations, (e) mental complexes.

On the basis of the above list of circumstances and conditions Cyril Burt

1. Burt, C., The Causal Factors of Juvenile Crime, *British Journal of Psychol* (1923), pt. I, pp. 12-27.

tried to discover the causes of juvenile delinquency. Some circumstances were noted through observations while others were measured through testing. The most important cause of juvenile delinquency turned out to be emotional. And crime appeared to have intimate relationship with the presence of tuberculosis and other serious diseases in the physical constitution of the parents. In the environment, the status of the family was found to be the most important. Physical and mental conditions of the adolescent himself was found to be of secondary importance. Accordingly, Cyril Burt came to the conclusion that the main factors concerning juvenile delinquency were defective discipline, defective relations between the parents and emotional aberrations.

2. Case history method. Another important method of discovering the cause of Juvenile delinquency is the case history method. The statistical method does not reveal the singular and actual as it does not include a study of the personal life of the juvenile delinquent under consideration. In the case history method, efforts are made to collect all information concerning every aspect of the subject's personality, as well as most of the circumstances of his life. The observer collects all relevant information concerning the school, home, family and any other important field of the life of the subject. Knowledge of the subject's ambitions, frustrations and problems is gained through mental tests, personality inventories and actual interview. Detailed information is sought at the hands of the subjects' parents, near relatives and intimate friends by interviewing all of them. And, on the basis of all such information that comes to hand, a complete case history is developed. An example of one such study is the book called *The Jack Roller* by Shaw.[2] Study of the case history revealed many factors that could have led them to find crime attractive, for example, bitter criticism of all others unceasingly, blaming others, ostentatious desire to attract the attention of others, rationalisation instead of insight, inability to understand oneself and unfounded suspicion of others, etc.

3. Psychoanalytic method. The third and the most important method of discovering the causes of juvenile delinquency is the psychonoanalytic method in which the external circumstances of the subjects are not the only subject of enquiry. What is attempted is the analysis of his subconscious mind. Psychoanalysts have recourse to many methods such as dream analysis, word association and other psychological tests with the help of which they can probe the unconscious element in the individual's mind and uncover the hidden and submerged causes that compel him to a life of crime and disorder. In their *Roots of Crime* Alexander and Healy[3] have written that the criminal tendency cannot be understood by discovering certain incriminating things by the statistical method nor by making inferences from the results of individual method. To understand the criminal mentality we should understand those psychological processes that are in the background of all human behaviour. It need not be specially pointed out that psychoanalysis cannot be said to be the one method

2. Shaw, C.R., *The Jack Roller*, Chicago University Press (1930).
3. Alexander, F. and Healy, W., *Roots of Crime*, Psycho-analytic Studies, 1935.

that can discover all the causes of delinquent behaviour among juveniles. In fact, one of these three methods taken alone can help in probing the causes of juvenile delinquency, and it is best to be used of all these three methods. Such an approach is the best as it throws light on the causes of crime by highlighting the internal and external conditions, and the peculiarities of his personality.

CAUSES OF JUVENILE DELINQUENCY

According to the novel approach and concepts of modern criminology, the causes of juvenile delinquency have been divided into two classes — internal and social classes. In crime, two special factors are at work — personal and external. Internal factors include physical and psychological factors while the external factors consist of social elements. Criminals have been divided into two categories by the American criminologists — (1) social criminals, (2) personal criminals. Social criminals, in particular, are the result of social circumstances. Walter Recklace has pointed out two specific causes of crime — (1) constructive, and (2) circumstantial. Some other criminologists have divided the various causes of crime into two parts — (1) sociogenic; and (2) psychogenic. Here, the causes of juvenile delinquency will be divided into three classes for convenient study — (1) social causes, (2) psychological causes, (3) economic causes.

Social causes

Of the various causes of juvenile delinquency, the most comprehensive are the social causes. Among them, the main ones are — (1) family, (2) school, (3) criminal area, (4) bad company, (5) recreation, (6) war, (7) social disorganisation and (8) displacement.

1. Defects of the family. Of the causes of juvenile delinquency, Elliott and Merrill accept distorted family influence to be the most potent. Of 4000 juvenile delinquents in Boston Healy and Bronner found that about 50 per cent of them came from divided or broken families. The major situations in the family that cause it are: (a) broken families, (b) attitude of parents, (c) character and conduct of parents, (d) effect of criminal relatives. In order to understand the importance of family as cause of juvenile delinquency, it is necessary to comprehend these factors.

(a) *Broken families.* A study of juvenile delinquency has revealed that the greatest number of delinquents come from broken families. A broken family, as the term indicates, is one in which family ties have been destroyed. A family is not constituted by a number of people living together but by their mutual intimate relationships. Absence of this intimacy results in the breaking up of a family, and it is in broken families that juvenile delinquents develop. In any such family, a child is not looked after properly. In the opinion of some specialists, broken families are more apt to arouse criminal tendencies in females than in male juveniles. The Child Care Society of Bombay had 386 boys and 169 girls under its care in 1947. Of these children the parents of two boys and two girls were serving prison sentences, two boys and five girls were under the influence of extreme indiscipline, six boys and nine girls were the victims of moral insecurity. In a broken family the relationships of husband and wife, parents and children, brothers and sisters lose their healthy nature. Hence, it is only natural if the children choose the wrong path that ruins their lives.

(b) *Attitude of parents.* In the family factor in juvenile delinquency, another important condition is the relation between the two parents. According to the preface writer of *Women of the Street*, a probing and searching analysis of the prostitutes of London, the problem of the prostitute has its origin in the relationship between the child and parents. Often when the child is deprived of love and is scolded constantly on every occasion, he develops feelings of revolt and hatred so that he runs away from the house at the earliest opportunity and falls into a life of crime. Disregard on the parts of parents induces feelings of insecurity in the children with the result that they develop mental complexes. If the parents try to conceal many facts of their own life from children, the tendency towards crime is only aggravated. One of the most common query that children are apt to put before their parents is where did they come from or where their younger brothers and sisters have come from. When they are told all sorts of lies by their parents, while they learn the truth from their servants or other people outside the family, a sense of insecurity is induced to them, because they feel that their parents do many things which they fear to tell their children and this injures their feelings. This sense of insecurity leads many children to sex crimes.

(c) *Character and conduct of parents.* The child's personality is considerably influenced by the character and conduct of its parents. One rarely comes across a child who has been able to mould its behaviour according to socially accepted values and conceptions in the face of his parent's telling lies, hypocritical behaviour, sexual immorality and thieving. In a study conducted by Miss Elliott, 67 per cent parents in broken families and 44 per cent parents in united families were engaged in immoral behaviour. If the mother is already involved in prostitution, the child will have little hesitation in following suit and with the worst conceivable consequence.

(d) *Influence of brothers and sisters.* A child's personality is susceptible to the influence of his brother's and sister's personality apart from the personality and mutual relationship of the parents. This influence is more potent in the case of girls as they are not exposed to external influence as much as boys who remain in the home for a considerably less period of time. If the senior children in the family manifest criminal tendencies, the youngsters are invariably influenced by it. If the elder sister shows criminal tendencies or is engaged in immoral behaviour, the younger sister is more apt to follow her example.

2. Defects of the School. After the family, a child's personality is next influenced by the school. But one major form of juvenile delinquency is absconding from school. In 1947 Williamson found in his study that playing truant from school, theft and sex crimes were the major forms of juvenile delinquency, and even among those running away from school or roaming outside the school claimed the greatest attention and interest among children. Analysing the causes of such behaviour, Williamson came to the conclusion that it was caused by criticism at the hands of parents, gaining membership of a gang of criminals, punishment by the teacher, weakness in some subject, and level of education that is above the child's ability and capacity. Children who run away from the school usually spend their time in the worst sort of company and commit all kinds of crimes. This is one of the major problems confronting the teachers. It is for this reason that in most big cities, students are not allowed to view matinee shows in film exhibition but preventions of this nature do not help to solve the problems. One of the major causes of increasing indiscipline in the present time is that education is taken as stuffing the brain with information rather than building up character. It need hardly be said that it is these factors that make the child lose interest in study and try to avoid school with the result that one falls into a life of crime.

3. Crime-dominated area. According to the results of a study by Clifford, Shaw and Mckay, some areas are not appropriate for the development of children. It is a matter of common knowledge that the neighbourhood casts important influences upon the child. Using the statistical method, Maller came to the conclusion that in New York, juvenile delinquency was greatest in those quarters where the level of life was very low, child mortality was very high, there were no means of recreation, residences were not permanent. In a community that is unstable there are no social taboos or laws. Pickpockets are found in great abundance in and around hotels and other places where travellers stay since there is always some traveller or the other there. Clifford, Shaw and Mckay studied juvenile delinquency in nearly 15 towns to discover that the rate of juvenile crime was highest in the centre of the town and lowest at its furthest reaches. From this they concluded that the social traditions of backward and low economic status areas distinguish the pattern of crime from the average groups. And these patterns are maintained in juvenile delinquent groups. In this way, big towns have certain areas where there is an abundance of criminals, and these areas are called criminal areas or crime-dominated areas.

4. Bad company. According to the famous criminologist Edwin H. Sutherland, criminal behaviour is acquired through interactions with others. He says that an individual becomes a criminal when there is excess of conditions that promote the infringement of law over conditions that prevent such infringement.[4] And, among children, some get good company while others don't. The child who gets bad company progresses towards crime while the child who gets into good company progresses to become an able and useful member of society. An individual's behaviour is influenced to a considerable extent by the conduct of his companions. In order to induce the children to accept and respect the values and assumptions of adult society around them it is necessary to create such an atmosphere in which inspiration to criminal behaviour is reduced to the absolute minimum.

---

4. Sutherland, E.H., *Principles of Criminology*, New York, 1955.

5. (a) *Absence of recreation.* Means of recreation have an important place in the child's development. It is only a good and healthy atmosphere that can provide the right sort of inspiration to the children for sensible and healthy behaviour in their spare time after schools. The ability to make proper use of one's spare time is an added instigation to criminal behaviour. Play and games are essential elements in the socialization and ethical training of children. Inadequate, uncontrolled and improper recreation in a town is one of the causes of juvenile delinquency. In Thurston's study of 2507 juvenile delinquents it was found that their spare time had hung heavy on their heads.

(b) *Defective recreation.* In modern times, the one means of recreation available to big and small is the cinema, which is responsible for juvenile delinquency and anti-social activity to quite an extent. New patterns of crime are presented to an individual through scenes of adventure and romance. Some films have such potent influence upon the adolescents that after their screening in some towns, certain kinds of crime increased many-fold. But the reactions of children to films are determined and guided by patterns within the house or around the neighbourhood. And different children react differently to it. Scientific studies have determined that the direct influence of cinema upon the behaviour of children is very little. Actually, more important than the cinema is the child's reaction to it which keeps on functioning on the basis of the previous experience and reaction to social and cultural circumstances.

6. War and post-war conditions. Increase in the rate of juvenile delinquency has been found during war and post-war periods. In countries that actually participate in the war, the children's education is considerably hindered and affected. It often happens that in wartime the father is on the front fighting the war, while the mother goes to the factory to earn. Hence, children are not properly looked after. Lack of any control leads to much promiscuous mixing between girls and boys with the result that sexual crimes increase. In wartime, wherever there was bombing, it was the adolescents in that area who took the greatest part in looting smashed houses. Hence, the situation of war definitely encourage criminal tendencies.

7. Social disorganization. Social disorganization leads to disorganization of individuals. And disorganization of society leads to increase in criminal activity; hence it, too, is one of the causes of juvenile delinquency. In modern industrial society there is lack of synthesis and equality which creates tension. This tension inspires young men and women to crime.

8. Displacement. Displacement also influences juvenile delinquency. In studying the town Berkeley, Stuart discovered that juvenile delinquents lived in an area where there was considerable displacement, but as compared with their own respective families, they themselves were much less active and dynamic.

PSYCHOLOGICAL CAUSES

Till now, we have been discussing the social causes of juvenile delinquency, all data for which were collected on the basis of the statistical method. The application of the other two methods of discovering causes of juvenile delinquency — case history method and psychoanalysis — has led to some light being shed on the psychological causes of the phenomenon. Psychological causes concerning criminal activity are the following:-

(1) Intellectual weakness, (2) mental disease, (3) characteristics of personality, (4) emotional instability.

1. Intellectual weakness. Having rejected Lombroso's[5] principle, Dr. Goring advanced the theory that intellectual weakness is a cause of crime. Goddard was the main exponent of the notion that mental weakness is the cause of crime. In his book *Mental Efficiency and Levels of Intelligence*[6] he has written that the greatest single factor or cause of crime is mental weakness. After examining 4000 children for their intelligence, Healy and Bronner[7] came to the conclusion that 13 per cent of them had an intelligence quotient below 70. This conclusion is borne out by S.S. Glueck and E.T. Glueck in their book *Unraveling Juvenile Delinquency*,[8] who studied 1000 criminal children in 1934 and came to the conclusion that 13 per cent children have an intelligence quotient of below 70.

2. Mental diseases. Other criminologists have tried to establish a definite relationship between mental disease and crime. In the many studies carried out upon criminals, some mentally diseased individuals were also found. According to this view, a criminal is a kind of mentally diseased individual who is asmuch in need of treatment as in need of punishment. Some psychiatrists and neurologists believe that the psychopathic personality is a cause of crime. Psychopathic children are born in families where there is almost complete absence of love, affection and control. Concerning psychopathic child Tappan has written that he is very unsocialised, irritable, cruel, obstinate, suspicious, self-centred, lonely, full of feelings of revenge, backward and hyper sexual or uncontrolled in his sexual behaviour. He is extremely devoid of repentance over his own cruel doings and the pain or suffering of others. A psychopathic child of this nature has the existence of an uninvited guest in his own house. He is never loved by any one, but is instead the butt of every criticism and abuse in the house. It is only natural that the child should react to such behaviour with feelings of unhindered obstinacy and homicidal tendencies.

3. Characteristics of personality. Tendency to crime is also found to have close relationship with characteristics of the personality. Personality is the method of an individual's adaptation to environment. Criminal children resort to illegal modes of such adaptation. Hence juvenile delinquents have been found to possess some characteristic features of the personality that shed light on the causes of delinquency. In his book *Unraveling Juvenile Delinquency*, Glueck pointed out that the degree of freedom, irresponsibility, revolt, homicidal

5. Caesar Lombroso, *Crime, its Causes and Remedies,* Little Brown & Co., Boston (1911).
6. Goddard, H.H., *Mental Efficiency and Levels of Intelligence,* Princeton University Press (1936).
7. Healy, W., Bronner A.F., *New Light on Delinquency and its Treatment*, Yale University Press (1963).
8. Glueck, S.S. and Glueck, E.T., *Unraveling Juvenile Delinquency,* Harvard University Press (1940), p. 356.

tendency, suspicion, lack of control, some forms of sadism, emotional and social maladjustment, extrovert behaviour, etc., in juvenile delinquent is much higher than in normal children. Immaturity in sentiment and lack of emotional balance were found to be some eight times more than in the normal child. A normal child is comparatively well-behaved, less explosive, peaceable, obedient and social. The juvenile delinquent, on the contrary, is found to be naughty, explosive, anything but peaceful, disobedient and unsocial. Glueck also discovered considerable difference between the general interest and forms of recreation of normal and abnormal children. A delinquent child was found to take much interest in works of an adventurous or dangerous nature. They were found to take considerable interest in seeing pictures and films. Among his interest and modes of reaction were found such practices as cigarette smoking, gambling, staying away from home, breaking things and travelling without tickets, etc. He is often the member of one or the other gang. On the contrary, normal healthy children were found engaging in games. In some study it has been proved that female juvenile delinquents exhibited considerable emotional instability and immaturity.

4. Emotional instability. In this way, emotional instability is one of the most important causes of crime. A child's personality is rendered unbalanced through lack of love and affection, emotional insecurity, very strict discipline, feeling of insufficiency and inferiority, and reaction of revolt. Such a state of mind inspires the child to criminal behaviour. In their studies, Healy and Bronner saw that 93 per cent of all juvenile delinquents manifest symptoms of emotional imbalance.

ECONOMIC CAUSES

Crime and poverty are intimately related. Study conducted by Shaw, Mckay and Elliott revealed that among juvenile delinquents, majority belonged to families of unskilled labourers. This discovery has the support of Bonger and Fornasiri, as they, too, advocate that poverty acts as an incentive to crime. Concerning these juvenile delinquents Merrill has written that a low family income compels the children also to share the burden and to neglect their education. Atmosphere in the factory and mill is such that it leads to male and female child to crime. Sometimes children are entrusted with carrying messages to the homes of seniors where they often see all kinds of sexual practices. This has the worst effect on them and they become tendencious towards crime. Statistics show that among juvenile delinquents, employed youngsters involved in crime number ten times the unemployed ones. Girls working in hotels or restaurants are easily lured into sex crimes since their wages are low, their residences are dirty, hours of work are long, and there is no shortage of individuals who want to lure them to a life of crime. In fact, children in poor families have many desires that remain unfulfilled, and to satisfy them they turn to crime. Poverty also induces sense of dissatisfaction and inferiority, another spur to criminal tendencies.

The foregoing exhaustive treatment of the social, psychological and economic causes of juvenile delinquency makes it clear that the principle of specific causation does not properly apply to this phenomenon. In fact, no modern criminologist and psychologist can refute the fact that the causes of crime are many and varied. A person's activities are his modes of adjusting to his environment. And in this adjustment individuals who apply socially acceptable means are called healthy while those who use unsocial and abnormal means for this adjustment are called criminals. Thus a child becomes criminal through the cooperation of many causes, social and individual, familial, psychological and economic. Hence, in order to rehabilitate the juvenile delinquent as a healthy member of society, it is necessary to understand all these causes and to remove them. It is a matter of no little satisfaction that this fact has been experienced in all progressive nations with the result that juvenile delinquents are everywhere cured rather than punished.

Modern welfare states aim at reforming the juvenile delinquents so that they may become responsible citizens when they grow old. The following are the most important methods to realize this objective:

1. Probation. In this method the juvenile delinquent is kept under the supervision of a probation officer whose job is to look after the delinquent, to help him in getting established in normal life and to see that the delinquent observes the rules of bail bond. Thus the delinquent, not only gets a chance to reform himself but also gets advice and concrete help for this purpose.

2. Reformatory institutions. Institutions such as reformatory schools, certified schools, auxiliary homes and borstal schools are devised to reform inmate delinquents. These institutions aim at all-round progress of the delinquent.

3. Psychological Techniques. Whereas the above measures are adopted by the state, the psychologist adopts psychological techniques for the reform of juvenile delinquents. Of these the important ones are the following:

(i) *Play therapy.* In this technique the delinquent children are given opportunities to participate in such plays as give expression to their repressed motives and help in the development of creative energy. In play therapy individual as well as group plays are utilised.

(ii) *Finger painting.* In this method the child is given plain papers and some others. He is allowed to paint in his own way by his fingers. The purpose is not painting but expression of repressed motives in the child, which leaves him sensible and healthy.

(iii) *Psycho-drama.* In this technique the child is allowed to participate in different roles in group drama and thereby manifest his repressed motives.

Besides the above mentioned specific techniques, the psychologist can reform delinquents by creating healthy atmosphere in the family and by providing adequate, healthy recreation. Finally, cure of juvenile delinquency requires coordinated and concentrated efforts of teachers, guardians and the government.

4. Government Measures. Children Acts are in force in the states of Andhra Pradesh, Gujarat, Kerala, Madhya Pradesh, Tamilnadu, Maharashtra,

Karnataka, Punjab, Uttar Pradesh and West Bengal and all the Union Territories. The Borstal Schools Acts, which are slightly different in scope, are in operation in the states of Andhra Pradesh, Gujarat, Kerala, Tamil Nadu, Maharashtra, Karnataka, Punjab, Uttar Pradesh and West Bengal. The Reformatory Schools Act of 1897 has also been enforced in all the bigger states and some Union Territories.

The problem of juvenile delinquency is mainly the concern of State Governments. The Central Government, however, have sponsored a Care Programme under which the states are given assistance. Under this programme, 40 remand homes, 17 certified schools, 5 borstal schools, 15 boys' clubs and 5 probation hostels have been established.

Besides formal education, vocational training in a number of trades is imparted to the inmates of the certified, reformatory and borstal schools. Some of these institutions also provide juvenile delinquents on their release with implements and money to enable them to settle down in trades learnt by them in schools. Other institutions provide follow up services. The inmates of the certified schools are given training in citizenship and democratic living and are encouraged to take part in extra-curricular activities, such as sports, debates, dramas, music and scouting.

Recently, seventy-two children also escaped from the home at Majnu-ka-Tila, Delhi, making it the third escape this year. Sources confirm escapes are common. Recently some inmates also fled from another custodial home. As a matter of fact, most children do not want to remain in these homes.

The state-managed homes, set up under the Juvenile Justice Act, were created for the care, protection and rehabilitation of neglected and deviant children, who are "destitute or have unfit parents, found begging or living in/near brothels and are likely to be abused or exploited for immoral and illegal purposes." Reportedly, the number of such children (mostly from Bihar, Assam, Bengal, UP, Andhra Pradesh and also Nepal) are increasing daily. In Delhi about 500 children are picked up annually. The city has about 100 custodial institutions. According to one estimate, children's homes across the country have a capacity to house some 3,50,000 inmates while 80 million children remain outside schools.

Although the Juvenile Justice Act, which replaced the Children's Act 1960, is in line with the UN Standard Minimum Rules for the Administration of Juvenile Justice, the Indian juvenile justice system has totally failed to imbibe the spirit of the Act. The world of custodial institutions is murky full of horror and neglect that is most shocking. Some members of the committee, now set up to look into the functioning of the homes, say on condition of anonymity: "The food is extremely bad. The kitchens stink unbearably. The toilets and the drains have been found to choke with sewage. Many homes do not provide cots to the children who sleep on the floor with poor cushioning even in the cold winter months. In some homes the walls are stained with urine and betel juice. The sick are seldom attended to properly. The use of soaps and phenols are not quite evident though there are funds for these items."

Observes Sandhya Sharma social worker and member of the Juvenile Justice Board, "I think even two hours of sincere work would bring some improvement. As adult-child communication is zero, in the absence of any emotional anchor, the children run away. If children fail to go to school, no one is bothered. At one home there is only one bat in the name of sports. The officers-in-charge keep attending meetings, the ladies keep knitting or basking in the sun. Even as a Board member, I am not aware where all the money is spent."

The Juvenile Justice Act, however, states the homes are to provide services for the physical mental, moral and spiritual welfare of children and facilities for self-improvement. "Rather than providing custodial care like parents provide, juvenile homes have degenerated into jail-like custodial centres. The JJ Board, despite its authority, has remained a mute spectator to the pitiable conditions of the Homes," comments Amod K. Kanth, ACP, Delhi Police and Secretary, Prayas Juvenile Centre for Neglected Children. Kanth adds, "The Juvenile Justice Act strongly advocates that children should not be kept in lock-ups as juvenile justice is distinguished from criminal justice. Most children arrested are non-offenders but the two categories — neglected children and juvenile delinquents are wrongly clubbed together."

Admits Balbir Singh, secretary, Social Welfare, "We'll not dispute it — there are bound to be certain deficiencies as the homes were established a long time ago. But there are also deficiencies in our own homes. A committee will soon make proposals for making these homes meaningful and livable."

QUESTIONS FOR EXERCISE

1. Is juvenile delinquency a pathological symptom? What remedies do you suggest for its control?
2. What do you understand by Delinquency? Can it be prevented or cured?
3. Give a definition of juvenile delinquency and discuss its causes.
4. What are the chief causes of delinquency? How would you prevent a boy from stealing?
5. Describe some of the factors that have been found to be related to criminal behaviour and juvenile delinquency.
6. Analyse the determinants and consequences of juvenile delinquency in India.

5
Prostitution

PUBLIC ORDER CRIMES

Public order crimes are violations of public order and decency and are crimes without victims. Public order crimes do not involve real injury to other person. Rather they disturb the community, as in the case of prostitution, may be injurious to the individual as in drunkenness and drug addiction.

There are striking differences in the behaviour systems of various public order crimes. Most public order offenders do not regard their criminal behaviour as part of their life organization.

The extent of prostitution and the reaction of society to it has fluctuated over years. Prostitution is a sexual intercourse on a promiscuous and mercenary basis with emotional indifference. Prior to entering into prostitution many call-girls have had personal contact with some one professionally involved in call-girl activities such as pimps or other call-girls. Once a girl has become a prostitute her apprenticeship period begins under the direction of another call-girl or a pimp. Here she learns the call-girl subculture's major characteristic of it being how to develop a sizeable and profitable clientale. Girls who become prostitutes tend to develop attitudes and behaviour patterns which are part of their social role. They develop their own professional language, special acts and services. The prostitute is paid for her loss of social esteem. Many prostitutes are able to leave their occupation for marriage or, for employment as waitresses or sales girls. But for many who are affected by V.D., alcoholism and drug addiction the end is in a derelict life of crime and imprisonment. The prostitute rationalizes about commercial sex by the legitimate value of financial success in society. Arrests strengthen the self-conception of a prostitute and other associates.

Some public order offences such as prostitution and homosexual behaviour grow out of and are rather heavily supported by clearly defined deviant subcultures. Prostitutes can be classified according to their method of operation as individual common prostitutes, organized houses of prostitution, call-girl and high class independent prostitutes. New girls are brought into the house and they soon, learn various sex techniques. The call-girl often depends upon some organization to recruit her patrons or through the intermediary services of a ball hop, hotel desk clerk, a taxi driver etc., who expect a fee. Prostitution is associated with panderers or pimps. Some prostitution is permitted by shady business of commercial recreation such as nightclubs. Prostitutes have often been indoctrinated into the profession, Group solidarity exists for protection from Police.

Much of the behaviour of public order offenders is consistent with legitimate behaviour patterns of society. The prostitute's behaviour is simply one way of satisfying legitimate heterosexual needs and is a commercial occupation.

Public order offences are considered as contrary to the system of morals or standards of proper conduct but social condemnation is mild. Indeed there is a dilemma between criminal action as opposed to no action at all against behaviour such as prostitution. Attitudes toward prostitution have varied historically and today they differ widely. The attitudes toward and the social status of the prostitute according to Davis vary according to three conditions: (1) if the prostitute practices discrimination among customers, (2) if her earnings are used for some socially desirable goal, (3) if she combines with her sexual role other more acceptable roles. In Latin America prostitution is prohibited by law but people tolerate it in urban areas. Prostitution is opposed because of: (1) degradation of the prostitute, (2) effects on general law enforcement through police protection, (3) effect on marital relations, and (4) the patronage of prostitutes by youths.

CRIME AND SIN

For the sake of scientific study, the sin, the vice, the tort, the immorality etc. have been dealt with differently in criminology. A crime is an act against society or law or both for which it is penalised. Keeping this definition of crime in view, it will be beneficial to differentiate all these concepts from crime.

All the acts against religion are considered sins. Thus, sin can be defined as the transgression of divine laws. Its very base is religion, while the crime is based upon laws. The concept of sin is traditional, based on orthodoxy and rigidity. The final decision in sin is taken on the basis of religious books while in the matter of crime, it is taken by the law court. Darrow has defined sin in a most suitable manner. In his words, "Sin... is an offence against God, a transgression against the divine law and any thought, desire, word, act or omission against that law."

CRIME AND VICE

Vices are, often, included in the category of crimes, but many of them, sometimes, are not regarded as crimes. There is a lot of difference in their aims. The criminal cause harm to others while the vicious or the wicked causes harm to himself only. For example, the vices like gambling, drinking, prostitution or deriving pleasure out of illicit sexual intercourse, cause harm to the individual only. As the harm to the individual indirectly effects the society, the later therefore prohibits the vices and generally gives punishment for them.

CRIME AND TORT

The encroachment of the individual rights is known as tort. Underhill has included the following actions in tort.

1. Encroachment of fundamental rights for which one is really authorized.

2. Encroachment of rights for which one is to suffer from personal loss.

3. The encroachment of social rights of an individual. The losses which can be compensated are counted as tort. The torts can be compensated, but in a crime a due punishment is given compulsorily by the law itself. In tort the man who has been injured or damaged by the vicious act, applies to the court for the compensation while in the matter of crime, the state itself punishes the criminal. The expression, interpretation or any sort of article which defames a person for nothing, or trespassing by force are clear examples of torts.

THE CRIME AND IMMORALITY

All the actions against morality, social patterns or values, or those which are generally thought improper, are put into the category of immorality. It is not necessary that all the immoral acts are crimes. For example, telling a lie is not always a crime but it is in fact an immoral act. Immorality is decided by the intention, not by its result, while a crime is declared by its effect. To explain the immorality in detail is the subject matter of Ethics. The study of tort is conducted by the law. Interpretation of sin is the subject matter of religion. Therefore, here, only the vices shall be discussed. In the study of vices, from the sociological point of view, the study of sex vices is the most important one, as in social disorganization, it plays a very important role.

ANALYSIS OF SEX INSTINCT

The sex instinct is the natural human instinct. It is only due to this instinct that there is a great attraction among the individuals (male and female). This attraction develops into deep intimacy in the favourable circumstances. This intimacy inspires the individuals of opposite sex to love one another. This love, generally ends in sexual intercourse between female and male. If this intimacy does not end in intercourse, the love advances towards idealism or high type of sentiments for humanity. This mutual love can't be left free in the society because it does not confine only to that extent. Again as the result of mutual intercourse, inspired by love, there is always a danger of pregnancy. And in the near future the very issue which is to take root, has to become a good, responsible and a promising citizen of the country. In order to achieve this very aim, due care and nourishment is necessary. This role can be played more successfully only by a family than by any other institution. The institution of family has come into existence only to bring up the children and control the sex instinct. It has been observed that an uncontrolled sex instinct produces many acute social problems and disorganises the personality of an individual. On the other hand the suppression of this instinct strengthens some other injurious activities, like that of cruelty and violence. Therefore sex instinct can neither be left uncontrolled nor suppressed totally. Moreover, sex instinct may be called an animal instinct, but the same, in its cultured and well developed form inspires love in a wider sense, the best emotion in human beings. Thus for its proper development and right direction of marriage, control has been established by the society in some form or the other.

SEX VICES

Every human instinct can be divided into two forms — healthy and perverted. In a healthy form, it is advantageous and good for the proper development of the individual as well as of the society. This is included in good behaviour. Within the limitations of matrimonial ties, the male and female enjoying love and sexual pleasure, are called well behaved, cultured persons. But in its perverted form every instinct is harmful to both, the individual and the society. The instinct is a part of our structure. We get natural pleasure by its fulfilment. But its perverted form is harmful to both the individual and the society. Therefore, in the absence of love, all the sexual relations, based on any other ground or the sexual perversions are called sex vices. The foremost example of sex vices is the prostitution. In it the very basis of sexual relationship is either money or only sexual pleasure, not love. From the psychological point of view many sexual perversions are taken as sex-vices. The sex-perversions like Masturbation, Anal eroticism, Sadism, Masochism, Scaptophilia, Frotteurism, Exhibitionism, Homosexuality, Transvestism, Infanto Sexuality, Betio Sexuality and the Nacrophilia etc. are the signs of mental deformities.

All the above mentioned sex vices are responsible for the individual disorganisation and as more than one man take part in them, they cause social disorganisation. Most of them except prostitution, are the subject matter of the abnormal psychology and in these cases, mental treatment is needed. Hence, here, only the sex vice prostitution will be discussed in detail.

The sexual impulse is natural to man. Both man and animal feel attracted towards opposite sex due to natural and normal development of the sexual impulse. The mutual attraction makes persons come closer and this proximity of body and mind generates feeling and emotion of love. This feeling of love culminates in the proximity of bodies in mates and the result is the obvious bliss of sexual intercourse. In the absence of the opportunities to consummate sex hetrosexually, man may seek self-gratification or gratification through homosexuality. He may also succeed in sublimating the sex energy and canalize it to creative and constructive channels. The paradise of man and woman in an unfettered embrace is a dream of the visionary. As a matter of fact society tries to restrict and control the sexual contacts between man and woman. The main reason for this is that sex is not a mere play; it procreates. Man and woman multiply to produce their replica. The children born out of love and sex play cannot be left untended; otherwise there will be chaos in the society. They must be properly reared up, given adequate opportunities for development. For this purpose society has the institution of marriage. The purpose of family is not only to help bringing up of children but also to restrict the unfettered expression of sexual impulse. The experience shows that promiscuous and unbridled sex harms the personality and leads to personal and social disorganization. The free love also breeds violence and jealousy, rape and murder. Though unbridled sex is harmful, too much repression of sex is even more harmful. In order to strike balance between unbridled sexual indulgence and total repression, every society has invented the institution of marriage in one form or the other. The balanced sexual expression is only that which fits in well in the personality structure of man and also which is within the accepted social limits. These limits of course vary from one society to the other.

Each instinct of man has two sides, healthy and morbid. The healthy expression of instinct promotes individual as well as social welfare and also increases the sense of well-being. A married person enjoying marital bliss and procreating strong and healthy offsprings commits no vice. As a matter of fact he is doing his duty. This is a healthy aspect of sex. But the morbid and perverted sex is wasteful and harmful to both individual and society. Though sexual indulgence is no vice and each man has his own capacity for sexual indulgence, perverted sex which harms the personality of man and perpetrates cruelty and injustice on others is vicious. The prostitution is harmful inasmuch as in it the bond between sex and love is severed and the personality of others is exploited. Rarely does a prostitute derive true sexual bliss. As a matter of fact too much friction in her body may become painful in the end. Besides she or he risks venereal disease. A prostitute as a matter of fact caters to a number of perverted desires of man which he cannot satisfy with his wife. The main among these are :—

(1) A man may have himself masturbated or may masturbate a prostitute. There may be communal masturbation by digital or artificial methods.

(2) A man may commit cunnilingus on a prostitute. He may ask her to commit fellatio on him or they may indulge in soixanteneuf, i.e. Sixty-Nine.

(3) A man may commit buggery or sodomy, i.e., may enjoy her *per anum*.

(4) A man may have various types of sex shows performed by prostitute, may or may not participate in these.

(5) In some towns there are prostitutes specializing in dog-show, donkey-show, self-abuse session, group sex etc. They also specialize in sadism as well at masochism.

Thus we see that prostitution is a repository of the entire gamut of perverted sex.

WHAT IS PROSTITUTION?

For practical, law-enforcement purposes, the definition of prostitution has usually not been too difficult. The prostitute defines herself when she agrees to have sexual intercourse with a person (not her husband) who offers her money for engaging in the intercourse, which may be coital or extra-coital.[1]

1. Benjamin, H., *The Prostitute in Society*, Mayflower Books, London, 1964, p. 24.

The average person doubtless defines the prostitute rather similarly: She is a person who will enter into sexual relations with anyone, or with almost anyone, who is willing to pay her for so doing. In August 1951 issue of the *International Journal of Sexology*, Albert Ellis wrote, commenting on Benjamin's definition:

"Under this definition (given above), commercialized prostitutes would certainly be included, whether they accepted many or a chosen few paying partners. But also included would be girls who trade their sexual favours for food, entertainment, or other gifts; and wives who, having no love and no sex desire for their husbands, continue to have sex relations in order to maintain the socio-economic benefits of marriage." He then adds :

"Now if prostitution is seen in this light, so that all persons who barter sex favours for non-sexual gains are realistically viewed as prostitutes, then, I should think, it would be easier for writers on the subject to agree as to prostitution's desirability. My own feeling would be that anyone who engages in sex activities when he or she has no sexual or amative desire for the partner...is hardly in enviable position. At the same time, I should also feel that anyone who cooks or manufactures shoes, or writes a book, or does any other kind of activity, which he does not enjoy, but for which he derives other socio-economic gains, is also in an unenviable position, and ideally should certainly be looking for a more enjoyable occupation. Since, in this rather grimly realistic world in which we reside, we all tend to have to do many things which we do not like to do, it is difficult to see why prostituting ourselves sexually should be considered much worse than our prostituting ourselves vocationally, artistically, or otherwise."

Perhaps with an eye to the exclusion of such persons as wives, mistresses, and employee, and for other reasons also, the word indiscriminate (or, sometimes, promiscuous) is brought into play as a qualifying adjective — in some cases achieving such prominence in the minds of the definition-makers that a prostitute is defined by her promiscuity, whether she is paid for it or not (as in no less than sixteen states — at last-count — of the U.S.A.). For example, the Ohio law (U.S.A.), reads: "The term 'prostitution' shall be construed to include the offering or receiving of the body for sexual intercourse for hire, and shall also be construed to include the offering or receiving of the body for indiscriminate sexual intercourse without hire."

Henriques has suggested that ".....any satisfactory definition (of prostitution) would have to include the whole range of venal sex activity. A suggested form might be the following : Prostitution consists of any sexual acts, including those which do not actually involve copulation, habitually performed by individuals with other individuals of their own or the opposite sex, for a consideration which is non-sexual. In addition sexual acts habitually performed for gain by single individuals, or by individuals with animals or objects, which produce in the spectator some form of sexual gratification, can be considered acts of prostitution. Emotional involvement may or may not be present."[2]

2. Fernando Henriques, *Prostitution and Society*, Vol. 1, MacGibbon and Kee, London, 1962, pp. 17-18.

Henriques is correct in noting that "emotional involvement may or may not be present" — something denied by those who define prostitution in terms of the absence of emotional involvement, and especially of sexual responsiveness on the part of the prostitute — but otherwise he has opened a variable Pandora's Box. Objections to certain aspects of his definition have already been raised. We will mention some of them. What, for example, is to be understood by the words "habitually performed ?" The question is no new one. Mantegazza[3] has noted that St. Jerome (after Ulpianus) defined a prostitute as "she who abandons herself to many men." Montegazza takes note of the ambiguity present in the word "many" by remarking: "A certain medieval casuist, not at all parsimonious in such matters, would have it that no woman was to be looked upon as a prostitute until she had given herself to at least 23,00 men. Other would reduce this figure to form 40 to 60."

One notes that St. Jerome does not include in his definition the element of remuneration. Thus, he apparently includes promiscuous women generally. So, too, as we have noted, are promiscuous women defined (legally) as prostitutes in some sixteen states of the United States. Sherwin[4] has observed that there thus exists in those 16 states no adequate legal distinction between prostitution and fornication — although the penalty for one may be considerably more severe than that which may be imposed for the other.

Kingsley Davis[5] once remarked that "We cannot...define human prostitution simply as the use of sexual responses for an ulterior purpose. This would include a great proportion of all social behaviour, especially that of women.... It would include the employment of pretty girls in stores, cafes, charity drives, advertisements. It would include all the feminine arts that women use in pursuing ends that require men as intermediaries, arts that permeate daily life and, while not generally involving sexual intercourse, contain and utilize erotic stimulation.

Goldberg[6] argues that the so-called temple prostitutes were not really prostitutes at all. He says, "It is the motive that determines whether a sexual union is prostitutional or not. Certainly, the woman who came piously to a temple, waiting in prayerful mood to be chosen by anyone at all, be ever so unattractive physically, and receiving for herself no monetary or material compensation — certainly, this woman cannot be called a prostitute." One might compare this to a statement on the matter by Maryse Choisy,[7] who vigorously declares that "Between a sacred courtesan and a call-girl there is the same difference as between a priestess who offers holy wine and a bartender."

Nonetheless, Goldberg and Choisy are in a decided minority and the designations sacred prostitute and temple prostitute are still widely in use,

3. Paolo Mantegazza, *The Sexual Relations of Mankind,* Eugenics, New York, 1936, p. 255.

4. Rovert Veit Sherwin, *Sex and the Statutory Law,* Oceana, New York, 1949, Part II, p. 7.

5. Kingsley Davis, 'The Sociology of Prostitution,' *American Sociological Review,* October, 1937.

6. B.Z. Goldberg, *The Sacred Fire,* University Books, New York, 1958, p. 73.

7. Maryse Choisy, *A Month Among the Girls,* Pyramid, New York, 1960.

applied both historically and contemporaneously as in the case of the Devadasis of present-day India.

PROSTITUTE CUSTOMER RELATIONSHIP

An analysis of the nature of prostitute-customer relationship will help in arriving at a satisfactory definition of prostitution the following are the important points in this connection :

1. Commercial. Sexual intercourse with a prostitute, as distinguished from intercourse under almost any other condition, is unique by virtue of the fact that each coition or extracoital sexual act (or series of coitions or extracoital acts, as in all-night arrangement) is paid for separately and at the time, and usually in cash. Sexual relationships with wives and mistresses may be equally commercial, but only rarely is there payment for each sexual visitation.

2. Transient. Another characteristic of the typical prostitute customer relationship, as compared to most other sexual relationships, is its transiency (and, usually, brevity).

3. Impersonal. Typically, as is often noted, the relationship between the prostitute and her customer is comparatively impersonal, especially on the side of the prostitute. Anonymity is maintained in most cases.

4. Predetermined. Affection, tenderness, and mutual respect are often, though by no mean always, wanting. Only the customer, ordinarily, is motivated mainly by a desire for sexual pleasure. In a sense, for the participants, the relationship is unusually well defined. What is to be provided and what is to be received are predetermined and mutually understood to an extent seldom present in other sexual relationships.

These are some of the factors of Prostitute-Customer relationship which help to define prostitution and the prostitute. Consequently, we may only say that prostitution, typically, will overlap marriage at one point, be distinct from marriage at another, will overlap promiscuity at one point, be distinct from promiscuity at another, and so on.

The much-sought-after, clear, concise definition of prostitution one which will exclude all acts and persons not intended to be excluded probably remains to be formulated. We have not succeeded in formulating such a definition, and have only provided some criteria which should be helpful in evaluating individual cases. Nevertheless, we are faced with the practical necessity of sometimes speaking of "prostitution" and of "the prostitute" as if prostitution and prostitutes could be generally defined : "We, must, therefore, have some kind of operational definition, and there seems no alternative but to designate as prostitutes-qualifying where essential those persons who are regarded by our society generally, and by our society's laws in particular, as engaged in what is commonly and legally defined as prostitution (exclusive of those statutes which label prostitutional acts for which no payment is made or expected). At the same time, we will keep in mind the manifold deficiencies of the definitions."[8]

8. Benjamin, H., *The Prostitute in Society*, p. 31.

DEFINITION OF PROSTITUTION

It may be of some interest, before departing the subject of definitions, to give some representative specimens. The reader should by now, be able to detect their deficiencies.

1. *M. Choisy in 'A Month Among the Girls'.* "Prostitution starts when the giver becomes a seller. What is love if it isn't a gift?"

2. *G.R. Scott in 'History of Prostitution'.* "A prostitute is an individual, male or female, who for some kind of reward, monetary or otherwise, or for some form of personal satisfaction and as a part- or whole-time profession, engages in normal or abnormal sexual intercourse with various persons, who may be of the same sex, or the opposite sex, to the prostitute."

3. *A. Flexner in 'Prostitution in Europe'.* "Any person is a prostitute who habitually or intermittently has sexual relations more or less promiscuously for money, or other mercenary consideration."

4. *H. Ellis in 'Studies in the Psychology of Sex'.* "...a prostitute is a person who makes it a profession to gratify the lust of various persons of the opposite or the same sex."

5. *W.J. Robinson in 'Medical Sex Dictionary'.* "Prostitution is indiscriminate sexual intercourse for pay."

6. *M. Ploscowe in 'Sex and the Law'.* "...if the woman offers to satisfy sexually in any manner whatsoever any man who meets her terms and conditions, she is prostitute."

TYPES OF PROSTITUTES

The following report on prostitute stratification in China was given by Magnus Hirschfeld upon his return from a world tour in the early 1930s.[9]

"Chinese prostitutes, wrote the famed sexologist", may be divided into five groups:

"The sing-song girls, who correspond somewhat to Japanese geishas, may be seen in great numbers, very prettily dressed and bejeweled, with charming innocent faces, usually riding in their rickshaws two by two, later to disappear, tripping gracefully, into the restaurants and hotels.

"The lowest stratum are the 'wild chickens' or 'streetwalkers', who, from nine to one o'clock at night, occupy large blocks with their 'amahs' (older servants) usually standing on the sidewalk, but frequently to be taken along.

"Still lower in this lowest class of prostitutes are the 'salt-water girls' (also called pheasants), who only try for sailors and therefore take their stand near the harbor.

"Between the two extreme groups, the sing-song girls and the 'wild chickens', there are the 'private', 'semiprivate' and 'public whores'. The 'private

9. Magnus Hirschfeld, *Men and Women*, Putnam, New York, 1930, pp. 71-72.

whores' are mostly sing-song girls who have come down in the world; the 'public whores' have usually worked up from the lowest class of 'streetwalkers'."

He adds, "To the Chinese, the European way of despising girls whom one uses for sexual pleasure seems an inexplicable contradiction. That is why they are even less inclined than the Japanese to regard prostitution as a shameful trade."

Hirschfeld also observed the prostitutes aboard the famous Flowerboats, or floating brothels, of Canton. He saw rows of boats "like floating streets of brothels. On the brightly lit decks the prostitutes exhibit themselves before gaily painted backgrounds.... ".

According to H. Benjamin, writing in *The Prostitute in Society*, the following are the important types of prostitute found in modern societies :

1. The Call-Girl. Greenwald writes that: "While the dictionary defines the call-girl as independently operating prostitute, I am using the term in the special way in which I know it. The call-girls in this book are the aristocrats of prostitution. They live in the most expensive residential sections of our large cities; they dress in rich, good taste. They charge a minimum of twenty dollars per sexual contact."[10]

Because her income is greater and because she spends more time with each customer and because not so many men are able to afford her services, the call girl typically has fewer sex contacts than do other financially successful whores. She may exercise what Greenwald terms the call-girl's "prerogative of refusal" the right to turn down any customer who for one reason or another, is distasteful to her. Some call-girls deny that they are prostitutes precisely on this basis; the prostitute is indiscriminate; they, so they say, are not.

One recalls the old story of the woman whose maid admired her new coat. "Where did you get it?" inquired the maid, "I slept with a man and made him so happy that he bought me this 500 dollar," said the woman. Sometime later, the maid appeared wearing an identical coat, "Where did you get it ?" the woman inquired. "I slept with five hundred men and made them so happy that they gave me a dollar apiece (or a piece)," said the maid.

2. The Streetwalker. Streetwalking is probably the most ancient of prostitute operating methods. It is also the method most objectionable to many persons, because of the streetwalker's "high degree of visibility."

In the Nineteenth and early Twentieth Centuries, prostitutes were sometimes permitted to work in bawdy houses specifically with the aim of getting them off the streets, where they would not be able to solicit, or even have to be seen by, "decent people." Historically, since earliest times, the streetwalker has been regarded as being at or near the bottom of the prostitution ladder. Her fees have traditionally been lower than those 'received by most other types of prostitutes' and she has been, in general, a less attractive type, of course, there have been striking individual exceptions, and still are today.

10. Harold Greenwald, *The Call Girl*, Ballantine, New York, 1958, p. 1.

3. Bar Prostitutes. R.E.K. Masters talked over the past 15 years with hundreds of young bar prostitutes in most parts of the United States. Most of them are not full-time whores, but are girls supplementing incomes earned as barmaids, B-girls, waitresses, etc. Some "hustle" only when they are between jobs, or in case of financial emergency. Since the closing of most American brothels, this group may well constitute a majority of all white females presently engaged in prostitution in the South, South-west, and Midwest United States. Certainly, if one excepts a few large cities they constitute such a majority.

4. Brothel Prostitutes. There certainly exists and existed no single "type" of brothel prostitute, or brothel. Houses of prostitution traditionally have ranged from the most elegant, catering to the most affluent and best-educated members of our society, down to the most sordid, catering to the lowest levels of male humanity with all gradations in-between. Girls working in the various types of houses were selected by and large with a view to their capacities for meeting the needs of the respective clienteles.

5. Camp Followers. Camp followers, in the broad sense, are simply prostitutes who gather and operate where large numbers of soldiers, and other servicemen are stationed, and who serve principally the sexual needs of those males, although civilians are seldom discriminated against. They are usually prostitutes of the bar girl and brothel girl varieties, more attractive than the average street-walker, not up to the standard of the too expensive call-girls.

Edouard de Beaumont, in his curious volume *The Sword and Womankind*, remarked of the camp followers of the past:

"From times most remote, hoardes of women were want to follow armies in the field...'A portion of the booty made by Mars in war ever goes to the profit of Priapus,' is the moral appended to a certain Bithynian fable."

6. Interracial Prostitutes. A good many prostitutes have members of all races among their customers, but the customers are not solicited or accepted primarily on a racial basis. We will deal here mainly with those women who intentionally specialize in a race or races different from their own, taking advantage of such racial barriers as exist, or unconsciously exploiting the radical difference in the service of neurotic goals.

The great majority of interracial prostitutes in the United States are Negro females specializing in white males, and white females specializing in Negros and sometimes Latin and Oriental males.

7. The Fleabag. The "fleabag" or prostitute whose customers are skid row males, is the lowest of the low in the hierarchy of American whoredom. Typically, she is aging, unattractive, and alcoholic. She cannot, of course, afford to be a narcotics addict. She works skid row because she no longer can attract any but humanity's flotsam and jetsam. In some cases, she is probably the skid row male's female counterpart and feels at ease only with other derelicts.

Some of the fleabag prostitutes are 60, 70, even 80 years of age. Many are venereally diseased. Their fees are most often determined on a "What the traffic will bear" basic and the traffic usually won't bear much. Seldom will the prostitute receive more than 2 dollars from a customer, and sometimes she will have to settle for considerably less. Fifty cents is not an unusual price for a skid row pair to agree upon, often after much haggling. The customer may bring along a bottle of cheap wine to "liven up the party."

The fleabag leaves skid row and her "profession" only when she dies or is placed in an institution.

8. Dance Hall Prostitutes. There remain in some cities, although they are less numerous than in the past, dance halls employing "hostesses" who either dance or "sit it out" with males purchasing tickets entitling them to a stipulated number of minutes of the hostess' time.

Girls and women employed in these establishments range in age from the late teens and early twenties up into the forties and fifties, with a rather surprising number in the older age groups. Some hostesses are quite attractive, but most are only fairly so. A few are not bona fide females, i.e., are homosexuals and female impersonators who probably in all cases are thought by their employers to be women, but who in some cases are known by other hostesses to be males.

9. Beat Prostitutes. Some girls living as members of the "Beat Generation" and subscribing to the values characteristic of that sub-society, reportedly engage in prostitution as a matter of principle and in accordance with an ethic which may or may not be rigidly adhered to.

10. Eldery Prostitutes. Gerontophilia, or the desire for a sex partner much older than oneself, is a not uncommon aberration. Probably in most cases it attests to incestuous cravings: A young man unconsciously equates the older woman with his mother; a young girl equates an older man with her father.

Several years ago, in Italy, a "ring" of "grandmother prostitutes" was uncovered by the police. The "ring" clientele consisted almost exclusively of young men. It is such elderly females, trading on their age and on the aberrant desires of young males, that we have in mind when mentioning a category of "elderly prostitutes." National newspapers carrying matrimonial and get acquainted advertisements quite often carry ads by young men seeking older and elderly women. Neither are marriages between young males and much older females particularly rare. We might add that it is singularly fortunate for some of these grandmother types that such a deviation exists. Otherwise, most of them would long since have had to go out of business.

11. "Gimmick" Prostitution. What we have in mind here are special techniques for marketing prostitution and unusual *modus operandi* of prostitutes. These include auctions and raffles, billboard and newspaper advertisements and call-girl directories, credit card schemes, travelling brothels, window displays of harlots, and so on.

12. Fricatrice and Feliatrice. The Fricatrice or the prostitute specializing in masturbating her customers and Feliatrice or the prostitute specializing in fellating her customers are seldom to be found in the United States. The prostitute specializing in anal intercourse is so rare that we seem to be wanting a term with which to refer to her, so where she is mentioned at all she is likely to be (mis)called a pederast, a sodomite whore, analist, or by some other term that leaves much to be desired.

13. Fetishism and Sadomaschoism. Both many individual prostitutes and some brothels cater to almost the entire gamut of sexual deviations. And almost every kind of deviate, the extreme sadomasochist most often excepted, is able to find prostitutes willing to provide for his (or her) needs. The text books even recount cases of procuresses who have kidnapped women and children and placed them, for a substantial fee, at the disposal of lust-murderers.

14. Adolescents. A great deal is heard today about high school girls living at home with their parents and pursuing prostitution as an avocation, sometimes for "kicks", sometime for money, probably most often for both. The tendency seems always to regard this phenomenon as something unprecedented — which, of course it is not — and to serve it up as evidence of the "widespread moral decay" in U.S.A. Since comparatively few girls of this kind are ever formally charged with prostitution, or their activities otherwise recorded and the records made public it is impossible to say whether adolescent, school-girl prostitutes are more numerous now than at various time in the past.

15. Child Prostitutes. Child prostitution apparently is as ancient as civilization. Temple prostitutes were sometimes no older than 7 years, as in Babylonia, where they practiced their calling in temples of Venus at that age. In ancient Egypt, also, the prostitution of young girls was a religious practice, so that, according to Strabo, some of the most beautiful and highest born Egyptian maidens were forced into prostitution, and they continued as prostitutes until their first menstruation.

CAUSES OF PROSTITUTION

The causes of prostitution may be grouped under the following classes: (1) Predisposing, (2) Attracting, and (3) Precipitating factors.

1. Predisposing factors are such elements in the prostitute's background as the "broken home", parental (especially maternal) promiscuity, approval or tolerance of prostitution in the immediate social milieu, and trauma productive of certain types of neuroses.

2. Attracting factors are the comparative advantages of a prostitute's career for a particular individual : larger earnings, an easier life, a more interesting or exciting life, for some the expectation of sexual gratification, and so on.

3. Precipitating factors include economic pressures, no chance for a desirable marriage, enticement or persuasion by a pimp or other prostitutes, an unhappy love affair, a good opportunity, *et cetera.*

According to Harry Benjamin and R.L. Masters, the most important and decisive of these advantages, which may also be reasons why women become prostitutes, may be summarized briefly as follows :

1. Economic Rewards. The economic rewards of prostitution are normally far greater than those of most other female occupations. This comparatively high remuneration is not only for actual services rendered, but also for the chance the women is taking when she engages in illegal activities. Some feminists, law makers, and other favouring equal punishment of the prostitute's customer, overlook this point — that the prostitute is paid so much for doing so little precisely because she is required to take risks that the customer does not share. We do not insist that, when the driver of a truck carrying explosives is blown to bits, his employer should share his fate. Logically, where prostitute and customer are alike punished — share the same risks — prostitute fees should be reduced considerably. Should this occur, and in the likely event that few customers were deterred by possible penalties, the probable effect would be an increase in the number of contacts with prostitutes because customers would have more money to spend for such contacts. Imposing penalties on customer of prostitutes might conceivably deter a few cautious or undersexed individuals; but probably an equal number would regard the danger as a challenge. Most, of course, would simply ignore the law such as the laws against adultery and fornication. An attractive, fairly intelligent girl, when working in a large American city as a call-girl with good connections, may earn several hundred dollars a week. A few earn considerably more.

2. The opportunity for adventure. What is regarded by the potential or actual prostitute as the excitement and glamour of the life is often a decisive factor. Many prostitutes, especially when they are working for a "high-class" madam, call house, or brothel, or are working for themselves in a wealthy neighbourhood, meet some intelligent, prominent, and affluent males with whom they would never get acquainted under ordinary circumstances. So long as a girl is able to remain in the upper, or even middle, echelons of whoredom, her life may be in fact much more interesting and exciting than that of the average secretary, hope-girl, or other working female.

3. Attractive and Busy Life. Prostitution seems to many an attractive, easy, undisciplined way of life. A minimum of intelligence and initiative are required from the prostitute who is content to simply "get by". Thus, the field naturally is a catch-all for the lazy, the mentally deficient, the inadequate but not necessarily severely disturbed personalities, etc. The contemporary streetwalkers, and the girls who solicit in taverns, are largely free to choose their own working hours and are accountable to no employer for their behaviour. Often they are able to choose customers to whom they are in some way attracted. The Voluntary Prostitute, not atypically, speaks of the pleasures of being able to "do as I please", of "not punching any damned time clock", and of "getting paid for screwing a guy I liked anyways" i.e., would probably have accepted as a bed-partner without charge under other conditions.

4. Sexual Pleasure. A small minority of prostitutes are so highly sexed that they enjoy many or most of their sex activities. Such women may find a life of prostitution virtually ideal — and otherwise would be adulterous wives or fornicating single women, and in either case more or less promiscuous. Kinsey and his associates found that, although most women are not so easily aroused as men, 2 or 3 per cent are far more interested in and responsive to erotic stimuli and sex relations than any male. It is likely that some prostitutes are members of this minority.

CAUSES OF PROSTITUTION IN INDIA

The social researches made so far into the causes of prostitution in India reveal that females are drawn into it for a variety of reasons. A study of Kanpur prostitutes has revealed that though a majority of prostitutes have taken to their profession due to extreme poverty and hunger, there are many who have willingly adopted it after a series of love exploits. Though the economic factor is quite important it is liable to be overemphasized. The citing of hunger and poverty as reasons for prostitution seems to absolve the prostitutes of all blame and they feel that this way they can win over the sympathy of society. Like the causes of prostitution the causes of prostitution mongery are also varied. The main cause of prostitute mongery is lust for novely in the field of sex. Too much familiarity breeds contempt. This is nowhere more true than in the case of sexual instinct. Repetitive sex is extremely boring and depressing. Through his monumental researches into sexual behaviour of American men, Dr. Kinsey has reported that people go to prostitutes because this is the most economical means of having variety of sexual experience. Compared to the marriage, concubinage, adultery and illegitimate liaisons, going to prostitute is safest, least risky and least complicating. The chief causes of prostitution can be classified in the following categories:

(I) Economic causes

(II) Social causes

(III) Psychological causes

(IV) Biological causes

(V) Religious and cultural causes.

(I) Economic causes

Though the economic compulsions constitute the major factor in the causation of prostitution it is by no means the only and exclusive causes of the phenomenon. It is not the cause that every prostitute accepts money for her services or that all prostitutes hail from indigent homes. There are many prostitutes who hail from well-to-do families. In India, of course, there are many prostitutes who are compelled to adopt prostitution to feed themselves and their dependents. However, poverty is not the only economic factor, there are many other factors which are economic. The economic factors are comprised of: (1) Poverty, (2) Under-age employment, (3) Unhealthy working conditions, (4) The pollution and corruption in Industrial centres, and (5) Immoral traffic in women and children.

1. Poverty. As referred to earlier the poverty is the main economic factor responsible for prostitution. A woman who is unable to get any gainful employment and who has no supporter must either starve to death or earn her livelihood through prostitution. The illiterate and semiliterate women cannot easily get employment. More often than not they have to sexually gratify their prospective employers. Many parents feel so utterly helpless that they prostitute their own children. The maidservants are often objects of the lust of their employers. The concept of poverty however is relative. A woman may prostitute herself in order to live well and give first-class education to her children.

2. Under-age employment. Many females have to work in hotels, offices, industry and shop at immature age. At this impressionable age they are easily misled by lust-seekers.

3. Bad working conditions. In India many women are able to get employment through intermediaries. These intermediaries and agents recruit women and keep them under their mercy. Whenever opportunity offers itself they exploit it fully and often succeed in receiving sexual bribe. Once a woman falls prey to their lust they in no time make a professional out of her.

4. Pollution and Corruption in Industrial Centres. The living conditions in most of the industrial centres are barbarous in India. Living accommodation is scarce and whatever is available is in slums. Due to paucity of accommodation most of the workers are compelled to leave their family and live alone. In the absence of family cinema going, gambling etc. make prostitute mongers of these persons. The industrial towns have busy brothels and innumerable prostitutes. In India women are paid less wages than men. Therefore contractors make it a point to recruit maximum number of women in the labour force. These women are easy prey to the lusts of contractors and their friends. Due to poverty and habit the labour women wear scanty clothes and often their raw bodies are exposed to full view of these lust-seekers. In slums the unmarried girls have to witness sexual activities of their relatives and are often seduced prematurely. The precocious development of sex often drives women to prostitution.

5. Immoral Traffic in Children and Women. Many tender girls are kidnapped from their homes by unscrupulous gangsters. They properly train them in the art of prostitution and when these girls mature they are sold.

(II) The Social Causes

The social causes are extremely important factors in encouraging and promoting prostitution. The social factors are comprised of: (1) Family causes, (2) Marital factors; (3) Bad neighbourhood, and (4) Illegitimate motherhood.

1. Family Factors. A study of London Prostitutes published as *Women of the Street* reveals that most of the prostitutes are connected with family troubles. Their parents were either living separately or their family relations were so strained that as children they were left to their own machinations and received no love. An unloved child when she grows up offers all of herself to any one showing any degree of love and affection. The children of criminals show a marked tendency to become prostitutes. If the mother is characterless and has to carry her clandestine liaisons, she rarely escapes the eager eyes of her daughter. Often it happens, that a man sleeping with mother succeeds easily in seducing the daughter.

2. Marital Factors. Many a superstitions prevalent in India force women into prostitution. For example widow-remarriage is still frowned upon. But as a recent Hindi film 'Phir Bhi' depicted even a middle aged woman is unable to eliminate and repress her physical needs and that the more you fight against them the more passionate and demanding these become. Therefore the widows unable to remarry due to social stigma may fulfil their physical needs by self-abuse, seducing of young etc. But as these are poor substitutes for the real sex, they may choose to become prostitutes. Secondly, in India it is still common to marry persons very young. If these girls become widows they often do so when they are very young. In Indian homes, particularly in villagers and poor, the illicit connections are common. Even brothers stoop so low as to have sex connections with their sisters. As a matter of fact there is no relationship so sacred that it does not get sometimes consumed by the fire of passions. Evidently these illicit connections are temporary and do not meet the sex needs of young women fully. Therefore, they seduce their servants or expose themselves to outsiders. Due to the irregular sexuality, unable to satiate their desires, they take prostitution as a last resort.

3. Bad Neighbourhood. The children living near brothels or in the company of immoral persons become so used to seeing sex trade that they come to accept it as normal. The brothel keepers usually haunt these areas for their prey. The children who get exposed to sex business want to have these exhilarating experiences at the first available opportunity. The young boys are lured to serve as sex slaves of wealthy sex crazy women. A recent survey of an American slum revealed that a woman of more than fifty would lure couple of boys to her apartment, offer them food and drink. Thus in a subtle manner she would develop intimacy and engage in weird sex circus with them. She would have them play with her and was able to satisfy five boys at a time.

4. Illegitimate Motherhood. The women who become pregnant as a result of their liaisons and who cannot get abortion get exposed in society. No body wants to marry them but everybody wants to enjoy them sexually. Desperately such women prefer to become regular prostitutes.

(III) Psychological causes

There are some psychological facts which tend the person towards prostitution. A woman who is frigid becomes desperate. She tries one man after another. Because of frigidity she is unable to experience pleasure and becomes a prostitute by trial and error. Some women are incapable of submission. In order to assert their independence they consort with other men. There is a psychological abnormality known as troilism. A husband who suffers troilism wishes to watch her wife submitting to the embraces of another man, sometimes he wants another woman to embrace his wife sexually and at the same time he sodomises her. It is not possible to go into the full range of psychological factors.

(IV) Biological Factors

The persons born with defective sex organs or overactive glands may feel compelled to seek sex gratification in a bizarre manner.

(V) Religious and Cultural Factors

In India there has been religious sanction to prostitution. In South, every family was supposed to offer one daughter to the temple where apparently she was supposed to serve gods with total dedication. They were known as Devadasis — god-slaves. But in actual practice they lived a life of prostitution. In ancient and medieval India prostitutes enjoyed the status of courtesans, that is, a pleasure girl of courtiers and kings. These courtesans enjoyed high status in society. There are certain religious sects in India as well as abroad in which the priest has the right to deflower every newly married girl. The polyandry and polygamy sanctioned by many societies are sophistications of prostitution. A man with numerous wives has to countenance lesbianism and illicit liaisons with servants in his family. Even eunuchs are used by such women to obtain relief. It is natural that if a person lives in a highly lascivious and erotic atmosphere his or her desire is multiplied and seeks release in normal as well as abnormal channels. In many cultures a guest is honoured by the offer of wife or daughter by the host.

All causes enlisted above contribute more or less to prostitution. The prostitution has a very long and varied history. As a matter of fact it is considered to be the oldest profession in the world. In modern times it is becoming fashionable to consider prostitution a necessary part of the society. Many favour development of the art of prostitution on the pattern of geisha girls of Japan. That prostitution is and may be a preferred profession and avocation with some people is clearly shown by the following remarks of George Ryle Scott, "In many cases the mother is a prostitute herself, the father is a pimp and they send their daughters in the streets with slightest compunction, often themselves initiating her in sexual intercourse."

DISADVANTAGES OF PROSTITUTION

Just as the advantages prostitution affords may help induce some women to become, and especially to remain, prostitutes, so the disadvantages of being a prostitute induce some women to quit "the life." These disadvantages are in the main evident. Probably the worst aspect of the profession in many parts of the world is its illegality which forces the girls and women of the demimonde (half-world) into the underworld, where they are likely to become truly demoralised. There, they may be preyed upon by hoodlums, who extort money from them for "protection" or simply demand "a cut" without offering anything in return but the prostitute's safety from the hoodlums themselves. Police officers are sometimes included in the ranks of these hoodlums.

The illegality of prostitution means for many women frequent jail terms. For some, it also means venereal infections from time to time. Underworld associations tend to lead to alcoholic and narcotic addiction. In some cases, a large portion of girl's earnings is paid out in attorney's fees. Much of what is left may be squandered on a succession of pimps and other exploiters.

For the lower level prostitutes, prisons and hospitals may alternate. With every arrest and conviction, a more hardened, resentful personality is likely to emerge. These frustrations and miseries also are conducive to alcoholism and drug addiction — for many, the end of the road.

For psychological as well as practical reasons, a prostitute's expenditures tend to be high. Some women, who entered the profession, intending to store up a "nest egg" and then retire or go into some other business, recognize eventually that the nest egg is difficult or impossible to amass, even though earnings are large. Such girls understand, too, that the longer one remains in "the life", the more difficult it becomes to make a satisfactory new life outside it in the "respectable world". Prospects of later exposure and disgrace, as consequence of past arrests and an everbroadening circle of former customers, increase. And finally, the woman with foresight is aware that her profitable years in the profession are definitely numbered. She will remain attractive only so long. After that, she will sink lower, and lower, receiving less and less money from more odious males. If she is to marry, or otherwise make some provision for her later years, it must be accomplished while some attractiveness remains.

There exist no firm data concerning "what happens" to most prostitutes: how many die in the profession, and from what causes : how many leave it otherwise; and the circumstances under which the latter depart. It is probable, however, that most white prostitutes who are neither drug addicts nor alcoholics leave the profession by way of marriage-proposals of marriage, many of course unacceptable, being received by almost every prostitute. Harry Benjamin interviewed in U.S.A. Most former Negro prostitutes probably end upon the welfare rolls. Of those who die in the profession—white and Negro—most are undoubtedly alcoholics and/or drug addicts. They must continue to engage in prostitution as long as possible to finance their liquor and drug habits. These are the women who die of exposure, general physical debilitation, infections etc. An unknown number of the drug addicts are murdered by "pushers" — by means of the "hot shot", an overdose of heroin, or narcotics laced with strychnine or some other, lethal poison. According to addicts, such murders are numerous; but they seem almost never to be mentioned in the newspapers. The addicts explain this by saying that the police policy is to consider "a dead junkie good riddance," and never to bother with investigating such homicides or listing them as such. One has, of course, no means of determining the truth of this contention. And deaths of this kind are in any case not caused by prostitution; they are a problem for the investigator of addiction. Mortality, is high among junkies and alcoholics generally.

Some of the more strong-willed and less neurotic prostitutes do just decide to get out of "the life" and find some other sort of employment — a decision much more likely to be effectively carried out when made by the prostitute herself with no official coercion involved. Some women manage to save enough money to retire or to go into a legitimate business. When brothels were common, many of the more intelligent prostitutes eventually became madams; but that opportunity for advancement is rare today.

As for those who do not marry, take other jobs, die, retire on their earnings, or sink to skid row prostitution, the same fates await them as await other aging unemployables: the welfare rolls, charity and mental hospitals, and other public-supported institutions. Women whose later lives are lived out on such a basis, usually have remained in prostitution as long as they were able to earn a living in it. Then, unfit for anything else, they become burdens on society. This, one notes, might be avoided were prostitution a legal occupation and prostitutes obliged to provide for their futures through Social Security or some other kind of pension plan. An enormous amount of misery, as well as expense to the taxpayer, might thus be avoided.

PROSTITUTE "REHABILITATION"

The acquired craving for the excitement of the prostitute's life-stated negatively in many instances by way of assertions that any other sort of life is intolerably dull — is encountered by almost every investigator of prostitution; and most dramatically and frustratingly and disillusioningly by those who attempt the forcible or coercive rehabilitation of prostitutes.

One of the earliest known attempts at prostitute rehabilitation was that made by the Empress Theodora, wife of Justinian, emperor of the Roman Empire of the East. Herself a former prostitute, Theodora was determined to "redeem" other women of her one-time calling. At great expense, she had constructed on the south shore of the Bosporus a palace wherein harlots were to be confined and re-educated. One night, in Constantinople, 500 whores were seized upon her orders and forcibly conveyed to the palace. They were well-treated there, and given whatever they wanted with the exception that no males were permitted to enter the establishment and no prostitute was permitted to go outside it. It is recorded that many of the girls perished of sheer ennui, or escaped that lingering death by suicide. The experiment eventually had to be abandoned as a total failure.

In the 1830s, in New York City, a somewhat similar attempt was made by a Mr. McDowell and a group of women supporters. So-called Magdalen asylums were established for the proposed rehabilitation of harlots. All day long the prostitutes were kept busy singing hymns, praying and listening to sermons—massive dosage of what we might now term brain-washing. But those unfortunate women, too, would have perished of sheer boredom had not most managed, by night, to slip out of windows and unguarded door and engage in the practice of their profession. Even so, only four girls remained at the asylum for a full month, rehabilitation was claimed in only one case, and the experiment was terminated. Of course, one must admit the possibility that all-day praying, hymn-singing, and listening to sermons, would soon prove unendurable whatever ones profession and might drive even a pillar of virtues into harlotry, if not to attempted homicide upon the would-be reformer.

Most prostitutes definitely prefer "the life" and even when they do not will stubbornly resist any attempt by others to reform them. Many, however, and particulary those of the Voluntary Prostitute group, do leave the profession voluntarily.

PROSTITUTE REHABILITATION IN INDIA

In India prostitution is a grave problem. Though exact data in not available, the number of registered prostitutes must be well over a million. In Mumbai there are 269 brothels and 12,058 prostitutes. In West Bengal there are 5,095 brothels and 45,000 prostitutes. In Bihar, in Mirzapur and Patna there are 100 brothels. In Motihari and Champaran there are 14 and 12 brothels respectively. In Orissa, in Ganjam city alone there are 200 brothels. In U.P. there is a sizable number of prostitutes in Allahabad, Banaras, Kanpur, Meerut cities. As a matter of fact there are sizable number of prostitutes in every big town in India.

Social and Moral Hygiene and After-Care Programme

The Social and Moral Hygiene and After-Care Programme undertaken on the recommendations of the Advisory Committee on After-Care Programmes and of the Social and Moral Advisory Committee, is aimed at the after-care and rehabilitation of rescued women and adults and children discharged from correctional, non-correctional and care institutions. The programme is implemented by the State Government with Central assistance, with the Central Social Welfare Board and the State Social Welfare Boards being associated with it in an advisory capacity. Forty-six after-care homes, providing training to 1,794 inmates and meeting other needs of the inmates, and 89 district shelters, receiving the discharged persons and sending them to the homes established under this programme, were sanctioned till the end of February 1962.

India being a welfare state, all our effort is underway to control and eradicate the curse of prostitution. Several laws have been enacted for this purpose. In 1956, Suppression of Immoral Traffic in Women and Girls Act was enacted, under which it was declared a legal offence to keep brothels, to entice girls and women and use them for prostitution.

All the provisions of the Act have been enforced throughout India from May 1, 1958. The Act prescribes punishments for brothel-keeping, for living on the earnings of prostitutes, for detaining a woman or girl in premises where prostitution is carried on, for prostitution in or in the vicinity of public places and for seducing or soliciting for the purpose of prostitution. The setting up of an adequate number of protective homes for the rehabilitation and the educational and vocational training of women and girls recovered and detained under the Act is also envisaged.

Rescue Homes and Reception Centres established under the After-care Programme can also be utilised as Protective Homes. About 100 Protective Homes (Government as well as private), having a total capacity of 4,419 inmates are reported to be functioning in the country.

Besides there are 80 Rescue Homes and 32 Rescue shelters to enable the stray women and prostitutes to find a place where they can receive preliminary training for rehabilitation in society. In the 3rd Five Year Plan five Protection Centres were opened in U.P. Besides above mentioned agencies, following other agencies are active to help and reform prostitutes and find them useful work. The Women Home, Chennai; Shardhanand Anath Ashram, Mumbai; The Good Shepherd Home, Chennai; Chrispins Home, Poona; The Salvation Army Home, Bengal; The Fendal Home, Bengal; All Bengal's Women's Union Home, Bengal; Khushalbagh Mission Orphanage, Gorakhpur; Mahila Anathalaya, Varanasi, are some of the important centres for rehabilitation of fallen women. But the measures being adopted to check prostitution are inadequate. It will need a concerted effort on the part of both public and government if the problem of prostitution is to be controlled.

QUESTIONS FOR EXERCISE

1. What is public order crime? Evaluate your answer with reference to prostitution as a public order crime.
2. Write short note on Prostitution.
3. Write short note on Causes of Prostitution in India.
4. Define Prostitution. What is being done by the state to eradicate prostitution?
5. Evaluate the efforts currently being made in India to curb Prostitution.

6
Suicide

Every six minutes a person commits suicide in the country and the total number of such deaths was 89,195 during 1994, an increase of 5.9 per cent over the previous year.

There were nearly 5,000 more suicides in the country in 1994 compared to 1993 and the suicide deaths increased at a compound growth rate of 6.2 per cent per annum against the population growth of 2.1 per cent, the National Crime Records Bureau (NCRB) said in a report.

West Bengal, which ranks fourth in the country's population, accounted for the highest number of incident of suicidal deaths consecutively for seven years, recording 12,389 suicides during 1994.

Followed by West Bengal, the other top risk states which reported high rate of suicides were Maharashtra with 10,782 suicides, Tamil Nadu (9,248), Karnataka (9,050) and Kerala (8,533).

Uttar Pradesh, India's most populous state, accounted for 7.8 per cent (6,938) of suicides in the country.

Among the Union Territories, Delhi and Pondicherry had maintained the status of reporting the highest and the second highest number of suicidal deaths during 1994. While Delhi reported a total of 803 suicides, Pondicherry accounted for 589 suicides during 1994, the report showed.

Lakshadweep reported one case of suicide during 1994, the NCRB said.

A study on suicidal tendencies revealed that undesirable conditions at home, like use of intoxicants, immorality, lack of parental love, poor parent-child relationship, too much of disciplining induce persons to take extreme step, the NCRB said.

Too harsh treatments, authoritarian attitude, parental discrimination in favour of a child and personality clashes affect the emotional balance adversely and may force persons to resort to taking the extreme step, the NCRB added.

Among the 14 specified causes, "dreadful disease" is the most important cause having 13.5 per cent share in total suicides, quarrel with parents-in-law or with spouse together account for 10.7 per cent of the suicides, implying that the three causes were responsible for nearly one-fourth of all the suicides in the country.

Poison remained, as in the past, the prevalent means for committing suicides. It accounted for 34.8 per cent of suicidal deaths followed by hanging (23.4 per cent), fire/self-immolation (11.5 per cent), and drowning (9.4 per cent).

The four means accounted for 82.8 per cent of the total suicides leaving 17.2 per cent share to other means, the NCRB side.

The study showed that 18 per cent more males committed suicides than females during 1994 and in the state of Jammu and Kashmir females outnumbered males.

The cause profile of minors (under 18 years of age) showed a different scenario with highest suicides due to "love affairs" (13.2 per cent) followed by 'failure in examination' (9.4 per cent) and 'dreadful disease' (8.8 per cent), it said.

The highest incidence of suicides for both the sexes occurred in the age group of 18 to 30 years (43.8 per cent) followed by 30 to 50 years with 32.2 per cent.

In rural areas, girls work on an average of nine hours a day, 315 days a year and shoulder manifold responsibilities notably sibling care as early as at the age of six or seven.

Early marriage, also thrusts a girl into the role of a wife and mother at a time when she is still a child herself, the NCRB said, adding that unable to cope up with the tension and vagaries of life she is sometimes forced to take the drastic step of suicide.

Stating that it was a serious concern that very large number (11.2 per cent) of children were driven to commit suicides, the study said that perhaps children feel more neglected and emotionally vulnerable than before due to changed scenario of social order.

"There is an immediate need to take up extensive studies in this sphere so that remedial measures could be taken to curb this high rate of suicides amongst children", the NCRB noted.

WHAT IS SUICIDE?

Man naturally wants to live. He wants to maintain his body and prolong his life by all means available. In fact he spends good deal of his energy and resources towards finding ways and means to extend to the uttermost limit his longevity of existence on this planet, nay he dreams and wishes to conquer death and reverse the processes of ageing. He wants to avoid even minor injuries. It is often observed that a man involved in a major accident or a soldier injured by multiple bullet injuries when admitted to hospital is asked by the doctor: your left and right arm are affected by gangrene and these must be amputated to prevent general poisoning of the body immediately. May we proceed? The patient may feel depressed and, for a while, may think about the futility of life. But soon he recovers himself and asks of the doctor: Shall I be able to live and feel healthy? The doctor nods and the patient willingly consents. The self-same story is repeated again and again in the Emergency operation theatres of the hospitals all over the world. This confirms the fact, if ever a confirmation was needed, that this urge for survival is most deep-rooted and fundamental in man. As a matter of fact, instinct of self-preservation is primordial and pivotal of all other urges; because, without survival nothing can be worthwhile. All these facts, notwithstanding, some persons do put an end to their lives. Then there are some persons who individually and rationally choose to die. Such persons commit suicide, that is, sui (self)+cide (killing). Such cases are no doubt few and such persons are somehow abnormal; their reactions to life and certain events are extremely uncommon, not to be found in average man. Though these reactions to life and such individuals are very few and far between, they are to be found at all times in every clime and every society. Thus the act of suicide is universal and timeless; there is no society and no time where the acts of suicide are non-occurrent. However, suicide, besides being personal, is also a social event and is profoundly affected by social influences. This is why suicide has been universally considered a social problem. The study of sociology includes study of both social organization and social disorganization. In social disorganization we study those problems which disturb the social organization and are productive of subversion in society. Suicide is one such problem. Therefore, the study of suicide and an investigation of its nature and prevention form the subject matter of sociology.

DEFINITION OF SUICIDE

1. Encyclopaedia Brittannica defines suicide as "the act of voluntary and intentional self-destruction." This emphasizes two salient features of the act of suicide: (1) that suicide involves there "will" of the person, which consents and acquiesces in willing self-destruction; and (2) "Knowledge" that death is being preferred to a life and that reason in person concerned is aware of and has acknowledged this as a fact and accepted it as inevitable and non-avoidable. Another important fact brought out by this definition is that there is some sort of purpose behind the act of suicide and that without purpose suicide is not possible. Without desire there can be no intention; and desire presupposes some object or goal, that is, some purpose which has to be attained. Ruth S. Caven has defined suicide as "the intentional taking of one's life or the failure when possible to save one's self when death threatens."[1]

2. Suicide is an Act which Affects whole Society. If someone indulges in self-destruction or commits suicide, not only the members of his family but society as a whole is affected. This is true more or less in every case of suicide; but this is particularly so if the suicide is committed by an eminent scientist, scholár, artist, writer, social reformer etc.; because their death deprives the society of their valuable services and may mean an irreparable loss to the society. This fact is illustrated by suicides in recent years by eminent personalities Marilyn Monroe and Dr. Shah etc. by consuming an over dose of sleeping pills. Recently a Japanese writer of world renown and a recipient of Nobel prize

1. Caven, R.S., *Suicide*, Chicago, 1928, p. 3.

killed himself by cutting his throat. The loss of such persons is deeply regretted by society because society is poorer on account of their deaths.

3. Suicide is Symptomatic of Personal Disorganization. Only if there is total disintegration of the personality of man and he has lost his equilibrium, a person commits suicide. There cannot be an urge to put an end to one's life so overwhelming as to suppress or counter the deep-rooted instinct of self-preservation unless there is some fundamental spiritual unrest and the soul, so to say, undergoes sea-change and is topsy-turvy. The suicide implies complete loss of sense of values in the person and the consequent feeling of emptiness and unwholeness of everything every aim or object of living. There is so much mental and physical disintegration that the ultimate escape through death appears to be the only way out.

4. Suicide is Symptomatic of Social Disorganization. Besides, being a case of personal disorganization, suicide also indicates or is symptomatic of social disorganization. The personal disorganization as a matter of fact, is disorganization of a social unit; and inasmuch as a change or deterioration in the unit spell change or deterioration in the whole, individual disorganization is a product of and as well as produces social deterioration. Therefore, the fact of suicide entails some definite disorganization in the society. In the least, it clearly foreshadows following facts: the norms and values which underlie and govern the society are being seriously questioned and challenged in some quarters and that society lacks the flexibility to cater to or accommodate the serious dissent.

PSYCHOLOGICAL ANALYSIS OF SUICIDE

The problem of suicide is highly complex; it can be approached in numerous ways and from various standpoints. A number of eminent psychologists have discussed suicide from the view point of psychology. Among them Freud and Bunsel are the most prominent. Below we shall discuss the views of these authorities of the world of psychological learning and accomplishments.

(A) *Freud's Viewpoint.* The famous psychologist, and the father of Psychoanalysis, Freud has discussed the problem of suicide from his peculiar point of view and in the light of his remarkable psychoanalytical account of the whole gamut of human behaviour. According to him there is a fundamental biological urge which expresses itself in paradoxical and bipolar manner in which there is constant pull in opposite directions. Eros and Thanatos, i.e., an urge to live and wish to die are fundamental impulses which pull man in opposing directions and they fight for dominance. If, for some reasons, the wish to die gets precedence over the urge to live and overwhelms it, man's urge to live becomes dim and ineffective and he considers death to be a more basic mode of existence. To explain the fact of suicide, Freud makes use of one of the fundamental concepts of psychoanalysis, namely, identification. Identification is a mental process by which man considers some object, some goal or some idea to be so intimate that he would live only for the sake of them and without them everything is useless, devoid of meaning and value. Usually death-wish expresses itself in the form of aggression, hatred and kill-joy; but when and if the urge instead of remaining externalized becomes internalized, man identifies himself with his own destruction and commits suicide.

(B) *Karl Menninger's Analysis of Suicide.*[2] The theory of Menninger regarding suicide is, infact, a corollary of Freud's theory. He has analyzed only the Thanatos, i.e., the wish to die. According to him, the wish expresses itself in three forms: (1) the wish to die; (2) the wish to kill; and (3) the wish to be killed. Menninger has tried to explain suicide on the basis of this tripartite expression of the Thanatos, the Death-wish. According to Menninger the wish to die must be strong and pervasive in a man who commits suicide. Besides, he must have a pronounced aggressive urge be an urge to kill. Now, for some reasons personal, or impersonal, the urge to kill must be utterly frustrated. The urge to kill must be very intense and forceful but its expression must be balked by some countervailing objective factors. This would understandably generate extreme tension, which would be resolved only by internationalization of the kill-urge, transforming it into a wish to die, leading ultimately to suicide. In the process of internalization of the death-wish there results an identification of the man committing suicide with the object of his wish to kill.

(C) *Bunzel's Analysis of Suicide.* According to Mr. Bunzel, the psychological processes leading to suicide are exactly the same that lead to the disintegration of his personality. Following are, according to Bunzel, the reasons of personality disintegration:—

(1) Fear and Anxiety. The emotions of fear and anxiety are very dangerous inasmuch as the man who is afraid and anxious is ever indecisive. The balance and harmony of his wishes and desires is badly disturbed; he fails to think objectively and is liable to overreact. This overreaction to fear-stimuli results in development of phobias — the morbid fears. Mr. Bunzel has specifically referred to acrophobia, the fear of high places, in this connection. A man affected by phobia is not so much fearful of the stimuli as of his own impending death. He perceives death everywhere.

(2) The Inferiority Complex and its Fulfilment. A person affected by the feeling of inferiority totally undermines and saps the confidence of man in himself. He becomes convinced of his own futility and life is devoid of all meaning. Such a person is driven by inches to a situation where suicide seems to be the only possibility. When a person fails to get recognition for himself but finds that his mates and co-workers are eminently successful he feels he is worthless and that there is no point in his life. A gradual build-up of this feeling results in suicide.

(3) Hatred and Aversions. Every man has his dislikes and aversions; these assume the form of intense hatred of and opposition to certain things or persons. But, sometimes, by a psychological process of identification and internalization the hatred gets internalized and self-hatred leads ultimately to suicide.

2. Menninger, Karl A., *Man Against Himself*, New York, 1938.

(4) Criminal Sentiment. Sometimes a person suffers from deep guilt complex and feels himself a sinner or a criminal. At times this feeling of guilt becomes so pervasive that life to him is nothing but shameful and disgusting. Therefore suicide seems to be the only honourable way out of the misery of life.

CRITICISM OF PSYCHOLOGICAL EXPLANATIONS

Some general points emerge from the above discussion. All psychological explanations are as a matter of fact based upon imaginary concept. For example these are not empirical facts but merely figments of imagination that man has in him as fundamental instincts like the wish to die or an urge to kill. No empirical evidence can be adduced to confirm or disconfirm such assumptions, which are purely speculative. Therefore these psychological explanations are at most possible though unconfirmable. They may prove out to be clever guesses and, therefore, ultimately true.

The psychological explanation of suicide has been criticized from another point of view. It is asserted in psychological theories that emotions like fear and anxiety, complexes like inferiority and guilt, instincts like Eros, Thanatos, aggression, self-esteem etc. are responsible for suicide. But, as a matter of fact, all these things are to be found present in each and every individual. Therefore all should commit suicide. This not being the case, some factor or factors other than the above mentioned must be crucial in determining suicide.

CHIEF CAUSES OF SUICIDE

A person who commits suicide must be doing so under extreme pressure and in a very complicated and involved set of circumstances. When, due to some reasons, the condition of a person becomes utterly miserable and forlorn and all hopes die before him he feels driven to a precipice of life where a plunge into abysmal sea of nothingness seems to be the only possibility and hope. It is certain that there is no single factors. Of course, in some cases, a particular factor may prove crucial and decisive and in others, a different factor may fill the bill. It is not easy to enumerate and study all the factors involved in suicide. Some of the important factors are the following:

(1) Psychological Causes of Suicide. The psychological factors play a vital role in causing suicide. In majority of the cases of suicide, the persons committing suicide, are mentally disturbed or mentally imbalanced. The chief psychological factors leading to suicide can be classified as follows :

(A) *Abnormal Feelings*. There are certain feelings and emotions, which are universally present but in acute and abnormal form these produce unsettling and upsetting effect upon man. For example, fear, anxiety, frustration, hatred, violence, vindictiveness, guilt and inferiority feelings can assume such dimensions that man loses his sanity. Overwhelmed by anyone or a combinations of these he loses his capacity for discrimination and rational thought. Consequently, he becomes abnormal and over-reacts to various stimuli. In the result, what will not even move an average man, produces deep tremor and earthquake in over-reactive person.

(B) *High level of Intelligence*. Compared to the individuals of average abilities and intelligence, far more suicides are committed by persons of bright intelligence and high talents. It is a commonplace that highly talented doctors, scientists, writers and artists are usually the persons who commit suicide. The suicides committed by practical-minded persons of average talents are relatively fewer number. The main reason for this is of course higher level of intelligence; but, besides, the life-problems of such individuals are far more complex, intricate and involved. It is precisely on account of life that these persons commit suicide.

(C) *Peculiarity of Personalities*. The various surveys conducted regarding the personality structure of the individual committing suicide reveal that those individuals who commit suicide are introverts and serious. Extroverts and social-mixers are rarely found to commit suicide. Whereas the extrovert persons are social and have many friends they share their joys and sorrows and rarely take anything to heart, the introvert persons are in the habit of feeling deeply and internalizing various emotions to which they are subject. Thus introverts are many more times suicide-prone than extroverts.

(D) *Mental Illnesses*. There are mental illnesses which become important factors in suicide. The mental illnesses and abnormalities are resultants of the loss of emotional equilibrium and frustrating life situations which imbue deep anxiety, dismay, despair and forlornness. The chief mental illnesses are Schizophrenia, Melancholia, Depression, Mania, acute Paranoia etc.

(2) Geographical Factors. Certain climatic and topographical factors are considered contributory to the phenomenon of suicide. The incidence of suicides is much higher in colder climates and mountains than in the warmer and tropical climates and plains. Many reasons are given for this phenomenon.

(3) Economic Factors in Suicide. The economic factors, too, play very important part in inciting suicide. Many other factors too are attached with the economic factors and act like adjutant causes or subsidiary factors. For example, the rise and fall of economic status lead to corresponding rise and fall in the prestige of a man. It is, therefore, not unusual to find that loss of fortune leads to suicide by a businessman. But actually the economic factor does not operate directly, because loss of fortune may not, and usually does not, mean that the man is going to starve. Then why commit suicide ? The real reason is that the prestige and social status enjoyed by a multi-millionaire is different from that of a millionaire. Therefore even when a multi-millionaire finds himself reduced to the status of a millionaire he suffers a loss of face and feels so depressed that he commits suicide. Below we shall discuss some of the categories of persons who commit suicide because of economic factors :

(I) *Suicide in Businessmen*. The pursuit of business is directly governed and influenced by economic factors like supply and demand, market trends, public tastes, governmental policies, war and peace etc. Due to any of these factors, change in government, outbreak of war or cessation of war, there can be havoc and great upheaval in the economic fortunes of businessmen. Suppose there is revolution and the new government divests businessmen of their economic possessions, to-day's multi-millionaire becomes a commoner. Unable to cope with the economic catastrophe, many a businessman commit suicide. Again, outbreak of war with a neighbouring country may spell in disaster of a businessman who has all his business contact with that country. The loss of fortune means loss of face, too; and loss of face so upsets certain individuals that they prefer death to dishonourable life. In business many evil practices flourish. The defection of funds, blackmail giving and taking bribe sea-laden entertainment of high business executives and officials etc. are some instances of them. Anyone who is found and caught may find his image darkened overnight and then life looks meaningless. In such circumstances, too many people commit suicide.

(II) *Special Occupations and Suicide.* Persons involved in certain special occupations are suicide-prone. Generally highly mobile persons commit suicides. An English survey reveals that the incidence of suicide in England is very high among hoteliers. In Germany and France call-girls and pornographers often commit suicide. Some of them commit suicide on such trivial matters like death of a pet animal. Middle-aged prostitutes are very much suicide-prone. The bankers, the playboys, the cinema and theatre personalities and artists are also very much suicide-prone. Another category of professionals who are predisposed to suicide are military top brasses; they always prefer death to professional disgrace. The harakiri of Japanese army generals is proverbial.

(III) *Unemployed Suicides.* Another category of persons who are forced to commit suicide on account of economic factors are persons who are unemployed and feel therefore wretched and failures. A talented artist, engineer, scholar or scientist, if unable to secure employment, feels deeply let down and this produces in them symptoms of manic-depression and the person feels he has no alternative except death. In India the incidence of suicides in this category is progressively rising on account of growing unemployment among highly educated.

(4) Family factors in suicide. By family factors in suicide is meant divorce, marital incompatibility, death etc. The various factors shall be discussed below:

(I) *Suicides due to love.* Since times immemorial there has been a strange attraction, a feeling and an urge to commune, between sexes. This has taken numerous forms such as courtship among young boys and girls, a strange desire to be near, to possess each other. Marriage is an institution invented by society to control this impulse and regulate it into socially acceptable channels; but there have always been some people who have defied the bonds imposed by the society and pursued their instincts unwaveringly. These people have to put up with the guiles and deceptions of lovers or beloveds. There are cases in which a lover is jilted by the beloved or she cheats him to settle the score. In these cases, some persons of highly emotional type are unable to suffer separations or the shock of deception and they put end to their lives. In certain cases, a young girl allows full rein to her natural instincts and in the process gets pregnant. She is shocked, asks the lover for marriage; but the lover quietly gives her a slip. Under these circumstances, many girls are known to have committed suicide. Still there is another category of cases in which the social conventions, parental prohibitions or difference in religion, social and financial status come in the way of successful romance, young couples are driven to suicide. Many Mumbai films are based upon this theme.

(II) *Marital Problems and Suicide*. In India, marital problems at times assume vicious proportions and produce a lot of mental ills. According to religious sanctions and social conventions and traditions, the parents of bride are required to pay handsome amount of cash, ornaments, clothes, furniture and many other things by way of dowry. In some communities this involves exorbitant expenditure and the parents of many a young women are unable to marry their daughters on account of fabulous sums involved in dowry which they simply cannot afford. Many such girls are condemned to prostitution and many of them put an end to their lives on account of the miseries they undergo. When some of these girls happen to remain unwed for a long time they feel highly depressed. This is because an unmarried woman is looked down upon by the society. Unable to cope with social contumely, calumny and disgrace, many of these unfortunate women put an end to their existence.

(III) *Suicide in Marriage*. There are occasions in the marriage span when suicide appears to be inevitable. In accordance with the Indian traditions marriage in an overwhelming majority of cases are arranged and the boy and the girl have had no chance of any premarital acquaintance. They are utterly ignorant about the habits, likes and dislikes of each other. There are some cases where these habits are so divergent, that quarrel between husband and wife becomes inevitable. There are cases where the mates are sexually incompatible. This incompatibility leads to an ever-increasing psychological tension and dislike. This mutual recrimination gradually becomes more and more vicious and in certain cases are a source of so much unrest that the person concerned commits suicide. Sometimes sexual habits, performances and failures can be a great source of shock, disturbance and disequilibrium, all of which leads man to commit suicide. If a person is weak in sexual performance or incompetent or impotent, the contempt of his spouse may become unbearable and he may end his life. Similarly, a barren wife is subject to great deal of ridicule and such a sensitive wife may commit suicide unable to cope with social obloquy.

(IV) *Suicides in women due to Family Causes*. In many Indian homes the condition of women is not satisfactory. In many homes women are maltreated. They are severely ridiculed for insufficiency of dowry, for failure to conceive, for bringing ruin to the family. The bitter and persistent quarrels of mother-in-law-bride, sister-in-law-bride are proverbial in Indian homes. These become so vicious that the bride may feel so utterly humiliated as to commit suicide. A widow in Indian Society has very hard time. She is not supposed to marry, she is not to dress properly, but must remain shabby. If the widow is young, she is prey to evil impulses of many. Being human, she craves love and thus is easily seduced. All these factors in certain cases lead the widow to commit suicide. A barren-woman is a queer phenomenon in Indian Society. She has no relief, no escape from constant social calumny, contumely and ridicule. She seeks help from quacks, fakirs and god-men but all this increases the burden of her heart and she ultimately embraces death as the only honourable course open to her.

(V) *Bodily causes of Suicide.* Many individuals commit suicide under the impact of certain physical affections. As regards the suicides induced by physical conditions one thing must be borne in mind, that is that in India more women than men make attempts to commit suicide even if they are not always successful. A survey regarding suicides reveals that maximum number of attempts at suicide are made by women between the age of 15 to 25. This is the age when a women discovers her sexuality and is greatly perturbed by the complicatedness of her sex-mechanism. A regular monthly discomfort and feeling of ill-at-ease mark the life of the women. This biological phenomenon upsets quite a few and they attempt to finish their lives. Besides this there are many chronic diseases which are incurable and a source of unrelenting mental and physical pain. The sufferings of cancer, paralysis, diabetes, impotence, and certain mystery diseases prove so uncomfortable that life becomes a continuous drama of pain having no episodes of pleasures. Under these conditions many persons finish their existence by committing suicide.

(VI) *The Religious Factor in Suicide.* There are some religious causes of suicide, too. The true religion always dissipated the urge to suicide. All great religions of the world condemn suicide. Only in Greek religion, which is really pre-historical, was suicide considered admissible. No true religion, however, sanctions suicide; it considers it a heinous sin. The line of argument is that since man has no power to make life; he has equally no right to take life whether his own or of somebody else's. Therefore killing whether homicide or suicide is a sin. But with the decline in the sanctity of religion in modern times, the people do not have such implicit faith in religious beliefs as they used to have in past. Consequently, religion no longer acts as a powerful prohibition against suicide.

(VII) *The Social and Cultural Factors in Suicide.* The social structure and cultural system under which an individual happens to live greatly affect and influcncc his beliefs, ideas and behaviour. A well organised and balanced social system help a man a great deal in leading normal and useful life. On the contrary, a disorganised society and divided or contradiction-ridden culture have the opposite effect, that is, due to cultural and social conflicts the individual also suffers from contradictory hopes and fears and in the process he becomes like a house divided against itself. If there is any cultural lag in a society it has adverse and injurious effect upon the individual. This adverse effect is at times so cataclysmic that it leads to suicide. Below we discuss some of these factors category-wise in order to appreciate the cultural impact fully:—

(i) *Social Disorganization and Suicide.* Consequent upon social disorganization, every social norm and value becomes a casualty. Along with disintegration in the social fabric, there is chaos in values. This chaotic situation of social norms and moral sanctions leads to relaxation of social control over human behaviour. In the result, there is rising spiral of crimes in society. Drug-addiction, religious and moral experimentalism, prostitution, violence, theft and dacoity become the order of the day. In such a vicious and polluted social atmosphere, the day-to-day life becomes chaotic, a senseless movement. In the extreme cases of individual disorganizations suicide results.

(ii) *Urbanization and Suicide.* The ancient India was a country of villages. Now there is rapid urban development and big towns and cities are springing up fast. With the rapid industrialization and urbanization the basic rural structure of society with its norms and values has undergone sea-change, all around there are crises, in particular the crisis of values. The intimacy and communal character of living so characteristic of the rural society has undergone overnight change and given way to informality aud aloofness characteristic of urban life. Thus life and behaviour has become artificial. This outward artificiality seeps into the soul of man and renders his life rabid and meaningless. A gradual change from rural to urban society would not produce so much social and personal disorganization as is the case if this change is rapid and sudden. The rapid and sudden change produces varying degree of imbalance in individuals. Some are able to absorb the change and make adjustments with it, while others fail and cave in. The extreme cases of those who are unable to make adjustments are potentially suicide-prone.

(iii) *War and Suicide.* The wars also have direct impact upon suicides. The period of war is a period of great excitement and thrills, particularly if the war is not directly involving the populace. The cessation of war suddenly leads to depression because all of a sudden quiet and slow movement replace excitement and thrills of war. Certain individuals are so deeply affected by this change that they commit suicide. Besides, in vanquished the sense of defeat, depression and failure is pervasive and may induce an urge to end the sorry state of affairs by plunging into the abysmal sea of nothingness.

(iv) *Unbalanced Socialization and Suicide.* The incidence of suicide is also directly affected by the processes of socialization, their proper and improper ways and means. If the socialization of the child is not proper and according to social standards and expectations, his mental and emotional development is retarded. Under these circumstances the child grows into an unbalanced, ill-adjusted person who feels himself a misfit everywhere. Driven by desperation of constant humiliation and failure such a man commits suicide.

The above discussion makes explicit some of the major factors of suicide. As a matter of fact, suicide is a complex phenomenon; there is a variety of factors and numerous causes responsible for it. In a particular instance of suicide, psychological factors may be dominant, but in other instances social or cultural factors may be dominant and still in another ease the cause of suicide may be stoppage of ·var or fall in the share value. Therefore, it is not possible to assign primacy as a causal force to anyone of these factors. Therefore we may conclude by saying that it is not possible to assert that this or that is the most crucial factor in suicide. We need to analyze the cases individually before we can say what are the factors of suicide in a particular case.

REMEDIES TO SUICIDE

The problem of suicide poses serious danger both to the individual and the society. As the social organization becomes increasingly, complex, the rate of incidence of suicide also rises. In India, consequent upon industrialization and urbanization the social organization is rapidly changing and this leaves many individuals maladjusted. On account of the increasing maladjustment, the incidence of suicide is showing an upward trend. The suicides have adverse effect upon the society and the nation, because, due to suicides, the nation loses the invaluable services of many persons. In critical social situations, as a rule, the suicides are committed by persons of high sensitivity, intelligence and talent. Naturally, it is a matter of grave concern to any nation if it starts losing its elite in suicides. However, suicide also has a chain reaction impact. If some notable personality commits suicide many more persons who are somehow holding themselves together, are deeply affected and their impulse to suicide is further strengthened. The suicides by famous scientists, writers, artists and politicians produce chain-reaction. On account of these incontrovertible facts it is the duty and obligation of the society and the nation to find correctives to the problem of suicide. But the important question is, what are these correctives? What steps can a society take to prevent occurrence of suicide ? Towards this end we have to eliminate those causes which lead to psychological and social tensions, cultural contradictions and produce personal and social disintegration. Following are the suggestions calculated to reduce or eliminate those irritants which induce suicide :

(1) Elimination of Factors Inducing Social Disintegration. In a disorganized and disintegrating society the incidence of suicide rises; therefore it is the duty of every nation and society to stem disintegration of the society and evolve ways and means which would produce social harmony and promote social peace and tranquility. The society should try to check and control crimes like violence, drug-addiction, sex offences, and marital infidelity etc. as these lead to rapid personal disorganization.

(2) Economic Reform. The economic factors play an extremely important part in causing suicides. The wide economic disparities and consequent class distinctions play havoc with the life of individuals. Due to widespread disparities society is divided into rich and poor. In such a society the money-power comes to play so vital a role that the social class, prestige and reputation rise and fall with economic possessions and dispossessions. Such a society cannot be harmonized; it will always breed conflicts and contradictions, till the society eliminates aggressive economic competition and reduces the overwhelming role of money and wealth.

(3) Religious Preaching. Indeed religion is always opposed to suicide and considers it to be a sin, a violation of the will of God. However in the modern society the spirit of religion is becoming weak and the restraint which was exercised by religious injunctions upon human behaviour no longer holds. Therefore it is of fundamental importance for every society that the spirit of religion should be revived and it is made to play the role of preaching love and harmony, forbidding violence and hatred. For this it is essential that various religious institutions should use their influence to propagate the sanctity of life and the value of love and harmony.

(4) Reform in the Institution of Marriage. A number of suicides in India are due to defective and retrograde traditions and conventions of marriage. For example, due to the institution of dowry, many deserving females are condemned to live the life of spinsterhood. This is obviously an abnormal condition of a nubile young damsel; but what is worse, such persons are socially stigmatized. Consequently, many such girls, unable to cope with the insistent natural urge become unwed mothers. Therefore, they are left with no alternative to suicide. Obviously, it is the duty of every society to remove from its social fabric irritants like these and also all other orthodoxies and harmful conventions which plague the society and undermine the moral and natural health of its members.

(5) Social Acceptance of Unmarried Persons. Our society is highly orthodox and conservative and in this society marriage for every young man and girl is considered in inevitability and anyone stepping out of this social barrier is subject to ridicule, calumny and contumely. However, it is now recognized by every enlightened person and society that the belief that marriage is an inescapable destiny of every man and woman is false and illconceived. There are in every society some persons whose fundamental nature and habits are incompatible with the institution of marriage. If such persons are forced to marry because of social pressure they find themselves in hell and to avoid and escape from the disgust and shame of life they commit suicide. No society has any right to interfere with the natural development of man and force upon him some artificial pattern. On the contrary society, must recognize the peculiar needs and urges of its members and suitably cater for these.

(6) Reform in Retrograde Social Traditions and Conventions. Generally the social traditions and conventions facilitate smooth movement of social life; but with passage of time they grow into orthodoxies and their observance becomes an end in itself instead of being a means of smooth social intercourse. These orthodoxies become hindrances in the way of social and personal developments. In Indian society evil customs like dowry, taboo on widow remarriage, casteism and untouchability destroy the real purpose and value of education and help increase psychological and social tension. The customs and traditions are indeed blots on the society and must be eradicated if there is to be peace and progress in the society and if the society is not to crumble under the weight of modernization, urbanization and industrialization. These orthodoxies are the chief causes of cultural lag and backwardness.

(7) Promotion of Healthy Entertainment. Entertainment is as necessary for the healthy and happy life as good food, home and other things. Entertainment is a great source of dissipation of tensions. Bad or sex-laden entertainment may thrill and produce temporary euphoria but in the long run it tells upon the mental health of the man. Therefore, it is the duty of the society to check wild pornographic display of dance, drama and cinema and to provide good natural and refreshing entertainment.

From the above discussion, it becomes plain what steps are necessary for the prevention of suicide. Indeed, the main cause of suicide is personal disintegration and the consequent imbalance of personality. Therefore all our efforts should be directed towards checking the factors which produce imbalanced and disintegrated personality.

DURKHEIM'S THEORY OF SUICIDE

Durkheim, the eminent French Sociologist, has made extremely minute and detailed study of the phenomenon of suicide. He has given his considered views and opinions in his world famous book *Suicide*.[3] In this book he has given a fine sociological analysis of suicide which is based on the theory of Sociologism or Collective Mind. In collectivism it is believed that each and every act of man is determined and influenced by the group or society. Indeed the individual acts are merely representative of the collective action and interaction. According to Durkheim Society is primary and the individual secondary; therefore society plays a primordial role and the individuals merely reflect or mirror those roles. Durkheim has studiously rejected the rival theories of psychologism etc. before propounding his theory of sociologism.

In putting forward his views on Suicide, Durkheim emphasizes the pivotal role that society plays in the life of the individuals. According to him, it is the social circumstances and the influence of the collective consciousness which are, in the main, responsible for the phenomenon of suicide. He says, "Suicide is an act which society disapproves although the collective conscience does approve of certain suicides of expiation."[4] Durkheim also showed that all other views regarding suicide are as a matter of fact conditioned by the prevailing social conditions and mirror the collective consciousness. All the alleged causes of suicide except Durkheim's own view are revelatory of the inner conscious workings of the collective mind. Some scholars have propounded the Geographical theory of suicide. According to them the incidence of suicides rises in summer months of May-June when compared with the winter months of December-January; but according to Durkheim though the stated facts are in order, that is, it is true that the number of suicides is higher in May-June in comparison with December-January, the weather conditions are not the true causes, they appear to be so to a superficial observer. But the real reason lies in the fact that inner social workings in individuals increase considerably in summer months. Therefore, it is not the heat but the social influences which

3. Emile Durkheim, *Suicide*, John A. Spaulding, New York, 1966.

4. *Ibid.*

account for suicides. Again, the psychological or sex factors alleged to be the causes of suicide have been explained by Durkheim on the basis of social conditioning. It is said that more men than women commit suicide. This is alleged to be due to sex difference; but, according to Durkheim, the real cause is not the difference of sex between men and women but the fact that men are more responsive to social conditions. Similarly, a depressed man commits suicide not because of depression but due to heightened sensitivity to social conditions in a depressed man.

The personal and psychoanalytical theories are similarly disposed of by Durkheim. As a matter of fact the psychological and personal factors are the resultant of social conditions and not *vice versa.* The indifferentism, hostility, aggression and hatred are also the responses to social conditions rather than being stimulator of social change.

Durkheim has classified different types of suicide on the basis of different types of personalities of men. He has recognized following three to be the fundamental:

(1) Egoistic;

(2) Altruistic;

(3) Anomique.

The main reason behind all the different types of suicides is the same, namely, social breakdown. A person commits suicide when there is disharmony and mal-adjustment between the personality of the individual and the social needs. When a person feels that he is a misfit in the society he feels impelled to commit suicide. Below we shall discuss briefly the different types of suicide.

(1) Egoistic Suicide. The suicides committed by persons who are self-centred and to whom self-regard is the highest regard are called egoistic suicides. On account of their self-centredness and lack of altruistic feelings, a sense of respect and regard for others, the egoistic persons are usually aloof and cut off from the main-stream of the society. They can never take whole-hearted interest in social projects. An overwhelming sense of self-regarded needs and heightened sense of self-importance leads to aloofness and in differentism and this grows into social alienation. This social alienation produces apathy. Being basically a gregarious animal, man is unable to cope with social alienation and feels impelled to commit suicide. Durkheim has tried to explain the egoistic suicide by illustrating its nature by various examples. According to him those persons who have none or few emotional attachments are more suicide-prone than those who have strong emotional attachment. Obviously, a man of strong attachments will always have a reason to live and can never experience the kind of apathy and vacuity felt by unattached individual. Generally single male or female are more suicide-prone than married persons. Widows or widowers are obviously predisposed to suicide. Similarly, persons who are issueless commit suicide in greater number than persons who are fathers or mothers. This fact can be proved true in fields other than family. Durkheim hastened to prove that all suicides connected with war are basically due to social causes. He freely grants the observation that there is sudden rise in the incidence of suicide upon the cessation of hostilities; but according to him, it will be very superficial to see war as the cause of this change in the suicide rate. Actually, there is great cohesiveness in social relations during war and a sense of common purpose and goal unite into well-knit social wholes. During war each person appears to be complementary to the other and co-operation is very real. But with stoppage of war all this is shattered. Soldiers who fought hand-in-hand are separated by wide distances. Nurses and soldiers whose romances flourished, all of a sudden everything comes to a dead stop. The social cohesion gives way to disharmony and discord. These social factors are the true causes of increase in suicide. Due to sudden disruption of routine in mutual relationship among soldiers, some soldiers, too, commit suicide.

The above discussion makes it very clear that the chief causes of egoistic suicide are social. It also is plain, upon Durkheim's analysis, that society is mainly responsible for suicide.

(2) Altruistic Suicide. According to Durkheim the second type of suicide is altruistic suicide. Such suicides are committed by individuals having a peculiar types of personality. An altruistic suicide is a form of sacrifice in which a person puts an end to his life by some heroic means in order to promote or further the interest of the cause or idea dear to him. According to Durkheim the persons committing altruistic suicide are those who attach great value and importance to the need and imperative of control. Compared to the value of society and its cause they consider their own personal life of no worth. For them the worthwhileness of their life lies in the maintenance and promotion of social forms of which they are shadows. Once such an outlook develops and takes firm hold of the man, such a person easily and willingly sacrifices his life for social causes, ends and purposes. As a matter of fact such a person considers himself only a reflection of the society and, therefore, of no worth and value in himself. Durkheim has illustrated altruistic suicide by the examples of suicides by soldiers which are due to rigorous and stentorian discipline. The ancient customs of *Sati*, in which a wife would willingly jump into the funeral pyre of her husband and thus end her life, is an example of altruistic suicide and can be explained as being due to rigorous social control acquiesced to.

(3) Anomique Suicide. According to Durkheim, the third type of suicide is *Anomique*. The type of suicides are concerned with social disorganization and imbalance. At the time when society is in a crisis, the social relations are disturbed and even disrupted; and at such periods and under the fluid and critical social conditions the personal and social ethics both become casualties. The values crumble and life becomes devoid of its guiding light. At such times the outlook of some persons suddenly undergoes critical change and results in dangerous developments. Durkheim has tried to illustrate this fact by giving examples from economic life. In critical periods there are sudden changes in the economic fortunes of people; multi-millionaires may become pauper overnight. Due to loss of financial fortunes many persons commit suicide. Now the fact is that neither economic prosperity nor economic poverty themselves can be causes of suicide. A sudden change must be producing repercussions and having reverberations on the social relations and conditions; and actually, it is these things which cause suicide and not the loss of economic possessions. What actually happens is that : man's social relations, status, regard and dispositions are affected by his riches or lack of them. Now a multi-millionaire is used to a particular status. He is honoured, respected and listened to by others. But if he loses his fortune his social relations are disrupted. If the change is gradual one adjusts to it with ease; but in case of sudden change no such adjustment is possible. Under these circumstances many people commit suicide. To a superficial observer the suicide is because of loss of fortune; but though there is loss of fortune, it is sudden and has social ties disrupted therefore, actually it is the social disruption that has caused suicide and not the loss of fortune.

CRITICISM OF DURKHEIM'S THEORY

Durkheim has given importance only to social factors in suicide and tried to relegate other factors to social factors and thereby has tried to establish the exclusiveness of social factors in the etiology of suicide. But this is a one-sided view. If it is possible to reduce non-social factors to social factors, it is equally possible to reduce social to non-social factors. For example, if we say that Mr. A committed suicide not because his wife slept with his boss but because his social ties with his boss were disrupted, we can also say that disruption of social ties is due to the character of man because Mr. B under similar circumstance did not commit suicide but settled the score by sleeping with his boss's wife.

QUESTIONS FOR EXERCISE

1. Define suicide. What are the main factors of suicide?
2. Discuss the causes of suicide.
3. Examine critically Durkheim's theory of suicide.
4. Write short-note on Suicide.
5. Discuss briefly Durkheim's theory of Suicide.

7

Alcoholism and Drug Addiction

Though alcoholism does not invariably lead to personal disorganization, it is undoubtedly an important cause of personal disorganization. In particular, the drinking habit among the poor and labour class has generated serious problems all over the world, and alcoholism among poor is dangerous morally, socially and economically. The poor drink usually to escape from their besetting worries which are largely due to indigency; but as is obvious, drinking can help only to perpetuate poverty and insolvency and by no stretch of imagination can be regarded as a solution of this problem. The excessive drinking robs man of his sense of discrimination; he is unable to distinguish between good and bad, right and wrong. This leads to loss of control and behaviour becomes involuntary and capricious. Thus alcoholism produces personality disintegration and is a chief cause of family disorganization. The poor in India remain permanently poor on account of alcoholism; their will to improve collapses and they accept their despicable existence as ordained and irretrievable. Thus alcoholism causes poverty and leads to huge waste of national wealth. The broken homes are invariable concomitants of alcoholic habit. In particular alcoholism affects the life of children and women very badly.

FORMS OF ALCOHOLISM

Some people take to liquor because of mental afflictions and emotional complexes; others drink though they suffer from no mental or other disease. Following are the main types of alcoholism:

1. Daily Liquor Consumption. With the exception of certain specific diseases this is invariably harmful. The liquor reduces tensions, dilates arteries and produces euphoria. In some exceptional cases its moderate daily consumption relieves nervous tension and induces good sleep. However medical advice is necessary in all these cases and it must not be self-prescribed.

2. Escapist Drinking. Some persons take liquor because under its euphoric spell a sense of well-being supervenes and thus they become oblivious of their nagging problems and worries. Though liquor does provide temporary relief it makes the problems worse because forgetting a problem does not mean that it has been solved. As a matter of fact man's capacity to cope with life situations becomes less and less due to the use of liquor. Thus poor remain poor or even become worse — moral degenerates and financial bankrupts.

3. Addictive Drinking. We may begin consumption of liquor for any reason but gradually it enslaves the man and he cannot kick it in spite of his best efforts. It is like a dangerous animal which as an infant looks so harmless, even charming; but as it grows it eats up the man.

The consumption of liquor is widespread in India. In Holi and other festivals a sizable majority of villagers and labourers drink. Even otherwise the habit is very widespread. Not only is liquor consumption common in India; but other intoxicants like Ganja, Charas, Bhang, Dhatura and Opium and its derivatives are widely used.

Though the rate of liquor consumption is very high in India, but undoubtedly there is some reduction in it due to prohibition policy of the government. But of late there are determined attempts to scrap prohibition and there is growth of liberalism and collapse of traditionalism. These factors are fast pushing up the sales of liquor in all states in India.

HARMFUL EFFECTS OF LIQUOR

The use of liquor and other intoxicants is harmful for every progressive and growing individual and society. It is harmful inasmuch as it impoverishes intellectually and morally softens and spiritually deteriorates the person addicted to liquor. Without weaning the poor from liquor no great economic or social progress in any country is possible. The following is the list of its harmful effects:

1. The Wastage of National Wealth. It has been estimated that a successful enforcement of Prohibition Policy would increase the purchasing capacity of people by rupees 140 crores; of this rupees 44 crores will be invested for productive purposes. It is obvious, therefore, that prohibition would save the country from huge wastage of national wealth.

2. Low Standards of Health. The consumption of liquor leads to deterioration of health. This may happen due to any of two following reasons:

(i) Liquor is narcotic and leads to nervous degeneration, liver cirrhosis, high blood pressure and host of other diseases and (ii) money spent upon liquor reduces one's resources and may not leave one with sufficient funds to buy nutritious food. The money which can buy gallons of milk is wasted on litres of liquor. The country-made liquor is often a great health hazard. Only in last two years several thousand people have died after consuming poisonous liquor in various parts of India.

3. Lowering of Efficiency. With fall in the standards of bodily health and mental agility, the fall in efficiency is but a corollary. The alcoholic is whimsical and incapable of sustained attention, concentration and putting in long hours of work.

4. Mental Imbalance. A man under the influence of liquor has no control over his will and is fickle minded. He is unable to think and work constructively. His vision and thinking gets blurred if intoxication is strong.

5. Increase in Poverty. In India the villagers and labourers drink in spite of their poverty. This obviously increases their poverty though it may provide them temporary well-being and euphoria.

6. Individual Disorganization. The consumption of liquor makes a man wayward in habits and whimsical in moods. He also loses all control over his will and his desire to grow and progress becomes feeble. He grows careless and indifferent and feels little difference between morality and immorality. All this produces personality disintegration.

7. Family Disorganization. More homes are broken due to drinking than any other single cause. This is easy to understand. As the moral sense of man is destroyed and his inhibitions removed, prostitution mongery and adultery are normal consequences of alcoholism. An alcoholic shows little respect to his wife or children. This leads to divorce and constant family tension.

8. Increases in Crime. Under the influence of liquor people act in unsocial ways as their inhibitions are removed. This includes murder, rape and other crimes. Moreover in order to meet the expense of drink a man may take to gambling or even theft.

9. Social Disorganization. All the above factors lead to social disorganization.

PROHIBITION IN INDIA

The Indian Constitution enjoins on the State to endeavour to bring about prohibition of the consumption of intoxicating drinks and drugs. In December 1954, the Prohibition Enquiry Committee was appointed to suggest a programme and a machinery for the implementation of the directive in the light of the experience of the State in implementing their prohibition policies in the past. The committee's main recommendation that schemes of prohibition be integrated with the country's development plans was affirmed by resolution of the Lok Sabha on March 31, 1956. The resolution recommended the formulation of a programme to bring about nationwide prohibition speedily and effectively.

The Third Five Year Plan has laid emphasis on prohibition being a voluntary social welfare movement, whose success depends upon (i) its acceptance as public policy accompanied by concrete administrative steps to make the policy a reality, (ii) support of large section of public opinion and active participation of social workers and voluntary organization, (iii) finding practical solutions to problems arising out of it, such as employment, and (iv) enabling State Government to meet possible loss of revenue on account of progress of prohibition.

A Central Prohibition Committee has been set up to review the progress of prohibition programmes, co-ordinate the activities in different States and keep in touch with their practical difficulties. The Committee also suggests ways and means to intensify propaganda in favour of prohibition, promotes research on the economic and social implications of prohibition and recommends measures to encourage and assist official and non-official agencies devoted to prohibition and temperance, propaganda, care and rehabilitation of alcoholics and drink addicts and scientific research in respect of problems associated with prohibition.

The progress in the enforcement of the prohibition policy in the different States and Union Territories of the Indian Union is briefly dealt with in the following paragraphs:

(1) Andhra Pradesh. Complete prohibition is in the districts of Anantapur, Chitoor, Cuddapah, East Godavari, Guntur, Krishna, Kurnool, Nellore, Srikakulam, Visakhapatnam and West Godavari. In the other districts, toddy and liquor shops have been shifted from populous areas.

(2) Assam. The dry law is in force in the districts of Kamrup and Nowgong, covering 19.2% of the area and 15% of the population of the State. In the other districts, measures to discourage the sale and consumption of liquor have been set in motion the more important of which relate to increase of rates of duty on both foreign and country liquor, stoppage of issuing new liquor licences, removing of liquor shops from industrial areas and tea gardens, the prohibition of serving liquor in public places and closure of liquor shops on national days.

Total prohibition of opium has been in force throughout the State since 1947. Seven opium addicts' treatment centres have been opened. With effect from July 1959, consumption of ganja and bhang has been totally prohibited.

(3) Bihar. A Prohibition Board to consider details of policy and to review the programmes of its implementation has been established. The work of preparing a phased programme has been entrusted to a technical committee. Among other steps taken to introduce gradual prohibition and to prepare the ground for total prohibition, mention may be made of the enhancement of duty and retail prices of counter spirit, introduction of the sliding scale system of settlements in respect of distillary liquor and drug shops, stoppage of sale on national days and closure of liquer shops for a period of 8 days in a month in certain areas of the State and a reduction in the sale hours of country liquor shops.

The supply of opium for oral consumption, except on certificates granted in limited numbers by approved medical authorities has been completely withdrawn since April 1, 1959.

(4) Gujarat. There is complete prohibition in the whole of the Gujarat State. Taluk prohibition drive committees and sub-committees of the block advisory committees have been set up. Similar committees at the village level are being formed with the help of the Panchayats.

(5) Kerala. Complete prohibition has been in force in the whole of the Kozhikode, Palghat, Cannanore and Trivandrum districts as also five taluks in the Quilon and Trichur districts and Fort Cochin area of Ernakulam district covering 58.8% of the area and 56% cf the population of the State. Advertisement and public inducements relating to drink have been prohibited. No fresh licences for liquor shops are granted. A State Advisory Board has been set up. Six

District Advisory Committees have also been established to enlist public co-operation for prohibition in the dry areas of the States.

All opium and ganja shops in the State have been closed with effect from April 1, 1959.

(6) Madhya Pradesh. Prohibition is in force in the districts of Sagar, Damoh, Narsimhpur, Hoshangabad, Khandwa and Vidisha, districts and portion of Bilaspur, Raipur and Durg districts and covering 16.4% of the area and 19.8% of the population of the State. A system of permits has been introduced in one tehsil of the Jabalpur district and one of Betul district. Among other steps taken are progressive reduction in the number of liquor shops, ban on advertisements relating to drink, prohibition of liquor, drinking in public places, progressive increase in the number of days on which liquor shops remain compulsorily closed, shifting of liquor shops from industrial and populous areas, enhancement of the price of intoxicants and encouragement of the consumption of healthy and refreshing light drinks.

The oral use of opium, except on permits issued by competent medical authorities, has been totally banned with effect from April 1, 1950.

(7) Tamilnadu. Total prohibition has been in force throughout the State since October 2, 1958. The enforcement of the prohibition law has been strengthened by providing enhancement of sentence, summary trials and control over sale and transport of molasses.

(8) Maharashtra. Total prohibition has been in force since April 1, 1961. Besides a State Prohibition Board, Taluk prohibition sub-committees have been set up in district development boards. Taluk prohibition drive committees and special committees of the block advisory committees have also been established. Efforts are now being made to establish similar committees at the village level. Subsidies are paid to welfare institutions, cooperative societies, village panchayats and municipalities for conducting Sanskar Kendras (Recreation Centres) for prohibition propaganda.

(9) Karnataka. Prohibition is in force in the entire State except in the district of Bangalore, Gulberga and Raichur. The dry area accounts for 81.1% of the area of the State and covers 79% of the production. To facilitate the successful implementation of the prohibition policy of the Government of Maharashtra, a ten-mile dry belt zone on the Maharashtra-Karnataka border in the Gulbarga district was created in July 1959. A Prohibition Board has also been set up for advising the State Government in the matter of effective implementation of the prohibition policy.

The sale of ganja, except for medicinal and scientific purposes is totally banned in certain districts of the State. Consumption of opium, except for medicinal purposes and by addicts on medical certificates, has been completely banned from April 1, 1959.

(10) Orissa. The dry law operates in the districts of Ganjam, Koraput, Cuttack, Balasore and Puri. Sale of foreign liquor to addicts in these districts is limited through licensed shops and on production of permits. In the non-prohibition areas, steps have been taken to reduce progressively the number of liquor shops and to increase the number of days on which liquor shops remain closed.

Oral consumption of opium has been prohibited since April 1, 1959, and all opium shops in the State have been closed.

(11) Haryana. Total prohibition exists in whole of Haryana. The Government of Bansi Lal, Chief Minister of Haryana, has enforced vigorously total prohibition in all parts of Haryana.

(12) Rajasthan. Prohibition is in force only in Abu taluk in the district of Sirohi. A phased programme has been put into effect since April 1, 1956. Among the more important aspects of this programme are the ban on serving drinks in public places, closure of liquor shops on pay days and other important national days, reduction in the number of country liquor shops, removal of liquor shops from populous areas and enhancement of duty on liquor and licence fees. A Prohibition Advisory Committee has been established to consider the question of introducing prohibition by stages.

(13) Uttar Pradesh. There is total prohibition in the three pilgrimage centres of Brindaban, Hardwar and Rishikesh and the districts of Badaun, Etah, Farrukhabad, Fatehpur, Jaunpur, Kanpur, Mainpuri, Pratapgarh, Rae Bareli, Sultanpur and Unnao. This covers 17.05% of the area and 21.4% of the population of the State.

The sale of ganja has been prohibited throughout the State and oral consumption of opium has also been banned with effect from July 1, 1959.

(14) West Bengal. Prohibition has not been introduced in any area of the State. Among steps taken to discourage the drinking habit are the declaration of dry days in industrial areas, reduction in the hours of transaction in excise shops and in the grant of licences for retail sale, enhancing the rates of taxation on liquors, etc.

(15) Union Territories. A policy of gradual prohibition is in operation in the Union Territories. All toddy and liquor shops have been closed, liquor shops are closed for five days in a week and import of foreign liquor is banned in the Andaman and Nicobar Islands.

In Delhi restrictions on the saleable strength of country liquor and the number of country liquor shops have been imposed. Advertisement relating to liquor consumption have been banned and various steps have been taken to stop public drinking. Sale of liquor in clubs is restricted to members only, the number of dry days has been increased and duty on all varieties of country liquor has been enhanced. With effect from April 1, 1959, the supply of opium is available only to addicts on production of medical certificates.

There is total prohibition in the Bilaspur district and subdivisions of Mahasu, Mandi and Chamba districts covering nearly one-fourth of the population in Himachal Pradesh. In other areas of the State the quota of country liquor has been reduced, as also the number of liquor shops. Drinking in public places has also been banned. An Advisory Board has been set up to advice the administration and prohibition committees are being constituted in all the districts.

In Manipur, the issue of licences for local distillation of country liquor has been discontinued since 1958 and special permits are issued to individual tribals for local distillation of liquor on festival and religious occasions. Public drinking and advertisements relating to drinking have been banned and a district prohibition committee has been set up to ensure the successful implementation of the prohibition policy and to seek public cooperation. The oral consumption of ganja, bhang and opium has been prohibited.

In Tripura, excise shops are closed for one day in the week and selling hours have been reduced. Advertisements relating to drinking have been banned. Steps are being taken to remove excise shops away from populous areas. The sale of ganja through government agencies have been completely withdrawn with effect from April 1959.

After coming into power, the Janata Government has planned to impose total prohibition in most of the country. This will cause a huge loss to exchequer, which will be partly met by central aid and partly by new taxes. Most of the states have already launched a phased programme to bring complete prohibition in four years.

In India alcoholism is the curse of the poor strata of society. While it shatters their health it further aggravates their poverty so much so that their wives and children do not get even the bare necessities of life. Alcoholism also leads to violence, marital conflict, family disorganization and increase in mental tensions and diseases. In the West, on the other hand, Alcoholism has not much relationship with poverty. Drinks are very much a part of their life and alcoholism is the result of excess. While it does affect the physical and mental health of the person concerned it does not create so much hardships for wife and children as in the case of India.

India is a poor country. Most of the people are even below subsistence level. Nutrition is not sufficient even for the middle class people. Hence alcoholism creates too much hardship. It is, therefore, absolutely necessary that the sale of wines and intoxicants should be limited to card-holders and every one should not be allowed to indulge into it.

ALCOHOLISM AND CRIME[1]

Abstinence, as we employ the term here, does not mean that an alcoholic beverage has never passed the person's lips. We include persons who drink a small amount once or twice per year. An example would be the man who has one drink at a wedding or the man who will allow a drink to be pressed upon him by friends rather than risk being impolite by adamant refusal.

Our next category is that of slight to moderate use of alcohol. By this we mean anything from a few drinks a year up to a drink every two days. Infrequent

1. Paul H. Gebard and others, *Sex-offenders*, pp. 739-40.

drunkenness, such as an annual intoxication at a New Year's party, would not exclude a man from this category. Except for two, all the sex-offender groups have from two to three-fifths of their members in this category of moderate drinkers. Non-sex offenders come close to marking the extremes of the range, the control group having the three-fifth figures and the prison group the two-fifths. The only observable clustering is that the homosexual offenders have rather large proportions (52 to 63 per cent) of moderate drinkers, the proportion being larger among those with older partners. This situation may reflect the fact that they frequent bars for sexual purposes.

The next category is that of frequent use of alcohol, i.e., from a minimum of one drink per day up to but not including alcoholism. We include a man who regularly got drunk once every month even though his drinks, if prorated, might not attain a daily average. We include in this group those who use alcohol habitually, and those to whom alcohol has some importance, but who are not alcoholics. The groups with the fewest frequent users are the control group and the homosexual offenders *vs.* adults, both with 18 per cent, while the aggressors *vs.* children have the most, nearly one-third. In general the various groups cluster around proportions of one-fiftn to one quarter. The only trends noted were that the homosexual offenders tend to have rather few frequent users and the aggressors tend to have many.

Alcoholics, are those who habitually use alcohol to such a degree as to interfere seriously with their social relationships and employment, or those who drink on the average of one-fifth of whiskey (or equivalent liquor) a day even though they may be able to maintain their social and economic status.

There is a great variation among the comparative groups in incidence of alcoholism, the proportions ranging from the 6 per cent of the control group and the offenders *vs.* adults up to the 40 per cent of the aggressors *vs.* children. In all the tripartite groups those whose objects were children have larger proportions of alcoholics than those whose sex-offense objects were aged twelve or older. In two of the four tripartite groups these differences are quite large. There is also a tendency for those whose sexual objects were minors (age-period 12-15) to have more alcoholics among their members than those involved with adults.

An additional and anticipated finding was that never less than half, and generally two-thirds to all, of the offenses committed while drunk were committed by frequent drinkers or alcoholics. Moreover, of the drunken offenses (including aggression) against children, from half to four-fifths were committed by just the alcoholics. Only about one-fifth to two-fifths of the drunken offenses against adults were by alcoholics. Conversely very few (0 to 5 per cent) of the offenses committed while sober were committed by alcoholics and not many more (0 to 17 per cent) by frequent drinkers.

In summary, while the use of alcohol is more important among the sex offenders than among the control group, it is more important still to the prison group. Alcohol as a group phenomenon does not seem to be any greater a factor in the predisposition to sex-offense behaviour than in predisposition to non-sexual criminality. Intoxication inclines persons to legally punishable behaviour, but it does not determine the form that behaviour will take.

DRUG ADDICTION[2]

The use of drugs of all types has long been taboo in American society although formal control, first through medical prescription and then through traditional criminal sanctions, has a shorter history. The complex of psychological and social resistances to the use of drugs is not a matter to enter into here, but it is important to recognize the emotional and intellectual horror that use of drugs invokes in the citizen who does not use them. The general climate of opinion among the public is often one of hostility and anger when the subject is broached.

Thus the combination of drug use and sex offenses provokes a stronger emotional response than either event singly. The "dopecrazed sex fiend" is a traditional figure in the mass media, and the drug-provoked "sex orgy" is a traditional event in our newspapers and magazines. Personifications of such stereotypes are actually very infrequent.

TYPES OF DRUGS

The chief drugs of interest here may be grouped into three classes.

1. Opiates. First are the opiates, both natural and synthetic. These are clearly addicting drugs to which there is major physiological adjustment and whose absence in the addicted individual causes an identifiable syndrome of withdrawal. Such physiological involvement may be taken as the distinguishing aspect of addicting as opposed to habituating drugs. The natural opiates range from smoking opium to the chemically extracted or refined products such as morphine and heroin (diacetylmorphine). The synthetic opiates which have comparable analgesic effects and addiction liability may be used as substitutes for the natural opiates.

Opiate users in the various sex-offender and control groups are of two types. Aside from persons with no experience, there are those with experimental experience, i.e., "joypopping" or "skinpopping," and those who are truly addicted or "hooked." From the best evidence available, and it is none too good, it is fairly clear that persons addicted to opiates seldom fully refrain from future use. Recidivism is marked and proceeds at a very high rate.

2. Marijuana. The second class of drugs consists of a single item, marijuana. This drug is smoked in cigarette form and is non-addicting. The use of this drug is often claimed to be a precursor of opiate use and addiction, but the data in this area are very poor. There is surely more experimentation with marijuana than there is with the opiate drugs, and it is unlikely that most marijuana users go on to opiate addiction. The patterns of marijuana, use are often considerably

2. Paul H. Gebhard and others, *Sex-offenders*, Institute for Sex Research, New York, 1965, pp. 734-37.

different from the patterns of the opiate users, being more sporadic and involving less criminal activity. For the purposes of this study marijuana users have been divided into experimenters and habitual users.

3. Other Drugs. The third class of drugs is a heterogeneous one containing a variety of drugs with a variety of effects. They are non-addicting but habituating. The barbiturates, the amphetamines, and other prescription drugs ordinarily used as either sleeping tablets or stimulants are part of this group. Use of these drugs for their ostensible medical purpose is not included here. Our concern is with use of the drugs for their euphoric, stimulant, or escape effects known in the subcultural group of the users as "kicks." Also included in this group of drugs is cocaine. A strongly hallucinatory drug, it is non-addicting, and presently its use is rather rare. It has been employed by some sophisticated addicts when available as a part of "speed ball", i.e., a mixture of heroin or morphine with cocaine, but such use is not frequent and given its non-addicting characteristics cocaine is included in this miscellaneous category. Certain esoteric drugs are not included, such as peyote, mescaline, or LSD-25.

Opiate addiction is much less marked among the sex-offender groups than it is among the prison group, and although there is generally a little more experimentation with opiates and actual addiction in these groups than among the control group, it does not appear to be related in any way to specific or generalized sex-offense behaviour.

Use of marijuana is a more widespread phenomenon than use of opiates. A single experience or a few experiences with marijuana are not unusual among persons in certain subgroups in the general population. It is like experimenting with alcohol, and generally with less consequence to the individual. Marijuana is not easily come by, and its illegal status makes habitual use somewhat difficult and expensive.

While the sex-offender groups generally use marijuana more extensively than does the control group, only in two cases does their use surpass that of the prison group. Neither the experimental nor habitual use of this drug seems to be associated with any particular or general type of sex offense. Marijuana use, like opiate drug use, is not an agent in precipitating any specific sex offense, nor does it appear to be a long term predisposing factor.

None of the specific types of drugs seem to bear any weight in the analysis of the various sex-offense groups, but if the total proportion of any group who have ever used drugs of any kind, experimentally or otherwise, is examined, two groups appear sharply different from the others. Two groups that are very similar to the prisoners are the heterosexual aggressors *vs.* children and minors.

If drug use may be assumed to stand in some relation to the "try anything once" attitude, then it is clear that the aggressor groups in general, and the aggressors *vs.* children and minors in particular, have a highly experimental and possibly impulsive relationship to the world. In this search for "kicks" they are similar to the prison group and their attitude is probably more related to a general delinquency than to the specific type of offense.

The use of drugs of any type could be either an index of different attitudes and situations than are usual among persons in the lower social classes, or a precipitating factor in the specific offense. There is no evidence for this latter hypothesis as far as these data go. What is evident is that most of the sex-offender groups are more exposed to all types of drugs and are more often users than are their non-delinquent peers. But since their exposure is usually no greater than that of the non-sex-offender delinquents, it is not a special characteristic of the sex-offense groups. Thus drug use is here a measure of an attitude of experimentation and general delinquency.

QUESTIONS FOR EXERCISE

1. What is Alcoholism? How far can this problem be resolved by the enforcement of prohibition?
2. Write short note on — Alcoholism.
3. How is Alcoholism a social problem?
4. Discuss the problem of Alcoholism in India. How is it different from the problem of Alcoholism in Western countries?
5. Discuss the Problem of Drug Addiction.

REFORM AND WELFARE

REFORM AND WELFARE

1
Socio-Religious Reform Movements

BACKGROUND OF RELIGIOUS REFORMS

After the British empire had been established in India it appeared that they had got a firm foothold in the country. The British analysed the social life of the Indians as it then existed and came to the conclusion that the Hindus were lagging behind all others in the religious, social, political and economic fields. This encouraged them in the attempt to impose their own culture and civilization upon the local population, believing that under the circumstances the people of India would be more receptive than otherwise. By this time, most of the social malpractices that had been introduced in Indian society from time to time, such hideous rituals as the hypocracy of pandits, child marriage, performance of sati, bigamy, caste discrimination, purdah, had all matured and come to their full growth. It was in this milieu that the Christian missionaries started preaching their own religion through the medium of Hindi, a task which was supplemented by the government, which tried to convert Indians to a Western culture through the use of English language. That the British succeeded in their design is evident from the rapidity with which the local population accepted this foreign culture and language. One immediate effect of this religious brain-washing was that the more rigid and fanatic Hindus exerted their energies to oppose any reform in their own religion while another section of Hindus immediately took to the English culture and were heart and soul in favour of adopting it without delay. The latter group of people was attracted primarily by the scientific development taking place in the West. At the same time another group of people separated itself from either of the two fanatic and external thinkers and advocated a synthesis between Indian culture and the new British culture, particularly the latter's work in the field of science. This particular group of thinkers opposed any kind of dogmatic inflexibility where religion is concerned, but they also objected to being made slaves of science. It was their declared aim to find some kind of synthesis between the two. And most of the movements for social or religious reform that occurred in the nineteenth century are the result of the energetic working of this group.

BRAHMO SAMAJ AND RAJA RAM MOHAN RAI

The first chief religious reformer of the nineteenth century was Raja Ram Mohan Rai, whose efforts in his chosen field left a deep impression upon contemporary social, political and religious thinking. Ram Mohan Rai was born in a small village named Radha Nagar in Bengal in the year 1772. He belonged to a family of Brahmins. He was a linguist who mastered Sanskrit, English, Hindi, Persian, Hebrew, Greek and Latin. He made use of his knowledge to study the religious books in each of these languages and thereby he became quite knowledgeable on the subject of religion. He realized that if Hindu religion was to retain its life and strength it must undergo some modifications, and it was with this end in view that the Brahmo Samaj was established in 1822. The principles of this society avoided all rigidity, stressing the importance of universal brotherhood and equality and the existence of a single God. In the social sphere Ram Mohan Rai opposed all inequality, child marriage, sati, bigamy, caste discrimination and the rest of problems that beset Hindu society. In the field of religion he could not and did not support the practice of priestly hypocracy, worship of stone idols, the elaborate rituals, human and other sacrifices made as part of yagya, etc. He pointed out the need for widow remarriage and the education of women. He did not oppose the western style of education since he was aware that the gulf of scientific learning that existed in Indian society could be filled only by this form of education. He exerted himself for the improvement and advancement of Indian literature and culture. He wanted the people to restrict themselves to constitutional methods in fighting for their freedom. Brahmo Samaj achieved wide popularity among the Bengalis, and after Ram Mohan Rai it was further propagated by such great figures as Rabindranath Tagore and Keshava Chandra Sen. After some time the Samaj broke up into two groups on account of differences on basic principles resulting in the formation of the Adi Brahmo Samaj led by Tagore and the Brahmo Samaj headed by Keshab Chandra Sen. Later on the latter became prominent and progressive when such eminent persons as Jagdish Chandra Basu, Vipin Chandra Pal, C.R. Das and Aurobindo Ghosh joined it.

PRARTHANA SAMAJ

Keshab Chandra Sen, creator of the ordinary Brahmo Samaj, had toured the country to impress upon people the importance of his own faith. In 1807 another society, the Prarthana Samaj sprang up in Maharashtra by the efforts of Sen. It was an institution which did not intend to follow the Christian religion or to establish its own sect by deviating from the Hindu religion. Its aim was to make worship part of every one's life, a worship not made through superstitious acceptance of a religious norm, but a prayer suggested and advocated by reason and intelligence. In the social sphere this society was no less revolutionary than the Brahmo Samaj of Raja Ram Mohan Rai. Its chief leaders were Atmaram Pandurang, Ramkrishna Gopal Bhandarkar who was a Sanskrit scholar and Mahadev Govind Ranade. At about the same time a female scholar, Rama Bai, laid the foundations of an Arya Mahila Samaj which resembled the Prarthana Samaj in its essentials. In 1905 Gopal Krishna Gokhale laid the foundation of another society named the Servants of Indian Society.

DAYANAND AND ARYA SAMAJ

Both the Brahmo Samaj and the Prarthana Samaj showed clear influence of Western thinking on their principles, since both admittedly wanted to arrive at some synthesis between the East and the West. It was Dayanand Saraswati, who was born in Gujarat, who tried to revive the Indian traditional philosophy and to modify it to suit the contemporary situation. He was in favour of improving present day society in the light of accepted ideals of old, since he accepted the Vedas as the basis of all social and religious change that he advocated. It was his desire to revive the Vedic religion, since, as he pointed out, there is nothing in the Vedas to support such repugnant institutions as restrictions on widow's remarriage, child marriage, sati, caste discrimination, etc. He agreed that all such malpractices should be eliminated from Indian society at the earliest, and pointed out that to do so would be in no way inconsistent with Indian cultural tradition. He established his Arya Samaj in 1877 with the intention of reviving the ancient Vedic religion and culture. Under his guidance the Samaj started a social revolution to root out all the evils that could be found in contemporary society. Its main achievement lay in the possibilities that society had opened up to those people who had abandoned Hindu religion and gone over to Christianity and Islam to return to Hindu religion. They helped to purify the converts and to bring them in Hindu religion. Dayanand wrote the famous work *Satyarth Prakash*, which is an elaboration of principles of this society as well as a refutation of the hypocritical notions of other religious groups. He contributed much to the development of Hindi language and education in general.

RAMAKRISHNA MISSION

The creator of the Ramakrishna Mission was Ramakrishna Paramhansa although his disciple Vivekananda achieved even greater fame than he himself did. Branches of his mission have been established in many important towns in the United States, at New York, Boston and Washington. Among the objectives of this mission are a steady realization of the glory of ancient Hindu culture and religion, and the attempt to guide on the path of progress and development. Ramakrishna Paramhans was a Bengali, having a considerable followings among people of his own state. After his death the control of the mission and its works passed into the hands of Vivekananda, who succeeded in achieving fame in other countries for the Vedanta philosophical system. The lectures that he delivered on the subject during 1823 are very famous. He stressed the importance both of spiritual and of physical power.

THEOSOPHICAL SOCIETY

Madame Blavatsky and Colonel Olcott established the Theosophical Society in 1875 at New York. They came to India later on and established their centre at Adyar in Madras. Dr. Annie Besant did very valuable work for this institution. Members of the society held disciples of every religion in equal respect, and believed in the principles of *karma* and rebirth, advocating that peoples of different nations should endeavour to lead the best possible life by adopting all best qualities of every religious and social system. They were also desirous of educating people in the study and understanding of philosophical, scientific and natural laws and in the necessity of mutual cooperation, of which there could never be too much.

OTHER REFORM SOCIETIES

The foregoing account does not exhaust the list of reform societies that sprang up during this period. It was a very fertile period for reform work. In 1861 Shivdayal, a businessman belonging to Agra, established the Radhaswami Satsang. This group makes no distinction of caste or creed, and treats the guru as an incarnation of God. This group continues its existence in Dayalbagh at Agra. In 1807 the Dev Samaj was started by Shivanarain Agnihotri who had originally been one of the staunch followers of Brahmo Samaj. In 1873 another Sanatan Dharma Rakshini Sabha was born in Calcutta, its avowed aim being to propagate the Sanatan Hindu religion.

MUSLIM REFORM MOVEMENT

It would appear that all the movements for religious reforms during the nineteenth century centred around Hindu society, but this is not precisely true since the Muslim society also had its fair share of such movements. Religious awakening overflowed from the Hindu section of society to the Muslim section. In Delhi the people were advised to fashion their lives on lines indicated in the Koran, by Shah Abdul Aziz. Sir Saiyed Ahmed Khan tried to put an end to many of the malpractices that had spread among the Muslims, while Karamat Ali Jaunpuri succeeded in organising the Muslims of East Bengal in the religious revolution, His followers encouraged the Muslims to turn to western methods of education. Similar reform work was done by Maulvi Chirag Ali who was opposed to the practice of bigamy among the Muslims. He was all in favour of education and the pursuit of knowledge. In the 19th century Abdul Ahmed started the Ahmedia movement by emphasizing the importance of moral and spiritual teaching. He claimed to be the messenger of God. But the most important reform movement was initiated by Sir Saiyed Ahmed Khan which made him the leader of progressive Muslims in India during the present period. He pointed the need for a westernized education and methodology of thinking among the Muslims. It was he who established the Muslim University at Aligarh. He also wrote a commentary on the Koran.

QUESTIONS FOR EXERCISE

1. Review briefly the social reform movement in India and indicate its success.
2. Write note on Social Reform.
3. Write note on Religious Reform.

2

Labour Welfare

WHAT IS LABOUR WELFARE?

1. The Oxford dictionary. Labour welfare includes "efforts to make life worth living for workmen."

2. A paper — submitted on behalf of the Latin American countries to the International Conference of Social Work held at Munich in 1956. Labour welfare includes "Services rendered to workers and their families by an industrial enterprise with the purpose of raising their normal material, social and cultural levels and to adjust to a better life."

3. At the ILO (SEA) session held at New Delhi in 1947. Workers' welfare was understood "as meaning such services, facilities and amenities, which may be established in, or in the vicinity of undertakings to enable persons employed therein to perform their work in healthy, congenial surroundings and to provide them with amenities conducive to good health and good morale."

4. The Rege Committee report submitted to the Government of India in 1946. "We prefer to include under welfare activities anything done for intellectual, physical, moral and economic betterment of workers, whether by employer, government or other agencies, over and above that provided by law or under some contract and what is normally expected as a part of the contract for service."

5. The Royal Commission on Labour (1931). "The term welfare, as applies to the industrial worker, is one which must necessarily be elastic; bearing a somewhat different interpretation in one country from another, according to different social customs, the degree of industrialization and educational development of workers."

6. Encyclopaedia of Social Sciences. "Labour welfare implies the voluntary efforts of the employers to establish within the existing industrial system, working and sometimes living conditions of the employers beyond what is required by law, the custom of the industry and the conditions of the market."

HISTORY OF LABOUR WELFARE IN INDIA

The following are the different stages in Labour Welfare movement in India.

1. Development since 1870 to 1914. The first industrial undertaking in India was established in 1854. During the following fifteen years, cotton textile, jute and coal industries and railways made considerable progress and employed a sizeable work force. The industrial progress was accompanied by usual inhuman conditions of work and exploitation of women and children. Major Moore published his report on 'the Administration of Bombay Textile Department' in 1872. Public response to the shocking findings of Major Moore expressed itself into organised labour work on one hand and agitational activities on the other. A *Brahmo Samaj* preacher, Mr. P.C. Majumdar established eight night schools for industrial workers of Bombay in 1872. In Calcutta, the *Brahmo Samaj* established a Working Men's Mission in 1878 which preached practical religion and established nine schools for working men and Depressed Classes for promoting education and social welfare activities among the jute mills' workers. Mr. Sasipada Banerjee also started the Baranagar Institute during the same year.

Agitational Activities

Agitational activities to press for demands for legislative provisions regarding health and safety of mill hands was started by Mr. S.S. Bengalee and his colleagues in Bombay in 1872. In 1874, Miss Carpenter, founder of the National Independence Association of Bristol, visited India to enquire into the conditions of factory employees and published her report. This led the Government of India to set up a Factory Commission in 1875 and enact the Factories Act, 1881 on the basis of its recommendations. In 1890, the first International Labour Conference met at Berlin and recommended the regulation of women and child labour. The Government of India was forced to amend the legislation in 1891 and introduced protective clauses in respect of women and children. In 1905 the Berne Conference the forerunner of the ILO made recommendations pertaining to hours of work and working conditions. Armed by these recommendations, the British industrialists pressed the government once again and prevailed upon the latter to enact the Factory Act, 1911 introducing measures to regulate hours and conditions of work. During three decades following the first Factory Act in 1881, voluntary action in the field of labour welfare also made considerable progress and moved from individual to organised group efforts. Formed in 1897 the Amalgamated Society of Railway Servants of India and Burma started a number of friendly benefit schemes. Organised in 1905 and 1907 respectively the Printers Union Calcutta and Postal Union, Bombay introduced mutual insurance schemes, night schools, educational stipends and funeral allowance for their members. In Bombay in 1910 the *Kamgar Hitwardhak Sabha* (Workers Welfare Association) was established to help workers in a variety of ways such as the payment of compensation for accidents to industrial workers and improving labour housing conditions.

2. Between Two World Wars. During the period the labour welfare movement got established on a continuous and regular basis. The important factors were the formation of the ILO, All India Trade Union Congress in 1919, the emergence of the Labour Party and the British Trade Union Congress in

Britain, the new orientation of the Freedom movement under Mahatma Gandhi's leadership, the increase in industrial activity and the size of work force and the militant mood of organised labour. Reforms in labour legislation were made in many directions. The Workmen's Compensation Act was passed and enforced. A significant development during the twenties was the beginning of labour welfare activities by the leading companies. The Royal Commission of Labour (1931), and the assumption of office by the Congress ministries in most of the provinces exercised great influence. The Royal Commission recommended shorter and convenient working hours for women and children, health insurance, maternity benefits, creches, elaborate health rules, labour welfare officers, minimum wages, etc. The Congress ministries, particularly of Bombay, Bengal and U.P. pursued a vigorous policy for setting labour welfare programmes in major industrial cities in their Provinces in 1937, 1939 and 1940 respectively. In 1936 Sir Dorab Tata School of Social Work, now known as the Tata Institute of Social Sciences, was established in Bombay.

3. Second World War. The Second World War proved a boon to the development of Indian industry and of the labour welfare movement. In 1942, the Central Government appointed a Labour Welfare Adviser and a few labour welfare officers in the Department of Labour. Provisions were made for the establishment of canteens, creches, rest rooms and ambulance rooms in establishments by amending the Factories Act, 1934. Labour welfare funds were started in establishments run by various government departments. The Mica Mines Labour Welfare Fund and the Coal Mines Labour Welfare Fund were constituted for providing housing, medical, recreational and educational facilities to workers and their families employed in mica and coal mines, all over the country. In 1942, a special officer was appointed in the Department of Labour to draft a scheme of health insurance for factory workers. Maternity benefits, pithead baths and creches were introduced in the mining industry.

4. Independence and After. The labour welfare movement acquired a new perspective after Independence. The Indian National Congress had made many commitments to industrial workers. It naturally tried to honour them. The Labour Department of the Central Government worked out a five year programme in 1946. This was followed by three Five Year Plans. The First Five Year Plan provided Rs. 6.84 crores for labour welfare which was increased to Rs. 29 crores in the Second and Rs. 71.08 crores in the Third Plan. Labour Welfare Advisory Boards now function in all States.

PATTERNS OF LABOUR WELFARE SERVICES

1. Basic Standards. Activity of the State in relation to the creation of basic welfare standards for workers employed in undertakings, culminated in the passing of the Factories Act, 1948; Mines Act, 1952; Plantation Labour Act, 1951 and similar other enactments regulating working conditions in other groups of industries like railways, sea-farers, CPWD, shops and commercial establishments and banks and insurance companies.

2. Activities to Meet Particular Needs. Principal measures concerning the general welfare of particular groups with special needs include Coal Mines (Pithead Bath) Rules, Mines Creche Rules, Coal Mines Labour Welfare Office Establishment Rules, Tea Districts Emigrant Labour Act, 1933 and Dock Workers (Regulation of Employment) Act, 1918. Owners of all coal mines are required to construct bath rooms near the head of pits and to provide adequate quantities of water and soap for workers to bathe after they come out of the pit. Likewise, all mine owners are required to provide a creche at the premises wherein women workers can leave their children below the age of six during working hours. The rules lay down standards of services and staff as well as specifications of accommodation. The Tea Districts Emigrant Labour Act, 1933 regulates the recruitment of plantation labour, its movement to Assam and repatriation. It abolished the 'indenture' system and thereby stopped gross exploitation of this class of labour. The Dock Workers (Regulation of Employment) Act, 1948 is a scheme of providing guaranteed minimum employment and welfare facilities to dock workers.

3. Particular Labour Welfare Services. Labour welfare services of a specialised nature pertain to indebtedness, housing and industrial co-operatives. Indebtedness Relief Acts of most of the States provide that industrial workers in respect of wage of less than Rs. 100 per month will not be subject to imprisonment under Section 51 of the Code of Civil Procedure, except where the debtor has been proved to be both able and unwilling to pay.

The need to improve the housing conditions of industrial workers was suggested for the first time in 1919 by the Indian Industrial Commission. The Royal Commission on Labour laid further stress on this need in 1938. Later the Bombay Textile Labour Enquiry Committee, the U.P. Labour Enquiry Committee, the Kanpur Labour Enquiry Committee and the Bihar Labour Enquiry Committee pointed out in their reports, the deplorable housing conditions in most of the industrial centres and made various recommendations for improving them. The Labour Investigation Committee suggested that the State Government should provide necessary finance for housing while the recurring expenses should be borne by the parties concerned. The problem was discussed at the seventh meeting of the Standing Labour Committee in 1915 and an Industrial Housing Sub-committee was appointed to go in the details of the problem. The report of the Committee was discussed and improved by the Standing Labour Committee in July, 1946. Various schemes and enactments were framed both by Central and State Governments for providing housing accommodation to industrial workers.

The first housing enactment was passed in the shape of the Land Acquisition (Amendment) Act, 1933 which enabled employers to secure land for construction of houses for their employees. The Mica Mines Labour Welfare Fund Act, 1946 and the Coal Mines Labour Welfare Fund Act, 1947, provided for the constitution of Housing Boards for the respective mining industries.

The Plantation Labour Housing Scheme was introduced by the Central Government in April, 1956. The Scheme has provisions for the grant of loan assistance to planters, through the State Government, to the extent of 80 per cent of the cost of a house subject to a maximum of Rs. 2,400 in North India and Rs. 1,920 in South India at a reasonable rate of interest recoverable in 30 annual equal instalments. The Scheme is designed to help planters to meet their statutory housing obligations under the Plantation Labour Act, 1951. Since loans under the Scheme were available to the planters only on furnishing security, considerable difficulty was experienced by them. In order to overcome this difficulty, the government introduced a 'Pool Guarantee Fund'. In cases where the planters were not in a position to furnish the normal security required for obtaining loans, the State Government may charge additional interest at 2 per cent per annum from the planters over and above that payable by them to the Government of India. The resultant realisation is deposited into a 'pool' which would indemnify the State Government against any bad debts. With the introduction of the 'Pool Guarantee Fund', security conditions have been relaxed.

The Railway Board and various Port Trust authorities have their own schemes of providing housing facilities to their employees. So far as the State Governments are concerned only the State Governments of erstwhile Bombay, erstwhile Saurashtra, Mysore, Madhya Pradesh, erstwhile Hyderabad, Uttar Pradesh and the Punjab have enacted legislation to provide suitable housing accommodation to the working classes. The U.P. and the Punjab enactments make provisions for the appointment of Housing Commissioners for control and management of houses constructed under the subsidised Industrial Housing Scheme of the Government of India.

4. Protection of Children and Women. One of the major concerns of the state is to protect and safeguard children and women against exploitation and victimisation. It was in 1881 that concrete steps were first taken to regulate working hours for children. The Factories Act, 1881, defined 'child' as a person below 12 years of age and prohibited the employment of children below 7. Child workers were to work nine hours a day. Through repeated amendments, the conditions of work were made more favourable to children. The Factories Act, 1934 introduced the concept of adolescent (between the age of 15-17 years) as a 'protected' person and required that children do not work for more than 5 hours a day with a maximum spread-over of 7 hours. The position was made still better in the Factories Act, 1943. This Act defined child as a person who has not completed 12 years of age and prohibited the employment of children below the age of 14 in factories. Young persons (between the age 15-18) could be employed in factories subject to certain conditions. The occupier of a factory, before employing a young person, must be in possession of certificate of age of the young person certifying that the person concerned is above the age of 14, and a certificate of medical fitness issued by the certifying surgeon, on the general physical fitness of the 'young person'. The 'young person' must be issued a token marked 'P' (protected person) which he must carry on his person during all working hours. He will work one relay only and shall not be allowed or required to work for more than 5 hours a day. He also earns leave with wages at the rate of one day for 15 days of work. Again, a young person cannot be employed in cleaning, oiling and repairing jobs as well as in hazardous occupations. He is also not allowed to work during night. The Mines Act, 1952 make provisions for 'young persons' which are similar to those made in the Factories Act, 1948. Further, it prohibits the employment of 'young persons' below ground and requires that they be given safe work under the supervision of adult workers.

In 1938, the Government of India enacted the Employment of Children's Act prohibiting employment of children in certain occupations. It laid down that no child who has not completed 15th year of age shall be employed or permitted to work in any occupation connected with the transport of passengers, goods or mail on the railways and in ports. It also prohibited the employment of children below the age of 14 in any workshop where bidi making, carpet weaving, cement manufacturing, printing, dying and weaving of cloth, cutting and smelting of mica, manufacturing of matches and fireworks, shellac works, soap making, tanning and cleaning of wool, are carried on.

The Act also prohibited night work for children. It does not apply to those establishments where manufacturing process is carried on by the occupier with the aid of his family members.

Another Act that protects children against exploitation is the 'Pledging of Children Act, 1938'. This Act declares an agreement to pledge the labour of children whereby the parent or guardian of a child, in return for any payment or benefit to be received, undertakes to cause or allow the services of a child to be utilited in any employment, to be void. However, an agreement made without detriment to the interest of the child and not made in consideration for any benefit other than reasonable wages to be paid for child's services and terminable at a week's notice will not be deemed illegal. The Tea Districts (Immigration of Labour) Act, 1933 lays down that no child shall be employed and immigrated to the districts unless accompanied by his parents and guardians. The Mines Act, 1952 holds the guardian responsible if a young person is found engaged in double employment on any one day.

Most of the Acts make special provisions for women workers. The Factories Act, 1948 provides for separate toilet, washing and resting facilities for them. It prohibits their employment during night and in hazardous occupations. It makes special safety provisions by disallowing them to clean, oil or repair moving machinery or to lift heavy weights. If a woman has a young child whom she has left in the factory creche, she has to be given time off at stated frequencies to go and suckle her baby. The Mines Act, 1952 makes all of the above provisions besides prohibiting their employment below ground. The Indian Merchant Shipping Act prohibits women to take employment on board of sea-going ships, except as nurses.

LABOUR WELFARE FUNDS

The labour welfare funds are one of the two major activities of the state. In 1946 the Government of India initiated a scheme to finance welfare activities in industrial undertakings out of specially created funds. In pursuance of this scheme, a number of enactments were made. The Mica Mines Labour Welfare

Fund Act was passed in 1946 followed by the Coal Mines Labour Welfare Act in 1947. The Government of India also framed rules to introduce such funds in industrial undertakings owned and controlled by them. Similar funds have also been instituted by some of the State Governments. The principal amongst these are the Bombay Labour Welfare Funds, the U.P. (Sugar and Power Alcohol Industries) Labour Welfare Fund, and the Gorakhpur Labour Welfare Fund.

LABOUR WELFARE CENTRES

The labour welfare centres are one of the common activities of the Labour Departments of different State Governments. Started in 1936 in Bombay, the idea has spread resulting in the establishment of similar centres in the principal industrial cities. Such centres are found in Bombay, Delhi, Kanpur, Calcutta and a few other places.

WELFARE ACTIVITIES OF EMPLOYERS

Welfare services provided by the employers vary from place to place depending upon the location, size and financial position of the undertaking, manufacturing process, structure of work force, philosophy of the management, etc. Little is known of the welfare activities in small and medium size undertakings. So far as big employers are concerned, they provide a variety of services. It will not be out of place to mention a few outstanding examples.

Tata Iron and Steel Company, Jamshedpur, maintains almost the whole of the city including dwellings, a general hospital, two dozen primary schools, a training institute, parks, roads and a local broadcasting system. Social services provided by the Company are in addition to those run by the State Government. The Company has special funds to give grants for tribal and *Harijan* welfare and to employees for educational needs of their children. The Company has a department of urban community development which runs ten urban centres in the town.

The Delhi Cloth and General Mills, Delhi has a department called Welfare Trust. The Trust undertakes to grant scholarships to the children of employees who are in educational institutions. It also maintains a Daughter's Marriage Fund. An employee can make monthly contributions towards it. At the time of the marriage of his daughter, he gets back his own money with interest plus employer's contribution.

Many companies provide lunch and transport to their employees at subsidised rates. Nearly ten thousand industrial consumer co-operative societies function in India where workers can buy consumer goods at prices much lower than the market prices. The Associated Cement Company in some of its works gives land to workers, provides technical know-how and encourages workers to form and supplement their wages.

WELFARE ACTIVITIES OF TRADE UNIONS

Though all unions keep an account head 'welfare of members' in their expenditure statement, yet very little appears to have been done by them in this direction. The Textile Labour Association, Ahmedabad is an exception. This union runs a number of adult education and literacy centres, provides free legal assistance to members in case of death, sickness in the family or other similar calamities.

From a brief description of the labour welfare practice given so far, it will be seen that trade unions either lack resources or are too occupied with the problems of their existence, to do any labour welfare work. A few exceptions apart, the employers cannot be said to have done much by way of labour welfare which they were not required to do either under the law or due to the essential imperatives of industry itself. The State has emerged as the principal agency for the promotion of labour welfare in the country. It will not be wrong to say that labour welfare in India has been imposed from above by the State and by and large it has a legal base. One need not go far to find justification for this state of affairs. Experience of industrialization in the West has shown that technical development is always rapid and the social evolution lags behind, with the result that there are always some groups of men who pay the price in terms of and forlornness unhappiness for rapid technical progress. To forestall adverse social effects of accelerated economic and industrial development; the Government of India planned labour welfare measures to be introduced along with industrial expansion. Apart from the fact that in the final analysis, legislative action is less expensive and yields results relatively quickly, a planned economy is temperamentally more orientated towards legislative and direction-giving action. Legislation by itself is also a great educational force which is borne out by the history of the development of labour welfare in India. Many welfare measures like canteens, rest rooms and health provisions that were forced on employers in early fifties have come to be accepted as normal accessories to industrial units now-a-days. Today, the debate is centred not on whether labour welfare services should be provided or not but on the share of responsibility that each of the parties should take for providing such services. And this great change in the attitude of the interests concerned has come about in barely ten years.

LABOUR WELFARE LEGISLATION

Most of the Constitutional Directives in the matter of protection and welfare of workers have been followed up through Central and State legislation, except for the right to work and the right to public assistance in case of unemployment. The benefits are available to workers and employees in mines, docks, plantations, factories, industries, motor transport industry, shops and hotels. The workers working with building contractors are still not entitled to all the benefits of labour laws. The laws making provisions for the welfare of labour can be classified into five categories and they are considered here.

1. Provisions related to hour of work, conditions of work, leisure, health and safety. These are to be found in the Factory Act, 1948, Dock Workers (Regulation of Employment) Act, 1948, Delhi Shops and Establishment

Act, 1962 (similar Acts have been passed by State legislatures), Motor Transport Workers Act, 1961, Coal Mines (Conservation and Safety) Act, 1952.

2. For regulating payment of wages, bonus, etc. The Minimum Wages Act (1948 and 1961) is the principal piece of legislation. This is followed by the Bonus Act of 1965.

3. Measures of social security and labour welfare. These includes Fatal Accidents Act, 1955, Employees' State Provident Fund Act, 1952 (amended in 1960, 1962), Employees' State Insurance Act, 1946, Maternity Benefits Act, 1961 and Coal Mines Labour Welfare Fund Act, 1947.

4. Collective Bargaining. Trade Union Act, 1926, and Indian Trade Unions (Amendment) Act, 1960, are the chief enactments dealing with right of association for collective bargaining.

5. Industrial disputes. These governed by the Industrial Disputes Act, 1947. The Industrial Disputes Banking and Insurance Companies Act, 1949, provides machinery for the disputes between Bank/Insurance workers and the management.

6. Social welfare. From the point of view of social welfare these post-independence enactments are very significant. The present economic development of our industries cannot take the burden of old age and survivors' pension. Therefore, the scheme for the Contributory Provident Fund has been introduced by the Employees' Provident Fund Act, 1952. Cash benefits and medical aid, half-salary during the period of disablement and pension to widows and children in case of death are some of the important benefits conferred by the Employees' State Insurance Act, 1948.

7. Social Justice. Labour laws are being extended to more industries and places of employment as a part of acceptance of the doctrine of social justice.

In a recent case (*Hindustan Antibiotics Ltd.* v. *Their Workman*, L.L.J. 1967 S.C. 114) the Supreme Court has held that there should be no distinction between the industries in public and private sector in matters of application of industrial and labour laws.

Under the Factories Act, 1948, a factory is defined as any permises including the precincts thereof where 10 or more workers are working or were working on any day of the preceding twelve months and in any part of which power is used for the manufacture. Where power is not used the number of workers should be 20 or more.

A worker is defined in the Act as a person, employed directly or through any agency, whether for wages or not, in any manufacturing process, or in cleaning any part of the machinery or premises used for a manufacturing process or in any other kind of work incidental to or connected with the manufacturing process, or the subject of the manufacturing process.

In 1971, the working population of India was about 10.04 crores or about 32.92 per cent of the total population of India. Of the working population only 10 per cent was in the organised sector and the rest in the traditional sector. Cultivator and agricultural labourers formed the bulk of the traditional workers, 43.34 per cent and 26.33 per cent respectively.

However, reliable data are available only for the organised sector of India's economy. Most of the Acts passed by the government for the welfare of workers relate to workers in this sector. A number of social security schemes are also in operation for these workers. These include factory acts, wages acts and social security schemes like employees state insurance, employees' provident funds, death relief and family pension for workers and their families. Some acts and rules have also been framed for the unorganised sector. The Minimum Wages Act, 1948 is also applicable to many categories of workers in this sector.

WORKING CONDITIONS

Working conditions in factories are regulated by the Factories Act, 1948 which prescribes a 48-hour week for adult workers and forbids the employment of children under 14 in any factory. Minimum standards of lighting, ventilation, safety, health and welfare services which the employers must provide in their factories have also been laid down. Factories with more than 250 employees have to provide canteens for their workers.

A report of International Labour Organisation defined labour welfare thus: "Workers Welfare should be understood as meaning such services, facilities and amenities which may be established in, or in vicinity of, an undertaking to enable the persons employed there to perform their work in healthy congenial surroundings and provided with amenities conducive to good health and high morale." Thus the labour welfare schemes aim at the maintenance and betterment of workers' health and raising of their moral standards and efficiency. A report of Labour Investigation Committee set up by the Government of India has observed, "We prefer to include under welfare activities anything done for the intellectual, physical, moral and economic betterment of the workers whether by employees, by Government agencies or by other agencies over and above what is laid down by law or what is normally expected as part of the contractual benefits for which the workers may have bargained. Thus, under this definition we may include, medical and educational facilities, nutrition (including provisions of canteens) facilities for recreation, cooperative societies, day nurseries and creches, provision of 'sanitary accommodation', holidays with pay, social insurance measures, undertaken voluntarily by employers alone or jointly with workers, sickness and maturity benefits schemes, provident funds, gratuities, bonuses and pension etc." Thus, all the above-mentioned definitions of social welfare agree on this point. It includes all voluntary acts by employers aimed at improvement and betterment of workers' social, moral, economic and intellectual conditions. Those acts which the employer is compelled, on pain of legal action, to undertake, however beneficial these may be for the workers, are not included in the provisions of labour welfare. By welfare schemes the industrialists give evidence of their moral and social enlightement and help all-round development of workers. This, in turn, helps him in the long run, because, as it has been well observed, a well-paid and satisfied worker is an asset and the low-paid unsatisfied worker is a liability.

TRADE UNIONISM IN INDIA

Trade Unions Act of 1926 conferred a legal and corporate status on registered unions and granted them certain immunities in regard to trade disputes. The Act makes provisions for three matters — (1) conditions governing the registration of trade unions, (2) the obligation to which a trade union is subjected after registration and (3) the rights and privileges accorded to registered unions to be spent for the conduct of trade disputes and for the provisions of benefits to its members.

The amended Act of 1947 contains a provision for compulsory recognition of representative unions by employers. The redeeming feature of the Act is that Labour Courts are to be appointed to hear and decide disputes arising from the refusal of employers to recognize any particular union. The Act specifies certain acts as unfair practices on the part of recognised unions and certain other acts as unfair on the part of employees. It also declares as unfair practice for any executive of a union to instigate a strike and unfair for a majority of members to take part in an irregular strike.

There are at present 5 central all-India trade union organisations in India: *Indian National Trade Unions Congress, All-India Trade Union Congress, Hind Mazdoor Sabha, United Trade Union Congress* and *Centre of Indian Trade Unions.* AITUC having become manifestly Communist since December 1929, the Indian National Congress leaders organised their own trade union — the INTUC. The Praja Socialist Party organised the HMS, CPI(M) has made a separate union, the CITU in 1970.

Though the five national organisations dominate the Indian trade union movement, not all trade unions in India belong to them or follow their leadership. The striking examples of these are *Ahmedabad Textile Labour Association* and *National Federation of Indian Railwaymen. The United Trade Union Congress* have no open political affiliations.

LABOUR WELFARE SCHEMES IN INDIA

1. Standing Mines Safety Equipment Advisory Board. This was set up in June 1963 and is composed *inter alia* of representatives of mine owners, mine managers, mine workers and the Government Department concerned. The functions of the Board are: (a) to make annual assessments of future requirements of mine safety equipment and material; (b) to review position regarding import of such equipment and materials; (c) to keep track of the progress of indigenous production of such equipment and material, and (d) generally to advise on the availability of mine safety equipment.

2. National Council for Safety in Mines. This was set up on July 11, 1963, to promote safety, education and propaganda in mines. It includes representatives of mine owners, workers and mine managers.

3. Coal Mines Labour Welfare Fund. This established in 1944, for improving the living and social conditions of workers in the coal mining industry.

4. Dock Workers (Regulation of Employment) Act, 1948. Dock Workers (Regulation of Employment) Schemes framed under the Act are at present in operation in the major ports of Mumbai, Calcutta, Cochin, Chenai, Mormugao and Visakhapatnam. These schemes seek to regulate the employment of certain specified categories of stevedore labourers. These schemes are administered by Dock Labour Boards which are tripartite bodies consisting of an equal number of representatives of (i) Central Government, (ii) Dock Workers, and (iii) the employers of Dock Workers and Shipping Companies.

5. Mica Mines Labour Welfare Fund. This provides medical, educational and recreational facilities for mica mine workers.

6. Plantations Labour Act, 1951. Under this all plantations are required to provide housing accommodation to the workers and their families in their residential quarters and to maintain hospital or dispensaries. Most States and Union Territories are running a number of welfare centres.

7. Motor Transport Workers' Act, 1951. This provides for the welfare of motor transport workers and regulates the condition of their work.

8. Iron Ore Mines Labour Welfare Cess Act, 1961. This provides for the levy and collection of a cess for promoting welfare of the labour employed in this mining industry. It came into force from October 1, 1963.

9. Mines Act, 1952. Safety measures in mines are undertaken under the Mines Act, 1952 and the regulations and bye-laws made thereunder. This Act provides for the regulations of labour and safety in mines.

10. National Commission on Labour. The National Commission on Labour, appointed in December 1966, consists of 12 members besides the chairman and member-secretary, the Commission include 4 independent members; one of whom is an economist, and four each to represent employers and workers.

The Commission was expected to review the existing legislative and other provisions intended to protect the interests of labour, to assess their working and to advise how far these provisions, served to implement the Directive Principles of State Policy as embodied in the Constitution and the national objective of establishing a socialist society and achieving planned economic development.

11. Wages Act, 1936 and the Minimum Wages Act, 1948. The former Act applies to persons employed in any factory, is defined by the Factories Act. 1948 and in any railway, and in receipt of wages which average below Rs. 400 a month. Minimum Wages Act, 1948 empowers the appropriate Government to fix minimum rates of wages payable to employees in industries specified in the Schedule. Wages Census Scheme has been formulated for envisaging collection of occupational wage rates and earnings data in respect of workers in major factories, mining and plantation industries. Steering Group on Wages, consisting of nominees of the Union and State Governments and representatives of workers and employers, studies the trends in relation to wages, production and price.

12. Wage Board. In the organised industries, wages are determined mainly through tripartite wage boards. The following names are the various Wage Boards set up so far.

Cotton Textiles, Cement, Sugar (1st Wage Board), Jute, Iron and Steel, Coffee Plantations, Tea and Rubber Plantations, Non-Journalists Employees of Newspapers, Working Journalists, Iron Ore Mining, Limestone and Dolomite Mining, Coal Mining, Second Wage Board for Cement Industry, Heavy Chemicals and Fertilizers, Cotton Textiles, Engineering, Port and Dock Workers Wage Board, Leather Goods Industries, Road Transport and Electricity Undertakings and Second Sugar Wage Board.

INDUSTRIAL RELATIONS IN INDIA

The Central Government has framed model rules under the Industrial Employment (Standing Orders) Act, 1946 for adoption by industrial establishments employing 100 or more workers. The Act, as modified in 1961, *inter alia* empowers the appropriate Government to extend its provision to establishments employing less than 100 workers.

1. Code of Discipline. A Code of Discipline has been drawn up to avoid breaches of the Code by settling the disputes between employers and workers by constitutional methods rather than by direct actions.

2. The Central Evaluation and Implementation Division. This persuades the parties to withdraw the cases pending in higher courts or the Supreme Court. The Central Employers and Workers Organization have set up committees for dissuading their affiliate members from filing appeals in higher courts against judgments of Industrial Tribunals or Labour Courts.

3. Industrial Tribunals. There are 7 Industrial-cum-Labour Courts at present for dealing with disputes in the Central sphere. Of these, 3 are located at Dhanbad, 2 at Bombay and one each at Calcutta and Jabalpur. The Industrial-cum-Labour Court at Delhi which is under the Delhi Administration also deals with some cases in the Central sphere.

4. Labour Courts. There is one whole-time Central Labour Court at Dhanbad. The Labour Courts set up by State Governments/Administrations, except those in Goa, Daman and Diu, Bihar, West Bengal, Manipur and Tripura have also been specified as Labour Courts for the determination of the money-value of benefits under the Industrial Disputes Act, 1947. The State Government/Administration Labour Courts at Delhi, Calcutta, Quilon and Bangalore have also been specified as Labour Courts for dealing with questions relating to application or interpretation of certified standing orders under the Industrial Employment (Standing Orders) Act, 1946.

5. Industrial Disputes Act, 1947. Under Industrial Disputes Act, 1947, 893 Works Committees in the Central undertakings are now functioning.

6. Tripartite Machinery. Tripartite Machinery at the Centre mainly consists of the Indian Labour Conference, the Standing Labour Committee, the Industrial Committees and the Committee on Conventions. There is also the Labour

Minister's Conference which is closely associated with the machinery, though not tripartite in character.

7. Conciliation Machinery. The administration of Industrial relations in the Central sphere undertakings rests with the Chief Labour Commissioner.

8. Workers' Participation in Management. The scheme of workers' participation in management has made some progress. Joint Management Councils are functioning in 80 establishments — 31 in the public sector and 49 in the private sector.

RESPONSIBILITY OF LABOUR WELFARE

Having discussed the problem of Labour Welfare, the question that is likely to come up in anyone's mind is: who is responsible for Labour Welfare ? Whose moral obligation is it to promote labour welfare ? The most popular view in this regard is that it is the duty of the employer to look after the social welfare of the workers employed by him. This seems to be the most responsible and well considered view because though the industrialist has to make big investment in the labour welfare schemes, it is by no means dead investment. A well-fed, well-clad and satisfied worker is an asset. He makes no loss of man-hours by absenteeism, strikes, slow tactics etc. Besides, he feels a sense of allegiance to the organization in which he works. Therefore though an investment, it pays very rich dividends. It is a moral duty of every mill owner or industrialist to provide fully for the food and other amenities for the families of the workers who suffer grievous injury in accident in course of performance of duties. He must also provide medical benefits, pensions, bonuses, incentives etc. However, the industrialist alone is not responsible for labour welfare. It is also the duty of welfare states to look after zealously the interests of the workers and initiate schemes for improvement in their working conditions, raising their morale etc. The Government should strictly enforce the benefits provided by law. It should also prevent any instance of exploitation of women workers and an abuse of children. In all progressive countries the workers have their Trade Unions which look after and safeguard and promote the interests of the workers. They can compel government and employers to agree to improve benefits for the country. An example of this is the recent announcement of Government of India to allow for 8.33% bonous to all industrial workers. All three, that is the employer, the Government and the Trade Unions are jointly responsible for labour welfare.

QUESTIONS FOR EXERCISE

1. Write short note on Labour Welfare.
2. Write short note on Employment Exchanges.
3. Write short note on Government schemes of Labour Welfare in India.
4. Write short note on Industrial Relations in India.

3

Rural Reconstruction

AIM OF RURAL RECONSTRUCTION

The term rural reconstruction means construction of the village in a new way or beginning all over again. The rural problems will be solved in this reconstruction. This will create radical changes in the life of villages and the economic system will be renovated or improved. The importance of rural reconstruction is apparent from the aim of rural reconstruction. The objectives of rural reconstruction are very comprehensive. The objectives include the eradication of poverty, improvement in the economic condition, improvement in the methods of agriculture, the organisation of a co-operative economic system by removing indebtedness, regeneration of cottage industries, donation of labour, development of communal feeling, spread of education, progress of health, sanitation, arrangement of residential quarters, progress in the means of transportation, establishment of co-operative societies, establishment of local administration, arrangement for recreation, removal of social malpractices like untouchability and caste distinctions and other aspects of an integral progress comprehending the social, economic and political aspects of rural life. The non-violent Swaraj of Mahatma Gandhi was based upon the idea of this rural reconstruction.

IMPORTANCE OF RURAL RECONSTRUCTION

Rural reconstruction will establish a non-violent Swaraj, which has been described by Mahatma Gandhi in just so many words. In a non-violent Swaraj nobody will be the enemy of any one else, everyone will mind his own business, no one will be illiterate, gradually everyone's stock of knowledge will be increased. There will be less diseases among the people, no one will be extremely poor and the laborious or willing person will always get work. There will be no scope whatsoever for gambling, wine, corruption on class struggle. The rich people will use their wealth prudently and will not waste it in increasing their comforts and enjoyments. In Swaraj such a state, in which a handful of wealthy people live in jewelled houses while thousands upon thousands live the life of animals in dark and airless slums should not exist. This constitutes Mahatma Gandhi's description of Swarajya, the aim of rural reconstruction. The government of India are also making continual efforts towards rural reconstruction. By rural reconstruction a socialistic system will be established in the country, exploitation will be eliminated and the rural population will undergo social and economic development. Thus the importance of rural reconstruction cannot be over-stressed. Indian culture will be regenerated and will further develop through rural reconstruction. Rural reconstruction will lead to the development of agricultural and cottage industries which will solve the food problem of the country and save millions of rupees in foreign exchange which goes towards the import of foodgrains, and it will also increase the national income. Adequate raw material will be made available to the industries in the country through rural reconstruction. Finally, rural reconstruction will result in the establishment of a true democracy in India, because most of the population lives in the village.

IMPORTANCE OF RURAL PLANNING

In the words of Planning Commission, "Planning is essentially a way of organising and utilizing resources to maximum advantages in terms of defined social ends". In this way the plans of rural reconstruction will try to take maximum advantage from the available resources, keeping in view the objectives mentioned above. It is obvious that planned reconstruction is the most superior method. Thus in order to make the best use of rural reconstruction it is necessary to avail of planning. Actually, the importance which has been attributed to rural reconstruction in the preceding paragraph is also the importance of rural planning because these objectives cannot be obtained in the absence of planning. In this way rural reconstruction and rural planning are of the utmost importance in a predominantly agricultural country like India.

GOVERNMENTAL EFFORTS FOR RURAL RECONSTRUCTION

At present the government of India is making strenuous efforts to remove the defects in the rural structure and is attempting rural reconstruction by solving social, economic and agricultural problems of the villages. The specific efforts in this direction are the following:

1. Land reforms, 2. The Five Year Plans, 3. Co-operative movements, 4. Community development projects, 6. Reorganisation of village panchayats.

Besides these government projects rural reconstruction is also being attempted through the Bhoodan Movement under the direction of Vinoba Bhave. The amount of efforts made to solve the problems of the villages under the Five Year Plans can be seen or estimated by studying the development which is the result of the first, second and third five year plans.

In most of the states in India the zamindari abolition laws have succeeded in eliminating the intermediaries from between the farmer and the government. Agriculture is being improved. New methods and new tools together with the methods of using them are being exhibited on the government farms. Arrangements have been made for growing better kinds of seeds on the government farms, which are distributed to the farmers through the government godowns. In the different states laws have been formulated for preventing the extreme subdivision and fragmentation of farms while efforts have also been made to reorganise the scattered farms. The central and state governments have made major and minor plans for the development of the means of irrigation. Many tubewells have been bored and numerous canals constructed. Factories have been set up for producing chemical manure in the country. Methods of protecting the crops from insects are also being developed. Arrangement for the distribution of seeds and the sales of the product is being made through government societies. Money is now available from the cooperative banks at a low rate of interest. In particular, cottage and small scale industries are being encouraged. The means of transport and communication are also being encouraged. New roads are being constructed while thousands of miles of roads are being cemented besides which new rail tracks are being laid. Efforts are being made to assist the villagers in buying, selling and increasing their knowledge of agriculture, industry and other subjects through organising exhibitions and fairs. New trees are being planted, this process being given a festive look by making it an occasion for celebration. Laws have been also made relating to the forest wealth. The village panchayats have been invested with great authority in the form of comprehensive rights. The panchayat courts have been given the right of looking into minor civil and criminal matters of the village. Attempts have been made to provide as many villages as possible with panchayat radios. Great effort is being exerted towards the development of primary and adult education. The villagers are being taught the lesson of self-dependence and cleanliness through movement for labour contribution. By encouraging the Bhoodan movement efforts are being made to provide the landless labourers with land. Through community development projects and development blocks a comprehensive effort is being made in the direction of rural reconstruction. Family planning is being encouraged and made popular among the villagers. The number of hospitals and maternity homes is continuously increasing. People are trying to bring the maximum possible number of improved bulls and buffaloes into the villages.

It is evident from the foregoing description that attention has been paid to the solution of all the serious problems of the village in the plans which are currently operating but the facilities provided by these plans are not available in the villages and neither has the progress achieved by these plans been satisfactory. The facility of hospitals and maternity homes has been provided in very few villages. Free and compulsory primary education is still a possibility which has yet to materialize. The attempts that have been made towards the solution of the problems of the low breed of cattle are inadequate and the condition of agricultural labourers remains unimproved. The measures for the prevention of floods and famines etc., are definitely inadequate. Even today thousands of villages do not have means of irrigation. The condition of panchayats is not satisfactory and in some places the panchayat courts have served to increase the quarrels instead of decreasing them. The amount of money spent upon the construction of roads in the villages is out of proportion to the quality of the roads which have resulted. Proportionate benefit does not accrue from the money spent in exhibitions. Not much improvement has been achieved in the sphere of cottage and small scale industries.

Nevertheless, the intensity of the rural problems is continually decreasing. Many projects for co-operative societies, co-operative banks, community development projects, development blocks, zamindari abolition, education, the popularization of radio, etc., have been definitely and really beneficial. Actually, the rural problems of India are so diversified and profound that the common measures to solve them cannot produce the desired results. Only radical efforts by the government and the public can bring about the desired improvement in the conditions of the villages.

COMMUNITY DEVELOPMENT PROJECTS

Meaning of Community Development

The Planning Commission has defined the community development project in these words: "Community development is an attempt to bring about a social and economic transformation of village life through the efforts of the people themselves." In this way the community development projects indicate or mean those projects for social and economic reconstruction in the village which are implemented with the co-operation of the public itself. In the words of Sri A.R. Desai, "The Community development project is the method through which Five Year Plan seeks to initiate a process of transformation of the social and economic life of the villages." In this way, community development project is a process controlled by the community itself. Here community implies rural community. Elucidating the meaning of community development project it has been laid down in 'India 1982', published by the Government of India, "It is a programme of aided self-help to be planned and implemented by the villagers themselves, the Government offering only technical guidance and financial assistance. Its objectives are to develop self-reliance in the individual and initiative in the village community. Community thinking and collective action are encouraged through people's institutions like the Panchayat, Co-operative Societies, Vikas Mandals, etc."

Aims of Community Development

Prof. S.C. Dubey, writing in his book '*India's Changing Villages*' has recognised the following two aims of community development projects —

1. To manage or achieve an adequate increase in the country's agricultural produce and a progress in the means of communication, rural health, cleanliness and rural education.

2. To initiate and to direct a process of synthetical cultural change aimed at transforming the social and economic life of the village.

The following major aims have been recognised by the Ministry of Community Development of the Government of India publication '*A Guide to Community Development*' —

1. To create a change in the mental outlook of the masses.

2. To develop responsible and active leadership in the village.

3. To make the villages self-dependent and progressive.

4. To modernize agriculture on the one hand and to develop cottage industries on the other hand in order to raise the economic status of the villagers.

5. To improve the condition of the women and families of the villagers in order to make the suggested improvements practicable.

6. To develop properly the future citizens of the nation.

7. To protect the interests of the rural educators.

8. To raise the standard of health among the rural populace and to protect them against disease.

(1) Short term objectives. The aims of the community development projects have been divided into two parts — Short term objectives and Long term objectives. The short term objectives are the following:

1. The maximum possible increase in agricultural production.

2. To solve the problem of unemployment in the villages.

3. To develop the means of communication in the villages.

4. To improve the centres of the primary education, public health and recreation in the villages.

5. To improve the conditions of houses.

6. To encourage cottage industries and indigenous handicrafts.

(2) Long term objectives. The long term objective of community development projects is the complete planned development of all physical and human resources. In it arrangement will be made to provide all villagers with full employment. The goal of community development project is the development of villages in such a way that the citizens of the country may not lack anything, which is the ideal of a welfare state, and that every one should get adequate food and that every one should progress socially, morally and financially.

In this way, in brief, the community development projects aim at the integral development of the village through the efforts of the villagers and the assistance of the Government.

Importance of Community Projects

Describing the importance which the community projects have for rural life the Planning Commission has written in the Second Five Year Plan, "It is a problem, briefly, of changing outlook of 70 million families living in the countryside, arousing in them enthusiasm for new knowledge and new way of the life and filling them with the ambition and the will to live and work for a better life. Extension services and community organisation are among the principal sources of vitality and democratic planning and rural development projects are the means by which through co-operative self-help and local effort villages and groups of villages can achieve in increasing measure both social change and economic progress and become partners in the national plan."

Social development projects will involve improvement in all the aspects, social, economic and other of rural life. The main effects which development projects have upon rural life are the following —

(1) Agricultural development. Agriculture in the foundation of rural economic life. The happiness and the prosperity of the village depend upon the progress of agriculture. The main cause of poverty in the Indian villagers is the backward condition of agriculture. The main problems of Indian agriculture are old techniques of agriculture, dearth of new tools, absence of manures and fertilizers, excessive subdivision of land, dearth of the means of irrigation, shortage of good seeds, etc. The community development projects have made efforts to solve all these problems which beset Indian agriculture. New techniques of farming are exhibited in the villages and manures, seeds, tools and fertilizers distributed. The community projects also undertake the repairing of old wells, supplementing them by sinking new wells in order that the farmers may have available the necessary facilities for irrigation. Efforts are made to protect the land from soil erosion and other maladies.

(2) Economic progress. The greatest problem of rural life in India is its poverty. The community development projects have encouraged cottage industries and handicrafts. Unemployed people are provided with work through auxiliary and useful services. Although these efforts are as yet quite inadequate, it is hoped that a continuous increase in them will lead to rural life in India becoming more prosperous in future.

(3) Development in respect of animals. Another major problem and obstacle to progress in the Indian villages is the deplorable condition of the animals which are even today employed in ploughing the fields. The ox is used for this purpose. In order to improve the strain of the species the community development projects have made use of good oxen. Improved poultry have also been arranged for the development of poultry farming.

(4) Development of education. Most of the people residing in the villages of India are uneducated and illiterate. At the same time they lack modern knowledge. Without the spread of education in the rural areas of India no progress of any kind whatsoever can possibly be expected. The community development projects have paid the desired and necessary attention to the education of children and adults, men and women. Schools for primary and adult education have been opened. Arrangements have been made for social education.

(5) Training for development. In the villages of India social and economic development cannot take place in the existing circumstances. It is necessary to have people trained and skilled in rural development. Under the community project arrangements have been made to train village workers, both male and female, block development authorities and other people concerned with the programme of rural development.

(6) Developments of the means of transport. In the villages of India there is a dearth of the means of transport, serious enough to prove great obstacle to industry and business. The community development projects have repaired the old roads and also managed to construct new roads. At various points small culverts have also been provided. These measures will not only improve business but will also serve to maintain the contact of the villagers with the world at large.

(7) Cleanliness. Dirtiness reigns supreme in the Indian villages. It is the cause of the spread of many kinds of diseases and it lowers the general standard of health. The community development projects have not forgotten to arrange for the purgation of the villages. A considerable length of drain have been constructed and steps have been taken to purify and keep pure the drinking water of the wells.

(8) Protection of health and the maintenance of a certain standard. In the villages of India epidemics and many less wide spread diseases carry off many men, women and children every year due to the almost utter absence of medication and facilities for delivery. The condition of the health of women and children is extremely dissatisfactory. Arrangements have been made for one health centre in each development block. Mobile dispensaries have also been arranged for. Midwives and nurses are also being trained to staff all the new dispensaries.

(9) Arrangement for residences. Most of the houses in the village are old fashioned and small. The community development projects have decided to assist the villagers in building houses and also arranged for providing them with modern plans and the building method of good and cheap houses.

(10) Social welfare. The community development projects have also given due attention to social welfare in the villages, making arrangements for games, variety shows etc., for the entertainment of the public. Gramophone, radio and cinema provide the villager with entertainment and also serve to enhance his stock of knowledge.

Criticism of Community Development

Looking at the above statistical details of the progress, both social and economic, achieved by the community development projects in villages, it becomes apparent that these projects have completely ignored many social and economic problems like the problem of the condition of the landless labourers, the problem of the backward condition of village and cottage industries, etc.

Secondly, even those social and economic problems which have received attention in these projects, are not being solved in an appropriate manner. For example, the arrangement of free and compulsory education is, as yet a thing of the future. The Programme Evaluation Organisation established by the Planning Commission put forward numerous criticisms of the community development programmes in its reports, of which the major ones are given below:

(1) Lack of the solution of local problems. There is a lack of the solution of local rural problems in the community development projects. This not only hinders the progress of the development programme but it also decreases the faith of the public in these projects.

(2) Dearth of Harmony within the Government Department. The community development organization is not in harmony with the other governmental departments.

(3) Shortage of Necessary Implements. There is an acute shortage of required necessary in implements in the development programmes and as a result even the work which is started cannot be completed.

(4) Shortage of trained personnel. Much effort has been made for training the officials in community development projects but the trained people are not available in required numbers.

(5) Absence of proper public co-operation. The community development programmes could not become public movements. At present they are not getting the proper active co-operation of the public.

(6) Shortage of female village workers. There is a great need for trained female workers for the emancipation of the rural women but, at present, they exist in very small number.

Suggestions

Actually, there is an urgent need for increasing the awareness of the public towards the plans for the success of the community development projects. Some suggestions, of which a few are given below, have been made in this connection.

(1) Greater emphasis upon local problems. The pattern of the community development projects should not be the same everywhere. These projects should lay more stress upon the solution of problems peculiar to the locality.

(2) Appointment of officials acquainted with rural conditions. Another way of arousing the interest of the public towards the community development project is to appoint officials who are acquainted with the rural culture and its ways and are also sympathetic and respectful towards them, in order that they may be able to mix with the villagers and to make these plans the projects and aspirations with the people.

(3) Appointment of workers, both male and female, selected from the villages as far as possible. Another way of awakening the sense of ownership in villagers towards the projects is to appoint or select the male and female village workers from among the villagers themselves.

(4) Organisation of the maximum possible training camps in the villages. If a maximum possible number of training camps are held in the villages, the villages will undoubtedly reciprocate heartily and will take a greater interest in the projects.

(5) More work and less propaganda. The officials detailed for the implementation of the development projects should adopt the principle of "More work and less propaganda". It will result in public showing greater faith in the projects.

(6) Establishing youth organisations and eliciting their co-operation. Before starting the programmes of development in the villages, youth organisations should be established and the programmes of development should be started with their co-operation when such organisations are well underway. The result of this move will be that the whole village will soon start taking interest in these programmes.

COMMUNITY DEVELOPMENT IN INDIA

The programme was launched on October 2, 1952 in 55 selected projects. Agriculture receives the highest priority in the programme. Other projects are communications, health and sanitation improvements, education, better housing, measures for women's and children's welfare, development of cottage and small scale industries etc. The Panchayat, Co-operative and school are the basic institutions at the village level to carry out the programme. The elected Panchayat has the charge of all development programmes in the area.

The programme is implemented through units of blocks, each comprising generally 100 villages, an area of 150 or 200 sq. miles and population between 60 and 70 thousand. There existed 5092 Community Development blocks into which the entire rural India was delimited as on 2 April, 1973.

Administrative Set-up. The Ministry of Food, Agriculture, Community Development and Co-operation is responsible for overall control of the programme. The basic policy matters are referred to the Central Committee, consisting of the members of the Planning Commission and the Ministry of Food, Agriculture, Community Development and Co-operation under the Chairmanship of the Prime Minister.

State Administration. Implementation of the programme is the responsibility of the State Government which works through State Development Committees. The executive head of the programme is the Development Commissioner who co-ordinates activities of all development plans.

Direct Administration. The newly created statutory Zila Parishads are responsible for the implementation of the programme in the districts. The Parishads consist of elected representatives of the people, including the Presidents of the Block Panchayat Samitis and M.P.s and M.L.A.s of the district.

Block Administration. At the block level, Block Panchayat Samiti is incharge of the programme. The administrative personnel consisting of a Block Development Officer and eight Extension Officers, work under the direction of the Samiti.

Finance. Resources for the programme are drawn both from the people and from the Government. For each block area, development schemes are conditioned by a qualifying scale of voluntary contribution from the people in each in kind or labour. When State assistance is offered for execution of such projects, expenses are shared by the Central and the State Governments equally, in respect of recurring items, and in proportion of 3 : 1 in the case of non-recurring items. For productive work like irrigation, reclamation of land, etc.

Funds are advanced by the Central Government to the State Government in the shape of loan. The Central Government also bears half of the expenditure on all personnel employed by the States in blocks.

Training. The National Council for Study and Research in Community Development supervises the entire training programme implemented through a network of training centres.

The National Institute of Community Development is an autonomous body, fully supported by the Ministry of Food, Agriculture, Community Development and Co-operation. It is engaged in (1) conducting orientation courses for different categories of high level personnel involved in development administration; (2) the analysis of problems of social change and rural development in which it undertakes research; and (3) issuing publications. It is situated in Hyderabad.

There are 12 Orientation and Study Centres mainly for the training of Block Development and Block Extension Officers, 8 Centres for the training of Social Education Organisers and 10 centres for Mukhya Sevikas.

There are other centres conducted by the respective State Governments under the supervision of the Government of India, where training to Gram Sevaks and Gram Sevikas as well as refresher training to Extension officers is given.

Tribal Orientation and Study Centres extend training in tribal life and culture to the staff working or to be posted in Tribal Development Blocks. There are 4 such centres at Bhubaneshwar, Jabalpur, Udaipur and Ranchi.

CO-OPERATIVE MOVEMENT IN INDIA

The co-operative movement in India began in 1904 as a measure for the relief of chronic rural indebtedness. The scope of the Act of 1904 was confined to the formation of credit societies only. But during the operation of the Act a number of serious defects were found : so in 1912, another Act was passed, which permitted for the first time the organization of non-credit societies in India. In 1914, the Maclagan Committee was appointed for the further improvement of co-operative movement. According to its recommendation, the Montford Reforms of 1919 made co-operation a provincial transferred subject. From 1925 Provincial Governments began to enact separate Co-operative Societies Act. But the matter did not improve and progress in India was very slow. In 1935, the Reserve Bank of India organised Agricultural Credit Department, as an important wing of its activities. The Government of India appointed the Co-operative Planning Committee in 1948, which recommended that primary societies should be converted into multipurpose societies and that efforts should be made to bring 50 per cent of the villages and 30 per cent of the rural population within the sphere of recognised societies within 10 years.

In 1951, the Reserve Bank of India appointed a Rural Credit Survey Committee to report on the whole structure of co-operative movement in India. In 1954, the Committee recommended an integrated scheme of rural credit. The main recommendations were — (1) State partnership in co-operative institutions at all levels, (2) full co-ordination between credit and other allied economic activities, specially marketing and processing, (3) development at the base of viable primary agricultural credit societies, (4) establishment of warehousing organisation, (5) nationalisation of the Imperial Bank of India for providing vastly extended remittance, facilities for co-operative and other banks.

The Reserve Bank of India Act was amended to provide funds to Co-operative Societies and National Agricultural Credit (long term of operation) Fund was established in February 1956 with an initial contribution of Rs. 13 crores. Subsequently in July 1950, a National Agricultural Credit (Stabilization) Fund with an initial capital of Rs. 1 crore, was also established.

The Government also set up a National Co-operative Development and Warehousing Board in September 1956 to promote the development of co-operative activities and to assist in the progress of processing, marketing, storage, warehousing and import of agricultural produce through co-operative societies and warehousing corporations. The Board administers two funds called Co-operative Development Fund and Warehousing Fund, to build up large non-credit societies and a chain of warehouses all over the country.

Two Other Corporations. Central Warehousing Corporation and State Warehousing Corporation have also been set up.

Training. There is All-India Co-operative Training College at Poona for training senior officers of the co-operative departments and institutions. There are 5 Regional Training Centres for the training of intermediate grade personnel and 3 institutions for the training of block level co-operative officers working in the community development blocks. Training schools also exist in the state for the training of junior co-operative officers.

Co-operative Farming. A National Co-operative Farming Advisory Board has been set up for planning and promoting the programme of co-operative farming in the States.

Co-operative Banking Organisation. It owes its origin to the Co-operative Societies Act of 1904 as amended by the Act of 1912. Under this Act, all classes of registered societies are spoken of as 'Societies'. In actual practice, however, primary units are, in some States known as banks and in others as societies. Co-operative banks comprise State and Central Co-operative Banks and registered non-agricultural (urban) co-operative credit societies with limited liability, each having minimum paid-up capital and reserves of Rs. 1 lakh. They are sub-divided into two classes, namely 'A' bank or bank with capital and reserves of Rs. 5 lakhs and above each, and 'B' bank or banks with capital and reserves ranging between Rs. 1 lakh and Rs. 5 lakhs each.

The co-operative banking system consists of the Provincial Banks at the apex, the affiliated Central Banks, and lastly, the primary societies affiliated to the Central Banks. According to the rules under the Act, these banks cannot generally lend to the non-members. The Central Co-operative Banks' principal function is to act as the balancing centre of their affiliated societies and to channel funds to the primary societies.

The functions of co-operative banks are as follows —(1) attracting deposits from money-lenders and professional classes, (2) lending money to the primary co-operative societies, (3) taking away excess fund of a co-operative society and utilising it for making up deficiencies in the funds of others, (4) supervising and guiding the actions of affiliated societies.

Central Land Mortgage Banks are the pivot of the structure of long term finance of the agriculturists through the primary land mortgage banks and raise their funds mainly by the issue of debentures. The defaulters are guaranteed by the State Governments in respect of the repayment of interests.

BHOODAN AND GRAMDAN MOVEMENT

Need for Rural Economic Revolution

The contribution of the Bhoodan movement towards the development of the Indian villages is very important. Bhoodan movement, as is obvious from its name, is the movement for donating land to the landless people. Through this movement it has been planned to bring about a non-violent revolution in the economic field within the country. In any country it is fundamentally impractical to talk of equality and brotherhood where millions of people are landless while a handful of people have large tracts of land. In order to put the democratic ideals into practice in the country it is essential to make a proper division so that no person may be in possession of land for the cultivation of which he needs manual help and also that no man should possess such a small piece of land upon which he cannot cultivate economically. In a society in which millions of farmers are landless and plough the fields of others, the public of the country does not have complete freedom. A large number of the landless farmers spend a life which is in no way better than the life commonly led by a slave. Thus there have been revolutions for the proper distribution of land in all the progressive countries of the world. In Russia and other Communist countries violent and bloody revolutions were initiated for the proper distribution of land. The violent revolutions have the advantage of affecting the improvements without delay but the improvements which transform only the external structure and not the psychology of the public should not be termed revolutionary in the real sense of the word. As a matter of fact the real social revolution takes place in the hearts of the public. It is a question of a change of heart. As long as the feelings of the different classes do not change and as long as these feelings do not approximate, the changes made in the external structure cannot be permanent. And even as it is wherever changes in the social and economic structure have been brought about violently these changes have either proved temporary or making them permanent has necessitated constant efforts over a long period of time.

Background of the Bhoodan Movement

In the modern age there is need for an economic revolution, not only a political revolution, in India. The country has become independent and continuous economic progress through the Five Year Plans is taking place but as long as the land is not properly and equally divided, the condition of millions of farmers cannot be any better than their condition in pre-independence era. The Zamindari Abolition Act in the various States of India is a solid step in the direction of the proper distribution of land, because these laws have given propriety rights to the farmers over the land which they were cultivating. Compensating the Zamindars in various proportions, their rights over the lands were taken from them. As a result of this official step the farmer gained a lot of advantage and the economic structure of the village experienced a revolution at least in its outward form. But as far as the question of a change in heart is concerned economic revolution is a thing of the future. The Zamindars did not happily part with their land so that their hearts were filled with hatred for the farmers and the Government. As a result of the increase in this hatred the mutual relations between the village people deteriorated whereas what was needed was that the people of the village should feel that the land of the country was everyone's property and that it should be used for the benefit of everyone. The Bhoodan movement was started in order to spread this ideal among the people.

Aim of the Bhoodan Movement

Describing the aims of the Bhoodan movement, its founder Acharya Vinoba Bhave has pointed out that everyone should have a right upon the land in a just social system based upon equality. Therefore, he does not beg for donations but asks for a portion which according to justice belongs to the poor. The main aim of the Bhoodan movement is to spread this correct idea so that economic and social inequality may be removed without any major revolution. With this objective, Acharya Vinoba Bhave started on tour of the country and going to places on foot, appealed to people to donate land. The Bhoodan movement started on 18th April 1951. Its aim was to acquire 500 lakh acres of land in order to provide every rural family with some land for agriculture. As the movement progressed the government and many illustrious leaders actively cooperated.

Other Kinds of Donations

As time went by movements for many other kinds of donations joined the Bhoodan movement. People were asked to donate wealth for the poor through the wealth donation movement. Through the intelligence donation (बुद्धिदान) movement appeals were made for the use of intellectual capacities for the attainment of the ideals of Bhoodan. Through the life donation (जीवनदान) movement appeals were made to the people to devote their lives to the attainment of the ideals of Bhoodan. Other kinds of movement include house donations and donation of means.

Gramdan

The Bhoodan movement is now gradually taking the form of the Gramdan movement. In Gramdan, as is obvious by the name, people think in terms of donating the entire village so that it may be regarded as a property of the rural community. The level of co-operation for rural development is very high in the villages acquired under the Gramdan movement. In a conference organized by the All India Service Organization at Palwal in Karnataka State, emphasis was laid upon the need for close co-operation between community development project and the Gramdan movement. An executive group of the Community Development Ministry deliberated upon this question and in May 1958, after the conference of Commissioners, certain practical decisions in this respect were taken. Now more importance will be given to the villages given in Gramdan than to other villages while opening community development blocks and while starting other programmes of community development. So far 41,76,814.93 acres of land has been received while the number of Gramdan and Zila Dans stand at 1,68,103 and 47 respectively.

In this way, the Bhoodan and Gramdan movements aim at fulfilling the aim of a non-violent revolution under the direction of such leaders as Acharya Vinoba Bhave and with the support of the Central and State Governments. Not only Indians but even many politicians, thinkers and scientists of Europe and America, Africa and Asia have shown interest in the application of this non-violent revolution. The success of this experiment benefits not only the population of India but will make evident to the entire world the possibilities of non-violent economic revolutions. At this stage it cannot be said as to how far the Bhoodan movement will be able to solve the problems of the Indian agriculturist but it can still be said that the present level of achievement of the Bhoodan and Gramdan movement is not negligible. Even if this experiment does not succeed it can serve as a source of inspiration for future movement of the same kind. Here it is necessary to remember that the Bhoodan movement has as yet not achieved any success which can encourage such enthusiasm. Most of the land donated is not cultivable and the intentions of the donors do not seem to be entirely selfless. Even the land so far received falls far short of the expected quantity. But in spite of these difficulties this movement is worthy of praise and deserves co-operation.

ROLE OF PANCHAYAT IN RURAL RECONSTRUCTION

The reconstruction of rural life in India depends upon the village panchayats. The economic, social and political reconstruction of the village can be brought about only through the panchayat. Mr. Nehru has rightly said that three factors are necessary for the solidarity of India, community development projects, superior village panchayats, and good village cooperative societies. If these three are properly developed the foundation of our country will be so strong and solid that it will face all kind of political and economic catastrophies, fearless even of the atom bomb.

(1) Decentralization of administrative authority. The administrative power was decentralised in India by the village panchayats and village people obtained the rights of self-Government. According to the U.P. Panchayat Raj Act of 1947, 36,239 panchayats and 8,543 panchayat courts had been established by 15th August, 1949. There are at present 2,22,054 village Panchayats in India, covering a population of 41-51 crores. In addition, there are 4,095 Panchayat Samitis and 232 Zila Parishads. These panchayats had been given the rights to all kinds of reconstruction in the village. The Government officials were anxious to give them assistance and suggestions.

(2) Social reconstruction. The Gram panchayat cultivated in the village people the habit of working together, owing responsibility for the various activities of the village, understanding things of public interest and living in co-operation and charity. The panchayati court taught them to resolve misunderstanding through mutual negotiations. The panchayat did much towards increasing the communal feeling by decreasing the effects of urbanization which had been manifested in the village youths in the form of a lack of responsibility, selfishness and impetuousity. The tendency to look upon the entire village as a family was born in the village people as a result of the communal contribution of labour in the construction of roads, lanes, drains, tanks, schools and panchayat houses. In this way the panchayat has a major role in removing the irresponsibility which had been the outcome of the disintegration of the joint family and the removal of caste panchayats. By arranging for radio sets and lectures etc., the panchayats created awakening in the villages. Thousands of primary schools were opened in the villages to spread education among the village children. In order to educate the older members of the community, adult education centres and night schools were opened. Literacy weeks were celebrated and resolute efforts were made to remove illiteracy from the country.

(3) Economic reconstruction. The economic condition of the villages of India are by no means satisfactory. The responsibility for this reconstruction also rests with the panchayats. Before the panchayat courts were instituted much of the hard earned income of the villagers was ill spent on litigation. Even the most trifling quarrels were taken to the courts and it sometimes took months and even years before any decision was arrived at. The cases were always postponed while a major part of the villagers' earnings found its way into the pockets of the advocates, peons and agents. In spite of all this, justice was at a premium because it was not particularly difficult to get false witnesses. Some villagers had even adopted bearing false witness as a lucrative profession. During the British rule the rural cottage industries of India suffered a devastating blow. Some cottage industries breathed their last because they could not compete with the cheaper foreign goods on the one hand while on the other they did not get any assistance from the government. The industries of the village came to grief also as a result of urbanization which resulted in the transportation of most rural commodities into the town and also a lack of demand for rural products. On account of this condition of the rural industries the artisans came to work in the urban factories. The village panchayat provided a cheaper means of getting justice and also encouraged the rural industries. Thirty-three per cent of the cases are settled by mutual negotiation and understanding. Bearing false witness became impossible because the matter now was solved without delay. The village panchayat assisted the cottage industries. It arranged for the sale of the produce by organising exhibitions, markets and fairs. It introduced new methods into the villages through radio and other modern innovations. As a result of the spread of education the people came to know many new facts regarding production, sales etc. in cottage industries. Besides the cottage industries the village panchayat also encouraged agriculture. India is predominantly an agricultural country. The reconstruction of the villages of the country is dependent upon agriculture. As a result of illiteracy the methods of farming, tools etc. had remained antique and the yield per acre was low. The panchayats arranged for modern agricultural implements and co-operative societies for superior seeds, superior manure and sales etc. It increased the knowledge of the specific aspects of agriculture in the people through radio, exhibitions and speeches and got financial assistance from the government. Besides these activities towards economic reconstruction, the village panchayats participated in the work of economic uplift through many other activities like arranging for pastures for animals, plantation of forests for firewood and wood for architectural purposes, and improving the breed of the cattle etc.

(4) Political reconstruction. The panchayat generated a social and national consciousness among the people of the villages in the modern individualistic and egoistic age. In the villages there are panchayat houses in which the people can congregate and discuss over the progress of the village. In thousands of villages Gandhi squares have been constructed so that the ideal of Gandhiji are constantly remembered and the patriotic feeling is always awake. At the same time the sense of self-dependence and co-operation is being developed in the villagers through the influence of the co-operative movement. A considerable length of roads, wells, schools etc. have been constructed with the help of voluntary labour. The elections of the panchayats and panchayat courts educate the villagers in the democratic method. As a member of the panchayat their ability of administration increases in arranging for the village. In spreading the democratic qualities of liberty, equality and fraternity the gram panchayats have played a major role.

(5) Centres of rural reconstruction. Actually the village panchayats are the centres of all kinds of reconstruction in the village. They provide the villagers with the opportunity of meeting at one place, sitting together and thinking as well as working cooperatively, solving their quarrels mutually, arranging for their own village and making efforts for their mutual progress. The responsibility of making the village ideal rests almost entirely with the panchayat. It is through their efforts that poverty, illiteracy, narrow-mindedness, disunity, frivolity and disorganisation can be removed from the village. Only these can make the villagers the ideal citizens of free India. Only these can give material shape to the dreams of Swarajya and Ram Rajya of Mahatma Gandhi, the Father of the Nation.

Suggestions

The panchayats are making considerable progress in the direction of rural development but this progress cannot be said to be entirely satisfactory. It is true that the villages of India are in such a backward state that much time must lapse before they can be developed democratically, but nevertheless some suggestions may be given in this respect. The Gram Panchayat can mould the life of the rural community into the right channels by removing its defects and fulfilling the needs of the modern changing life. For this there is need for some change in management and right etc. of the panchayats. In this regard some suggestions follow:

(1) Education of panchayat in administrative function. In the village education is not very wide spread. Many of the panchas elected by the villagers are only normally literate. Most of them are completely ignorant of administration and justice. More often the revered elders are elected who have not the least idea of modern changes, democratic thinking and scientific researches. It is true that the officials of the government can assist them in this respect but then it no longer remains the administration of the panchas but rather becomes the administration of government employees, annihilating in the progress the very ideal of panchayat. Thus there is every need for educating the panchas in respect of administration, of adjudicating justice, scientific outlook and democratic ways of thinking, etc. After being elected they should be educated in the training centres and their knowledge increased through national and international exhibitions. They should be brought into contact with the leaders of the nation in order to remove and dispel their dogmatism. It is a matter of satisfaction to know that the state government are working in this direction. Some time back many panchas came from Rajasthan to see the international agriculture fair at Delhi and gained inspiration by meeting the Prime Minister. Prior to this a trainload of villagers had travelled around the country. Much work is still needed in this direction.

(2) Decrease in the intervention of the government. Besides educating the panchas the interference of government officials in the activities of the panchayats should be decreased in order to attain a state in which the panchayats should be given full rights in matters of the village. The government officials sometimes intervene unnecessarily in these activities of the panchayats. This not only hinders the work of the panchayat but also detracts from the respect of the panchas and deprives them of their enthusiasm for the work. It is usually seen that the panchayat officer and panchayat inspector is given the most respected place when he adorns the meeting, while even sarpanch occupies a position of comparatively lower status. This is very improper. The government official, no matter what his rank, is always a paid and hired servant of the public. He has the freedom of making use of rights in serving the public, but he will always be given a position lower than the representative of the people in the government of the people and even more so when this representative is an honorary leader. The government officials should try to increase the respect of the panchas in the eyes of the villagers but this can happen when there is adequate education spread among them and they understand their rights.

(3) Control over formation of political parties. Democracy is the government of the people but there is just that much more opportunity for party politics. As in the state and central elections the elections of the panchayats are also infested with the formation of parties on the basis of caste, class and other mean interests, and even after the election, work of the panchayats is interrupted due to this party politics. This defect is found not only in respect of panchayats but in all kinds of elections in the country. There is need for a strong revolution to root out this evil. Without this revolution the foundations of democracy can never be strengthened in India.

(4) Increase in the rights of the panchayats. The rights of the panchayats should be increased for rural reconstruction. The panchayats should be given the right to demand exemption from payment of taxes in the event of any famine or disaster in agriculture.

SOCIAL EDUCATION

What is Social Education?

Inaugurating the Village Adult Education Seminar of UNESCO in 1949 Maulana Abul Kalam Azad, erstwhile Education Minister defined social education by pointing out that it means education for the entire man. It will make him literate so that the knowledge of the world may become available to him. It will tell him exactly how he has to adopt himself to his environment and how he has to derive the maximum benefit from his physical conditions. It will teach him the modern methods of handicrafts and production, so that he may be able to affect his financial improvement. It will teach him about the science of immunity from disease, of individual and community, so that his domestic life may be prosperous and happy. Finally, this education will impart to him the education of citizenship so that he may be able to assist his government in the decision for making the country strong and establish in peace after he has acquired some knowledge of the corporeal things. Originally, the meaning attached to social education was merely literacy of adults but now it has come to include all kinds of education for the adults. In the words of Biharee, "Social education is the stimulation in each citizen of a greater awareness of the advantage of the pattern of society as conceived in the constitution and a persistent desire for progress towards such a pattern socially, economically and culturally."

Aims of Social Education

In the words of Pt. Jawaharlal Nehru, "To educate the adults in the 3 R's, and the affairs of world, a network of social education organisation has been set up". In this way while social education aims at removing illiteracy it also endeavours to acquaint the adults with the problems af this world. In the words of K.G. Saiyeden, "The aim of the movement is to create a spirit of friendship between people by bringing together men and women of different nationalities." In this way the aim of social education is both individual as well as social. It seeks to elevate all the various kinds of standards of life, be they physical, mental or intellectual, in order that people may be in a position to make active contribution in all spheres of national progress. It teaches them about the reconstruction of the village.

The programme for social education has been divided into the following five phases—

Programme for social education. (1) Spread of literacy, (2) Acquainting people with the laws of health and sanitation, (3) Improvement in economic level, (4) Encouraging the sense of citizenship and imparting awareness of rights and duties, (5) Healthy recreation concurring to the needs of society and individual.

Characteristics of Social Education

The main characteristics of the above mentioned programme of social education are the following:

(1) Spread of literacy. Social education spreads literacy among the adults.

(2) Advancement of handicrafts and cottage industries. Besides spreading literacy, social education makes handicrafts and cottage industries popular.

(3) Training in self-administration. Social education trains adults in self-administration.

(4) Training for ideal citizenship. Social education tries to make the adults ideal citizens.

(5) Education in health and cleanliness. Social education informs the villagers about the laws of health and cleanliness.

(6) Knowledge of the problems of the world. Social education imparts the knowledge of the problems of the world to the adults.

(7) Integral development. Social education directs its efforts into achieving the integral development of the adults.

(8) Organization of healthy recreation. Social education besides formal education organises healthy recreation through the medium of radios and cultural programmes.

(9) Contribution in rejuvenation. One of the major characteristics of social education is that, besides education, it contributes to every programme for rejuvenation.

Methods of social education. It is on the basis of these characteristics that the method of social education has been developed. Hence night schools have been arranged in the village centre for teaching the adults. Social education is not limited only to adult males. This education is imparted even to adult women as well as to young men and adolescents, boys and girls and the syllabus laid down for them concurs harmoniously with their peculiar psychology. In order to increase the attraction of the programmes such means as the movies, education vans, posters and charts are employed. A characteristic of this method is the broadcasting of programme over the radio. Community consciousness and nationality are popularized and communicated to the people through social acting, folk dances and folk songs. The people are also informed about the scientific means of agriculture and handicraft and attempts to develop the qualities of leadership are made. At regular intervals sports competitions and development fairs are organised. Educational excursions are also arranged periodically. Programmes for composing adult literature are made and mobile and permanent reading-rooms are also arranged for.

Problems of Social Education

In India, there are many problems which plague social education. The major ones are the following:

1. The rural people are not very spirited in their approach to social education.

2. Often the adults do not show much of an inclination towards social education.

3. The night schools are terminated during the peak season in agriculture.

4. There is a serious absence of proper literature for social education.

5. Being brought up in an urban atmosphere, most of the workers are unable to take proper interest in social education.

6. Other programmes beside literacy are not emphasised properly.

7. Proper and adequate means for social education are not available.

Suggestions advanced by the Planning Commission

The Planning Commission had made some very important suggestions for the solution of problems which infest social education, the more important of which are given below:

1. In social education, education of life, health, recreation, domestic and economic education should also be given the necessary attention.

2. After imparting the knowledge of language, efforts should be made to strengthen this knowledge through films, radio, libraries and reading-rooms etc.

3. The programmes for social education should be adopted and modified according to the local needs.

4. Much care should be exercised in the selection and training of the personnel for social education.

5. The Teachers Training College should carry out research about the ways of making people literate.

6. There should be a suitable administrating machinery for maintaining a certain standard in the work of social education. It must have become quite obvious from this brief description of the different aspects of social education that this plan has some predetermined objectives which are immensely beneficial to the country. There can be no two opinions on the subject that the Indian villages are in great need of social education and it is the only means to their redemption. As it is made obvious by the survey of the progress of social education in India, there is need for much work in this direction. But there is no doubt that the present progress of social education is not entirely

dissatisfactory. The suggestions made by the Planning Commission for the solution of the problems of social education are very useful. In India social education is still in its infancy. But nevertheless, "If today the villages of India are humming with greater activities than ever before some credit for this must go to the social education movement."

QUESTIONS FOR EXERCISE

1. What is rural reconstruction? Give an ideal plan for rural reconstruction in India.
2. Evaluate the impact of the welfare activities of the Government on village life in India.
3. Explain the importance of planned rural development in India.
4. Assess the contribution of Community Development Programme in rural reconstruction.
5. Evaluate the role of community development programmes of the Government of India in the promotion of social welfare.

4

National Emotional Integration

The unity of a nation depends upon the extent to which its various members look upon themselves as members of the same group. National unity or integration does not automatically follow upon living within the same geographical boundaries. Emotional integration is necessary for this unity. As is evident from the term itself emotional integration is the unity, identity or similarity of emotions. If it exists, then individuals feel related to and concerned with each other, despite any external differences. It is emotional integration which keeps members of a family organised. In colleges, this emotional integration is generated through various communal programmes. It promotes a sense of community and impedes the progress of disorganizing tendencies.

In India one finds marked differences in the living standards, dress, customs, religion, culture, etc., of the various people existing in different parts. India's large size is emphasized by these differences, but one result of this that when a person goes from one part of the country to another, he is almost a foreigner there. This had led to regionalism, expressed in the desire of people of one region to promote their own regional interests at the expense of the interests of other regions. Regionalism has gained tremendous momentum because it has been linked with linguism. Linguism is the prejudice of the speakers of a particular language to develop their language, to the detriment of any and all other languages spoken in different parts of the country. Casteism or racial distinction between the Hindus and Muslims had led to deterioration of social organisation in the country. Untouchability is an offshoot of casteism. Religious communities have been known to come into violent conflict with each other, thus leading to considerable damage to public and private property, and bloodshed on a large scale. Communalism is responsible for the hatred which one religious group fosters for another. Putting it briefly, regionalism, linguism, casteism, communalism, etc., are the disruptive and disorganisation influences which have divided Indian society into various groups. It is impossible to hope for a solution of the problems in the absence of emotional integration. And, if these problems remain unsolved, democracy will also remain a dream.

Unity in Diversity

Generally speaking, the extent of diversity found in India tends to create the impression that it is not a country but a sub-continent. But this does not imply that unity or integration is impossible in such a situation. One finds distinct and different racial characteristics among the inhabitants of different parts of the country, because differences of complexion, size, shape, etc., are clearly evident. It can be clearly seen that there is gradual decline in the physical stature of the inhabitants as one moves from Punjab to Assam. If other examples are necessary, it can be seen that there are all kinds of complexions in this country. In the north complexion varies from darkly wheatish, dark, yellow, pink and even runs into mixtures of these colours. Inhabitants of the Andamans are jet black while those of the South Dravidians is a shining black, in direct contrast is the rosy white complexion of the Kashmiris. Turning to languages, one finds that the Indian Constitution has granted recognition of Urdu, Bengali, Assamese, Oriya, Punjabi, Gujarati, Marathi, Sindhi and numerous other languages, in addition to Hindi. Besides, Telugu, Kannada, Tamil and Malayalam have been accepted as the four Dravid languages. Sanskrit has also been given special consideration, as the original Aryan language. Differences exist not only at the level of language but also in respect of dress, religion, culture, etc. Tribes of the north-east, central districts and the south differ from each other in their modes of life, their social and psychological characteristics, etc., to such a great extent that one can find among them different cultural and social regions. If one travels from east to west, and then back again, one will find clearly perceptible differences in complexion, dress, customs, modes of life, dietary habits and other aspects of culture, even at very short distances. But despite these differences of region, race, language, tribe, etc., the existence of a national unity cannot be questioned. One finds this inner unity or integration in all the people spread over the landmass limited by Himalayas on the one side and the Indian Ocean on the other, the Burma Hill on the east and Pakistan on the west. This inner unity is the basis of emotional integration. Despite the more obvious and superficial differences, prosperity increases. It is this inner unity which Sir Herbert Rizely described when he commented that, at the root of the apparent diversity of physical and social type, language, custom and religion that immediately strikes the observer coming to India, is a definite similarity or identity or inner unity of life from the Himalayas to Cape Comorin. This inner integration or unity is the basis of Indian culture. All the saints of the past were aware of this unity, although they were no less aware of the obvious differences. It is for this reason that India has always been treated as a single unit, even in the remote past. It has been customary to refer to all the people residing in different parts of the country as Indians, even though one could see the differences of religion, culture, languages, etc. In fact, the very name Bharatvarsha denotes not merely geographical boundaries but actually the ideal of a cultural unity. During the Middle Ages, India was always treated as one unit. That India is accepted as the mother by all Indians is only due to a feeling of oneness and identity.

Efforts at Increasing Emotional Integration

It was this question of emotional integration which inspired the Central

Education Ministry in 1961 to organise a committee for emotional integration under the chairmanship of Dr. Sampurnanand. This campaign to increase emotional integration had the solid foundation of belief in the principle of unity in diversity. All that is needed is that the younger generation should be educated in this direction through various kinds of programmes. Speaking at the inauguration of the Indian Integration Committee, Shri K.L. Shrimali, explained the significance of education and commented that if we want to generate national consciousness in our people, we will have to plan our education accordingly. Education must be so designed as to encourage each participant to think of himself as a responsible part of the Indian nation. Education must take upon itself the responsibility of awakening the younger generation to the truth that, despite obvious external differences, all Indians are the same, emotionally.

Keeping in mind the objective outlined above, the Emotional Integration Committee gave the following suggestions:

(1) Reorganization of Syllabi. In order to reorganise and reshape the syllabi of colleges and universities to accord with the needs of the nation, the committee made the following suggestions:

(i) At the primary stage, stress should be laid upon nationalistic stories, poems, songs, etc.

(ii) At the secondary stage, in addition to the other subjects being taught, special attention should be given to the study of national literature, social studies, moral and religious guidance and extra-curricular activities.

(iii) At the university level, the syllabi should include the various social sciences, languages, literatures, cultures and arts. Teachers and students should be given facilities to travel to various parts of the country.

(2) Encouragement to extra curricular activities. Besides imparting formal knowledge to the students, the teachers must provide them with the opportunity to take part in such extra-curricular activities which are important from the standpoint of emotional integration. Besides, such programmes must also represent the entire nation. Such programmes help in the development of 'we' feeling, a feeling of unity and sympathy. One example of such programmes is the Inter University cultural festivals, in which teachers and students participate from all parts of the country.

(3) Improvement of textbooks. It is desirable that textbooks on various subjects, and especially on history, should be amended and improved. They should be designed to encourage a sense of emotional unity with people living in other part of the country. This will also help to check the growth of communal feelings. But it should also be remembered that such amendments should not be made at the cost of truth because such violence to truth is not necessary. That the country is one is an undeniable truth. What is required is an expression of this truth.

(4) Improvement concerning language and script. In this connection the Committee on Emotional Integration made the following recommendations:

(i) The use of the Roman script should be permitted to increase knowledge of Hindi in certain areas.

(ii) International numerals should be used in every field of knowledge.

(iii) Arrangements should be made to teach the Devanagri script where it is not known.

(iv) Hindi textbooks should also be provided in the regional scripts. Dictionaries using both Hindi and the regional languages should also be prepared.

(v) At the university level, study of Hindi and English literatures should be encouraged so that integration is encouraged and divisive forces checked.

(vi) The rights of the minorities should be protected in formulating a language policy.

In addition to the above list of suggestions, the Committee for Emotional Integration also made certain other suggestions. In schools the daily programme should be started after a community prayer and a ten minute talk, either by the principal or by some respected persons, on some subject which may encourage emotional integration. Another way of encouraging emotional integration is to organise a mass meeting of the school once a year and asking the students to take an oath to increase emotional integration. Besides, all subjects and activities likely to lower awareness of differences should be encouraged. In this manner it is possible to create a climate in which all people feel that they are members of one nation. On the negative side, all efforts must be made to destroy all elements which tend to obstruct the growth of emotional integration.

Suggestions for Improving Emotional Integration

Apart from the suggestions outlined above, education can be used in the following suggested ways for improving emotional integration in the country:

(1) Development of an All-India language. The first condition for increasing emotional integration in the country is that an All-India language should be evolved. Hindi is the only language capable of performing this role. Hence, it is desirable that knowledge of this language be made compulsory for every citizen. Government should extend every facility for developing Hindi literature. The development of a national language will not prejudice the interests of regional languages. They should be allowed to pursue their own course. But all communications between the Centre and the States should be conducted in the all-India language. Applicants for administrative jobs in the government should be required to know Hindi, although they may be allowed to take the examination in their regional language.

(2) An All-India educational policy. Education is the most effective tool for spreading emotional and national integration. For this reason a national educational plan should be devised. This plan should aim at providing every child with knowledge of the ideas of great men, poet, leader, religious thinkers, etc. Textbooks should he prepared under the supervision of the Central government and provided by it, so that the younger generation may be brought up in an atmosphere of nationalistic fervour. Rules for the appointment of teachers, their pay scales and their conditions of working should be common all over the country. The same syllabi should be applicable to all institutions in the country at the primary, secondary and university levels. All-India organisations like the N.C.C., Scouting, Girl Guides, etc., should be given appropriate encouragement. University education should be through the medium of the national language, even if the students are permitted to answer questions in their mother tongues. In this manner, the objective of national unity or integration can be achieved by evolving an All-India educational plan.

(3) Programmes for increasing national unity. Many kinds of programmes can be devised for increasing national unity. For example, the cinema can be used to spread the feeling of national unity. Radio and television can also be used equally effectively. All-India competitions and meetings can be organised in various parts of the country to increase national unity. Such programmes help people living in different parts of the country to meet residents of other parts and learn their ideas and understand them. Travel-facilities should be made more common and delegations and tours encouraged. During the last few years special trains made up of farmers of different areas, students and members of parliament toured the entire country. This helped the cause of national integration. Other programmes similar to these can be organised.

(4) Development of inter-cultural understanding. In all the programmes outlined above, intercultural understanding will be promoted. This helps people to achieve liberality of attitudes to other cultures, an essential precondition of national unity in a country in which there are many cultures.

(5) Efforts by teachers. Success of most of these programmes for increasing national unity depends upon teachers. As long as the teachers themselves do not rise above their petty narrow mindedness and create lofty national ideals, there is little hope of the students developing any emotional unity. Hence, it is desirable that national consciousness should first be stirred in the students. For this, teachers from various parts of the country should be encouraged to meet each other. This can be done through the All-India Teachers organisation. Even otherwise, most of the problems of teachers are common all over the country, and when they meet each other they will get an opportunity to think over these problems and exchange ideas. At the same time, a national consciousness will be awaken in them. Yet, attention must be paid to forestalling the development of a class consciousness among the teachers. The government can make a positive contribution in this direction by organizing lectures from time to time and distributing literature of this kind.

(6) Governmental efforts. Governmental effort is essential for bringing success to all the projects outlined above, because without official blessing there is little that education can achieve. This cannot be doubted because there are many agencies which are working against the development of emotional integration. So long as the government fails to check agencies which encourage linguism, communalism, religious bigotry and other disruptive forces, education will not be able to achieve the goal. One of the first steps in this direction is control over disintegrative political parties. In every part of the country laws should be enacted to prevent any individual from giving expression to linguism, communalism, regionalism, casteism, untouchability, etc. This should be followed up by a strict application of these laws.

It is evident from the foregoing description of the measures for increasing emotional integration that these measures must be both positive and negative. Adoption of all these measures would be a positive step. The negative step of destroying all obstacles in the way of emotional integration is no less important. For this, teachers, administrators and guardians will have to work collectively.

QUESTION FOR EXERCISE

1. Discuss the problem which Indian Nationalism is facing these days and assess how emotional integration of Indian people is achieved by state action in India.

5

Welfare of Backward Classes

Department of Women and Child Development in the Ministry of Human Resource Development is responsible for formulating policies and programmes for women and children besides coordinating, guiding and promoting the activities of both governmental and non-governmental organisations working for the welfare and development of women and children. The major thrust of the programmes of the department is towards ensuring the well-being of children and women, particularly those of the weaker sections of society and for raising the status of women and bringing them into the mainstream of development. The Department is comprised of the Nutrition and Child Development Bureau and the Women's Development Bureau. While the Nutrition and Child Development Bureau is responsible for the overall development of children, the Women's Bureau works to improve the lot of women. The National Institute of Public Cooperation and Child Development (NIPCCD), a society registered under the Societies Registration Act, 1860, functions under the department. Its activities include research and evaluation studies, organisation and conduct of training programmes for programme functionaries, organisation of workshops/ seminars and conferences in the area of women and child development. NIPCCD is also responsible for the training of functionaries of the department's most significant programme, the Integrated Child Development Service (ICDS). The Central Social Welfare Board (CSWB) which is a registered body under the Indian Companies Act of 1956, works as an apex body to promote voluntary action in the field of women and child development by extending financial support to various non-governmental organisations in the country. It reaches even to the grassroot level organisations through its state boards.

CHILD DEVELOPMENT

Integrated Child Development Services

Following the adoption of the National Policy for Children in 1974, the scheme of Integrated Child Development Services (ICDS) was initiated in 1975 as a Centrally sponsored scheme. The scheme provides a package of services, namely: (i) supplementary nutrition; (ii) immunization; (iii) health check-up; (iv) health referral; (v) pre-school non-formal education; and (vi) health and nutrition education for mothers. The target group consists of children in the age group 0-6 years and pregnant and lactating mothers.

The number of projects (Centrally sponsored) sanctioned as on 31 December 1992 stood at 2,571 and 194 state sector projects (rural/tribal blocks and urban blocks). Over 182 lakh (children and mothers) are receiving supplementary nutrition, while about nine lakh children are receiving pre-school stimulation under the scheme. The integrated package of services as mentioned above is delivered through the focal points of *Anganwadis* (one anganwadi in one village generally) in which sanctioned number is over 3.9 lakh. Several evaluation studies have brought out that ICDS is currently fulfilling a major national need and there has been a decline in infant mortality rates and birth rates, better health and immunisation coverage and larger acceptance of family planning in ICDS areas.

In 1992-93, the financial provision for ICDS was Rs. 356.74 crore. This account for all components on projects expenditure except the nutritional component, which is funded by the state governments. For nutrition component, apart from state government's contribution, food aid is also available from Cooperative for American Relief Everywhere (CARE), World Food Programme (WFP) and through the erstwhile Centrally sponsored Wheat Based Nutrition Programme. A beginning was made to institutionalise a special set of interventions for adolescent girls through ICDS infrastructure. These interventions for adolescent girls were sanctioned in 507 ICDS projects. The services provided include health and nutrition cover, functional literacy and upgradation and improvement of home-base skills.

World Bank Assisted ICDS Projects

The Centrally-sponsored, World Bank assisted ICDS projects sanctioned during 1990-91 for predominantly tribal areas of Andhra Pradesh and Orissa, continued its operation during 1992-93. The project provides additional inputs for women's income generation. Women's Integrated Learning of Life (WILL), services for adolescent girls, strengthening of health components, experimentation with nutritional rehabilitation centres and therapeutic food, construction of anganwadi buildings and godowns-cum-CDPO's offices on a selective basis and enhanced inputs in the spheres of communications, training, project management, equipment, monitoring, evaluation, etc. Another World Bank assisted ICDS-II project, for certain areas of Bihar and Madhya Pradesh is being launched.

Training of ICDS Functionaries

The effective delivery of the package of services envisaged under the significant programme of ICDS depends on proper training and orientation of the functionaries at all levels. Accordingly, a comprehensive programme for the training of ICDS functionaries has been undertaken concurrently by this department. The National Institute of Public Cooperation and Child Development (NIPCCD), other selected training institutions and voluntary organisations recognised by the state governments have been involved in the training of ICDS functionaries, namely, the anganwadi workers and helpers (the grassroot level functionaries of the ICDS scheme), supervisors and the child development project officers (CDPOs). There are 290 anganwadi workers training centres (AWTCs) for imparting training (job course as well as refresher course) to anganwadi workers/helpers and 20 middle level training centres (MLTCs) for imparting training (job course as well as refresher course) to supervisors. The job course training and refresher training to the CDPOs is given by NIPCCD and its three regional centres located at Bangalore, Lucknow and Guwahati.

Balsevika Training Programme

With the rapid expansion of welfare schemes in the country such as the Integrated Child Development Services Scheme the demand for the grassroot level functionaries is on the rise. The Balsevika Training Programme was started in 1961-62 to meet the requirement of the trained personnel for the institutions implementing welfare programmes for the pre-school children. The Programme is being run by the Indian Council for Child Welfare (ICCW) with cent per cent grant assistance. There are at present 25 *Balsevika* training institutes (BSTIs) in the country, each conducts this training course of 11 months duration for 50 trainees.

The syllabus of the Balsevika training programme covers the fields of nutrition, health, education and pre-school education and social work. Since the inception of the Balsevika Training Programme, a total number of 30,559 Balsevikas have been trained till March 1992.

Creches/Day-centres for Children

Under the scheme, the services available to the children include sleeping and day-care facilities, supplementary nutrition, immunization, medicines, entertainment and weekly medical check-ups. It is being implemented by the Central Social Welfare Board through voluntary social welfare organisations and by Indian Council for Child Welfare and *Bhartiya Adimjati Sevak Sangh* all over the country. During 1992-93, assistance was continued to be provided to support the existing 12,470 creche units.

Early Childhood Education (ECE)

ECE has been designed to improve the children's communication (language) and cognitive (social, emotional, intellectual and personality development) skills as preparation for entry into primary schools. The programme is in implementation in the nine educationally backward states of Andhra Pradesh, Assam, Bihar, Jammu and Kashmir, Madhya Pradesh, Orissa, Rajasthan, Uttar Pradesh and West Bengal and at present 4,365 ECE Centres are functioning in these states with over 1.50 lakh children beneficiaries.

Special Nutrition Programme (SNP)

This programme was launched in 1970-71 for children below six years of age and for expectant and nursing mothers. Under the programme, supplementary feeding is given for 300 days a year to the beneficiaries. Every child receives 300 calories and 8-10 gm of protein and every expectant and nursing mother 500 calories and 20-25 gm of protein per day. The programme is in the state sector.

Wheat Based Nutrition Programme (WBNP)

The Wheat Based Nutrition Programme is being implemented in 16 states and three union territories to cover about 31 lakh beneficiaries in ICDS areas. The programme has been transferred to the state sector with effect from 1 April 1992.

Infant Milk Substitutes, Feeding Bottles and Infant Foods Act, 1992

The Infant Milk Substitutes Bill, 1992 regulating the production and supply of breast milk substitutes, for the promotion of breast feeding was passed recently in Parliament.

National Plan of Action for Children

India reaffirmed its commitment to the cause of children, keeping in with the pledges made in the World Summit for Children by drawing up for implementation a decodal National Plan of Action for Children. The Plan identifies quantifiable goals to be achieved by 2000 AD in the spheres of health, nutrition, education and related areas.

Balwadi Nutrition Programme

Balwadi Nutrition Programme (BNP) is being implemented since 1970-71 through the Central Social Welfare Board and four national level voluntary organisations. About 5,600 *Balwadis* are being run by these five agencies to implement the programme. About 2.29 lakh children in the age group of 3-5 years are covered under this programme. Apart from nutritional supplementation, the balwadis look after the social and emotional development of children.

National Awards for Child Welfare

National Awards for Child Welfare were instituted in the year 1979, the International Year of the Child, as state's recognition for the voluntary action for the cause of child welfare. Five awards are given to institutions and three awards to individuals annually for the best work done in the field of child welfare. The award carries a cash prize of rupees two lakh and a citation for the awardee institution and Rs. 30,000 and a citation for the individual awardee.

United Nation's International Children Emergency Fund (UNICEF)

Department of Women and Child Development is the nodal department for UNICEF assistance in the country. UNICEF assistance has been available for the programmes which has focus on children. The programme areas, included the integrated child development services, urban basic services, women development, health, nutrition, education, water supply and sanitation.

WOMEN DEVELOPMENT

The Constitution of India guarantees equal rights and opportunities for both men and women. Towards this, efforts are being made through development planning to raise the status of women besides mainstreaming them into the process of national development on par with men. The programmes for the development of women include employment and income generation programmes, welfare and support services and programmes to create awareness generation, etc.

Hostels for Working Women

The scheme seeks to provide cheap and safe accommodation for working women belonging to low income group. The scheme was modified in 1980 to provide assistance for day-care centres for children attached to working women hostels. An outlay of rupees six crore has been made for 1992-93 to sanction 80 additional hostels to provide accommodation to 3,400 working women. Since inception of the scheme 640 hostels with an intake capacity of 41,813 women with day care facilities to 5,726 children in 221 hostels have been established.

Employment and Income Generating Training Production Units

The NORAD (Norwegian Agency for International Development) assisted programme started during 1982-83 to train women belonging to weaker sections of the society and to provide them employment on a sustained basis. The programme is implemented through public sector undertakings/corporations/autonomous bodies/voluntary organisations. Under this, training is imparted to women in selected non-traditional trades such as electronics, watch manufacturing/assembly, printing and binding, handlooms, weaving and spinning, garment making, etc. A budget provision of Rs. 4 crore was made for the year 1992-93. So far, about 300 projects have been sanctioned to benefit over 26,000 women.

Condensed Courses of Education and Vocational Training for Women

This programme is implemented by the Central Social Welfare Board (CSWB) through voluntary organisations. Under this programme, women in the age group 18-30 years who have had some schooling, are coached for 2-3 years to enable them to appear at different levels of examinations like middle school/secondary school/matriculation. The component of vocational training was added to this programme during 1975. During 1992-93, a provision of Rs. 8 crore was made for conducting 1,200 courses. During the year 1992-93, 893 courses to cover 22,375 women beneficiaries have been sanctioned till 31 January 1993.

Socio-economic Programme

Under this programme, the Central Social Welfare Board gives financial assistance to voluntary organisations for undertaking wide variety of income-generating activities and provide opportunities for work and wages to needy women belonging to the category of poor and the downtrodden, widows, destitutes, disabled, etc., particularly from economically backward and underdeveloped areas. Small industrial units, handlooms and handicrafts units, dairy units and other animal husbandry programmes like piggery, goat rearing, ship breeding, poultry units and also self-employment units are set up under this programme. A new thrust has been given identifying new sector of income-generating projects. Under this scheme, 3,642 women have been benefited till 31 January 1993 during the year 1992-93.

Support to Training-cum-Employment Programme

This programme of Support to Training-cum-Employment for Women (STEP) living below poverty line, was launched in 1987 to strengthen and improve the skills and employment opportunities in traditional sectors where majority of women are already working. The sectors include agriculture, animal husbandry, dairying, fisheries, handlooms, handicraft, cottage and village industries and sericulture. The focus is mainly on marginalised and assetless women from households of wage labourers, unpaid female workers, marginal labourers, female-headed households and other dispossessed groups in order to integrate them into the mainstream of development. Since the inception of the programme, about 81,000 women have been benefited.

Women Development Corporations

The Scheme for setting up of Women Development Corporations (WDCs) was formulated in 1986-87. These corporations are expected to play a catalytic role in identifying the women entrepreneurs; provide technical consultancy services; facilitate availability of credit; promote marketing of products; promote and strengthen women's cooperatives; arrange technical facilities, etc. So far, the corporations have been set up in the states of Andhra Pradesh, Goa, Haryana, Himachal Pradesh, Jammu and Kashmir, Karnataka, Kerala, Madhya Pradesh, Maharashtra, Meghalaya, Punjab, Tamil Nadu, Uttar Pradesh, West Bengal and in the Union Territory of Chandigarh. The scheme has been transferred to the state sector during 1992-93.

Short Stay Homes for Women and Girls

Government gives grant-in-aid to voluntary organisations/institutes to assist/run short stay homes for women and girls. The scheme was started in 1969 with the objective of providing temporary shelter and rehabilitation to those women and girls who are in social and moral danger due to family problems, mental strain, social ostracism, exploitation or other causes. Each home at a time accommodates 20-30 inmates. There are 201 short stay homes sanctioned in different states/union territories.

Awareness Generation Projects for Rural and Poor Women

This programme is implemented by the Central Social Welfare Board through voluntary organisations. Under it, awareness generation camps are conducted for the rural and poor women. The number of participants in each camp is 25 women. Since the inception of the programme, over 4,000 projects have been sanctioned benefiting about one lakh women.

Education Work for Prevention of Atrocities against Women

Assistance is given under the programme to the organisations for education work for the prevention of atrocities against women through propaganda/publicity and research work of related issues.

Information and Mass Education

Public awareness about social problems and consequent efforts to bring the desired behavioural changes are envisaged to be achieved through the use of mass-media including electronic, print, traditional media and outdoor publicity, utilising the outlets of Information and Broadcasting Ministry which include AIR, Doordarshan, Field Publicity, DAVP, Song and Drama Division, etc. Voluntary organisations and related institutions are also involved in creating public awareness about social evils and public perceptions towards child care, health, nutrition as well as women's development. Documentary films, TV coverage with a focus on the girl child, women's issues and social problems like dowry, etc., are also being made to sensitize the public and project positive image of the girl child.

Rehabilitation of Women in Distress

The major objective of the scheme is to rehabilitate destitute women and their dependent children through vocational training and residential care and make them economically independent. The expenditure is shared among the Central Government, the state governments and the voluntary agencies in ratio of 45:45:10. A provision of Rs. 15 lakh has been made during the year 1992-93. This Centrally sponsored scheme has been transferred from 1 April 1992 to the state sector.

National Commission for Women (NCW)

A National Commission for Women was set up on 31 January 1992 to monitor the matters relating to constitutional and legal safeguards provided for women to monitor the implementation of legislations made to protect the rights of women, review the existing legislations concerning women and suggest amendments, wherever necessary and look into the complaints and take *suo moto* notice of cases involving deprivation of the rights of women. The Commission has since started its activities.

National Plan of Action for the SAARC Decade of the Girl Child (1991-2000 A.D.)

In fulfilment of the commitment made by the Heads of the Government/States/SAARC countries at Male in 1990, the Department had prepared a National Plan of Action for the SAARC Decade of the Girl Child. This Plan of Action draws its inspiration from both the National Policy for Children (1974) and the National Plan of Action for Children (1992). The girl child, being an integral part of the target group of children, she will derive the fullest possible benefit from the general plan of action. However, her gender-specific needs and requirements will be taken care of by this Plan of Action.

WELFARE OF THE DISABLED

According to the estimates of the World Health Organisation (WHO),10 per cent of the population in the world has one or more physical or mental disabilities. In a sample survey conducted in 1981 by the National Sample Survey Organisation of India, the total number of disabled persons in the country may be about 120 lakh who suffer from locomotor, speech, hearing and visual disabilities. No precise estimate in respect of mental retardation is available. However, studies undertaken by research organisations have indicated the extent of mentally handicapped persons between 2 to 2.5 per cent of the population. The Ministry of Welfare continued to implement special programmes for the early detection, education, training and rehabilitation of various categories of disabled persons.

Rehabilitation Council

Rehabilitation Council, an apex body to enforce uniform standards in training of professionals in the field of rehabilitation of the handicapped in the country has been set up as an autonomous body during 1992-93. The council prescribes minimum standards of education and training of professionals; recognises certain institutions for conducting training programmes leading to degrees or diplomas. The council also recognises foreign degrees or diplomas or certificates on reciprocal basis and maintains Central Rehabilitation Register of persons who are allowed to practise or seek employment in rehabilitation services for the handicapped.

Rehabilitation Council has finalised the standardisation of 43 courses. The Council is also organising the joint entrance examination on all India basis for the course in physiotherapy, occupational therapy, prosthetic and orthotic engineering and diploma in mental retardation in respect of institutions under the control of the Ministry of Welfare. The Council has been converted into a statutory body through the Act of Parliament. The Act has received the assent of the President of India on 1 September 1992.

PROHIBITION AND DRUG ABUSE

In keeping with its nodal responsibility for drug abuse prevention, the Ministry of Welfare has been sponsoring a variety of research studies on the subject through major academic and research institutions. Recently, a nationwide project covering 33 cities and in-depth survey of drug prone areas was commissioned by the Ministry to ascertain the nature and extent of the problem, to delineate the major socio-economic factors contributing to it, to identify areas and population groups affected or susceptible to it, and to assess adequacy or otherwise of the available services. Though the studies were based on the perceptions of informed persons and affected individuals, the findings thereof provided some important clues for a better understanding of the problem and of its ill effects on the individual, the family and the society at large.

Article 47 of the Constitution enjoins that the state shall endeavour to bring about prohibition of consumption except for medicinal purposes, of intoxicating drinks and drugs which are injurious to health. Responsibility for fulfilling the Constitutional obligation in regard to prohibition rests largely with the state governments. The Centre has, however been continuously making efforts to educate people about ill effects of drinking through mass media and also encouraging voluntary organisations through grants for educative publicity.

During 1992-93, there has been spectacular expansion of drug counselling and de-addiction services to cover more beneficiaries. As against 111 counselling centres during the last year, the number has increased to 145. Similarly, as against 49 de-addiction centres last year, the number has increased to 84. The number of after-care centres has increased to 14 from 10 as compared to previous year. In spite of financial constrains the number of all the services in the field of de-addiction has been expanded.

Street Children

The term 'street children' is broad enough to include children not only of the street with no familial support or with no families but also those who have their families but are found on the street under various kinds of compulsions. Many of the street children have to struggle hard for their survival, mostly by earning on their own through meagre sources such as rag picking, vending newspapers, shoe shining, hawking, auto-washing, etc. While the boys among them are quite visible, the street girls also exist.

It is for the first time after independence that the Ministry of Welfare has launched a new scheme for the welfare of the street children. The scheme provides integrated community based non-institutional basic services for the care, protection and developments of the children who live on the streets or pavements with or without their family. An amount of rupees eight crore has been provided for the scheme in the Eighth Five Year Plan. The scheme is to be implemented through voluntary organisations by providing grant-in-aid and is to cover initially 24,000 beneficiaries in 11 most populous cities. The scheme will be operated through 40 NGOs through a network of about 240 centres.

WELFARE OF THE AGED

The problems of the aged are acquiring larger dimensions and complexity due to the fact that the number of aged is on increase. According to 1981 census, the population of the aged persons (60+) was 4.45 crore. It is estimated to have increased to 5.48 crore in 1991. The proportion of the old people to the population has increased from 6.2 per cent in 1981 to 6.5 per cent in 1991. This may go upto 7.6 per cent by 2000 A.D.

Article 41 of the Constitution enjoins on the State to make effective provision within the limits of its economic capacity and development for public assistance in case of old age. Government is assisting voluntary organisations to establish old age homes and day care centres in providing diverse services to the aged. It is also making all efforts to provide and enlarge old age pension scheme implemented by different states and union territory administrations.

For the first time, a new scheme under Central sector has been launched by the Ministry for the welfare of the elderly people. The scheme is to be implemented through voluntary organisations and provides services like foster-care, day-care, old age homes, mobile medicare, etc. An amount of Rs. 10 crore has been provided under the scheme during the current Five Year Plan. The response to the scheme all over India continues to be overwhelming.

DEPARTMENT OF PENSION AND PENSIONERS' WELFARE

The Department of Pension and Pensioners' Welfare was set up in March 1985. Its responsibilities include formulation of policy and co-ordination of matters relating to the retirement benefits of all Central Government employees. The department has also provided an integrated approach to matters relating to post-retirement benefits.

A revised integrated pension structure was introduced on 1 January 1986 based on the recommendations of the Fourth Central Pay Commission. Pension for full qualifying service of 33 years is now uniformly calculated at 50 per cent of average emoluments drawn during the ten months preceding retirement. Benefit of the revised formula has also been extended to pre 1 January 1986 retirees and their pensions have also been improved upon. Minimum pension/ family pension is now Rs. 375 per month. Pension structure for pre 1 January 1986 retirees as well as those retiring on or after 1 January 1986 is now linked to average Consumer Price Index (CPI) 608 (1960 as base) and a system for grant of relief against inflation beyond CPI 608 has been introduced. Provisions relating to retirement gratuity/death gratuity and family pension have also been improved upon. Procedure for sanction and disbursement of pension has been streamlined. Central Pension Accounting Officer (CPAO) has been set up from 1 January 1990. Action commences 24 to 30 months in advance of the date of retirement to ensure that retirement benefits are paid from the very date of retirement.

The revised procedure eliminates a number of intermediate agencies. The format of the pension payment order has been revised to indicate full particulars of service which go into the calculation of retirement benefits. The pension payment order also includes details regarding family pension; based on these details, payment of family pension is commenced by disbursing officers without requiring fresh sanctions from administrative authorities.

The Department of Pension and Pensioners' Welfare also plays a useful role in the redressal of pensioners' grievances. Pensioners' grievances received in this department are taken up with the respective ministries for appropriate remedial action. Qualified officers in this department also attend to pensioners' grievances in person; pensioners can meet the concerned officer on any working day between 4 PM and 5 PM without prior appointment. Pension *Adalats* are also held by the Ministry of Railways, Department of Posts, Department of Telecommunication and Ministry of Defence at places where there is a large concentration of Central Government pensioners in order to sort out pensioners' grievances on the spot.

Research and Publication

On research side, about 15 new studies have been sponsored to evaluate on going programmes of the Ministry in the field of handicapped, drug abuse, ageing, etc. About five conferences/workshops have been funded on various subjects dealt by the ministry. Translation of Encyclopaedia of Social Work in Hindi is in progress and likely to be completed shortly. In addition, six new publications are likely to be brought out by the Planning, Research, Evaluation and Monitoring Division (PREM) of the ministry, namely: Social Work Education Facilities in India, Summary of Research Reports, compilation of Social Welfare Statistics, Directory of Voluntary Organisations, A pocketbook on Social Welfare and Development, etc.

QUESTIONS FOR EXERCISE

1. What is the meaning of Integrated Child Development Services? What steps have been taken by the Government of India for Child Welfare?
2. Explain the need of women development. What steps have been taken by Indian Government in this direction?
3. Write short note on Welfare of Disabled.
4. Explain the need of Welfare of Aged in the Indian context.

Bibliography

Anjaria, J.J. and Manilal B. Nanavati, *The Indian Rural Problem*, Indian Society of Agricultural Economics, Bombay, 1960.

Baden, Powell, B.H., *The Indian Village Community*, Harf Press, New Haven, U.S.A., 1957.

Banerji, D., *Family Planning in India,* New Delhi, People's Publishing House, 1978.

Bhattacharya, S.N., *The Village on the March,* Delhi, Metropolitan, 1959.

Banerjee, G.R., *Sex Delinquent Women and their Rehabilitation,* Tata Institute of Social Sciences, Bombay, 1953.

Bhattacharya, V., *Some Aspects of Social Security Measures in India*, Delhi, Metropolitan Book Co., 1970.

Chatterjee, B.B., *Impact of Social Legislation on Social Change,* Calcutta, Minerva Associate, 1971.

Chowdhry, D.P., *Voluntary Social Welfare in India*, Sterling Publishers, New Delhi, 1971.

Chandrasekhar, S., *Population and Planned Parenthood in India,* George Allen and Unwin Ltd., London, 1955.

Desai, A.R., *Rural India in Transition,* Popular, Bombay, 1961.

Gangooly, B.N., *Problems of Rural India,* Calcutta University Press, Calcutta, 1921.

Govt. of India Publication, *Report of the Study Team on Prohibition*, Vol. I and II, New Delhi, 1969.

..................*India*, 1982.

I.L.O., *Working Women in Changing India,* New Delhi, 1963.

Kuppuswamy, B., *Social Change in India,* Vikas, Delhi, 1972.

King, J. (Ed.), *The Probation Service*, Butterworth, 1958.

Pillay, A.P., *Welfare Problems in Rural India,* D.B. Taraporevala Sons & Co., Bombay, 1931.

Sharma, R.N., *Rural Sociology in India*, Munshi Ram Manohar Lal, New Delhi, 1978.

Sharma, R.N., *Social Disorganisation* (Hindi), Rajhans Prakashan Mandir, Meerut, 1976.

Sharma, R.N., *Criminology and Penology,* Rajhans Prakashan Mandir, Meerut, 1979.

Sharma, R.N., *Indian Social Problems,* Media, Bombay, 1982.

Sharma, R.N., *Indian Society,* Media Publishers, Bombay, 1979.

Sharma, R.N., *Contemporary Indian Society* (Hindi), Saraswati Sadan, New Delhi, 1976.

Sharma, R.N., *Principles of Sociology,* Asia, Bombay, 1968.

Singh, Sita Ram, *Nationalism and Social Reform in India,* Ranjit Printers, Delhi, 1968.

Sinha and Bose, *History of Prostitution in India*, The Bengal Social Hygiene Association, Calcutta, 1933.

Srinivas, M.N., (Ed.), *Social Change in Modern India,* Orient Longmans, New Delhi, 1972.

Spencer, H.D., *Towards Freedom from Want,* Oxford University Press, London, 1949.

Thakur, U., *The History of Suicide in India*, Munshi Ram Manohar Lal, New Delhi, 1965.

Thomson, W.S., *Population Problems,* McGraw Hill Book Co., New York, 1953.

Venu Gopal Rao, S., *Facets of Crime in India*, Allied Publishers, Bombay, 1967.